NATIONAL
GEOGRAPHIC

TRAVELER

amsterdam

NATIONAL GEOGRAPHIC
TRAVELER

amsterdam

by Christopher Catling &
Gabriella Le Breton

photography by Yadid Levi

National Geographic
Washington, D.C.

CONTENTS

TRAVELING WITH EYES OPEN 6

CHARTING YOUR TRIP 8

History & Culture 13
Amsterdam Today **14**   Feature: Food & Drink **24**
History of Amsterdam **26**   Architecture & Arts **36**

Nieuwe Zijde 45
Introduction & Map **46**   A Walk Through the Heart of Amsterdam **60**
Feature: A City of Keels & Wheels **68**

Oude Zijde 71
Introduction & Map **72**   Feature: Sex & Drugs in Amsterdam **82**
A Waterside Stroll **96**

Jodenbuurt, Plantage, Oostelijk Havengebied, & Environs 99
Introduction & Map **100**   Feature: The Genius of Rembrandt **106**
Exploring Plantage & Maritime Amsterdam **116**

Northern Canals 127
Introduction & Map **128**   A Stroll Through the Jordaan **140**
Feature: Brown Cafés & Dutch Gin **148**

Southern Canals 157
Introduction & Map **158**   Feature: Houseboats **185**
A Walk Along the Amstel River **186**

The Museum Quarter, Vondelpark, & De Pijp 189
Introduction & Map **190**   Feature: Vincent van Gogh **201**
A Walk Around the Museum Quarter & Vondelpark **204**

Excursions 211
Introduction & Map **212**   Biking in Waterland **214**
A Drive Through the Bulb Fields of Haarlem **224**

Travelwise 235
Hotels & Restaurants **242**   Shopping **256**   Entertainment & Activities **262**

INDEX 265   **CREDITS** 270–271

Pages 2–3: Amsterdam's canals are largely a legacy of the Dutch Golden Age.
Opposite: Certain tulips from Amsterdam will survive the long trip home.

TRAVELING WITH EYES OPEN

Alert travelers go with a purpose and leave with a benefit. If you travel responsibly, you can help support wildlife conservation, historic preservation, and cultural enrichment in the places you visit. You can enrich your own travel experience as well.

To be a geo-savvy traveler:

- Recognize that your presence has an impact on the places you visit.

- Spend your time and money in ways that sustain local character. (Besides, it's more interesting that way.)

- Value the destination's natural and cultural heritage.

- Respect the local customs and traditions.

- Express appreciation to local people about things you find interesting and unique to the place: its nature and scenery, music and food, historic villages and buildings.

- Vote with your wallet: Support the people who support the place, patronizing businesses that make an effort to celebrate and protect what's special there. Seek out shops, local restaurants, inns, and tour operators who love their home—who love taking care of it and showing it off. Avoid businesses that detract from the character of the place.

- Enrich yourself, taking home memories and stories to tell, knowing that you have contributed to the preservation and enhancement of the destination.

That is the type of travel now called geotourism, defined as "tourism that sustains or enhances the geographical character of a place—its environment, culture, aesthetics, heritage, and the well-being of its residents." To learn more, visit National Geographic's Center for Sustainable Destinations at *nationalgeographic.com/travel/sustainable.*

amsterdam

ABOUT THE AUTHORS & PHOTOGRAPHER

Christopher Catling, a member of the British Guild of Travel Writers, has worked as an author for 21 years. He has written more than 40 guidebooks, including top-selling titles on Venice and the Veneto, and Florence and Tuscany. He is also a major contributor to websites and multimedia products such as *Expedia, Encarta,* and *AutoRoute Express.* Catling first fell in love with Amsterdam and its easygoing ways in 1987, when he was sent there to write a city guide for business travelers. He has since returned numerous times, allowing him to indulge his passions for art, architecture, and archaeology. Catling's mission in life is to encourage others to view the cultural environment as a resource equally worth preserving as the natural world. When not traveling or writing, Catling can be found walking with his family, playing the violin, or perfecting his surfing.

Co-author **Gabriella Le Breton** was born in Cape Town, South Africa, to an English father and a Dutch mother. Her family traveled across the globe while she was growing up, resulting in an education at schools in Prague, Zürich, Vienna, Singapore, and England. Le Breton has written for U.K. national newspapers including *The Daily Telegraph* and *Sunday Telegraph, Financial Times,* and *The Times,* and for magazines such as *The Spectator, Harper's Bazaar, Condé Nast Traveller,* and *Food & Travel.* She also researched and co-wrote the *Skiing Europe* guidebook for Footprint Travel Guides. Despite her peripatetic lifestyle, Le Breton has made regular visits to family and friends in the Netherlands, and to Amsterdam in particular, since childhood, giving her a thorough understanding of the Dutch people, country, and traditions.

Photographer **Yadid Levi** is based in Tel Aviv and Buenos Aires, and has long been fascinated by travel and by other cultures. His work has appeared in publications such as *National Geographic Traveler, Travel & Leisure, Condé Nast Traveler, Sunday Times Travel Magazine, Wall Street Journal,* and *Bon Appétit.*

Charting Your Trip

With its iconic canals, fringed by 17th-century gabled homes and crossed by more than a thousand bridges, world-class museums, music and theater venues, and cosmopolitan hotels and restaurants, Amsterdam is every inch a modern city. Yet the diminutive size of the Dutch capital, combined with the welcoming, liberal attitude of the locals, gives Amsterdam the intimate feel of a large village.

Getting Around

One of the joys of Amsterdam is its compact size, which makes it extremely easy to get around on foot, by bicycle, or with the assistance of the city's very efficient public transportation system. The most popular means of transport for locals is the bicycle, but cycling in the city takes a little getting used to (see p. 69). Trams are ideal for inner-city transport, crisscrossing the city and stopping often, but there is also a metro, buses, and ferries. The I amsterdam City Card (see sidebar p. 10) gives unlimited use of all this public transport, and electronic OV-Chipkaarten (PT Smart Cards) are available for single or multiple journeys and multiday passes.

If You Have Only a Week

Start your week with Amsterdam's definitive landmark: the canal belt. Head for Centraal Station on **Day 1** and begin with a canal cruise. Once you're back on land, start exploring the southern canals and make your way to Het Grachtenhuis Museum (Canal House; 1 mile/1.7 km south of Centraal) to familiarize yourself with the history of the canal belt, a UNESCO World Heritage site. Then stroll along the Gouden Bocht (Golden Bend), dip into a *hofje* (landscaped courtyard) or two, relive the Golden Age in one of the other canal museums, peruse the shops of the Negen Straatjes, and have a drink in a traditional brown café like De Twee Zwaantjes (see pp. 148–149).

A visit to the Amsterdam Museum on **Day 2** will situate you in Nieuwe Zijde (0.7 mile/1.1 km south of Centraal; Tram 1, 2, 4, 5, 9, 16, 24, or 25), where you'll discover the ancient heart of Amsterdam. From the museum, walk north to the Koninklijk Paleis and Dam Square and then head northwest along the old medieval ramparts on Oudezijds Voorburgwal. This brings you into De Wallen, where you'll find Oude Kerk, Amsterdam's oldest church, the unmissable Ons' Lieve Heer op Solder

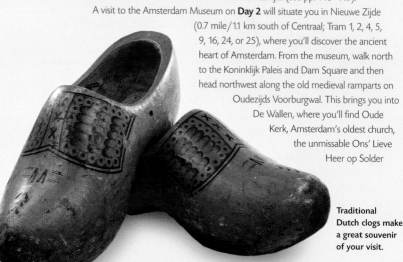

Traditional Dutch clogs make a great souvenir of your visit.

Museum, and the infamous Red Light District. After a taste of Chinatown in Zeedijk, walk back south on Oudezijds Achterburgwal toward the Amstel River for the floating flower market.

Day 3 will give you a rest from pounding the canals. Spend the morning in the Rijksmuseum (1.5 miles/2.5 km south of Centraal; Tram 1, 2, 5, 7, 24 or bus 170, 172, or 174) before picking up a picnic at Zuidermarkt, which you can enjoy in nearby Vondelpark. After lunch, window-shop in the boutique-studded streets around the park before visiting the Stedelijk Museum (0.6 mile/1 km north of the park) or attending a concert at the Concertgebouw (0.75 mile/1.2 km northeast of the park).

On **Day 4,** turn your attention to the Jewish Quarter (0.75 mile/1.2 km south of Centraal Station; Metro 51, 53, 54—all stop at Waterlooplein), visiting the Museum Het Rembrandthuis and Joods Historisch Museum. Once you've explored the monuments, walk southeast to the Hortus Botanicus gardens for lunch and decide between the Hermitage Amsterdam or the animals in the parks of Artis.

Day 5 brings you back to the northern canals, exploring the leafy Jordaan district (0.9 mile/1.5 km southwest of Centraal; Tram Westzijde 13 or 17, and get off at Westermarkt, or Tram 1 and get off at Dam/Raadhuisstraat). Arrive early at the Anne Frank Museum, from where you can wind your way northward to Noordermarkt (just north of the museum). If you're lucky, it will be market day (Saturday or Monday) but even if not, enjoy a slice of famous apple cake from Winkel Café. Stroll along the peaceful Brouwersgracht before crossing the canal and joining the popular shopping street of Haarlemmerstraat. At this point, you could hop on a westbound bus (22, 21, 48) for Westerpark Culture Park or a bus (18, 21, 22) to Spaarndammerbuurt, farther north, or you could decide to explore the picturesque Westelijke Eilanden on foot.

NOT TO BE MISSED:

A boat trip on Amsterdam's iconic canals **68–69**

A visit to Oude Kerk, the ancient heart of Amsterdam **84–85**

Paying your respects at the Anne Frank House **136–138**

A slow stroll along the canal belt's Golden Bend **176–179**

Getting lost among the riches of the Rijksmuseum **192–197**

A drive through the bulb fields of Haarlem **224–225**

Visitor Information

The Amsterdam Tourist Office website *(Iamsterdam.com)* provides a wealth of online information on hotels, restaurants, shopping, excursions, and anything else you need to know about visiting the city. See p. 240 for a list of other useful websites. The largest tourist office, by Centraal Station, has a friendly staff who will provide detailed answers to any questions you might have, and help reserve tours and tickets to attractions.

Focus on eastern Amsterdam on **Day 6.** Starting at Centraal Station, follow the "Route Oosterdok" footpath east to the Openbarel Library, NEMO science center, Maritime Museum, Muziekgebouw aan 't IJ, and the Eastern Docklands. Once you've had your fill of the modern architecture and quirky stores, return to Centraal Station and take a free ferry to Noord for a night on the Pancake Boat (see p. 49). Or head south and then west along the Lozings-kanaal for a locally brewed beer in the windmill of Brouwerij 't IJ.

Now that you're something of a local, **Day 7** is the time to explore De

Climate

Amsterdam's maritime climate does result in frequently gray, overcast skies and rain during the colder months of winter (Nov.–March). Indeed, the Dutch have almost as many expressions for rainy weather as the Inuit have for snow. A lightweight, waterproof coat is therefore an invaluable travel accessory in the city. However, summers are generally warm and virtually Mediterranean, or at least locals behave as if they are, with much alfresco dining and drinking in evidence along the city's numerous canals.

Pijp (1.7 miles/2.7 km south of Centraal; Tram 16 or 24 from Centraal, getting off at Albert Cuypstraat). Enjoy a hearty breakfast and stock up on silly gifts at the Albert Cuypstraat, then grab a tram (3, 12, 16, 24) from there to the Museumplein for the Van Gogh Museum, having saved one of the best Amsterdam experiences for last. Return to the city center for a final send-off at the Heineken Experience or stroll through the Spiegelkwartier, keeping an eye out for last-minute antique buys.

If You Have More Time

Being relatively small, many visitors feel they can "do" Amsterdam in a couple of days, but the city deserves closer inspection. By all means, visit the key museums, admire the canal belt, and walk along shopping thoroughfares like **Damrak** (just south of Centraal) and **Kalverstraat** (also south of Centraal), but try to make time for the little things as well: Enjoy the gardens of a tranquil hofje, haggle with the stallholders at **Waterlooplein** (Metro 51, 53, 54; 0.9 mile/1.5 km south from Centraal), eat fresh herring on **Haarlemmersluis** (just west of Centraal), go for a run in **Vondelpark** (2 miles/3.5 km southwest of Centraal; Tram 1, 2, 5 or bus 170, 172, 174), savor locally distilled gins in an authentic 17th-century *proeflokaal*, and hire a traditional *sloep* boat to explore the canals in your own time (Amsterdam Boats BV is 1.2 miles/2 km east of Centraal; Tram 26).

Amsterdam also boasts three exceptional cinemas: the modern **EYE Film Institute** in Amsterdam Noord (take the 901 ferry to Veer Buiksloterweg, just north of Centraal), the delightful art deco **Tuschinski Theater** in Reguliersbreestraat (1 mile/1.6 km south of Centraal; Tram 1, 2, 5, 9, 16, 24, 25), and **The Movies** in Haarlemmerdijk (0.7 mile/1.2 km northwest of Centraal).

Sports fans will know Amsterdam's successful soccer team, AFC Ajax. You can watch them play at their stadium, the Amsterdam ArenA in Bijlmer (5.5 miles/9 km

Buy an I amsterdam City Card

Make the very most of your time in Amsterdam with an I amsterdam City Card (*iamsterdam.com*). Valid for 24, 48, or 72 hours, the City Card provides you with unlimited use of the public transport system, free or discounted entrance to some 40 of Amsterdam's finest museums and attractions, a canal cruise, discounts and gifts at numerous restaurants, bars, and shops, and a detailed city map. An informative booklet comes with each card, detailing which attractions are included and how best to reach them. In addition to being the most convenient way to explore Amsterdam and discover its key sights, the City Card will also encourage you to visit as many of the city's museums and attractions as possible. Book online to qualify for a discount and pick up your card(s) at a tourist office, or purchase directly at local shops and newsagents.

A soccer match, lively debate, and plenty of great Dutch beer make for a good night out among locals at the Bruincafé 't Centrum, a traditional bar on Rembrandtplein.

southeast of Centraal; *amsterdamarena.nl*). Ice-skating and ice hockey are popular too. You can watch the local team, the Amstel Tijgers, in action at the Jaap Eden IJsbaan center (3.3 miles/5.4 km southeast from Centraal; *jaapeden.nl*).

Farther Afield

The Netherlands is barely twice the size of New Jersey, and many of its culturally significant cities are located a short hop from Amsterdam, making it a great base for further exploration. The cities of **Den Haag**, **Haarlem**, **Delft**, **Rotterdam**, **Utrecht**, and **Leiden** are all less than an hour away by train from Amsterdam. The long, sandy beaches of **Zandvoort** and **Bloemendaal aan Zee** are equally close to the city and make a great cycling day trip. Similarly, you can hire a bicycle, put it on the ferry to Amsterdam Noord, and find yourself pedaling through landscapes seemingly unchanged since Rembrandt immortalized them in 17th-century paintings. A visit to the jaw-droppingly intricate and colorful gardens of Keukenhof is a must for any green-fingered visitor, while the bulb fields surrounding the 80-acre (32 ha) park are a joy to cycle or drive around. ∎

Money Matters

Make sure you have some cash with you while you're out exploring, as most of the city's smaller cafés, restaurants, and shops don't have credit card facilities. Even the major supermarket chain Albert Heijn won't accept credit cards.

Tipping is a rare phenomenon in the Netherlands, but 10 percent is normal for good table service in smart restaurants; none is expected at bars. Taxi drivers expect a 10 percent tip if they assist with luggage or have to wait.

History & Culture

Amsterdam Today   14–23

**Experience: Browse the Markets
of Amsterdam**   16

**Experience: Celebrate King's Day
Like a Local**   19

Feature: Food & Drink   24–25

**Experience: Taste Amsterdam's
Café Culture**   25

History of Amsterdam   26–35

Architecture & Arts   36–44

**Experience: Explore the City's
Private Gardens**   41

**Experience: Take a Walking or Biking Tour
of Amsterdam**   42

The facade of Hotel De Doelen
Opposite: Vibrant venues such as
Supperclub make Amsterdam a
delight for night owls.

Amsterdam Today

Amsterdam is by no means a big city, yet it has made extraordinary contributions to our world. The designers of its canal belt pioneered large-scale urban planning; its 17th-century merchants brought us exotic spices, drinks, foods, and flowers that we now regard as everyday; the city gave us some of our best-loved artists, as well as the controversial policies of legalized prostitution and soft drugs.

Amsterdam's endless invention is driven by an indomitable spirit of freedom and tolerance. This, combined with an enduring sense of nostalgia, continues to shape the life of the city today. Scratch the surface of Amsterdam and you will uncover exceptional depth behind the dollhouse-perfect gabled homes, cafés, and parks.

A view of the city from the bell tower of Oude Kerk (Old Church)

The Making of Amsterdam

Amsterdam's picturesque labyrinth of canals is invariably considered its most distinctive and charming feature. And, with significantly more tree-lined canals and bridges than Venice, the 400-year-old canal system not only provides countless photo opportunities but has come to define the city and its people. However, what most visitors don't realize as they walk around Amsterdam is that much of it is reclaimed seabed. When you land at Schiphol Airport, you are actually below sea level and, as you admire the cutting-edge architecture of the Eastern Docklands or the attractive converted warehouses on the Westelijke Eilanden, you are walking on what was once water. As the great French philosopher René Descartes said: "God created the world but the Dutch created Amsterdam."

Amsterdam is the capital of the Netherlands (nearby Den Haag is the seat of Dutch government), which is not—as commonly thought—interchangeable with Holland. Holland has become a cozy, informal name for the country, but it applies only to two western provinces along the North Sea, Noord and Zuid Holland (North and South Holland). These encompass Amsterdam, Den Haag, and Rotterdam. Although most Dutch people accept the use of Holland as a generic term for the country, the independent-minded inhabitants of other provinces, such as Limburg and Friesland, resent being called Hollanders.

As the great French philosopher René Descartes said: "God created the world but the Dutch created Amsterdam."

The Big Village

At just 85 square miles (219 sq km) Amsterdam is virtually identical in size to Manhattan (site of the 17th-century Dutch colonial settlement of New Amsterdam). With more than 800,000 residents, it is one of Europe's most densely populated cities (although it's still a far cry from Manhattan's 1,585,000 residents). Each year, millions of tourists swell its population, yet Amsterdam retains the congenial feel of a big village, the key to its charm. Big-town bustle is to be expected on the touristy streets from Centraal Station down Damrak and along Kalverstraat to Rembrandtplein. But step aside from these major thoroughfares and you find yourself lost in the maze of Amsterdam's grachtengordel (canal belt), exploring quiet leafy streets and cloistered medieval courtyards. These are still very much residential streets—thankfully, the city center hasn't been totally colonized by offices and shops.

If you stay more than a few days in Amsterdam, you too will become part of this friendly village community.

Settling in is made easy by the sociability and linguistic dexterity of many Amsterdammers, who learn English, German, and French from an early age, and seem to have equal fluency in all three (not to mention their own language, Dutch). English is the one that Amsterdammers use most naturally, with more than 70 percent speaking it, happily mixing Dutch and English in the same sentence.

The Amsterdammers

Amsterdam was largely founded on trade, giving it a long history of investment, speculation, making money, and losing money. The Bank of Amsterdam was founded in 1609, when it offered loans at only 3 or 4 percent interest, thus enabling merchants to buy commodities in bulk, store them in warehouses, and speculate as demand and prices fluctuated. Investments didn't always go smoothly, however, with vast fortunes being swept away overnight, most infamously during Tulip Mania in the 1630s, when the city became the world center of furious bidding on the delicate flowers. Amsterdam banking continues to thrive today, although the interest rates are a little lower.

With its merchants ranking among the world's wealthiest people during the Golden Age, Amsterdam pioneered the acceptance of traders into the rarefied echelons of society typically reserved for royalty and nobility. As depicted in Frans Hals's painting, "The Banquet of the Officers of the St. George Civic Guard" (1616), wealthy traders were held in the highest esteem, selected by the Haarlem city council to serve voluntarily for the local militia with the bearing of nobles. This classless society could not have been more different to the hierarchical environments of France and England and remains a key part of Amsterdam society today.

Similarly, the unashamed accumulation of wealth is an integral part of every Amsterdammer's DNA. And, although a village in atmosphere, Amsterdam has always boasted global dimensions, remaining a hub of international trade, finance, business, and art.

EXPERIENCE: Browse the Markets of Amsterdam

The Dutch love a good market and there are no fewer than 21 regular markets in Amsterdam. Rub shoulders with the neighborhood locals, browse for old books, stamps, or coins, or adopt someone else's tat as your treasure. Some markets worth meandering through:

Albert Cuypmarkt: A mile-long (1.6 km) stretch of more than 250 stalls in De Pijp, selling everything from cheese and fish to clogs and radios (see pp. 206–207).

Bloemenmarkt: No visit to Amsterdam is complete without a stroll along the floating flower market on the Singel with its riot of bulbs, flowers, and houseplants.

IJ-hallen: With more than 750 stands, this monthly flea market in Amsterdam Noord is a treasure trove of jewelry, antiques, art, and kitsch.

Nieuwezijds Voorburgwal: This stamp and coin market is a must for collectors.

Noordermarkt: Twice a week, market stalls open at the foot of the Noorderkerk, selling local organic food and produce on Saturdays and vintage clothing on Mondays.

Oudemanhuispoort: A bustling book market tucked in a covered passageway between historical university buildings.

Rembrandt Art Market: Rembrandtplein becomes a lively market on spring and summer Sundays, with local artists creating and selling their works (mid-March–Oct.).

The lively thoroughfare of Utrechtsestraat runs from the Rembrandtplein to the Frederiksplein and crosses over three canals: the Herengracht, Keizersgracht, and Prinsengracht.

Looking back to their ancestors' boom and bust extremes, contemporary Amsterdammers have a healthy attitude toward work—they are industrious and entrepreneurial but rarely workaholic. They have also inherited a careful approach to spending, with flamboyant displays of wealth as frowned upon today as in 17th-century Amsterdam.

Doubtless a legacy of the sober doctrines of Calvinism, this disapproval of excessive behavior extends to all aspects of life, as indicated by the saying: *"Doe maar gewoon, dan doe je al gek genoeg,"* which translates loosely as "Just act normal, as that's crazy enough already." The only time normal isn't crazy enough is during the annual *Koningsdag* (King's Day) celebrations, when Amsterdammmers, like all Dutch people, succumb to *oranjegekte* (orange madness; see sidebar p. 19).

Liberal Attitudes

Openness, pragmatism, liberalism, and cultural pluralism have been core values for Amsterdammers since the city's beginnings. As early as the 17th century, religious freethinkers were welcomed, Jewish refugees given a home, printing presses encouraged, and brothels licensed and managed by civil servants. Locals will tell you this tolerance stems from a fierce love of individual freedom and a hatred of hypocrisy. The classic Amsterdam state of mind is "I don't like what you're doing, but I recognize I have no right to interfere with your rights if you don't interfere with mine." It's a logic that acknowledges that personal freedoms are only tenable if we don't seek to impose constraints on others.

> **The classic Amsterdam state of mind is "I don't like what you're doing, but I recognize I have no right to interfere with your rights if you don't interfere with mine."**

More than any other European nation, the Dutch—and Amsterdammers in particular—apply an extremely pragmatic approach to controversial issues: drugs, prostitution, homosexuality, euthanasia, and abortion. The basis for this pragmatism is that encouraging the forbidden, taboo nature of an issue will only worsen it—the subversive sale of narcotics and sex on the city streets leads to the development of gangs, corruption, hard drugs, people trafficking, and violence. But allowing it to exist in a controlled, regulated environment, while maintaining an open attitude and educating those involved, will achieve greater control. By and large, it seems to work: There are fewer pot smokers, drug addicts, and drug-related deaths in the Netherlands than in most developed nations, and the country performs fewer abortions per capita than any other country.

Amsterdam's permissive culture is further reflected in its role as the gay capital of Europe. COC, which originally stood for the euphemistic *Cultuur en Ontspanningscentrum* (Center for Culture and Leisure), is a Dutch organization for GLBT men and women. Founded in 1946, it is the world's oldest GLBT pressure group, and it continues to fight for GLBT rights, promotes AIDS awareness and education, and provides support and guidance. The world's first memorial to gays and lesbians persecuted during World War II, the Homomonument, was erected in Amsterdam in 1987.

Unique Style

For all their cosmopolitanism and Amsterdam's role as a global hub of contemporary art, design, and film, Amsterdammers retain a nostalgic affection for tradition: The pealing carillons that play hymns or snatches from Beethoven to mark the passing of the hours; the soft glow of *schemerlampen* (twilight lamps) in a café; the comforting vanilla scent of pancakes and waffles; coffee and cake shared with a friend.

This sense of simple, familiar conviviality goes by the name of *gezelligheid,* a word almost impossible to translate. Ask Amsterdammers to explain it and they are more likely to give you examples of gezelligheid, rather than a direct translation, because the English word "coziness" simply doesn't cover it. For a resident of the Jordaan, gezelligheid might be singing songs around a piano in a café. To a De Pijp local it might be perusing the Albert Cuypmarkt with a friend and having coffee afterward. For others, it might be savoring the first fresh herring of the spring or drinks with friends on a sunny evening in Vondelpark.

EXPERIENCE: Celebrate King's Day Like a Local

Once a year, on April 27, the entire Netherlands indulges in the raucous celebration of *Koningsdag* (King's Day), previously *Koninginnedag* (Queen's Day). Cities and towns become a sea of orange as people, pets, buildings, boats, and cars don the color of the Dutch royal family, the House of Orange-Nassau. People are known to succumb to *oranjegekte* (orange madness) on this rare opportunity for the typically straitlaced Dutch to let their hair down—and often dye it orange.

While the party rages all across the Netherlands, Amsterdam is the hub of Koningsdag, with its narrow streets and squares thronging to the celebrations of some 800,000 people who travel into the city for the big day. Boats of every size and shape jostle their way down the canals, blasting music for orange-clad, dancing passengers and for the revelers lining the streets.

Parties and concerts are also held the evening before Koningsdag, on *Koningsnacht* (King's Eve). Many Amsterdam nightclubs such as Melkweg *(melkweg .nl)* and Panama *(panama.nl/ nightclub)* organize all-night events, which are becoming increasingly popular. Suffice it to say, it's probably not the best time to get an early night in Amsterdam.

History of Koningsdag

The national holiday dates back to August 31, 1885, when *Prinsessedag* (Princess's Day) was held to celebrate the fifth birthday of Princess Wilhelmina, heiress to the Dutch throne. On her accession, the holiday acquired the name Koninginnedag. After Wilhelmina's daughter Juliana succeeded to the throne in 1948, the day was changed to April 30 in accordance with the new queen's birthday. Juliana's daughter, Beatrix, retained the celebration on April 30 in honor of her mother. Her son, King Willem-Alexander, who succeeded her to the Dutch throne, following her abdication in 2013 (see sidebar p. 55), decided that King's Day will be celebrated on his birthday, April 27 (unless this is a Sunday, as in 2014, when it will be celebrated on Saturday, April 26).

Koninginnedag Becomes Koningsdag

The year of 2013 witnessed unprecedented celebrations as the new king was sworn in, so midway through April 30, Queen's Day changed into the first King's Day in over a century. With the last Koninginnedag and first Koningsdag transforming the country, Amsterdam saw scenes of intense jubilation.

Koningsdag Free Market

In addition to live music, parties, dancing, food stalls, and street entertainers, Koningsdag is known for its nationwide *vrijmarkt* (free market). With their entrepreneurial spirit and history of trade, the Dutch adore a street market (see sidebar p. 16). The holiday is the one day of the year when the government permits citizens to sell products on the street without a permit and without paying Value Added Tax (sales tax). The result is a nationwide flea market, as streets are lined with real bargains in furniture, household items, or even Delft pottery. As a full-on party mood prevails, prepare for lots of good-natured haggling and breezy banter.

Amsterdam becomes a riot of joyful orange each year in late April.

Ice-Skating in Amsterdam & Beyond

The Dutch adore ice-skating, so join them at Amsterdam's largest and best-known ice-skating center, the Jaap Eden IJsbaan (*Radioweg 64, tel 694-9652, Tram 9, $$, jaapeden.nl*). The center is home to the Amstel Tijgers ice hockey team and incorporates a large outdoor and indoor rink. If you're wobbly on the blades, don't worry, there is also a beginner's corner. The center is open October through April, and there's even disco skating every Saturday evening, if you're feeling brave.

By far the most hotly anticipated ice-skating event in the Netherlands is the *Elfstedentocht* (Eleven Cities Tour). This 120-mile-long (200 km) skating marathon is held in the northern province of Friesland and passes through each of its eleven cities. The tour includes a speed skating race (with 300 contestants) and a leisure skating tour (with 16,000 skaters) and typically takes place in January or February. However, the natural ice along the entire course must be at least 6 inches (15 cm) thick for the event to go ahead. This can result in gaps of more than 20 years occurring between competitions. When the ice is deemed safe, the tour starts within 48 hours, sending the Netherlands into an ice-skating frenzy. The last Elfstedentocht took place in 1997, but its summer equivalent, *Fietself-stedentocht* (Eleven Cities by Bicycle) takes place on Whit Monday every year.

Vincent van Gogh captured the essence of Dutch gezelligheid: "I like to wander through Amsterdam's old, narrow, and rather somber streets, with their shops occupied by chemists, lithographers, and ships' chandlers and browse among the navigation charts and other ships' supplies. I cannot tell you how beautiful the city is at twilight."

As you follow in Van Gogh's footprints, wandering the little-changed canal belt at dusk, glancing into the softly lit, book-lined interiors of the antique shops and homes, you may conclude—correctly—that Amsterdammers are avid readers. The city leads Europe as one of its largest markets for books and is home to the continent's largest public library, the OBA. The fact that you can glimpse such intimate detail is another intriguing feature of the city, a peculiarly Dutch habit of leaving curtains and blinds open to reveal invariably chic, ruthlessly clean and tidy interiors. One theory is that this practice dates back to the Reformation, when citizens needed to show they were not praying in secret (see pp. 28–30). Although the Netherlands is now one of western Europe's most secular countries, the habit continues, implying that, today at least, it simply reflects a moralistic desire to prove you are a clean-living citizen—in effect saying, "Look through my windows; I have nothing to hide."

Project 1012

The windows of Amsterdam's infamous Red Light District are an altogether different story. Although part of the city's allure for some visitors, its seedy underbelly is a point of contention for many locals. The district vividly reflects Amsterdam's split personality, as it fights to uphold both its conservative moral ideals and the personal freedoms of residents. In a move backed by most Amsterdammers, Project 1012 was initiated by the municipal council in 2009 to address the district's growing criminal infrastructure. This billion-dollar project includes the limitation of prostitution to just two areas, the closure of a third of coffee shops and enforcement of stricter regulations on the remaining properties, and the reduction of businesses deemed conducive to crime (see p. 83).

While most locals welcome the move, others are concerned that it will oversanitize the city, stifling it and turning it into a living yet static museum. Fortunately, this is fairly unlikely for, as Rob Wagemans, founder of concrete, a contemporary architects' firm, says: "No matter how much we try to clean it up, Amsterdam is still sex, drugs, and rock 'n' roll, and I hope we will never lose that. Its presence here creates and embodies freedom, regardless of whether you choose to actively engage in that scene or not. It gives you the feeling that everything is possible."

Furthermore, as embodied by many of Wagemans's firm's projects, a particular aptitude of Amsterdammers is the ability to masterfully blend old and new, without damaging the former, or lessening the impact of the latter. This is artfully demonstrated in the reinvention of landmarks such as the Rijksmuseum, Stedelijk Museum, and Hermitage Amsterdam, and in concrete's repurposing of gracious old houses into slick new hotels, restaurants, and museums.

> **"No matter how much we try to clean it up, Amsterdam is still sex, drugs, and rock 'n' roll, and I hope we will never lose that."**

These innovative renovations include the Dylan, Canal House, Conservatorium, Het Scheepvaartmuseum, and Het Grachtenhuis. Amsterdammers also like to think globally: The firm's designs can be seen in locations from Stuttgart to Singapore to Seoul.

Art, politics, and the occasional profanity are all part of the streetscape of Spuistraat.

The iconic Ajax soccer club celebrates another championship at their Amsterdam ArenA home.

Ethnic Amsterdam

The Netherlands operated one of Europe's most open immigration policies through the late 20th century. Immigrants represented more than 20 percent of the country's population by 2012; that number was some 30 percent in Amsterdam. Ethnic communities have made many contributions to the city, such as the spicy cuisine of Indonesia, with a rijsttafel (an Indonesian meal of rice and mixed dishes) considered as much a national dish as pancakes and pea soup; the regeneration of Zeedijk by the Chinese; and the exotic Moroccan, Surinamese, and Indian fruits, spices, and vegetables on the stalls of Albert Cuypmarkt.

However, attitudes toward immigration started to change at the turn of the millennium: Critics cited numbers spiraling out of control and rising crime rates. The murders of politician Pim Fortuyn in 2002 and film director Theo van Gogh in 2004, both outspoken opponents of open immigration, in particular from Muslim countries, shocked the nation and gave focus to social unease and anxiety about multiculturalism. Nonetheless, the traditionally tolerant Amsterdammers were equally shocked when politician Geert Wilders and his openly anti-immigration, anti-Islam, Eurosceptic Party for Freedom became the third largest political party in the Netherlands. Immigration policies and Wilders's prominence in Dutch politics continue to be a source of heated debate in Amsterdam.

City of Artistic Endeavor

The Netherlands has provided the world with some of its greatest painters—Rembrandt van Rijn, Vincent van Gogh, Johannes Vermeer, Frans Hals, and Piet Mondrian to mention just a few—and has played a leading role in making art available to the public. Amsterdam became Europe's first commercial art market during the Golden Age, with art being sold everywhere and bought by everyone. The passion with which Amsterdammers followed the refurbishment of their much-loved Rijksmuseum, Stedelijk, and Van Gogh Museum, and the sheer number who renew their Museumkaart (an annual museum card, which costs under €50 ((U.S. $66)) and gives access to more than 400 museums in the Netherlands), is testament to their ongoing love affair with art.

Amsterdammers engage in many artistic and intellectual endeavors, from the performing arts to debating societies. The Concertgebouw and its orchestra celebrated its 125th birthday in 2013 and still rates among the world's finest classical music venues and ensembles. The new Muziekgebouw aan 't IJ, which incorporates the renowned Bimhuis jazz club, quickly established itself as one of Europe's finest music venues. The city hosts numerous internationally recognized festivals each year, from the classical music Grachtenfestival and performing arts Holland Festival to Gay Pride and the Roots Cultural Festival. A leading market for books, Amsterdam is also a major publishing center and home to many architects, composers, movie makers, authors, and journalists.

Ahead of Their Time

Members of one environmental group, the Kabouters, or Gnomes, were elected to the city council in the 1970s, and some of their bolder experiments have gone down in Amsterdam mythology. One was the idea of providing a free bicycle for anyone who needed one. Painted white (symbolic of peace), the bikes were to be placed at strategic points around the city. If you needed a bike, you just took the nearest one available and then left it out for the next person who needed a ride. The idea lacked nothing in terms of simplicity or logic, and it failed because meaner spirits stole the bikes and sold them for drug money.

Know the Local Lingo

Amsterdammers love giving things nicknames, particularly modern architecture. The city itself is affectionately known as Mokum (Yiddish for "safe haven"). The white, fiberglass extension on the Stedelijk Museum is *de badkuip* (the bathtub); the twisting red bridge spanning Sporenburg and Borneo Island is *de Pythonbrug* (the python bridge); the elliptical Kurokawa wing of the Van Gogh Museum is *de oester* (the oyster); and the glass ING building is *de schoen* (the shoe).

That other cities, including Copenhagen, have introduced white bikes successfully—computerized tracking devices deter theft—proves that such ideas were not impractically idealistic but simply ahead of their time. In many ways, that has been Amsterdam's role in the early 21st century—a city at the heart of Europe daring to be different and to challenge old thinking. From tolerating European integration, gay marriage, euthanasia, and all forms of consensual sexual activity, to the decriminalization of drugs and the rehabilitation of criminals and drug addicts, Amsterdam is a thoroughly modern city. It sees itself as a catalyst for change not just in the Netherlands, but in Europe as a whole. ■

Food & Drink

Dutch cuisine is often described as simple and straightforward, even "rustic," with many vegetables and little meat. The Dutch tend to skip the refinements but love *iets lekker* (something tasty). With national dishes generally involving potatoes, raw herring, cheese, and pancakes, few would argue that their national cuisine is worthy of tremendous pride.

Dutch apple cake (*appeltaart* or *appelgebak*), flavored with cinnamon or lemon juice, and served with cream

The Dutch, and Amsterdammers in particular, eat extremely well. Amsterdam's nine Michelin-starred restaurants and its wealth of diverse cuisines reflect its cosmopolitan nature, with everything from escargots and gnocchi to pad thai and satay available. The Dutch appetite for spice is a legacy of its colonial past and a rijsttafel, a medley of dishes from Indonesia, is a national dish. In addition to a rijsttafel, try these Dutch "delicacies" at least once:

—*Bitterballen:* little balls of beef or veal ragout in a crisp, deep-fried bread crumb coating, best enjoyed dipped in mustard along with a beer.

—*Kroketten:* like bitterballen but larger and oblong, typically served on bread.

—*Nieuwe Hollandse haring:* Dutch herring (see p. 151).

—*Pannekoeken* and *poffertjes:* the classic Dutch *pannekoek* (pancake) is large, light, and served with sweet and/or savory toppings (try bacon with spiced apple). Poffertjes are mini pancakes served with butter and powdered sugar.

—*Patat:* thick, crispy potato fries served with great dollops of mayonnaise. In a nod to their origin, they're often called *Vlaamse frites* (Flemish fries). The brave should try *patatje oorlog* (war fries), a stomach-churning mix of peanut satay sauce, mayonnaise, and onions. Amsterdam's best frites stand is Vleminckx *(Voetboogstraat 31),* near Kalverstraat, established in 1887.

—*Stamppot:* the epitome of hearty Dutch cuisine, consisting of mashed potatoes and vegetables like kale or carrots served with *rookworst* (smoked sausage).

–Stroopwafels: chewy syrup waffles known the world over but created in 18th-century Gouda. Buy them hot from the grill at food markets or warm them on your cup of tea or coffee.

Going Dutch

For something more gourmet, treat yourself to a meal prepared by Kees Elfring at Marius *(Barentszstraat 173, tel 422-7880, deworst.nl)*, Dennis Kuipers at Vinkeles *(Keizersgracht 384, tel 530-2010, vinkeles.com)*, or Ronald Kunis at De Kas *(Kamerlingh Onneslaan 3, tel 462-4562, restaurantdekas.nl)*. These three Dutch chefs are the leading lights of Amsterdam's food revolution. While remaining true to the roots of Dutch cuisine, they are by no means tethered to potatoes and butter. They have worked in some of the world's great restaurants and apply cosmopolitan influences to the Dutch larder.

Say Kaas

We can't talk about Dutch food without mentioning cheese. This is not just a cliché.

The Dutch are among the largest cheese consumers in the world, wolfing an average 50 pounds (22 kg) each annually. One of the country's best-known cheeses is Edam, which was the world's most popular cheese from the 14th to the 18th century, as its red wax coat ensured it aged and traveled well. This made it an essential in any Dutch ship's galley on a long sea voyage. Other stalwarts include Gouda, Leerdammer, Beemster, Friesian clove cheese, and Leiden cumin cheese. Cheese devotees should visit the Kaaskamer (Cheese Room; *Runstraat 7, tel 623-3483; kaaskamer.nl*) for further education in the ways of the Dutch gold.

A Drink with That?

The Netherlands' traditional drinks are *jenever* (gin) and beer (see pp. 148–149), coffee, and tea. These beverages have been distilled, brewed, and consumed in Amsterdam since the 15th century, and various traditions regarding their consumption endure. Spending time in cafés and bars establishing these quirks is half the fun of visiting Amsterdam.

EXPERIENCE: Taste Amsterdam's Café Culture

Known as the *volksdrank* (people's drink), coffee is consumed by the Dutch at a rate of more than 18.5 pounds (8.4 kg) per person each year. This is double that of their caffeinated counterparts in North America. Coffee rituals form an integral part of daily life, from entertaining at home to office breaks and enjoying a *lekker bakkie* (tasty "cuppa" coffee) in a café.

It is likely that this coffee-guzzling heritage dates back to the Golden Age, when Amsterdam was the European hub of tea and coffee trade. As in most old European cities, Amsterdam's cafés are historically social gathering points, where locals come to read the papers, discuss politics, literature, and art, and just to enjoy a good gossip. The Dutch remain very sociable and static in their coffee consumption, only

rarely enjoying a bakkie alone and virtually never on the go.

There is little complication in the preparation of coffee, and ordering your coffee of choice in Amsterdam isn't difficult. A *gewone koffie* (normal coffee) is a regular filter coffee, while a *koffie verkeerd* (literally "wrong coffee") is similar to a latte. Regardless of what type of coffee you order, it will be served with a glass of water and a biscuit, even if you chose to accompany it with a more substantial snack, such as a classic Dutch *appelgebak*—cinnamon-spiced apple cake served with *slagroom* (whipped cream). Bear in mind that cafés serve drinks and light meals while brown cafés (see pp. 148–149) also serve alcoholic drinks, and coffee shops sell marijuana (see pp. 82–83).

History of Amsterdam

One question fascinates everyone who studies Amsterdam's history: How did a bog-ridden, one-street town, founded as a squatter community by a bunch of lawless fishermen, grow to become the dynamic hub of one of Europe's most powerful mercantile nations?

Origins

Archaeologists date the origins of Amsterdam to around 1175. This was when the first settlers put down roots, living in fishing huts built on the low marshy banks of the Amstel River. This land belonged to the wealthy Bishops of Utrecht, but no previous attempt had been made to colonize it because it was subject to catastrophic floods. These early inhabitants lived a difficult life but they were free— owing no taxes or feudal duties to any landlord, either religious or secular.

The Amstel Gets Its Dam

Over the next 200 years, the squatter settlement was transformed into a thriving cosmopolitan commercial center, whose original shape can still be traced today.

Amsterdam stands at the point where the Amstel River joins the IJ (pronounced "eye"), then a shallow, fish-filled inland sea. Just before it joins the IJ, the Amstel splits into several branches. One of these is now paved over to form Damrak, the city's main street, but originally it was a waterway, which the first settlers sealed off by building a dam. Using sluices to control the level of the water on the river side, and a lock gate to allow boats in and out, Damrak thus became a natural harbor where boats could unload their goods onto the bank-side. This dam is what gave the city its rather prosaic name, Amsterdam (originally Amstellredamme), which simply means "the Amstel dam."

Archaeologists date the origins of Amsterdam to around 1175.

Several of the long streets running parallel to the Damrak include the place-name elements *voorburgwal* and *achterburgwal*, meaning "before the wall" and "behind the wall." They mark the line of the town's first defensive ramparts and palisade. The area within these walls is still known as De Wallen (The Walls).

This area was depicted in the earliest map of Amsterdam, a bird's-eye view drawn by Cornelis Anthoniszoon in 1534, now in the Amsterdam Museum (see pp. 64–67).

From Fishing Village to Cosmopolitan Port

The first documentary reference to the new settlement appears in a parchment preserved in the city archives, with the date of October 27, 1275. Bearing the seal of Floris V, Count of Holland, this grants "the people abiding near the Amsteldam" the right to travel freely within the County of Holland without paying tolls when using bridges and locks. Floris no doubt bestowed this privilege on Amsterdam

The front of Amsterdam's Centraal Station displays the *Groot Rijkswapen* (Greater Coat of Arms of the Realm), the personal emblem of the Dutch monarchy.

in order to gain the town's support in his bid to wrest territorial control from the Bishop of Utrecht. Floris wanted to extend the border of Holland northward to incorporate Amsterdam, but he was thwarted by the bishop, who sent in a henchman to assassinate him. This sparked a war in which Amsterdam unexpectedly took the bishop's side by giving refuge to the count's assassin. William II, son and successor to Floris V, took revenge by laying siege to Amsterdam, which surrendered after two weeks. William vented his anger by tearing down the walls and revoking the town's privileges. Later, magnanimous in victory, he relented and in 1300 the town received a new charter, granting the residents the right to elect their own council, pass their own laws, police their own streets, and try miscreants in their own courts.

These were substantial freedoms and privileges in a feudal age, and the charter was certainly one of the factors instrumental in Amsterdam's transformation from a fishing village to one of the most powerful cities in northern Europe. Here bankers, traders, merchants, craftsmen, and other members of the emergent urban middle class could live and prosper. In this increasingly liberal city, they could take control of their own lives, free of the feudal obligations that enslaved so many of their country-dwelling contemporaries.

The Ship of Trade

Another crucial factor that helped Amsterdam flourish was the invention in the 14th century of the cog—a sturdy, broad-beamed, seagoing cargo ship with a capacity ten times greater than that of existing vessels. It opened up a new era in European trade by making it cheap and safe to transport basic commodities over long distances by sea, so much so that historians have likened the impact of the cog to that of the jumbo jet in our own age.

Until the invention of the cog, most goods in Europe had traveled by coastal vessel or by packhorse and riverboat, attracting tolls and taxes en route that greatly added to their cost. Wool, grain, salt, and timber could now be transported much more cheaply by sea from northern Europe, where they were in abundant supply, to southern Europe, where

The Protestant Revolution

In the 14th century a series of purported miracles occurred in Amsterdam, turning what was a religiously minded city into a major pilgrimage center for Catholics. Indeed Amsterdam became important enough to attract visits from a succession of Holy Roman Emperors.

However, many Amsterdammers saw Catholicism as a corrupt force and resented the power that Catholics wielded over business as well as religious affairs. Calvinism, based on the teachings of the French Protestant reformer John Calvin (1509–1564) became the banner under which many middle-class citizens

fought for greater self-determination. Calvinism appealed to the citizens of Amsterdam because it reflected their values of sobriety, hard work, and discipline.

When the Catholic authorities tried to prevent people from attending Calvinist meetings, worshipers held assemblies in secret. Eventually the sheer numbers made this impossible, and huge open-air meetings often turned into riots as the authorities intervened. In many cases, however, militiamen simply refused to carry out their orders, believing that the punishments for open worship were out of all proportion to the crime.

they were in demand. These ships returned laden with luxury goods from the Mediterranean, from Arabia, and from the Orient—silks, spices, perfumes, wines, and dried fruits.

Amsterdam's entrepreneurial shipbuilders and merchants were quick to latch on to the opportunities presented by this new seaborne trade. At first, Amsterdam was simply one of several port towns located around the Baltic and the North Sea to enjoy growing commercial prosperity. Soon enough, however, it began to compete with the others by offering lower import duties and customs levies, thus eclipsing much bigger and far longer established places such as Antwerp and Bruges (Brugge).

Dutch Revolt

In addition to being a city of entrepreneurs, Amsterdam was a deeply religious city, with numerous churches, chapels, and convents. In 1555, the Habsburg Holy Roman Emperor Charles V put his son, the Spanish king Philip II, in charge of the Low Countries. At that time, the Low Countries included modern Belgium and parts of northern France, as well as the Netherlands. The Habsburgs, one of Europe's most powerful ruling families, had acquired control of the Low Countries in 1482, adding it to their vast empire.

Opponents of the Habsburgs rallied around the Protestant Prince Willem of Orange, and in 1572 he led an army of volunteers in the first conflict of the Dutch Revolt.

Philip was a fanatical, almost monklike Catholic, who made it his life's mission to stamp out the rise of Protestantism (see sidebar opposite) within the Habsburg colonies. In order to accomplish this goal, he appointed Spanish noblemen, including the so-called Iron Duke, Fernando Alvarez de Toledo, to powerful positions in the Netherlands.

Opponents of the Habsburgs rallied around the Protestant Prince Willem of Orange, and in 1572 he led an army of volunteers in the first conflict of the Dutch Revolt. Bitter battles ensued, but the desire for freedom inspired the people of the northern Netherlands to great feats of selflessness. By refusing to bow to repression, they broke the Spanish will and gave Willem time to gather reinforcements and defeat the Spanish.

The Alteration

Matters in Amsterdam came to a head in May 1578, by which time the Spanish were demoralized and in retreat. Calvinists loyal to Prince Willem entered the city and arrested the Catholic administrators, who were put on a ship and made to leave. The event has gone down in Dutch history as the *Alteratie,* the Alteration, a neutral term that gives no hint of its enormous consequences. Catholicism, not Calvinism, was now banned in the city, and the Calvinists occupied all the key positions of power. More important, the city was at peace, and citizens were again free to pursue the business of creating wealth.

It took another year before the Spanish accepted defeat. The final peace was signaled by the signing of the Treaty of Utrecht in 1579, whereby the seven northern provinces of the Netherlands effectively declared independence from the Catholic south (modern Belgium), and formed a new Republic of the United Provinces. They agreed to pool resources for mutual defense in the event of an external threat, but otherwise each province had a large degree of self-determination.

Having lost their grip on the Protestant north, the Spanish instituted a series of harsh measures in the Catholic south that further boosted Amsterdam's fortunes. A flood of Jewish and Protestant refugees fled Antwerp and other southern cities, ending up in Amsterdam. This mass migration created overcrowding, squalor, and a wave of anti-immigrant feeling, but ultimately it was to the host city's benefit. The newcomers brought with them the skills that laid the foundations for the city's preeminence in banking and in the diamond-processing industry.

Golden Age

The 1579 Treaty of Utrecht ushered in an era of peace and prosperity known as the Dutch Golden Age. The major landmarks of the Golden Age read like a catalog of astonishing achievement. By 1597, Dutch explorers had sailed to Indonesia and produced the necessary charts and maps to allow their fellow countrymen to follow in their wake. In 1602, the highly organized Dutch set up the United East India Company (Verenigde Oost-Indische Compagnie or VOC) to manage and coordinate trade with the Far East. The VOC established trading ports at strategic points along the route and all the way up to China and Japan and down to Tasmania, gaining a strategic foothold in southern Africa, too. By 1611, Amsterdam had usurped the position of the Spanish, Portuguese, and Venetians to become Europe's biggest importer of spices and other exotic commodities from the Far East.

In 1613 work began on the canal belt, part of a well-thought-out plan to control the growth of the city and to accommodate the demand for more warehousing and more berths for ships. At the same time it provided an opportunity for merchants to plow their earnings back into the local economy, encouraging them to build prestigious canalside houses. These they decorated with works of art that kept the city's artists busy and threw up some of the greatest talents of the age such as Rembrandt, Frans Hals, Johannes Vermeer, and Ferdinand Bol.

In 1616, Willem Schouten from Hoorn, the harbor town to the north of Amsterdam, rounded the tip of South America (which he named Cape Horn after his birthplace). That same year, Jan Pieterszoon Coen, another Hoorn

Naval Wars

The Dutch preeminence of the Golden Age was not to last for long. The English quickly copied Dutch innovations, from advances in ship design and the concept of trading shares on a stock exchange to the creation of low-cost marine insurance. Amsterdammers scarcely had time to enjoy their prosperity before English privateers were attacking their ships. In 1664, the English seized Manhattan from the Dutch, took control of the island's New Amsterdam colony, and renamed it New York. Such conflict continued between the two nations for the next century, not even stopping after the Dutch prince, Willem of Orange, was crowned King of England in 1689.

The English warship *Royal James* fires on Dutch vessels during a 1666 sea battle.

native, founded the city of Batavia (modern Jakarta) in Indonesia. As Dutch explorers continued to open up new trade routes overseas, Amsterdam saw the formation of the Dutch West India Company (Oost Indische Compagnie or WIC) in 1621, modeled on the VOC, and in 1626, Peter Minuit explored the Hudson River, where he purchased the island of Manhattan as a base for the company's operations.

Dutch entrepreneurs were everywhere, and Amsterdam was the place to which they brought back their exotic trade goods and their wealth. Shiploads of Ming-dynasty porcelain imported from China set first Amsterdam—and then all of Europe—alight with demand for the new and exotic vases, jars, and bowls. This led to the creation of an industry based just south of Amsterdam, in Delft, that was devoted to producing imitation Chinese porcelain, a product that would be known as Delftware. Visitors to Amsterdam during the Golden Age sent letters home expressing their astonishment at the sheer scale and excitement of a city entirely dedicated to making money.

Decline & Revolution

Amsterdammers prospered and some became extremely wealthy, building the palatial mansions that earned the southernmost part of the canal belt the nickname the Golden Bend. But, as often happens when one entrepreneurial generation hands on its wealth to the next, the upper echelons of Amsterdam society were full of people living on wealth rather than creating it.

Europe's mini Ice Age inspired idyllic winter scenes, but Dutch art often belied the real hardships suffered.

The scene was set for another Alteration as those who didn't share in this wealth suffered from a slow but steady decline in the economy, worsened by high taxation and a series of very harsh winters. Present-day Dutch galleries contain numerous paintings of snowy landscapes and skaters on the frozen canals of Dutch cities—evidence of the mini Ice Age of the latter half of the 18th century. The harsh reality behind these Christmas-card scenes is that many people died of starvation or hypothermia.

Also displayed in the art of the age are group portraits showing the dour trustees of various charitable institutions that existed to provide for the poor. Such charity came at a price, and many people preferred to starve on the streets rather than be subjected to the degradations of the almshouse.

When Revolutionary French soldiers marched into Amsterdam in the snowy winter of 1795, many residents went out to greet the invaders rather than defend the city. The old regime in Amsterdam scarcely put up any resistance when relieved of its duties as councilors and regents. In what has gone down in Dutch history as the Velvet Revolution, Amsterdam and the Netherlands became part of the French Empire.

Constitutional Reform

If Dutch intellectuals believed that France would lead them into a new, more enlightened age, they were badly mistaken. After the revolution came Napoléon, who installed his brother, Louis Bonaparte, on the newly created throne of the Netherlands. As king, Louis threw the citizens out of their town hall, which he turned into his palace, and relegated the city council to subservient status.

After the defeat of Napoléon, European leaders met at the Congress of Vienna to redefine the map of Europe, and the Dutch regained their independence and sovereignty. Still hungry for democratic reform, Amsterdammers took to the streets in a series of riots in the 1840s. The government responded by charging Johan Rudolf

Thorbecke with drawing up a plan for constitutional reform, and the new constitution, with provisions for the first directly elected Dutch parliament, came into force in 1848.

Economic Revival

At the same time as a measure of democracy was introduced, Amsterdam experienced a period of economic rejuvenation that came about largely as a result of farsighted investment in infrastructural modernization. In 1876, the 15-mile (24 km) Noordzeekanaal (North Sea Canal) was opened to shipping, providing a fast route from the city to the open sea. Now large modern vessels bearing tin, timber, tea, coffee, rubber, quinine, and other commodities from the Indonesian colonies were able to dock at new quays built on the western side of the city.

These ships, in turn, were able to complete their journey faster and more cheaply as a result of the opening of the Suez Canal. In addition, the discovery of major new diamond fields in South Africa boosted the city's diamond-processing industry.

In 1847, Amsterdam gained a rail link to Rotterdam, but this was only a temporary station. The city had to wait until 1889 before today's grand Centraal Station was completed, just one of several imposing buildings that were constructed at the time. Other architectural achievements of this era included the huge art-filled Rijksmuseum, Concertgebouw concert hall, and the commodities exchange—the iconic Beurs van Berlage. Serious consideration was given to a plan to fill in the city's major canals to create wide, Parisian-style avenues. Amsterdam owes a great debt to those conservationists who fought against such plans, ensuring the city survived with its beautiful 17th-century canal belt intact.

Early 20th Century

Amsterdam's economic rejuvenation led to a period of short-lived prosperity that was fractured by World War I. The Netherlands adopted a position of neutrality, but nevertheless suffered from food shortages. These were the result of the grim war taking place almost on its doorstep, as vast armies massed in the fields of Flanders and in Germany. In the interwar period, Amsterdam hosted the 1928 Olympic Games, building a stadium for the purpose in the south of the city in an area now full of factories.

During the Great Depression of the 1930s, many thousands of unemployed Amsterdammers were given work on job creation schemes, including the construction of the Amsterdamse Bos, a much-valued recreation park and green lung in the southern suburbs. It was at this time, too, that the city council produced what would prove to be a farsighted document, called the General Development Plan. This innovative program made provision for the controlled growth of the city over the remainder of the 20th century, including the establishment of Schiphol Airport, which grew from a tiny airfield on the reclaimed land of Haarlemmermeer to eventually become the fourth-busiest airport in Europe.

> **Amsterdam's economic rejuvenation led to a period of short-lived prosperity that was fractured by World War I. The Netherlands adopted a position of neutrality, but nevertheless suffered from food shortages.**

Nazi Occupation

The Netherlands tried once again to remain neutral at the start of World War II, but Adolf Hitler simply ordered the country to surrender to his will. He demonstrated the consequences of refusal by sending bombers to destroy the city of Rotterdam and threatened that the same treatment would be meted out to every city in the Netherlands, one by one, until the Dutch gave in. The cruelty of this inhuman act, which left 8,000 dead, 80,000 homeless, and Rotterdam a smoldering ruin, was compounded by the inevitablility and ignomy of the Dutch surrender to the German forces the following day.

Amsterdammers watched in stunned disbelief as the tanks and troops rolled into their city. A year later, when 400 Jews were rounded up in the city, dockworkers led a general strike, but the protest lasted only two days as the Nazis caught and shot the strike leaders. In 1942, Anne Frank and her family went into hiding and very nearly avoided capture (see pp. 136–138), but they were discovered and sent to concentration camps in the summer of 1944.

In 1942, Anne Frank and her family went into hiding and very nearly avoided capture (see pp. 136–138), but they were discovered and sent to concentration camps in the summer of 1944.

By the winter of 1944–1945, some parts of north Europe had already been liberated, and the northern Netherlands effectively became a buffer between the Allies and Hitler's Germany. Rail, sea, river, and road blockades designed to prevent food and supplies reaching Germany also isolated many in the Netherlands and left them to starve; gone too were supplies of gas and electricity to help Amsterdammers survive one of the coldest winters of modern times. Buildings were ransacked for timber to feed fires, and anything edible—including rats and flower bulbs—ended up inside the stomachs of desperate people at the risk of typhoid, diphtheria, and cholera.

Liberation & Radicalism

That is one reason why Liberation Day (May 5) is still celebrated in Amsterdam with such fervor, and why the city's flea markets are full of people mulling over bent and broken odds and ends. Nobody who lived through the war years in Amsterdam can break the habit of hoarding and trading anything that might be of use. Neither will the war generation ever forget the sight of American and Canadian B-17s dropping food crates from the sky in early May 1945, or their first blissful taste of bread, tea, Spam, and American chocolate.

The children of that generation, those born in the 1940s and 1950s, seem not to have been cowed by their parents' experiences, but rather inspired to create a new and better world. The 1960s and 1970s saw the rise of radicalism all over Europe, but nowhere more so than in Amsterdam. Here, in addition to fighting for the cause of nuclear disarmament and calling for an end to all forms of discrimination, the city's *Provo's* added a raft of novel demands to the political agenda.

These anarchists, who adopted the name Provo's after one newspaper branded them *provocateurs*, were a small group of radical thinkers who decided to influence Amsterdam politics through the use of humor and street theater. The wide sidewalks of Spui Square, in front of the statue known as Het Amsterdamse Lieverdje—the

Amsterdam Rascal—became the Saturday-night meeting place for young radicals who would try to stir up public feeling about grievances both real and imagined. Perhaps the most visible anti-establishment protest took place in 1966, when smoke bombs were set off in an attempt to disrupt the marriage of Princess Beatrix and Claus von Amsberg.

On Koninginnedag (Queen's Day) in 2009, a more deadly attack occurred at Apeldoorn, when a man drove his car into a parade that included Queen Beatrix, Prince Willem-Alexander, and other members of the royal family. Eight people were killed (including the attacker) and many injured, but none of the royal family were harmed.

A New King

Despite such incidents, the affection of the Dutch people for their royal family has never been in doubt. The Royals are seen as straight-talking and pragmatic, reflecting the characteristics of those they serve. In January 2013, shortly before her 75th birthday, Queen Beatrix announced her abdication after 33 years on the throne. Abdication is not unusual in the Dutch royal family, with both Beatrix's grandmother and mother previously relinquishing their crowns. Stepping aside in favor of her son, King Willem-Alexander, Beatrix cited her conviction that the "responsibility for our nation should now rest in the hands of a new generation."

Amsterdam bade farewell to Queen Beatrix and welcomed the new king Willem-Alexander in a series of celebrations in April 2013. There was the traditional Queen's/King's Day street market, canal parade, music, and dancing, but also a Royal Boat Parade along the IJ. Celebrated Dutch DJ Armin van Buuren hit the decks during the boat parade, joined by the Royal Concertgebouw Orchestra in a gesture that perfectly embodied the juxtaposition of treasured traditions and forward-looking energies within this unique city. ■

King Willem-Alexander, his mother, Princess Beatrix (formerly Queen Beatrix), and Queen Máxima

Architecture & Arts

Amsterdam has its own unique and very particular charm. With the possible exception of Venice, to which Amsterdam is often likened, no other city can match its architectural homogeneity. Unlike Venice, however, Amsterdam is a city not of grand effects but of small and intimate details.

Architecture

Like the music of Bach or Mozart, architectural Amsterdam is a city of repeated patterns, in which each variation from the main theme has the power to thrill. Spotting the endless variations is one of the great pleasures of strolling around this most elegant of cities.

The basic pattern is provided by the way that each building in the canal belt is of similar width and height, the result of deliberate and farsighted town planning. The city council's decision to control building standards was born of necessity. Like many other cities in medieval Europe, Amsterdam was largely built of timber, with roofs of reed or straw, the only exception being the churches. Dedicated to God and symbols of the city's aspirations, churches were considered special enough to warrant being built from expensive imported sandstone.

Combustible construction materials, combined with rudimentary chimneys and fireplaces, ensured that just about every town and city in Europe suffered a devastating fire at some stage in its early history. In the case of Amsterdam, fire struck twice in the 15th century, in 1421 and 1452, and on each occasion the city was all but destroyed.

> Like the music of Bach or Mozart, architectural Amsterdam is a city of repeated patterns, in which each variation from the main theme has the power to thrill.

Building Standards: The city fathers responded to the problems by issuing instructions that all buildings must in future be built of nonflammable materials, and, in typical Amsterdam fashion, they offered householders a subsidy to help underwrite the costs. Likewise, in typical Amsterdam fashion, some people ignored or found a way around the rules. The two oldest surviving buildings in Amsterdam (in the Begijnhof, see p. 62, and on Zeedijk, see pp. 90–91) are both built of timber—yet the first was built in 1477 and the second in 1550, well after the date when city ordinances demanded the use of brick for the walls and ceramic tiles for the roof.

Grachtengordel: The medieval city became increasingly crowded as the population of Amsterdam grew in the 15th and 16th centuries. When refugees from Antwerp began to flood the city in 1585, the city council decided to expand Amsterdam by digging the Singel (Belt) canal. The canal wrapped around the city, allowing for new buildings on both banks, with a mix of commercial, residential, and state-owned property, such as the city arsenal, as well as berths for ships and

Admiring the "Apollo from Olympia" sculpture, at the Allard Pierson Museum

even shipyards for their construction and repair. The period between 1585 and 1593 saw military and industrial activity shift to the Oostelijke Eilanden, artificial islands constructed in the harbor to the east of the city, where the Maritime Museum now stands (see pp. 118–120). This paved the way for the city to develop in a more genteel way, with residential areas explicitly designed for gentlemen, and a special district set aside for artisans.

The canal belt, dating from the 16th and 17th centuries, is now a UNESCO World Heritage site.

The man entrusted with working out how this should be done was a humble carpenter by the name of Hendrick Staets (1575–1649). Although he lacked paper qualifications in town planning, Staets came up with an elegant and logical plan: He would wrap three canals around the core of the old city, then use the soil removed during the canal excavation to create building plots. Little did he know that these plans would be recognized as a World Heritage site by UNESCO some 400 years later.

Staets calculated every single detail with a surveyor's precision. Each canal was to be precisely 82 feet (25 m) wide, broad enough to accommodate four lanes of barges, and 7 feet (2.1 m) deep. Housing plots were to have precisely 98 feet (30 m) of frontage. The maximum height was stipulated to ensure that properties backing onto each other did not steal each other's light. Back annexes (such as the one in which Anne Frank and her family hid) were permitted for accommodating servants. Shops and commercial activity were relegated to the short radial canals, so that anyone looking down the length of the canals would see an unbroken vista of palatial residences. Industrial activity was only permitted in the ironically named Jordaan (Garden) district, which explains why housing plots cost least on the Prinsengracht, facing the Jordaan, and most on the Herengracht, closest to the city and farthest from the smoke and smell. Altogether the canal belt would stretch for a length (including both canal banks) of 7.5 miles (12 km). Combined with the Jordaan, this would treble the city's capacity for growth.

Striking a Blow for Individuality: If the canal belt (*grachtengordel* in Dutch) had been built in strict military fashion according to these formulae, Amsterdam would now be a curiosity—but a deeply dull one. From the start, variations began to creep in. Wealthy merchants bought more than one plot and built very wide houses. Speculators and builders subdivided their plots into smaller proper- ties. Most of the houses were built with their main roof ridge at right angles to the canal. To finish off the ridge with a simple triangle would make the house indistinguishable from a common warehouse, so architects began to design ornate gables. The earliest ones took the form of stepped brickwork, but Philips Ving- boons (1608–1675) introduced the more curvaceous design known as a neck gable (resembling the neck of a wine bottle) in 1638, which was widely copied. Other designs soon followed, each consisting of a square or rectangular brick core, flanked by decorative scroll stones—the name given to the carved sandstone side pieces that give the gable its individual character.

If you were wealthy enough, you would commission your own designs, carved with motifs that advertised the fact that you were a successful merchant by depicting ships, bales of silk, dolphins, and flying fish—even slaves. Otherwise you would take whatever the stone mason supplied from stock, ready-carved— which explains why the same designs and motifs appear across the city.

If you couldn't afford a unique gable, you could commission a *gevelsteen* (gable stone). As the name suggests, these were initially set in the gable, but later appeared lower down on the house front, typically above or beside the front door. The small rectangular stone was carved with images that identified your name, house, or profession in a variety of different (and sometimes humorous) ways. Other ways to make your house stand out included oversize windows, ornate fanlights, heavily embossed front doors, and stoops, or staircases, leading to the front door, decorated with cast-iron balustrades.

Warehouses & Hoist Beams: People couldn't afford any of these stylistic flourishes without an income, and despite the aim of making the canal belt purely residential, warehousing was integral to many designs. In the oldest stretches of

What's On

Find out about local events in the *A-Mag*, a monthly pamphlet produced by the Amsterdam Tourist Board and sold at all tourist offices. *Amsterdam Weekly* is a free cultural newspaper, available from English-language bookshops (see pp. 256–257).

The Ticketshop on Leidseplein is the place to go for advice on Amster- dam's cultural events and attractions, and to buy tickets to see them. If you're feeling spontaneous, check to see what the Last Minute Ticket Shop desk has to offer—half-price tickets go on sale at noon each day for shows that evening.

Keukenhof (Kitchen Garden), also known as the Garden of Europe, the famous Dutch garden near Lisse

the canal belt, in the northern sector, you can see fine warehouses, now converted to apartments. They are easy to spot because of their sail-shaped shutters, often painted in distinctive colors to contrast with the surrounding brickwork.

Residential houses often had offices on the ground floor and warehouse space in the attic. Goods were winched up by means of the hoist beams that still project from many canalside houses and in many cases are still used to lift large items of furniture into the houses through the windows. In order to stop goods from bumping against the brickwork and windows, many houses were built with a facade leaning forward at an angle from the perpendicular. There were several other advantages to building house fronts "in flight," as this was called. Rainwater was kept clear of the facade, so the exterior timberwork did not rot and damp was reduced; soot and other airborne pollution was less likely to cling to the brickwork, so the building remained relatively clean.

Some house fronts leaned to an exaggerated degree, posing the real danger of the house collapsing, or of bricks falling away if the mortar rotted. Building regulations limited the tilt to a maximum of one inch in every three feet (25 mm in every meter), but this rule was widely ignored, as you can see by looking at the picturesque buildings on Reguliersgracht, at the spot known as the Seven Bridges. To reduce the risk of the gable falling down, iron clamps were used, attached to tie rods connecting the gable to the roof ridge. These can often be seen if you look behind the gable.

French Style & Modernism: Later buildings in the canal belt broke radically with the Dutch tradition. Instead of end-on gables, it became the fashion among wealthy families to build houses with wide frontages and ridges running parallel to the canal. These facades, often of sandstone, incorporate such classical features as cornices, balustrades, and pediments. After the lively and sometimes quirky design of the 17th century, these 18th-century buildings seem conventional and dull.

The same cannot be said for the style that swept Amsterdam in the early 20th century. By then, after a 200-year period of relative stagnation, the city had regained its place in international trade and began to suffer from major overcrowding. H. P. Berlage, the innovative designer of Amsterdam's new stock exchange (see pp. 52–53) was asked to draw up a plan for the city's expansion. He came up with a scheme that allowed for large houses for the city's wealthy in the garden suburbs of Amsterdam South, with working-class accommodations to the west and east. Although the sumptuous villas of the Museum Quarter and Amsterdam South are beautifully designed and still very desirable properties, Berlage and his followers—members of the so-called Amsterdam School—poured their creativity into producing innovative low-cost housing. Built around a series of courtyards, with bulbous corner towers and eye-catching spires, the housing complexes of Spaarndammerbuurt (west) (see pp. 152–153) and De Dageraad (see p. 209) are inspiring examples of the belief that cheap housing need not be dull.

Because it maintains a huge legacy of historic buildings, central Amsterdam offers relatively few opportunities for new architecture to flourish—with the exception of the redeveloped Oostelijke Havengebied (Eastern Docklands) and striking contemporary buildings such as the EYE Film Institute and Van Gogh Museum Annex. The suburbs house other examples of contemporary architecture. In Bijlmermeer, for instance, the ING Bank complex of 1987 was built without right angles in rejection of the boxlike form of most office buildings.

> **Amsterdammers' voracious appetite for art to hang on their walls created Europe's first commercial art market.**

Art & Commerce

Having built themselves such handsome town houses, the merchants and bankers of Amsterdam now sought to furnish them in similar style. Amsterdammers' voracious appetite for art to hang on their walls created Europe's first commercial art market. Astonished visitors to Amsterdam, encountering paintings for sale everywhere—in stores, artists' houses, street markets, and galleries—never failed to comment upon this fact. Elsewhere in Europe, art was the

EXPERIENCE: Explore the City's Private Gardens

Each year, on the third weekend of June, green-thumbed visitors get the chance to visit the gardens of some of Amsterdam's finest 16th- and 17th-century canal houses. Your inside take on Dutch horticulture comes courtesy of the city's **Open Tuinen Dagen** (Open Gardens Days) scheme (*opentuinendagen.nl*).

When you walk through people's kitchens, sitting rooms, and bedrooms to admire their lush urban oases, you'll glean intriguing insights into the mind-set of Amsterdammers. The program is overseen by the horticultural historian Tonko Grever, who is curator at the Museum Van Loon (see p. 183). Grever invites some 30 property owners to take part in the event each year. These include owners of private homes, offices, and museums. The small fee paid by visitors to access all the gardens over three days goes toward a different municipal horticultural project each year. While many of the gardens follow traditional canal-garden style, with trimmed buxus hedges in symmetrical shapes, others are a riot of roses, wisteria, and jasmine overhanging dense camellias, rhododendrons, and hydrangeas.

EXPERIENCE: Take a Walking or Biking Tour of Amsterdam

A fun and interesting way to appreciate the pioneering architectural works of the Amsterdam School is to take part in a guided walking or bicycle tour of Amsterdam Zuid. Organized by the visitor center at **De Dageraad** (*Burgemeester Tellegenstraat 128;* see p. 153), along with the **Het Schip Museum** *(hetschip.nl),* these tours introduce you to the theories and monumental works of leading architects of the Amsterdam School, Michel de Klerk and Piet Kramer. Advance reservations are advised for walking tours *(hetschip.nl),* and are required for bicycle tours.

prerogative of wealthy patrons—the Church, guilds, charitable institutions, monarchs, and powerful aristocrats—while in Amsterdam everyone could, and did, own a work of art.

Those who could afford it commissioned their own portraits, treating art as a form of photography, making a record of themselves at the height of their career or at a significant milestone, such as a wedding day. Others banded together to commission group portraits: It was common practice for guilds, civic guards, militia companies, and charitable institutions to hire one of the leading painters of the day to make a record of their membership, preserving their portraits for posterity.

Rembrandt and Frans Hals excelled in both group and individual portraiture, raising this static form to the heights of great art, but neither was fully appreciated in his own lifetime. Both died in poverty—Frans Hals in a home for the old and destitute in Haarlem, and Rembrandt in the Jordaan, to be buried in an anonymous grave—leaving it to future generations to judge how far these two artists towered above their contemporaries.

Off-the-Shelf Morality: Contemporary taste was not for Hals's and Rembrandt's bold monumental and expressive works of genius, but for minutely observed landscapes, cityscapes, interiors, and morality tales. Dutch art of the Golden Age is characterized by an almost fanatical devotion to clarity of draftsmanship and line, rendering in paint as close as possible a representation of the real world. Indeed, some patrons purchased art for its sheer technical bravado. Amsterdam's art galleries were (and still are) full of wintry scenes with snow on eaves and skaters on ponds, or the interiors of churches, demonstrating the artist's skill in using that most difficult of all colors, white.

Many paintings bought off the shelf from the city's art dealers (of whom Rembrandt was one) promote a specific morality. Amsterdam's art patrons seem to have liked paintings that either depicted virtuous behavior, or its opposite. Vermeer was the master of domestic scenes in which patient and modestly dressed women carry out their household duties with resignation and almost religious devotion, turning simple tasks, like pouring milk or sweeping a cobbled alley, into sacramental acts.

Deliberate Ambiguities: Vermeer's poignant portrait "Woman in Blue Reading a Letter" (ca 1663) in the Rijksmusuem, depicting an apparently pregnant woman reading a letter, is perhaps the most explicitly moral; a sea chart in the background suggests that the master of the house is abroad. This portrait of a faithful wife—keeping her love for her absent seafaring husband alive in her heart—could almost be Penelope waiting for her Odysseus to return from the Trojan Wars.

Jan Steen's morality tales depict virtue's opposite. His paintings, which show children drinking and smoking and adults neglecting their tasks, appear to be a warning against self-indulgence, but his rogues and wastrels are painted so lovingly that you cannot help but wonder whether licentiousness is being condemned or celebrated. That Amsterdam burghers sought out and bought these paintings in such quantities suggests they enjoyed the deliberate ambiguity.

Still Lifes: No such ambiguity surrounds the numerous still-life paintings in Amsterdam's museums. Typical of a Dutch still life is an assemblage of gorgeous and exotic objects: flowers and butterflies, imported fruits and spices, beautifully bound books, richly patterned oriental rugs. Nearly always, there is a worm or caterpillar slowly nibbling away at the pretty scalloped petal of a scented carnation to remind us of our mortality and of the transience of worldly luxuries—an apt moral for a city awash with exotic luxuries. Some objects have symbolic meanings: a watch for time, a musical instrument for order and harmony (though they can

Vermeer's "Woman in Blue Reading a Letter": Dutch art often served as a morality tale.

also symbolize indolence and idleness). Patrons would also have been privy to the pre-Freudian language of visual and linguistic puns deployed by artists to amuse their patrons. Jewelry boxes, vases, and candlesticks could stand for the male and female genitals; feathers, mirrors, and cut-glass decanters betokened vanity; dogs symbolized licentiousness; eggshells the frailty of the human condition. Reading a still life could be a stimulating puzzle and a perfect conversation piece, as well as being an uplifting aesthetic experience.

Performing Arts

Amsterdam is synonymous with the Royal Concertgebouw Orchestra, one of the world's great ensembles, displaying professional polish and interpretative flair. Reserve tickets well in advance to avoid missing the opportunity to hear the Netherlands Philharmonic Orchestra and Netherlands Chamber Orchestra perform at the Concertgebouw and accompany many of the productions presented by the Netherlands Opera in Amsterdam's famous Muziektheater.

Performing Arts in Amsterdam

Amsterdam has long been known in Europe as a nurturing incubator of the performing arts and is now home to three main theater buildings: the Stadsschouwburg Amsterdam on the Leidseplein, which hosts theatrical performances; Het Muziektheater, which is the principal opera house and home to De Nederlandse Opera and Het Nationale Ballet; and the Carré Royal Theatre, built as a permanent circus theater in 1887 and currently used mainly for musicals, cabaret performances, and pop concerts. In 1993, the popular improvisational comedy group Boom Chicago founded its own theater at Leidseplein, where it addresses political and social issues with satire and elements of cabaret.

Amsterdam has no pop, rock, roots, or jazz bands of global renown, but the city's vibrant independent rock scene has produced acts such as Fatal Flowers, The Outsiders, and Urban Dance Squad. Appreciative audiences for all forms of contemporary music ensure that it is a favorite venue for touring musicians. In the world of jazz and blues, such venues as Alto and Bimhuis (see p. 263) are legendary.

In Amsterdam's hippie heyday, the nightclubs Melkweg and Paradiso (see p. 264) were bywords for avant-garde and progressive rock; today they have settled into the mainstream. Melkweg, housed in a converted dairy, offers a varied daily performance program that ranges across reggae and roots, Latin and dance, video, circus, and puppetry. A similar mix with more emphasis on mainstream dance music, rock, and Europop characterizes most of the live performances at Paradiso, housed in a converted church.

Some of the city's smaller clubs are renowned not so much for the acts on stage as for the stylish dress of the clubbers who attend theme-party nights. People come to Amsterdam from all over Europe to party in an atmosphere of hedonistic eroticism. Gay Amsterdam has greatly influenced the inventiveness and outrageousness of some of the costumes and the displays of physique that you will see at these events. If you are not brave enough to take part yourself, you can always look at the photographs displayed outside the clubs in Rembrandtplein and Amstelstraat to get an explicit idea of just what an eye-opening experience a visit to a city club can be. ■

Amsterdam's fast-beating commercial heart: trams, tourists, bicycles, and barrel organs hurrying between grand churches, palaces, condom shops, and a sex museum

Nieuwe Zijde

Introduction & Map 46–47

Centraal Station 48–49

Experience: Ride the Museum Boat & the Pancake Boat 49

Damrak & Warmoesstraat 50–53

Dam Square 54–59

Experience: Attend a Free Church Concert 59

A Walk Through the Heart of Amsterdam 60–63

Experience: Relish Amsterdam's Largest Sandwich 62

Amsterdam Museum 64–67

Feature: A City of Keels & Wheels 68–69

Experience: Rent Your Own Sloep 69

More Places to Visit in Nieuwe Zijde 70

Hotels & Restaurants in Nieuwe Zijde 243–244

Clock face detail at Centraal Station

Nieuwe Zijde

From their names, you might be tempted to think that Amsterdam's Nieuwe Zijde (New Side) district is younger than its neighbor, the Oude Zijde (Old Side, see p. 71). In reality, the two parishes are roughly equal in age, but they were subsequently named after their respective churches, built in different centuries.

Oude Zijde's Oude Kerk (Old Church) was founded in 1250, so it is almost as old as the city itself. Nieuwe Zijde got its name from the grand Nieuwe Kerk (New Church), built in 1408 in flamboyant Gothic style to symbolize the city's growing status and prosperity.

The Nieuwe Kerk stands on one side of Dam, the city's main square and the site of the historic dam from which Amsterdam got its name (see p. 26). The church sits next door to the Koninklijk Paleis (Royal Palace), originally built as a prestigious town hall for the city in 1648–1665. Both the New Church and the Royal Palace look across to the Nationaal Monument, a very moving World War II memorial and the central focus of the city's annual Remembrance Day ceremony.

From this main square, Damrak, originally a branch of the Amstel River used as a harbor for fishing boats, lighters, and seagoing cargo ships,

NOT TO BE MISSED:

Morning coffee at Centraal Station's 1e Klas café **49**

A ride on the Museum Boat & the Pancake Boat **49**

Pondering the portraits in the Schuttersgalerij **62**

A visit to Amsterdam's famous floating flower market **63**

Familiarizing yourself with local history at the Amsterdam Museum **64–67**

Enjoying the peace and tranquillity of Begijnhof **70**

0   200 meters
0   200 yards

Area of map detail

station, Centraal Station, in the 1880s cut the city off from its harbor, signaling the city's decline as a global center of maritime trade. However, it kept the arrival point for most visitors to Amsterdam in the same place, with the elegant, Cuypers-designed station the bustling central point of the city today. Not only do international and national trains arrive at the railway station, but trams, buses, and ferries all throng around Stationsplein (Station plaza), the hub of Amsterdam's extensive transportation network. This is a good place to start a canal cruise and where you will find the free ferries that cross the IJ Bay to Amsterdam Noord. By 2017, Centraal Station will also welcome the Noord/Zuidlijn (North-South public transportation line), a metro and rail service linking North and South Amsterdam.

Despite the regeneration of Nieuwe Zijde, look closely throughout the district and you will still find ancient streets, buildings, taverns, and waterways redolent of the mercantile city of old. As you walk through these storied streets, it is not hard to conjure up the colors and noise of 17th-century traders from Russia, Persia, Turkey, China, and the West Indies haggling with local traders over the price of exotic commodities in the Beurs. Step back in time as you enter the tranquil, medieval Begijnhof (Beguines Court) or as you investigate the city's long and extraordinary history in the Amsterdam Museum. ■

cuts through the middle of the historic city center, dividing Nieuwe Zijde (to the west) from Oude Zijde (to the east). Following extensive regeneration, this once seedy thoroughfare now provides a red carpet of shops, restaurants, hotels, and galleries to lead visitors into the heart of the city.

A Harbor History

For centuries, the Nieuwe Zijde district was open to the sea. Anyone strolling around the area until the end of the 19th century would have seen a forest of masts and rigging, felt the sea breeze, and caught the scent of the salt-laden air. The construction of Amsterdam's main railroad

Centraal Station

Where sailing ships from Indonesia and Japan, Tasmania, and the Americas once unloaded their precious cargoes, commuters now pour through the imposing portals of Amsterdam's Centraal Station. As a visitor to Amsterdam, this is probably the first building you will see when you arrive.

The palatial Centraal Station stands as a grand entrance to the city.

Centraal Station

⬛ Map p. 47

Visitor Information

✉ Stationsplein 10

☎ 201-8800

🚇 Centraal Station Metro, all buses & trams to Centraal Station

🚢 Museumboot & Canal Bus to Centraal Station

iamsterdam.com

When the railroad age came to Amsterdam in the 1870s, several sites were considered for the station. The decision to build here was controversial because the harbor was still a potent symbol of the city's maritime origins and construction of the station would separate the city from its harbor on the IJ River.

To compensate for the loss, the city authorities hired P. J. H. Cuypers (1827–1921), the leading architect of the day, to design a station that would serve as a monumental gateway to the city. Completed in 1889, the station was built on a massive artificial island, resting on 8,700 wooden piles driven into the ground for support. Two huge towers flank the central portal of red brick with sandstone detailing. The western tower displays a clock, and reliefs dot the walls, depicting merchants from across the world offering goods in homage to the Maid of Amsterdam, a symbolic personification of the city.

Morning Coffee

Take morning coffee at two nearby cafés: **1e Klas** *(Stationsplein 15, 1012 AB, tel 625-0131, restaurant1eklas.nl)* is Centraal Station's original first-class waiting room on Platform 2b, now a stylish café. Art deco fittings, wood paneling, and lions flanking the entrance hark back to the golden age of rail. Exit the station and bear left, crossing Stationsplein (the paved area out front), and you'll spot a timber building on the waterfront, the **Smits Noord-Zuid Hollandsch Koffiehuis** *(Stationsplein 10, 1012 AB, tel 623-3777, smitskoffiehuis.nl)*. Built in 1911, it now houses the tourist office and an atmospheric café downstairs.

The North-South Line

Amsterdam has been subject to major disruption over the past decade, as the North-South public transportation line has been built under the city. While Amsterdammers are typically vocal in their frustration at years of construction along key roads, the line will undoubtedly prove popular when it opens in 2017. The metro and light rail service will pass under the IJ Bay and call at eight stations between Noord and Zuid.

To the Harbor

The station underpass leads beneath the platforms to the harbor. From here the view stretches westward to the docks lining the North Sea Canal, and east to the Eastern Docklands (see pp. 124–125). At the rear of the station a **ferry terminal** offers regular free rides across the IJ, to the Noord (North) area (see p. 126). ∎

EXPERIENCE: Ride the Museum Boat & the Pancake Boat

If seeing the canal-house facades and visiting the city's museums are high on your Amsterdam agenda, you'll find a canal cruise the most convenient and comfortable way to go. You'll also meet Dutch cruisers happy to share their knowledge of the city. Both major cruise operators, **Canal Bus** *(Weteringschans 26-1hg, tel 623-9886, canal.nl)* and **Lovers** *(Prins Hendrikkade 25, tel 530-1090, lovers.nl)*, offer 24-hour hop-on/hop-off tickets (Canal Bus also has a 48-hour option), which include discounts on admission to various museums. You'll have a choice of several routes, all of which run regularly throughout the day during peak season.

An excellent way to explore Amsterdam's harbor is aboard the **Pannenkoekenboot** *(Pancake Boat, Ms van Riemdijkweg, tel 636-8817, pannenkoekenboot.nl)*. This popular service leaves from Amsterdam Noord (see p. 126) and offers various voyages, such as a one-hour "all-you-can-eat pancakes" cruise and a two-and-a-half-hour cruise with pancakes plus a buffet of typical Dutch dishes. As you feast, the boat sails from Noord around the IJ Bay, passing the NDSM docks and the old Westelijke Eilanden harbors (see pp. 154–155), and reaching the quays and islands of the Eastern Docklands (see pp. 124–125). To reach the Pancake Boat, simply take the free, ten-minute ferry from Centraal Station to NDSM-Werf, which deposits you right next to the embarkation point.

Damrak & Warmoesstraat

As you emerge from Centraal Station, the main street of Amsterdam, called Damrak, lies straight ahead. Over to the left, glass-topped boats wait to carry visitors on canal-boat tours, mooring in the insignificant little pool also known as Damrak, once the busiest spot in Amsterdam. Warmoesstraat (Vegetable Garden Street), Amsterdam's oldest thoroughfare, runs parallel to Damrak. Once a prestigious address, it has benefited from an extensive recent face-lift.

Damrak Street, the busy main thoroughfare, gives many visitors their first impressions of Amsterdam.

On the occasions that Samuel Pepys (1633–1703), the London diarist, visited Amsterdam in the 1660s, he was thrilled by the hustle and bustle of its boat-filled harbor. His contemporary, Sir Thomas Nugent, recommended Warmoesstraat to English travelers on the grounds that its innkeepers were the only honest ones in town, and the Mozart family lodged here in 1766.

The Red Carpet

However, two centuries later, this area, located on the fringes of the Red Light District, had descended into a sorry state, lined with sex shops, seedy bars, and tacky souvenir shops. In an attempt to address the growing criminal infrastructure in the area, and the less-than-favorable first impression offered to visitors on this main thoroughfare, the municipal council initiated Project 1012 (named after the area postcode) in 2009.

This ongoing and successful strategy aims to discourage crime and corruption in the city center by reducing the types of businesses that are conducive to crime, permitting prostitution in just two areas, and enforcing stricter regulations on coffee shops. The scheme also introduces basic infrastructure improvements, like wider sidewalks and improved street lighting, and economic support for new hotels, boutiques, and cultural initiatives, lending it the name the red carpet.

Old-School Charm

A few pockets of gentility from the times of Pepys and Nugent can still be found in the district. A beguiling tavern called **In de Olofspoort** (In Olof's Gate; *Nieuwebrugsteeg 13, 1012 AG, tel 624-3918, olofspoort.com*), located at the end of Nieuwebrugsteeg (New Bridge Alley) to the left of Damrak, dates back to 1619. This is an authentic *proeflokaal,* or tasting bar, where you can sample different spirits, notably *jenever* (gin) (see p. 149).

A little further down the Warmoesstraat, the 16th century, former salesman's house at No. 139 has long been home to bars, clubs, and societies. In 1979, a group of young artists squatted in the then-derelict building. They subsequently turned it into an exhibition platform for new, raw artworks. Unaffiliated with any commercial gallery or museum, **W139** offers "room for risk" to young artists who are not yet ready to exhibit in established museums. After a renovation in the 1990s, this autonomous space has secured its place in Amsterdam's art scene.

Next, retrace your steps for about 150 yards (140 m) until you reach, on your left, the alley of Oudebrugsteeg. This brings you out onto the southern end of Damrak beside the **Grasshopper** café *(Oudebrugsteeg 16, tel 626-1259, grasshopper.nl).* Written in bold letters around the eaves of the café is this legend: *De Cost*

INSIDER TIP:

Buy Amsterdam's best bread at Gebroeders Niemeijer *[Nieuwendijk 35, gebroedersniemeijer .nl]*, **with its beautiful art deco ceiling.**

—PAUL RÖMER
Managing Editor,
National Geographic Traveler
magazine in the Netherlands

Gaet Voor de Baet Uyt. Colloquially translated, this means "You have to invest money to make money"—an apt motto for a spot that was the heart of mercantile Amsterdam in the 17th century.

Opposite the café lies the **Oude Accijnshuis,** an incongruously sedate classical building, built in 1683 to house the tax collector's office. Merchants later came here to pay duty on their

W139

- ✉ Warmoesstraat 139
- ☎ 622-9434
- ⏰ Sun. Noon– 6 p.m.
- 💲 Free
- 🚇 Centraal Station Metro, all buses & trams to Centraal Station
- ⛴ Canal Bus, Museumboot & Artis Express to Centraal Station

w139.nl

Flower Power & Tulip Mania

Of all the exotic imports that Amsterdam merchants brought back to the city, few were as popular, costly, or transient as the Turkish tulip bulb. The most highly prized blooms were those that suffered from an unusual viral condition in which the pigment in the petals broke into flame- or feather-like striations. Delft factories created special vases shaped like elongated pyramids, measuring up to three feet (one meter) tall, with a series of cup-shaped bowls up each of the four sides, in which to display tulip blooms.

Such was the desire among Dutch collectors to own fine specimens that the bulbs were traded on the Amsterdam commodities exchange. At the height of Tulip Fever, which gripped the city in the 1630s, bulbs were fetching higher prices than emeralds. Family fortunes were blown away in what was known as "the wind trade" (so called because speculation in bulbs was as insubstantial and as changeable as the wind), yet the bulb came to have an enduring and honorable place in Dutch culture.

goods before they were taken to be sold in the **Beurs van Berlage,** the commodities market (see below) that stands alongside the Oude Accijnshuis.

Retrace your steps up Oude-brugsteeg, and back on Warmoes-straat, at No. 141, you will find the **Condomerie Het Gulden Vlies** (Golden Fleece Condom Shop). This respectable establishment sells gift-wrapped condoms in every form imaginable.

Opposite the shop, Papenbrug-steeg takes you out onto Damrak, with the Beurs to the right and the city's biggest department store (built 1911–1913) to the left. Called **De Bijenkorf** (The Bee-hive), this is Amsterdam's answer to Macy's and *the* place to shop for fashion, toys, household goods, and furniture (see p. 257).

Beurs van Berlage

At least a quarter of the length of Damrak is taken up by the huge Koopmansbeurs (Merchants' Exchange), now known as the Beurs van Berlage, after H. P. Berlage, the building's architect. Merchants from all over the world came here to make

INSIDER TIP:

Discover *jenevers,* or Dutch gins, in Proeflo-kaal Wynand Fockink at Pijlsteeg 31 [near the Beurs; *wynand-fockink .nl*]. The distillery's olde-worlde tasting room is lined with antique, hand-painted bottles.

—JEREMY GRAY
National Geographic author

their fortunes, haggling noisily over the price of tobacco, sugar, silks, Chinese porcelain, spices, and even tulip bulbs, when the phenomenon of tulip mania hit the country in 1636 (see sidebar above).

The first exchange building was erected in 1607. Until then, merchants carried out their business on the quayside or in the surrounding streets. Berlage's building, constructed between 1898 and 1903, is the third on the site, and it established a new landmark in Dutch architecture. The architects of most buildings of this era (including Centraal Station and the Rijksmuseum) looked backward for inspiration, to the Gothic and Renaissance eras. By contrast, the Beurs was groundbreaking and modern, and accordingly it was initially derided. Nonetheless it was studied by the young architects of the Amsterdam School, who went on to build some of the city's most innovative, early 20th-century housing (see pp. 152 & 209).

The most prominent feature of the Beurs, the clock tower, bears the legends: *Duur Ur Uuur* (Await Your Hour) and *Beidt Uw Tyd* (Bide Your Time), demonstrating Berlage's antipathy to the fast-paced business that went on inside. His politics were further reflected in the building's interior friezes, which glorify the concepts of cooperation and communal ownership of wealth, in direct challenge to the raw capitalism of the free market that thrived inside.

Berlage's building now houses a series of concert, conference, and exhibition halls. Attending a concert or exhibition at the Beurs is one way of appreciating its palatial interior, dotted with murals, furniture, and tile pictures. However, joining a guided tour provides access to otherwise inaccessible rooms, and you'll hear a history of Dutch trading. Tours start at 10:30 a.m. on Saturdays and include an ascent of the 130-foot (40 m) bell tower, and coffee or lunch in the Beurs Café. ■

Beurs van Berlage Museum

- Map p. 47
- Damrak 243
- 530-4141
- $$
- Tram: 4, 9, 14, 16, 24, 25

beursvanberlage.nl

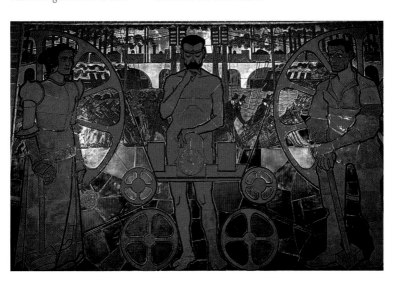

A detail from the interior of the Beurs van Berlage on the subject of labor and time

Dam Square

Dam Square is Amsterdam's principal public space, a large cobbled square dominated by the imposing Koninklijk Paleis (Royal Palace), built between 1648 and 1665 as the city's Stadhuis (Town Hall). The palace is a source of civic pride for Amsterdammers, and one of the city's best-loved architectural legacies from the Golden Age.

The Nationaal Monument, Dam Square, a popular meeting point

Koninklijk Paleis

The Stadhuis was built when Amsterdam was at the peak of its powers as a maritime trading nation, a fact celebrated in the decorations. The gilded weather vane is shaped like a Dutch *kogge*—cog—a small but sturdy ship that sailed the oceans, bringing back exotic commodities to make the city wealthy. The carved pediment shows the Maid of Amsterdam receiving homage from the oceans and continents of the world, symbolized by sea gods, fish, lions, and unicorns.

On the roof of the palace, the bronze figure of Peace holds an olive branch, a reference to the Treaty of Münster, signed in 1648, which ended the Eighty Years' War against Spain and ushered in a period of sustained growth and prosperity. Peace is flanked by Prudence and Justice, a reminder that this building served as a civil and criminal court, as well as being home to Amsterdam's city government.

The Stadhuis's conversion to a palace took place in 1808 when Napoléon invaded the Netherlands and put his brother, Louis Bonaparte, on the Dutch throne. The massive structure, Amsterdam's most prestigious public building, was designed by Jacob van Campen in the classical style that was fashionable in the mid-17th century. Classicism demanded at least the appearance of marble; the nearest material available to Van Campen was gray-white sandstone.

Visiting the Palace: Finding your way into the building can present a challenge. The entrance (which is through the right-hand arch in the facade arcade) was deliberately kept small and inconspicuous to make the building easier to defend. The cellars served as the city's arsenal, prison, and bank vault, and could be used for storing literally millions of gold florins.

Each visitor to the palace receives an audio tour. The first room you come to on the tour of the interior is the small **Tribunal.** It's the most highly decorated room in the whole palace, though the lack of any color hints at the chilling purpose to which it was put. Here the death sentence was pronounced, in full view of the crowds gathered in the square outside, on any citizen found guilty of a capital crime, such as murder, witchcraft, or treason. The sculptures, executed in clinical white marble, were intended to remind the judges to exercise Justice and Prudence.

Opposite the entrance is the marble seat of the secretary who recorded the death sentence in the city annals, and over it a plaque commemorates the laying of the first foundation stone when work on the Stadhuis began

Koninklijk Paleis

- 🗺 Map p. 46
- ☎ 620-4060
- 🕐 Open daily in summer & during school vacations; closed Mon. rest of year
- 💲 $$$
- 🚊 Tram: 4, 9, 16, 24, 25

paleisamsterdam.nl

Queen Beatrix's Abdication

In January 2013, the Dutch Queen Mother, Queen Beatrix, announced her abdication after 33 years on the throne. Abdication is far from rare in the Dutch royal family—both Beatrix's grandmother and mother abdicated too. The belief that the role of king or queen is neither God-given nor lasts a lifetime is another example of the pragmatic approach of the Dutch. Beatrix said: "I am not abdicating because this office is too much of a burden, but out of conviction that the responsibility for our nation should now rest in the hands of a new generation."

Those hands belong to her eldest son, King Willem-Alexander, who assumed the throne on April 30, 2013, at the high point of a year of celebrations that commemorated the end of the Napoleonic occupation in 1813. The kingdom of the Netherlands was established two years later. Willem-Alexander is the first Dutch king since Willem III, who reigned until his death in 1890. An ex-member of the International Olympic Committee, he is a trained pilot and water management expert. He was groomed for the throne for many years.

in 1648. A figure representing the city of Amsterdam stands above the plaque, flanked by the gods of the Amstel and IJ rivers.

The Universe in Miniature:

Coming out of the Tribunal, turn right to reach the main staircase, which leads to the **Citizens' Hall,** a huge and colorful room whose rich decorative scheme

---

Piles & Palaces

The construction of the Koninklijk Paleis involved sinking an extraordinary number of wooden piles deep into the ground, each 36 feet (12 m) long. The exact number is easily remembered by a formula taught to every Amsterdam schoolchild: Just put a 1 before the number of days in the year and a 9 behind—the result is 13,659.

---

represents the cosmos. The marble floor is inlaid with brass maps of the northern sky and the Eastern and Western Hemispheres, while a huge figure of Atlas, supporting a celestial globe, looks down from above the entrance to the Magistrates' Court. The ubiquitous Maid of Amsterdam is portrayed again, this time flanked by the gods of Wisdom (Pallas Athena) and Strength (Hercules).

Off this central room lie the smaller chambers that served as meeting rooms for the city council and various branches of the city's administration. Classical references abound, giving clues to the function of the different rooms.

Above the entrance to the **Magistrates' Court** stands a marble statue of blind Justice, holding an executioner's sword, and flanked by figures symbolizing Death and Retribution. Venus, goddess of love, looks across to the office where marriages were registered, while Icarus (who tried to fly but fell from the sky when the sun melted his wings of feathers and wax) plunges head first to the Earth in the relief atop the entrance to the office where citizens filed for bankruptcy. The decorative festoon above depicts poisonous plants, rats gnawing on unpaid bills, and an empty money chest.

Ceiling paintings and massive narrative artworks lend color and drama to many of the rooms. Again, these tell stories from classical literature and the Bible. Solomon prays for wisdom, and Moses appoints a council of 70 wise men to advise him in narratives depicted on vast canvases that hang in the **City Council Chamber,** there to remind its members that they were ultimately accountable to God.

From Napoléon to Today:

Here and there a few reminders survive from the era when the Stadhuis first served as a palace for the court of Napoléon (1808–1813). Empire-style chandeliers light several of the rooms, and the Bankruptcy Chamber has a suite of elegant furniture in the neoclassic style popular at the time.

Today, this splendid palace is no longer the home of the Dutch monarch—King Willem-Alexander's official residence is in Den Haag (The Hague)—but it continues to be used for state events, including the reception of foreign heads of state when they are invited on formal visits to the Netherlands.

Nationaal Monument: One annual ceremony performed by King Willem-Alexander is the laying of a wreath on the Nationaal Monument on Remembrance Day (May 4). The monument lies on the opposite side of Dam Square from the palace, in front of the NH Grand Hotel Krasnapolsky (see p. 243).

This fine obelisk of creamy travertine was erected to preserve the memory of the World War II dead. It contains earth from each province in the Netherlands, as well as from Indonesia (the former Dutch East Indies). The victims are represented by naked chained figures beneath the outstretched arms of the crucified Christ. Today the monument serves as a popular meeting place for both locals and visitors to Amsterdam.

Nieuwe Kerk

Modeled on the splendid Gothic cathedral at Amiens in France, the Nieuwe Kerk (New Church) on Dam Square dates back to 1408 and is only new in relation to the early 13th-century Oude Kerk (see pp. 84–85). It was

Nieuwe Kerk

- Map p. 46
- Dam Square
- 638-6909
- Occasionally closed for rearrangement of exhibitions
- $$$
- Tram: 1, 2, 4, 5, 9, 16, 17, 25

nieuwekerk.nl

Visitors learn Dutch history in the Citizens' Hall of the Koninklijk Paleis.

completed at the time when the medieval Gothic style was being eclipsed by the new Renaissance style.

To see the point at which Gothic yielded to Renaissance, walk around the outside of the church. As you circle it, heading to the right of the entrance (down an alley called Eggertstraat, then left onto Gravenstraat), you will pass several well-loved Amsterdam watering holes. **De Drie Fleschjes** (The Three Flasks) is a colorful old *proeflokaal* (tasting bar), and alongside is **Het Huys met de Gaeper** (The House with the Gaper), a *wijnlokaal* (wine-tasting bar). The "Gaper" in question is a wooden figure in a helmet, set above the door. He would once have adorned—and advertised—the premises of an apothecary, and he is opening wide so the apothecary can look inside his mouth and diagnose his complaint.

Continuing left brings you to the northern transept, the last part of the church to be completed. Looking up, you will see that the beautiful geometric Gothic tracery gives way to typical Renaissance shell hoods, niches, and columns. Note also a feature typical of Dutch churches: The attractive small shops built up against the church wall were constructed to generate an income for the upkeep of the church. Although it continues to be the national church of the Netherlands (and thus the place where the Dutch monarch is crowned), the Nieuwe Kerk is now mainly used as a concert hall and a venue for art exhibitions. Organ concerts are held Sundays at 8 p.m. from June through August. The church also boasts a lively café, **'t Nieuwe Café,** in the adjoining building, which is popular with local artists and musicians.

The baroque pulpit in Amsterdam's Nieuwe Kerk

EXPERIENCE: Attend a Free Church Concert

Amsterdammers love the uplifting chimes of a church carillon. The sound of bells pealing across the canals and echoing around the narrow, winding streets has been a constant here since the Golden Age.

In keeping with this age-old tradition, four of the city's nine 17th-century churches give a free carillon concert each week. The hour-long concerts encompass many types of music, from well-known classical and folk pieces to the occasional contemporary tune. Concert programs are typically posted the day before the event at the foot of the church bell tower.

To enjoy the carillon at its best, find a picturesque spot outside the church a few minutes before the concert is due to start. You will notice that many of the windows of nearby houses are opened to let the sound in. To bring the music of old Amsterdam to your ears visit:

Munttoren (*Muntplein*; see p. 63) Fridays from noon

Oude Kerk (*Oudekerksplein 23*; see pp. 84–85) Saturdays from 4 p.m.

Westerkerk (*Prinsengracht 281*; see p. 139) Tuesdays from noon

Zuiderkerk (*Zuiderkerkhof 72*; see pp. 94–95) Thursdays from 10 a.m.

The building's present appearance of Protestant austerity is a result of the Alteration of 1578 (see pp. 29–30), when this Catholic church was taken over by the Dutch Reformed Church and stripped of its medieval statues and frescoes. To emphasize the break with the Catholic past, the liturgical focus of the building was moved to the nave, with its immense baroque **pulpit** dating from 1648. Beside it is the **organ case** of 1645, which survived a fire that gutted the church in the same year only because it had been dismantled and removed to the organmaker's workshop for repair. Opposite is an imposing mid-17th-century baroque **choir screen,** with a marble base and exuberant barley sugar-twist columns of brass.

In place of the high altar, the ceremonial focal point of a Catholic church, the city fathers placed the splendid **tomb** of Admiral Michiel de Ruyter (1607–1676). De Ruyter won many sea battles in the Anglo-Dutch Wars of 1665–1667 and 1672–1674 before being killed fighting the French in the seas near Sicily. He was

INSIDER TIP:

Best sightlines of the roof of the Nieuwe Kerk? For a bird's-eye view take the Ferris wheel at Dam Square.

—PANCRAS DIJK
National Geographic *magazine in the Netherlands writer*

held up as a model citizen for his courageous service and given an elaborate state funeral. Allegorical figures of Power, Prudence, and Perseverance—reminders of his many sterling virtues—flank De Ruyter's massive monument. ■

A Walk Through the Heart of Amsterdam

Medieval and modern Amsterdam lie cheek by jowl in this walk, which passes through the historic core of the city, moving from the tempting window displays of Amsterdam's busiest shopping street to the quiet cloisters of the city's former orphanage and convent.

Flea markets abound in Amsterdam; this one is near the Royal Palace.

The walk starts on **Dam Square** (see pp. 54–59). As its name suggests, this square was built on the site of the original dam across the Amstel River, after which the city is named. Old paintings in the Amsterdam Museum (see pp. 64–67) show goods being carted across the cobbles in wheelbarrows and on sleds, and an arcaded building in the middle of the square. This was the 1565 Waag (Weighhouse), which was demolished in 1808 because the imperious King Louis-Napoléon deemed that the building obscured his view from the Royal Palace.

NOT TO BE MISSED:

De Papegaai church • Amsterdam Museum • Begijnhof • Bloemenmarkt

With the Royal Palace on your right, cross Dam Square to Kalverstraat. To your right is the Peek & Cloppenburg department store, with **Madame Tussauds ❶** on the top floor (see p. 70). Modern stores line pedestrian-only Kalverstraat, the city's main shopping street. On the right, just before Nos. 66–72, don't miss the tiny entrance to the splendid neo-Gothic church of 1848. The church is known as **De Papegaai ❷ (The Parrot),** after the bird carved in stone to the left of the entrance, and served as a clandestine church in the era when

---

🅰 See also area map pp. 46–47
► Dam Square
🕓 3 hours
↔ 1.6 miles (2.5 km)
► Dam Square

---

open Catholic worship was prohibited in Amsterdam (see also pp. 86–87).

Turn right down Sint Luciensteeg to the entrance, on the left, of the **Amsterdam Museum ❸** (see pp. 64–67). The entrance wall is decorated with *gevelstenen* (gable stones) rescued from demolished houses. These carved sandstone plaques were used to identify houses in the days before numbering was introduced, and usually gave a clue to the houseowner's occupation or name. Here you will see depictions of a milkmaid and a porter, and a plaque inscribed "de Swarte Molle" (the Black Mole)—perhaps marking the house of a furrier.

Rather than entering the museum here, go back to Kalverstraat and turn right. Look for another narrow entrance, set back on the right, with a leaning doorway dated 1581. The carvings on the doorway depict children, dressed in the red and blue uniforms of the city orphanage, seated around a table from which the Holy Ghost is rising in the guise of a dove. A bronze pillar topped by a moneybox, once used for collecting charitable donations, stands in front of the gate.

Passing through the arch, you come to the quiet tree-shaded courtyards where orphanage children once played, surrounded by a dignified set of buildings converted in 1580 from the former convent of St. Luciën. The city's foremost architects— Hendrick de Keyser and

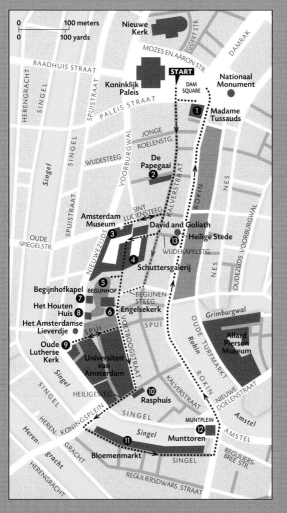

Jacob van Campen—were chosen to undertake this work, showing the high priority given to welfare projects by the city authorities in the Golden Age. The courtyard, the former convent dairy farm, is now a pleasant spot for lunch at the museum's **Café Mokum.**

Just beyond the café, on the left, glass doors lead into the **Schuttersgalerij** ❹ (Civic Guard Gallery). This is a public footpath that passes through the museum *(path open only 10 a.m.– 5 p.m.)*; if it's closed, go back to Kalverstraat, turn right, and take the first right, Begijnen-steeg, to continue with the walk. The gallery is lined with group portraits of members of the various militias—volunteer police forces responsible for maintaining law and order in the city from the 17th to early 19th centuries.

Tranquillity in the Begijnhof

Leaving through the glass doors at the far side of the gallery, continue down the alley to a small door in the wall on the right that leads into the courtyard of the **Begijnhof** ❺ (see p. 70), a peaceful residential enclave where people come to absorb the spiritual atmosphere of this former beguines court. Beguines were lay Christian nuns who led a religious life without taking vows of chastity or poverty. They lived in communities like this one (founded in 1346) and devoted their lives to caring for the sick and educating the poor. The church, rebuilt in 1727, is now known as the **Engelsekerk** ❻ (English Church) because it was used by the English community in Amsterdam. Lunchtime concerts are held inside (see the noticeboard by the door for details).

Opposite, at No. 30, is the delightful **Begijnhofkapel** ❼ (see p. 70), built in 1671 as a clandestine chapel and disguised as a house. Beside it, at No. 34, is **Het Houten Huis** ❽ (The Wooden House), the second oldest surviving house in Amsterdam, built in 1470, but not open to the public.

Leave the Begijnhof the way you came in and turn right onto the irregularly shaped square called **Spui.** Over to the right, in front

EXPERIENCE:
Relish Amsterdam's Largest Sandwich
Join the locals for lunch at the excellent **Eetcafé Singel 404** *(Singel 404, tel 428-0154).* This busy café serves huge and well-priced open *broodjes* (sandwiches), available hot or cold, hearty soups, fresh smoothies, and man-size cakes. Enduringly popular, particularly with students, the tiny interior and the tables lining the canal outside fill up from late morning through mid-afternoon, so patience is needed here. The wait is worth it, with imaginative and generous sandwich fillings ranging from a traditional Dutch Uitsmijter (a fried egg sandwich) with lashings of slow-cooked ham and cheese to smoked chicken with avocado, brie, and sun-dried tomatoes served on a wide choice of home-baked breads.

of the Athenaeum bookstore, stands the 1960 bronze statue of a scruffy urchin called **Het Amsterdamse Lieverdje** (The Amsterdam Rascal). It became a symbol of alternative Amsterdam in the 1960s and '70s when anti-establishment demonstrators gathered here on Saturday nights for street theater and impromptu demonstrations.

Cross the road over to the **Oude Lutherse Kerk** ❾ (Old Lutheran Church), now part of the University of Amsterdam library, then turn left and take the second right, down Voetboog-straat. This leads to **Heiligeweg** (Holy Way), so called because medieval pilgrims used to pass along here to the site of the Miracle of Amsterdam (see sidebar p. 85).

At the junction of the two roads you will see the preserved gatehouse of the **Rasphuis** ❿, the 17th-century prison where the inmates were set to work shaving brazil-wood with bladed rasps to make a powder used as dyestuff. Look out for the doorcase that depicts naked chained men on either side of the allegorical Maid of Amsterdam, and a cart piled high with timber pulled by snarling hyenas, lions, and boars.

The Floating Flower Market

Turn right onto Heiligeweg, cross the next bridge, and turn left into **Bloemenmarkt ⑪**, the floating flower market. The 15 florist shops lining the left-hand side of this street are based on floating barges moored in the Singel canal. The sight of such a variety of flowers, bulbs, topiary shrubs, and pot plants is colorful and absorbing. Standholders will advise you on what customs regulations will allow you to bring home, and what will grow best where you live.

At the end of the market, turn left to the **Munttoren ⑫** (Mint Tower), so named because it briefly housed the city mint from 1672 to 1673. The lower part of the tower, with its gunports and "bacon-strip" courses of alternate brickwork and sandstone, belonged to the ancient city walls, built around 1480. Until this time, the city had been defended by an earthen rampart. To defray the cost of rebuilding the defenses, petty criminals were given the choice of paying their fines either in money or bricks. City architect Hendrick de Keyser added the steeple in 1620. This has a fine carillon that plays a tune every 15 minutes.

As you go, look across to the gray classical building on the opposite bank. This is the **Allard Pierson Museum** of archaeological antiquities (see pp. 78–79). Just beyond, at Rokin 99, is a postmodern version of a gabled canal house, ironically called the **Oud Hof** (Old Court), built from pink granite and blue-tinted glass. Continuing down Rokin, leading you back to Dam, you cannot miss the 30-foot-tall (9 m) granite column in the middle of the sidewalk, just by Wijdekapelsteeg. The **Heilige Stede ⑬** (Holy Column) is all that survives of a chapel built on the site of the Miracle of Amsterdam, which attracted pilgrims in their thousands from 1345. Devout Catholics still commemorate the event with a silent candlelit procession (known as the Stille Omgang) around March 17, the anniversary of the Miracle.

You'll find a multitude of tulip bulbs for sale at the Bloemenmarkt (Flower Market) on Singel.

Amsterdam Museum

Amsterdam's former orphanage provides an atmospheric setting for the maze of rooms that make up the Amsterdam Museum. A wealth of innovative exhibitions recount Amsterdam's history from its medieval origins to the present day, encouraging travelers to connect with the city and its people, past and present.

Modern media meets paint on canvas at Amsterdam Museum (formerly Amsterdams Historisch Museum).

Amsterdam Museum

⬛ Map p. 46
✉ Kalverstraat 92
☎ 523-1822
💲 $$$
🚋 Tram: 1, 2, 4, 5, 9, 14, 16, 24, 25

amsterdammuseum .nl

To visit Amsterdam Museum (formerly Amsterdams Historisch Museum) is to learn something of an endlessly intriguing city that you hadn't known before. This is true even for residents, but the museum demands of the discerning traveler at least two visits: a quick familiarization tour to gain an overview of Amsterdam's history and a return visit once you know the city better. It is well worth taking advantage of the hour-long audio tour (available in various languages, including English), which you can pick up from reception. This audio tour will guide you through the highlights of the museum and add greatly to your experience of the galleries.

Amsterdam DNA

The permanent Amsterdam DNA exhibition comprises numerous pictures, objects, installations, and soundbites demonstrating the process by which Amsterdam grew from a small fishing settlement on the Amstel River delta to a city of more than 800,000 inhabitants during the course of its history of almost 800 years. You can explore the exhibition thoroughly in about one hour, gaining a solid understanding of the city's long and turbulent history, and gaining a sense of the rich, vibrant culture of Amsterdam.

The exhibition leads with Amsterdam's four key values: the Spirit of Enterprise, Freedom of Thought, Civic Virtue, and Creativity, and goes on to weave these into the city's history, breaking it down into seven different time periods from the year A.D. 1000 to the present day.

Thus, the exhibition begins with a contemplation of the slow and arduous colonization

INSIDER TIP:

For a quick fix of Golden Age paintings, visit the Schuttersgalerij [Civic Guards Gallery] in the entrance passage to the Amsterdam Museum. The awe-inspiring group portraits here are up to 20 feet [6m] long.

—JEREMY GRAY
National Geographic author

of the marshy terrain of north Holland in the 11th century. The displays reimagine life at the time, with artifacts such as fish spears, cauldron hooks, clogs, and saws suggesting a settlement of fishermen and boat builders who struggled to subsist among the reeds.

Next the visitor is transported to bustling medieval Amsterdam, where cesspits full of discarded rubbish provide archaeologists with a picture of

Guided Tours of Museums on Your Phone or Tablet

In partnership with the Waag Society and DOEN charity, the Amsterdam Museum has created the excellent free Museum App *(museumapp.nl)*. The app provides interactive, English-speaking tours of several of the city's leading museums, including the Amsterdam Museum, the Rembrandthuis (see pp. 103–104), the Joods Historisch Museum (see pp. 108–109), and Het Schip (see pp. 152–153). In addition to covering these attractions, the app offers guided walking tours of central Amsterdam and other parts of the city, such as the Plantage and the route to Haarlem, and separate tours of Den Haag (see pp. 228–229) and Rotterdam (see pp. 232–234). If you're concerned about racking up large international roaming fees on your cell phone, several of the museums offer iPhones preloaded with the app for a nominal fee.

a society of growing prosperity. The relics and religious memorabilia found also demonstrate Amsterdam's popularity as a pilgrimage center in this era of Europe's Dark Ages.

Be sure to admire Cornelis Anthoniszoon's extraordinarily detailed and accurate bird's-eye view of Amsterdam, which was drawn in 1538 and shows the gradual blossoming of the city.

It was some 50 years later, in 1578, that Amsterdam passed from adolescence into adulthood, when the city declared its independence and forced the Catholic city government to give way to the increasingly popular Protestant reformers.

Thus, the scene is set for the Golden Age, which can be explored in a separate permanent exhibition. This exhibit consists of a very impressive collection of artwork, including Rembrandt's celebrated "Anatomy Lesson of Dr. Jan Deijman," painted in 1656. Most of it was destroyed by fire in 1723, and what survives is the deathly white corpse, viewed in shortened perspective, that Dr. Deijman is about to dissect at the start of a public lecture on anatomy, sponsored by the city's Guild of Surgeons.

Modern City

The Amsterdam DNA exhibit continues through the Napoleonic era, the city's 19th-century decline, and the General Expansion Plan of 1935, a farsighted blueprint for the controlled expansion of the city.

A moving section of the exhibition documents the nightmare of the Holocaust and the so-called Hunger Winter of 1945, when several thousand citizens died from starvation and disease in the final winter of the Nazi Occupation.

In contrast with these horrors, the museum takes an affectionate look at the postwar era and the early 21st century,

The influence of Amsterdam's colonial history looms large at Amsterdam Museum.

focusing on the city's celebrated tolerance and its pragmatic approach to prostitution, homosexuality, and radical and anarchistic political movements.

The Sound of Amsterdam

The Amsterdam Museum prides itself on presenting pioneering installations and exhibitions, such as the Sound of Amsterdam. This enables visitors to experience how the largest square of the city, the Dam, sounded in 1895, 1935, and 2012. Facing a large painting of Dam Square by Breitner, dating back to 1898, the visitor can don headphones and become immersed in the soundscape of the city as it was then: horse-drawn carts clattering across cobblestone roads, sailors off-loading materials on nearby canals, and the carillon of Nieuwe Kerk. Moving aurally to the interwars year of 1935, you will hear the noise of trams, the foreboding whine of air-raid sirens, and static-interrupted snatches of radio broadcasts by the Dutch Resistance.

Amsterdam Close Up

Temporary exhibitions at the Amsterdam Museum, such as a portrait of the greatest Dutch soccer player, Johan Cruijff, enable visitors to delve deeper into the social and cultural fabric of Amsterdam. Further exhibitions of contemporary art, design, and fashion ensure the museum retains a young audience and a lively atmosphere.

Het Kleine Weeshuis

For those traveling with children, the Little Orphanage is a section of the museum dedicated to families with children of four years and up. Housed in the former home of the head teacher, the Little Orphanage re-creates daily life in the 17th-century orphanage, complete with rowdy dining rooms, classrooms, a crude toilet, and a cattle shed. The interactive exhibits whisper, and visitors hide from teachers and get involved with milking the cows, an activity guaranteed to ensure much merriment.

INSIDER TIP:

A good option for the determined sightseer is the Amsterdam 100 Highlights Cruise by Canal. This departs from the Holland International Canal every 15 minutes. There's an audio guide on board to steer your eyes in the right direction.

—HANNAH LAUTERBACK
National Georgraphic contributor

Mokum

Having taken the time to explore the Amsterdam Museum, you will be familiar with the etymology of Mokum (a Yiddish word for "safe haven" used by Amsterdammers as a nickname for their city). So take a little extra time to enjoy a cup of coffee or light snack in the popular **Mokum Museum Café,** with its sunny terrace. ∎

A City of Keels & Wheels

A guided boat tour of Amsterdam's famous canal belt is a must when visiting the city. A cruise is a fantastic way to orientate yourself, admire the grand canal houses, and appreciate the waterways that define Amsterdam's landscape and identity. While Amsterdammers happily navigate the canals in small boats, 490,000 *fietsers* (cyclists) also take to the roads of Amsterdam each day; cycling is as much part of daily life as the canals.

Travelers can best experience Amsterdam from the comfort of a canal cruise boat.

On the Water

Amsterdam is built around a network of 165 canals, which total 47 miles (75 km) in length and are spanned by 1,281 bridges. A complex system of sluices and mechanical pumps flushes the canals with fresh water from the IJsselmeer each night, replacing one third of the canal water.

A raft of firms offer guided canal tours throughout the canal belt with commentaries in various languages. Most of these firms operate from Centraal Station, with additional stops at the piers along Damrak and Rokin, and the Rijksmuseum. Most companies also offer a wide choice of cruises, from basic hour-long trips and the dedicated Museum Boat service (see sidebar p. 49) to 48-hour hop-on/hop-off tickets and candlelit dinner cruises (see sidebar p. 175).

For a more bespoke option, the rigid inflatable Water Taxi *(Prins Hendrikkade 25, tel 535-6363, water-taxi.nl)* enables clients to create their own itineraries and comes complete with a well-stocked bar. Journeys are charged for the boat by the minute, making it a particularly good option for larger groups (of up to eight).

Renting a boat for King's Day, or other holidays, requires an an all-day reservation, and reservations should be made well in advance. Also, keep in mind that the boating season in Amsterdam runs from March 1 through November 30.

On Your Bike

Cycling comes naturally to the Dutch, whose flat country is ideal for getting around by pedal power. There are over 18 million bicycles in the Netherlands—881,000 in Amsterdam alone, many of which appear to reside in Centraal Station's multilevel bicycle park—and some 22,000 miles (35,000 km) of *fietspaden* (bicycle paths).

You will discover an astonishing variety of bikes in Amsterdam. Some sport Hawaiian leis; others have child or dog seats, shopping baskets, or trailers; many carry an extra passenger on the rear seat; and still others (*bakfietsen*, or tub bikes) have flatbed trailers sticking out in front: these are used to stash everything from shopping and children to furniture and animals.

In addition to having dedicated lanes, cyclists have their own junctions, traffic lights, and regulations (relatively few of which are actually heeded). Cycling in Amsterdam liberates you to explore and feel like a genuine local, and rental bikes are available at low cost from a number of places (see p. 238). However, it takes practice and courage to become accustomed to the sheer density of cyclists and chaotic nature of the traffic. Pay particular attention if you're using rental bikes with old-fashioned backpedal brakes.

INSIDER TIP:

Do as the locals do, and *always* lock the frame of your bike to an immovable object. Don't make it easy for thieves by leaving your bike unlocked, even momentarily. They will help themselves and you will lose your deposit.

—PANCRAS DIJK
National Geographic
magazine in the Netherlands writer

EXPERIENCE: Rent Your Own Sloep

Once you've enjoyed an official guided canal cruise, and familiarized yourself with Amsterdam's canal rings, why not rent an electric *sloep* (a traditional aluminium boat, or sloop, but without a sail) and explore the canals by yourself?

Sloepdelen *(Planciusstraat 28hs, tel 419-1007, sloepdelen.nl)* is an excellent operation with a fleet of very well maintained boats moored in two locations in Amsterdam *(Nassaukade 69 in the Northern Canals and Borneosteiger 1 in the Eastern Docklands).*

You can simply book a boat online from the location most convenient for you, after which you will receive a code with which to access a key to a boat (stored in a locker on the dock), and off you go. The sloeps are very easy to drive, and the website provides clear instructions on how to use them, which can be downloaded and printed out. Each sloep can carry six people comfortably, and up to ten passengers maximum. The largely new fleet is electrically powered, making it quiet and environmentally friendly, and a fully charged battery lasts for 14 hours. Just don't forget to unplug your sloep from the mains before driving off.

You can make a booking on the day you wish to sail, so pick a sunny afternoon, invite some friends along, grab provisions from one of Amsterdam's food markets, and simply soak up the relaxed atmosphere of the city known as "the Venice of the North."

More Places to Visit in Nieuwe Zijde

Begijnhof

Separated from Spui, one of Amsterdam's busiest shopping streets, by no more than a high wall, the Begijnhof (see p. 62) is a place of spiritual calm amid the bustle of the city. So renowned were the Beguines (lay nuns) of Amsterdam for their charitable work and industrious way of life that they were exempted from the laws that prohibited Catholic worship and institutions when Amsterdam became a Protestant city at the Alteration of 1578 (see pp. 29–30). The last member of the order died in 1971. Today, the houses are rented at a nominal price to Catholic women—elderly widows and students from the city's university.

Among several buildings of note around the courtyard, the **Begijnhofkapel** at No. 30 is especially interesting. From the outside it looks like a house, but beyond the small front door lies a clandestine chapel whose interior is crammed with tier upon tier of wooden galleries, added as the Catholic congregation grew over the centuries since the church was first built in 1671. Hung around the walls are medieval painted panels depicting the Miracle of Amsterdam (see sidebar p. 85), and subsequent miracles experienced by pilgrims who came to the shrine in search of cures.
begijnhofamsterdam.nl.
🗺 Map p. 46 ✉ Enter from Gedempte Begijnensloot 🚊 Tram: 1, 2, 5

Madame Tussauds

This attraction mixes waxworks of international personalities—actors, pop stars, and politicians—with local content. For children, this can be a fun way to discover the Dutch Golden Age, through animatronic tableaus featuring Prince Willem of Orange and the Golden Age artists Rembrandt and Vermeer.
madametussauds.com/amsterdam
🗺 Map p. 46 ✉ Dam 20 ☎ 522-1010
💲 $$$ 🚊 Tram: 4, 9, 14, 16, 20, 24, 25

Sexmuseum Amsterdam "Venustempel"

To the outsider, Amsterdam can be a baffling mix of Protestant tradition, Dutch practicality, and sexual laissez-faire. So where better to establish the world's first sex museum? The Venus Temple explores the theme of sensual love with an extensive collection of erotic paintings, pictures, objects, recordings, and films, in a sensitive, educational, and humorous way. Delicate Japanese netsuke and 19th-century ladies' fans painted with

INSIDER TIP:

Most pedestrians dash along busy Kalverstraat, past the sign above De Papegaai [The Parrot] church that urges "Een kwartier voor God"—fifteen minutes for God. Why not heed the slogan and make time for the beautiful, once clandestine Catholic church?

—TIM JEPSON
National Geographic author

erotic scenes are displayed with tinderboxes carried by soldiers in the Napoleonic Wars featuring bawdy images, in an intriguing labyrinth of rooms spread between two connected houses. A minimum age of 16 years applies to all visitors.
sexmuseumamsterdam.nl.
🗺 Map p. 47 ✉ Damrak 18
☎ 622-8376 💲 $ 🚉 Centraal Station Metro, all buses and trams to Centraal Station ⛴ Canal Bus, Museumboot & Artis Express to Centraal Station.

The city's oldest quarter, peppered with crooked gabled buildings housing brothels, secret churches, and sailors' taverns

Oude Zijde

Introduction & Map   72–73

University Quarter   74–79

Red Light District   80–81

Feature: Sex & Drugs in
   Amsterdam   82–83

Oude Kerk   84–85

Experience: Walk in the
   Silent Procession   85

Museum Ons' Lieve Heer
   op Solder   86–89

Experience: Attend Mass at
   Ons' Lieve Heer op Solder   87

Zeedijk   90–91

Nieuwmarkt   92–95

A Waterside Stroll   96–98

Hotels & Restaurants in
   Oude Zijde   244–246

Stained-glass window in the
Oude Kerk (1555)

Oude Zijde

Oude Zijde (Old Side) is Amsterdam's oldest residential quarter. The area is also known as De Wallen (The Walls): Its two principal canals—Oudezijds Voorburgwal and Oudezijds Achterburgwal—were dug just within and outside the city's medieval ramparts.

Most of the streets and canals of Oude Zijde run parallel to these walls, but one street cuts right across them, pursuing its own wayward path. This is Zeedijk, and its name (Sea Dike) indicates that it follows the line of the original embankment that was built to protect medieval Amsterdam from flooding.

Zeedijk was, for many centuries, the rough end of Amsterdam—initially the rowdy haunt of bawdy 13th-century sailors, then of 20th-century drug pushers and addicts, no doubt with every type of nefarious activity known to mankind taking place in between. Today, thanks in large part to the positive influence of Amsterdam's Cantonese community, it is the vibrant hub of Chinatown, where antique shops and fusion restaurants sit cheek by jowl with jazz cafés and a splendid Buddhist temple.

Farther south, the quiet, leafy University Quarter borders on Amsterdam's infamous Red Light District. The world's oldest profession lies at the heart of this ancient city, and its continued practice here, in addition to the coffee shops that sell cannabis legally, speaks volumes about the famous Dutch traditions of pragmatism and tolerance.

In recent years, however, a major regeneration scheme has dramatically cut the number of windows, brothels, and coffee shops in the Red Light District, encouraging designers, art galleries, restaurants, and fashion boutiques to take their place. Exploring Amsterdam's ancient heart might have become less titillating, but it is also more varied and safe. ■

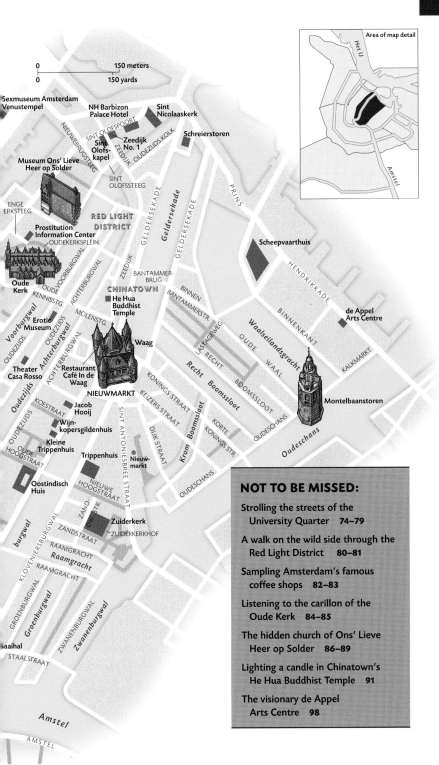

Area of map detail

Het IJ

Amstel

0   150 meters

0   150 yards

Sexmuseum Amsterdam
Venustempel

NH Barbizon
Palace Hotel

Sint
Nicolaaskerk

NIEUWEBRUGSTEEG

SINT OLOFSPOORT

Sint
Olofs-
kapel

Zeedijk
No. 1

ZEEDIJK

OUDEZIJDS KOLK

Schreierstoren

Museum Ons' Lieve
Heer op Solder

SINT
OLOFSSTEEG

PRINS

Scheepvaarthuis

ENGE
ERKSTEEG

RED LIGHT
DISTRICT

Prostitution
Information Center

OUDEKERKSPLEIN

GELDERSEKADE

GELDERSEKADE

VOORBURGWAL

ACHTERBURGWAL

ZEEDIJK

BANTAMMER-
BRUG

HENDRIKKADE

Oude
Kerk

OUDE
KENNISSTG

Voorburgwal

CHINATOWN

He Hua
Buddhist
Temple

BINNEN
BANTAMMERSTR

BINNENKANT

de Appel
Arts Centre

Erotic
Museum

OUDEZIJDS

OUDEZIJDS

ACHTERBURGWAL

MOLENSTG.

Waag

LASTAGEWEG

OUDE

RECHT

Waalseilandsgracht

WAAL

BINNENKANT

KALKMARKT

Theater
Casa Rosso

Restaurant
Café In de
Waag

NIEUWMARKT

Recht Boomssloot

BOOMSSLOOT

Montelbaanstoren

Oudezijds

KOESTRAAT

Jacob
Hooij

KEIZERS STRAAT

KONINGS STRAAT

Krom Boomssloot

KORTE
KONINGS STR.

OUDESCHANS

Oudeschans

Wijn-
kopersgildenhuis

Kleine
Trippenhuis

OUDE
HOOGSTRAAT

SINT ANTONIESBREE STRAAT

DIJK STRAAT

Trippenhuis

Nieuw-
markt

Oostindisch
Huis

NIEUWE
HOOGSTRAAT

OUDESCHANS

burgwal

KLOVENIERSBURGWAL

ZANDSTRAAT

ZAND-
STR.

Zuiderkerk

ZUIDERKERKHOF

RAAMGRACHT

Raamgracht

RAAMGRACHT

GROENBURGWAL

Groenburgwal

ZWANENBURGWAL

Zwanenburgwal

aaihal

STAALSTRAAT

Amstel

AMSTEL

NOT TO BE MISSED:

Strolling the streets of the
University Quarter   74–79

A walk on the wild side through the
Red Light District   80–81

Sampling Amsterdam's famous
coffee shops   82–83

Listening to the carillon of the
Oude Kerk   84–85

The hidden church of Ons' Lieve
Heer op Solder   86–89

Lighting a candle in Chinatown's
He Hua Buddhist Temple   91

The visionary de Appel
Arts Centre   98

University Quarter

Historically Leiden was the main center of learning in the Netherlands, with Amsterdam encouraging its young to acquire practical skills as surgeons, architects, artists, or soldiers, usually by joining a guild. Nevertheless, those with an intellectual bent formed the Athenaeum Illustre (Illustrious School) in 1632, from which the University of Amsterdam evolved.

Today, Amsterdam's university has over 30,000 students and some 300 study programs, many taught in English. One of Europe's largest comprehensive universities, it remains true to the city's traditions of open-mindedness, civic duty, and engagement with social issues. The University Quarter lies to the east of Dam Square and is reached by walking along Damstraat to the first bridge and turning right down the far bank of Oudezijds Voorburgwal. As you cross the bridge, look right to No. 187, dated 1663. The gable is flanked by the carved figures of an Indian and an African, seated on bales of tobacco. Merchants often used the figures of Africans, Turks, or Indians to symbolize the exotic origins of their stock.

Around the Former City Hall

Two blocks down on the left is the entrance to the courtyard of the **Grand Hotel** (*Oudezijds Voorburgwal 197*). Converted to a hotel in 1993, it was originally built in 1647 as the headquarters of the Admiralty and has symbols of war and justice carved in the pediment. In 1808, when King Louis Napoléon took the Stadhuis (Town Hall) on Dam Square as his palace, the city council moved to this building, where it remained until 1988, when the new Stadhuis and Muziektheater complex (see p. 105) was completed. Not all

The facade of the Oostindisch Huis (East India House) in the University Quarter

of the majestic Grand Hotel is in the 17th-century classical style: Coming out of the courtyard, the former City Hall to the left was built in the 1920s in the restrained art deco style of the Amsterdam School.

On the opposite bank of the canal stands the **Oude Vleeshuis** (Old Meat Market; *Oudestraat 119*), an 18th-century building whose gable is decorated with the heads of horned cattle. Farther along, heading south, across the next bridge and to the right, is a classical doorcase, carved with lion masks and cherubs, dated 1624. This once led to a tavern known as De Brakke Grond (The Brackish Ground), a reference to the terrain in the 17th century. Today **De Brakke Grond** is a Flemish culture house, with dynamic offerings in theater, performing arts, music, and film from Flanders. It also houses a Flemish café.

Uncle John the Pawnbroker

The next building on the left is the **Bank van Lening.** In this case, "bank" is a euphemism for pawnbroker, and the building provided warehousing for goods offered as security against loans. The inscription over the door tells those who already have gold to pass on by—this bank is for those who are in need. Established in 1578, the Bank van Lening provided an alternative to commercial pawnbrokers who charged extortionate interest rates. The loan rates here were set in accordance with the borrower's means, at a rate that took into account the individual's ability to repay. To Amsterdam's needy citizens, the institution was known affectionately as Oom Jan (Uncle John). Operated as the Stadsbank van Lening (City Bank of Loans) since 1614, it still extends loans to Amsterdammers today.

INSIDER TIP:

Indulge in fine wines and champagnes at Bubbles & Wines bar *[Nes 37, tel 422-3318, bubblesandwines.com].* With tutored wine tastings, 50 wines, and gourmet bites, there's plenty to keep you here.

—PAUL RÖMER
Managing Editor,
National Geographic Traveler
magazine in the Netherlands

Crossing the next bridge, look to the right, at No. 231, where the Agnietenkapel stands, fronted by a lively gateway of baroque strapwork, with the words "Athenaeum Illustre" worked in wrought iron across the top, referring to the body that evolved into today's university. Once part of the convent of St. Agnes, this simple but graceful chapel of 1470 was taken over by the Athenaeum Illustre in 1632 and transformed into a Renaissance lecture theater, in which to teach students philosophy and trade skills. The chapel is open to visitors but is no longer used as a museum.

De Brakke Grond
- Map p. 72
- Nes 43
- 626-0044
- Tram: 4, 9, 16, 24, 25

brakkegrond.nl

The Meeting of Three Waterways

Continuing down the canal, look across to the elegant classical facade of No. 316, designed by Philips Vingboons in 1655 and featuring a stucco panel of a sleeping pilgrim guarded by angels. At the bottom end of Oudezijds Voorburgwal stands the intriguing **Huis op de Drie Grachten** (The House on Three Canals; *Oudezijds Achterburgwal 329*) of 1609, with step-gabled facades facing each of the three waterways—Oude-zijds Voorburgwal, Grimburgwal, and Oudezijds Achterburgwal. To the south it looks across the graphically named Grimburgwal (Muddy Ditch Wall). Heading right at this point will take you to Oude Turfmarkt (Old Peat Market), where you will find the **Allard Pierson Museum** (see pp. 78–79; *Oude Turfmarkt 127*), the university's museum of antiquities. The museum is part of the gray-brick complex on the far bank of the Grimburgwal canal that houses the main university campus, built on the site of the city Gasthuis (Hospital). Over to the left, on the eastern side of Oudezijds Achterburgwal, you will see the original hospital gate, carved with elderly male and female figures flanking the city's coat of arms.

A short way up on the right is another old gateway, carved with a pair of ancient pince-nez spectacles. This leads through to the **Oudemannehuis,** founded in

Shopping, cycling, and café life: a classic Amsterdam moment on Spui Street

The Dutch East India Company

The Verenigde Oost-Indische Compagnie (United East India Company), or VOC, was established in 1602 as a chartered company when the States General of the Netherlands granted it a 21-year monopoly to carry out colonial activities in Asia. It grew to become the world's first multinational corporation, rapidly eclipsing all its rivals in Asian trade and appropriating unprecedented power—the VOC established colonies, waged war on nations, negotiated treaties, coined money, and sent almost one million Europeans to work in Asia. The Tulip Mania of 1637 (see p. 52) saw the VOC become the most valuable company in world history, driving its value up to a contemporary equivalent of $7.4 trillion. However, corruption proved the VOC's downfall, and it was declared bankrupt in 1800. The former VOC territories then became the Dutch East Indies, expanding during the 19th and 20th centuries to become the Republic of Indonesia.

the early 17th century as a home for elderly male paupers, rebuilt in 1754. Now part of the university, you can go through the glass doors into a corridor lined with booksellers' stands specializing in secondhand and antiquarian books. The gateway at the other end of the corridor, on Kloveniersburgwal, was carved by Anthonie Ziesenis in 1786 and shows two elderly men supported by the youthful female figure of Charity, holding a fruit-filled cornucopia.

The Women's Prison

Kloveniersburgwal is named after the *kloveniers,* the militiamen of the Guild of St. Adrian, who policed this district in the 17th and 18th centuries. If you turn left here, then take the third left, on Spinhuissteeg, you will find the preserved doorway of the **Spinhuis** *(Oudezijds Achterburgwal 185)* up on the right. Here, women who had been convicted of petty crimes were put to work spinning flax and making fishing nets—as shown in the 1645 carving above the door. One of the women in the frieze is being whipped, and the inscription, translated, means "My hand punishes but my intention is good."

As you emerge from Spinhuissteeg, look left at No. 187, which has a plaque dated 1727 carved with a rebus; the picture of the house and the man are a visual pun on the name of the owner, a Mr. Huysman. Turning right up Oudezijds Achterburgwal takes you past various faculty buildings to Oude Hoogstraat, with its shops selling new and antiquarian books, textiles, crafts, and clothing.

East India House

Heading right, from the exit to Oudemanhuispoort, look for a narrow gateway at No. 24, on the right. The highly ornate facade of the **Oostindisch Huis** (East India House), now part of the University of Amsterdam, faces you as you pass through into the courtyard. Though not large, it was the headquarters of the Dutch East India

Allard Pierson Museum

- ▲ Map p. 72
- ✉ Oude Turfmarkt 127
- ☎ 525-2556
- ⏱ Closed Mon., Sat. & Sun. a.m.
- 💲 $$
- 🚋 Tram: 4, 9, 14, 16, 24, 25
- 🚤 Museumboot

allardpiersonmuseum .com

Company, whose vast trading empire stretched halfway around the world (see sidebar p. 77). Nobody knows who designed the building, which dates from 1605, but the playful strapwork in the gable and above the windows, combined with the effective use of contrasting red brick and creamy sandstone, are all the notable trademarks of Hendrick de Keyser (1565–1621).

Allard Pierson Museum

The Allard Pierson Museum is devoted to the archaeology of the Romans, ancient Egypt, Etruria, Greece, southern Italy, Cyprus, and western Asia. The museum strives to make Mediterranean antiquity interesting and accessible not only to scholars but to a broader audience.

The collection, owned by the University of Amsterdam, has developed from humble beginnings to become one of

INSIDER TIP:

Regardless of whether or not you smoke, visit the Hajenius cigar and tobacco shop [Rokin 96, tel 623-7494, hajenius.com], which boasts magnificent art deco interiors dating back to 1915.

—GABRIELLA LE BRETON
National Geographic author

the world's largest university museums. Allard Pierson was the University of Amsterdam's first professor of classical archaeology in 1877. Although Pierson had a modest number of plaster casts, it was the extensive collection of books and antiques belonging to his successor, Professor J. Six, which became the basis for today's museum. When Six died in 1926, the Allard Pierson Foundation was established in order to purchase his collection. The foundation opened the museum in 1931 in the attic of the Institute of the Department of Mediterranean Archaeology and gradually augmented Six's collection, opening in the current venue in 1976.

Egypt: The entire first floor is dedicated to the museum's Egypt exhibition. This provides a chronological trip through ancient Egypt, from the earliest prehistoric pottery (5000 B.C.) to the colorful textiles of the Coptic era (5th to 11th centuries A.D.). In between are models of the pyramids of Giza, cases of

The Oude Turfmarkt

The stately building that houses the Allard Pierson Museum on Oude Turfmarkt (Old Peat Market) was built in 1868 and subsequently extended and redesigned by W. A. Froger in 1915 to serve as the headquarters of the Bank of the Netherlands. Froger introduced architectural elements inspired by Greek and Roman models, including pilasters, capitals, and marble floors.

Dionysus Sarcophagus, Allard Pierson Museum

fine jewelry, carved reliefs of Egyptian rulers in polished sandstone, and a room dedicated to the mummification process.

From Ancient Rome to Cyprus:
The museum's second floor is a treasure trove of artifacts from ancient Rome and Greece, Cyprus, Etruria, and western Asia, giving visitors a vivid sense of the daily life of these early people. Notable exhibits include a reconstructed Cypriot two-seat funerary chariot; reconstructions of Etruscan temples and houses based on models found in tombs; elegant water jugs with long spouts formed like an ibis beak from Iran; and a bathtub-size Roman sarcophagus dating from the 2nd century B.C. and decorated with men and women dancing in a naked, drunken frenzy, in honor of Bacchus, the god of wine. One outstanding exhibit—a graceful couch used for reclining at banquets—suggests the comfort of life for wealthy Romans.

The ancient Greek section consists largely of ceramics decorated with scenes from Greek epics and mythology. You will find a delightful case devoted to animals in antiquity containing terra-cotta frogs, bronze lions, stone cockerels, a ferocious wild boar, and a solitary grasshopper. Some are toys; others are offerings to the gods and represent some of the disguises these deities adopted when visiting earthbound mortals. ■

Red Light District

In the very heart of Amsterdam lies the city's infamous Red Light District. During the day it has the air of a fairly ordinary part of Amsterdam, but in the evening the facades are lit up by neon lights advertising sex shops and live shows. The city is actively reducing the number of brothels and "windows," many of which are found in beautiful yet neglected canal houses.

Direct marketing in Amsterdam's Red Light District

The far-reaching Project 1012 (see p. 83) is reducing much of the seedy, threatening nature of this ancient part of Amsterdam. However, be mindful not to take photographs of prostitutes in the Red Light District; it is not appreciated by them or their pimps.

Walk from Dam Square down Damstraat and turn left at the second bridge, onto Oudezijds Achterburgwal. Four doors down on the left you will find the **Hash Marihuana Hemp Museum.** A left turn in Stoofsteeg takes you to a bridge with vistas up and down Oudezijds Voorburgwal. On the other side of the bridge, to the right, No. 136 was the home of Admiral Maarten Harpertszoon Tromp (1598–1653), who scored many victories in naval battles against the English. He is depicted here resting on a cannon with a sunken ship in the background. On the opposite bank, note the run of bell gables (Nos. 101–107).

De Wallen

This part of Amsterdam is known as De Wallen (The Walls) because its streets marked the lines of the city's earliest defensive ramparts and palisade. The medieval **Oude Kerk** (Old Church; see pp. 84–85) on your left was the very heart of the original town.

The impact of Project 1012 can be seen here in the art galleries, the chic Restaurant ANNA (see p. 245), and the boutique brewery De Prael (employing people with long-term psychiatric disorders), all of which flank Oudekerksplein (Old Church Square).

If you are curious about the world's oldest profession, visit the **Prostitution Information Center,** to the north of the church. The mini-museum was founded by former prostitute Mariska Majoor in 1994. The center offers guided walking tours of De Wallen in English on Wednesday and Saturday evenings, providing a safe, informative way to explore the area. For the curious and brave, Majoor offers one-on-one workshops to understand how it feels to be on the other side of the glass.

Hidden Secrets

The next stretch of Oudezijds Voorburgwal contains some of the city's oldest surviving houses and, at No. 40, the delightful **Museum Ons' Lieve Heer op Solder** (see pp. 86–89). On the opposite bank, **No. 19** is a splendid sandstone house with a very tall neck gable and scroll stones carved in the shape of giant fish. On this side, **No. 18,** attributed to Hendrick de Keyser, has a plaque on its facade showing Egmond Castle, which is on the coast just west of Alkmaar. No. 14 is called **De Leeuwenburg** (The Lion Castle) after the sandstone carvings of lion masks set into the

---

Erotic Museum

The Erotic Museum (Oudezijds Achterburgwal 54, tel 627-8954, erotisch-museum.nl, $$) is packed from floor to ceiling with erotic pictures, from late 19th-century sepia-tint photographs to a series of self-portraits by the late John Lennon, sketched during his famous "bed-in" peace protest with Yoko Ono at the Amsterdam Hilton Hotel in 1969. The museum's new Sexy Art Gallery features erotic art from across the world.

---

brickwork. These reference the coat of arms of the Baltic port city of Riga, the original home of the first owner of this house. Built in 1600, the house retains several rare features, including the cellar shop, whose entrance protrudes from the facade into the street; the wooden window shutters on the ground floor, which could also be opened up to create an awning above and a shop counter below; and the tiny leaded windows filled with green-tinted glass.

Several carved gable stones have been reset in the wall that terminates the canal. To the right of the wall stands the sluice gate that controls the flow of water from the canals to the IJ River beyond. Turning left into Nieuwebrugsteeg takes you past the In de Olofspoort *proeflokaal* (see p. 51) and out onto Damrak and Centraal Station. ∎

Hash Marihuana Hemp Museum

- 🅰 Map p. 72
- ✉ Oudezijds Achterburgwal 148
- ☎ 624-8926
- 💲 $
- 🚊 Tram: 4, 9, 16, 24, 25

hashmuseum.com

Prostitution Information Center

- 🅰 Map p. 73
- ✉ Enge Kerksteeg 3
- 🕐 Open Weds. & Sat. p.m.
- 🚊 Tram: 4, 9, 16, 24, 25

pic-amsterdam.com

Sex & Drugs in Amsterdam

Amsterdam's pragmatic approach to prostitution is almost as old as the city itself—prostitutes in De Wallen were paying rent to the city bailiff in the 17th century. And, while the Dutch hemp heritage dates back to 15th-century sailors, the application of the *gedoogbeleid* (tolerance policy) to soft drugs in the 1970s is a liberal approach that continues to divide the Dutch today.

A nighttime walk in the colorful Red Light District is an eye-opening experience for any traveler.

The fundamental concept behind the tolerance of both prostitution and soft drugs in Amsterdam's ancient De Wallen (The Walls) area is that making them visible and legal in a regulated environment, in combination with education, should achieve better control and less abuse than criminalizing them. Prostitutes are licensed, receive regular health checkups, and pay income tax; their earnings are audited, and they have representatives in the local Chamber of Commerce. While soliciting is illegal, the law stipulates that what goes on in the privacy of the prostitutes' own homes is their own business. This explains the *"kamer te huur"* (room available for rent) signs seen outside the city's brothels.

Similarly, the law distinguishes between "soft drugs" (namely cannabis and excluding hallucinogenic mushrooms) and "hard drugs," allowing the personal use of the former in a limited, controlled way in designated coffee shops. These coffee shops sell various types of pot and hash, as well as drinks and snacks. (The place to go just for coffee or a beer is a café or a brown café.) Coffee shops are permitted to stock a maximum of 17.5 ounces (500 g) of cannabis at any time, and sell a maximum of 0.17 ounces (5 g) to any adult. Interestingly, fewer than half as many Dutch smoke marijuana per capita as Americans, and the country has fewer hard drug users per capita than most other European nations.

Project 1012

The Red Light District is an undeniable part of Amsterdam's tourist appeal. However, Project 1012, launched by the city council in 2009 (see pp. 50–51) to regenerate the district, addresses the growing issue of "tourist trash" and the growth of criminal activity in the area. As Lodewijk Asscher, Dutch deputy prime minster, says: "A civilized society cannot ignore sex trafficking. Behind a smile in a window in De Wallen there is often a lot of sorrow."

The billion-euro project has limited prostitution to two zones in the district, doing away with nearly half of the windows and brothels, and plans to close a third of its coffee shops. It is also replacing sex shops, massage parlors, and similar "low-quality" businesses with small hotels, boutiques, cafés, and offices. During the first two years of the campaign, the twin projects Red Light Design and Red Light Fashion saw the council replace sex windows with free exhibition spaces for young artists and designers, many of whom have since settled permanently in the area. The popular

If the sign says "coffee shop," you can be sure to find more than caffeine on the menu.

RL Radio station also broadcasts from a former window.

While many locals support the initiative to clean up De Wallen, ridding the city of its seedy underbelly, others claim such municipal control is the antithesis of Amsterdam's identity and long history of tolerance. Nowhere else in Amsterdam is the city's split personality—conservative/liberal, tolerant/judgmental—as apparent as here in the Red Light District.

Three Popular Coffee Shops

With legislation concerning Amsterdam's coffee shops changing so frequently, suggestions of which establishments to visit are prone to date quickly. In the spirit of "here today, gone tomorrow," and in the hope that some stalwarts might remain to keep the city's herbal tolerance alight, the coffee shops below are atmospheric and welcoming:
• **Paradox** (1 Bloemdwarsstraat, tel 623-5639, paradoxcoffeeshop.com) has been serving great coffee and healthy food in the heart of the Jordaan since 1991. It is a quintessentially chilled-out

coffee shop accurately proclaiming: "We're not big, loud or stupid, just small, quiet and knowledgeable."
• **Kandinsky** (Rosmarijnsteeg 9, tel 624-7023) is an enduringly popular spot, located in the southern canals district on a quirky street lined with vintage clothing and antique stores.
• **De Rokerij** (Lange Leidsedwarsstraat 41, tel 622-9442, rokerij.net/coffieshop /leidsestraat/index.html) comprises three large, spacious coffeeshops located on Leidseplein, near Centraal Station in the Jordaan district.

Oude Kerk

The city's oldest church was founded in the early 13th century, but most of the surviving structure dates from the rebuilding of 1306. Dedicated to St. Nicholas, patron saint of seafarers, the church contains the tombs of several admirals, as well as those of some of Amsterdam's most illustrious citizens.

This ornate organ in Oude Kerk, Amsterdam's oldest church, is one of four pipe organs in the church.

It is often said of Protestant churches that their white walls and vast windows symbolize the clear light of reason, but the beautiful Oude Kerk (Old Church) did not start out this way. Today's light-filled interior was the result of iconoclasm—Calvinists attacked this church in 1566, destroying statues, images, and works of art in a protest against laws that kept them from worshipping freely.

The iconoclasts did not destroy everything. As you enter you can see paintings in the timber vaults that survived because they were out of reach. Over to the right, on either side of the high altar, medieval choir stalls with carved seats (misericords) show scenes from popular moral tales, including *Reynard the Fox*, as well as peasants in the midst of some very basic bodily functions. Perhaps these examples of medieval humor survived because they appealed to the cynical Amsterdam frame of mind, which is also in evidence in the room off the south transept where marriages took place: The legend above the entrance reads "Marry in haste; repent at leisure."

Dating from the Protestant era are the box pews of city dignitaries in the nave. The organ, built in 1724, is the most ornate object in the church. If you attend an organ recital or a choral evensong (a schedule is in the church porch), you'll discover that it sounds as magnificent as it looks.

INSIDER TIP:

Watch out for the intricately carved wooden stalls in the Oude Kerk choir. Each illustrates a different proverb in typically graphic Dutch style, such as "Money doesn't grow out of my behind."

—JUSTIN KAVANAGH
*National Geographic
International Editions editor*

Bones & Bells

Every inch of the floor is covered with grave slabs, carved with names, symbols, and coats of arms of those buried beneath. The grave of Saskia van Uylenburg, Rembrandt's first wife, lies in the north aisle. Rembrandt painted many tender portraits of her and was devastated when she died in1642.

A memorial to Amsterdam-born composer Jan Sweelinck (1562–1621) rests in the opposite aisle. Sweelinck was the Oude Kerk's organist, and the Sweelinck-canotorij—Sweelinck Singers—perform here regularly and help to keep his music alive.

As you leave the church circle, turn to the right for a look at the massive bell tower of brick and sandstone. Rising high above the church, this intricate tower is topped by the imperial crown of the Holy Roman Emperor Maximilian I, who granted Amsterdam permission to use the crown in its coat of arms in return for generous bank loans. The tower can be climbed as part of a guided tour from April to September. Every quarter hour a tune is played on the carillon of 47 bells, installed in 1658. If this appeals, return at 2 p.m. on Tuesdays or 4 p.m. on Saturdays for a full carillon concert (best heard from the bridge).

Art in the Redlight

In September, the Oude Kerk hosts the Independent Art Fair and auction organized by the Art in Redlight (AIR) Foundation. The naves and chapels of the church are filled with the work of global contemporary artists, sold to support the Orange Babies charity. ∎

Oude Kerk

- ⬛ Map p. 73
- ✉ Oudekerksplein 23
- ☎ 625-8284
- 🕐 Closed Sun. a.m.
- 💲 $
- 🚊 Tram: 4, 9, 16

oudekerk.nl

EXPERIENCE: Walk in the Silent Procession

Each March, some 8,000 people take part in the **Stille Omgang** (Silent Procession; *stille-omgang.nl*), a silent nocturnal procession around Amsterdam that starts at the Spui and culminates at the Oude Kerk. The ritual started as a substitute for the Roman Catholic processions that were prohibited after the Reformation in the 16th century and commemorates the Miracle of the Host. This miracle happened on March 15, 1345, when a dying man was given Communion as part of the last rites. He vomitted and the mess was thrown into the fire, yet the next day, the Communion host was found pristine and intact. Visitors began reporting that the sick were being healed, along with other miraculous occurrences. Pilgrims soon began to flock to the site.

Museum Ons' Lieve Heer op Solder

Behind the ordinary facade of this 17th-century merchant's house in the Red Light District lies an extraordinary secret. Work your way up to the attic, passing through a number of rooms restored to their Golden Age glory, and you emerge in a glorious clandestine church, where Catholics worshipped in secret for centuries.

The hidden chapel at Ons' Lieve Heer op Solder Museum (Our Lord in the Attic Museum)

**Museum Ons'
Lieve Heer op
Solder**

 Map p. 73

✉ Oudezijds
   Voorburgwal 40

☎ 624-6604

🕐 Closed Sun. a.m.

$ $$$

🚊 Tram: 4, 9, 16,
   24, 25

opsolder.nl

The story of the Museum Ons' Lieve Heer op Solder (Our Lord in the Attic) starts with the wealthy merchant Jan Hartman (1619–1668). Hartman bought a prestigious property on the Oudezijds Voorburgwal, known then as the Fluwelen (Velvet) Burgwal for its luxurious homes, and extended the existing canal house to incorporate two rear houses. On the ground floor and basement he built a shop and storage room, adding a lavish reception room on the first floor to show off his status and receive guests. He then linked the third floor of the main house with the top floors of the other two to create a huge attic.

Secret Worship

Hartman was a Catholic and his son was training for the priest-hood. However, this was the era of the Reformation, and Catholics were banned from practicing their religion in public. The Protestant city council that resulted from the Alteration of 1578 (see pp. 29–30) voted to allow Catholic worship to continue in the city on condition that the churches did not look like churches and were not accessible from public roads. Thus, Hartman created a church in his house, and for over 200 years the local Catholic community worshipped in his attic, entering via a tiny door on the Heintje Hoeksteeg side alley.

In 1739 the priest Ludovicus Reiniers bought the house. He lived in the foremost house and improved access to the church by inserting a new staircase in the middle house. It was probably during the rebuilding of the front facade in the 19th century that the statue of a stag that surmounted it disappeared. Instead of the Hart, the church became known as "Our Lord in the Attic."

Museum

When the large Sint Nicolaas church opposite Centraal Station was consecrated in 1887, Our Lord in the Attic was superseded as the local parish church. In that same year a group of Catholics in Amsterdam bought the property, saving it from demolition. A year later, on April 28, 1888, Our Lord in the Attic was opened to the public on weekdays, making it the city's oldest museum after the Rijksmuseum. Today, the Oude Huis (Old House) is

INSIDER TIP:

The pink interiors of the Ons' Lieve Heer op Solder church are an accurate depiction of its decor in the 19th century, when it last served as a parish. The color was known as caput mortuum, or dead head.

—TIM JEPSON
National Geographic author

complemented by the Nieuwe Huis (New House), a neighboring canal house that incorporates the museum entrance, café, shop, and temporary exhibits. The two houses are linked by a subterranean walkway.

EXPERIENCE: Attend Mass at Ons' Lieve Heer op Solder

On the first Sunday of each month (from October through May), you can attend Catholic mass in one of the world's most unusual churches, the **Ons' Lieve Heer op Solder.** The so-called Solderviering (Attic Celebration) starts at 11 a.m. and continues the long tradition of active worship in this ancient church. You'll hear the hauntingly beautiful music of the Solderkoor (Attic Choir) and be served coffee in the museum afterward.

Midnight mass is held in the church on Christmas Eve but is very well attended and thus places must be reserved well in advance. Contact the museum for details *(opsolder.nl, email info@opsolder.nl).*

Het Oude Huis

You can equip yourself with an excellent audio guided tour and make the most of the museum's beautifully restored rooms as you approach its crowning glory. The Grachtenkamer (Canal, or Front Room) and Sael (Salon) boast opulent Golden Age artwork and furnishings, making the Tussen-kamer (In-between Room) half-way up the stairs to the church, where the chaplain lodged in the late 19th century, appear spartan in comparison.

The Main Church: The church itself is surprisingly large, comprising a nave and two galleries. The altar, flanked by two marbled columns with classical capitals, is the visual focus. The columns and arch frame a painting by Jacob de Wit, with the whole culminating in a stucco sculpture of God the Father and the Holy Spirit. A beautiful organ, built especially for the church by Hendrik Meyer in 1794, dominates the canal end.

Additional Altar: After leaving the main church, you reach a small additional altar to the Virgin Mary and the confessional, dating back to 1740. Descend through the Jaap Leeuwenberg room, which is named after the church's former director and benefactor and lined with religious devotional art. You reach the restored 17th-century kitchen, complete with a few added "modern" innovations from the 19th-century, such as the adjoining privy. ■

Amstelkring facade with simple spout gable

"The Baptism of Christ" (1716) hanging above the mock marble altar is by Jacob de Wit (1695–1754).

Wooden viewing gallery of church

Clandestine church

Rear house

The Sael, or main living room

Middle house

Our Lord in the Attic Museum

The Kapelaanskamer, the priest's secret hiding place

House on the canal

Zeedijk

Zeedijk (Sea Dike) was built in the early 13th century to prevent the city from flooding. Initially a well-to-do area, it entered a 300-year decline when visiting sailors adopted it as their haunt in the 17th century. By the 1980s it was a hotbed of crime known as "Heroin Alley," but the 1990s signaled its rebirth as the vibrant hub of Chinatown and an area of antique shops, jazz cafés, and Asian restaurants.

He Hua Buddhist Temple is an oasis for meditation and reflection on busy Zeedijk Street.

Zeedijk

Map p. 73

The Sailors' Quarter

Zeedijk begins to the east of Centraal Station, behind the NH Barbizon Palace Hotel and the huge twin-towered Sint Nicolaaskerk. The first section of Zeedijk is particularly attractive, especially at the junction with Sint Olofspoort (St. Olaf's gate), where the buildings lean in all directions. They were deliberately built like this so that goods could be winched up to the warehouse space in the gable without bumping against the front of the house.

Zeedijk follows the line of the medieval city walls (hence its serpentine shape on the map). Sint Olofspoort was one of the main city gates. The gate has now gone, but one of the city's oldest houses has survived. **Zeedijk No. 1** dates from 1550 and is one of only three medieval timber buildings left in Amsterdam.

It is now a colorful café, **In 't Aepjen** (In the Apes)—so named because an earlier owner kept monkeys *(aapjes),* given to him by sailors in payment for lodgings.

Opposite, at No. 2A, is the entrance to **Sint Olofskapel,** whose sculptures show a grim life-size skeleton and garlanded skulls. The chapel was built in 1425 and restored in 1992 and now serves as a conference and banqueting center for the NH Barbizon Palace Hotel.

Several buildings in the vicinity have gable stones (plaques). On the right, on Sint Olofsteeg, a plaque on the side wall of No. 3 shows a spotted leopard (perhaps this was once a furrier's). At the next bridge, on the right, another plaque shows the medieval St. Olof's gate and another opposite depicts a cooper at work. The winding gear below the bridge belongs to the locks that were once used to hold back the tidal waters of the IJ River, before it was closed off from the open sea. From this bridge there is a good view southward to the Oude Kerk's spire (see pp. 84–85).

Gay Amsterdam & Chinatown

The next stretch of Zeedijk is lined with upscale antique shops whose windows offer glimpses of rare and tempting treasures. At No. 63, on the left, the shopfront survives from Bet van Beeren's café, Café 't Mandje. Bet ran the café from 1927 to 1967 as a haven for lesbians and gays in an otherwise largely unwelcoming city.

Beyond lies Amsterdam's **Chinatown,** complete with authentic smells, restaurants, and stores selling rice cookers and coromandel screens. Here you can shop for temple dogs and gilded Buddhas, consult an acupuncturist, buy gold and jade, or eat Cantonese seafood. The **He Hua Buddhist Temple** is the largest palace in Europe in the Chinese Palace style. Built by the local Chinese community, using materials from China, it is a haven of spirituality in this bustling area. ■

He Hua Buddhist Temple
Map p. 73
Zeedijk 106–118
420-2357
Closed Mon.

What Does He Hua Mean?

The Chinese Fo Guang Shan He Hua Temple is symbolic in many more ways than its mere physical presence in the heart of medieval Amsterdam. More commonly called He Hua Temple (and pronounced "gguh ggwaa"), the name of this Buddhist sanctuary is heavy with meaning. *He* in Chinese translates into "lotus" in English, while *Hua* means "flower." As a symbol of enlightenment, the lotus flower is treasured in Buddhist cultures and is a fitting name for the temple. However, *Helan* is the Chinese word for "Holland" and has a second meaning, "Dutch flower." Thus, the temple's name also reflects the hope of the Chinese that Buddhism will blossom in the Netherlands.

Nieuwmarkt

Narrow and intimate Zeedijk leads out onto the windswept open space of Nieuwmarkt (New Market), where you'll find cafés, restaurants, and a daily market selling flowers, cheeses, fruits, and vegetables of every variety. The Waag (Weighhouse) is now a popular café and restaurant, with a summer terrace.

Street stalls at the Nieuwmarkt (New Market) with the Waag building in the background

Nieuwmarkt
Map p. 73

Restaurant Café In de Waag
Map p. 73
Nieuwmarkt 4
422-7772
Tram: 4, 9, 14, 16, 24, 25

indewaag.nl

The **Waag** began as Sint Antoniespoort (St. Anthony's Gate), built in 1488 to control the south road into the city. Almost as soon as the building's brick walls were completed, the city began to expand beyond the walls, and this gateway building became redundant. It next became a weighhouse where local merchants and manufacturers (especially those making cannon and anchors) could check the weight of their goods.

Meetings of the Guilds

The upper rooms of the Waag were used by the city's medieval guilds, each of which had a separate entrance. Facing Zeedijk (on the northwestern corner) is the entrance used by members of the masons' guild. The relief above the door, carved by Hendrick de Keyser in the early 17th century, shows various tools of the trade: In the central roundel above the door is a bearded figure holding a bricklayer's trowel, while there are roofers' tools to the left, plumbers' tools to the right, and masons' tools below.

Circling around to the right, the door of the painters', glaziers', and sculptors' guild shows their patron saint—the evangelist St. Luke—seated on his ox. Farther around, beside the entrance to the **Restaurant Café In de Waag**, the words "Theatrum Anatomicum" (Anatomy Theater) carved above the door signal the entrance to the surgeons' guild. In addition to lunches and dinners, In de Waag offers English-style afternoon teas (reservation required) and *jenever* (gin) tastings for groups (minimum eight people).

Cannon & Wine Coopers

This part of Amsterdam, as well as being the immigrant quarter, formed the city's first industrial district—one that resounded to the noise of metal- and wood-working in the 17th and 18th centuries. Two local manufacturers who dealt in iron, copper, lead, and armaments were the wealthy Trip brothers; their elegant house can be seen to the south of Nieuwmarkt.

To get there, turn your back on the Waag and cross to the right-hand (western) bank of the Kloveniersburgwal canal. As you make your way across, take note of the varied gables on the buildings on this side of Nieuwmarkt;

Nos. 34–36 boast a gable stone carved with knights on horseback.

Divert down the second alley to the right, Koestraat, to see the **Wijnkopersgildenhuis** (Wine Coopers' Guild House) on the left (No. 10). The wine coopers were merchants who sampled, bottled,

Anatomy Lesson of Dr. Tulp

Rembrandt's first major public commission—one that helped establish his reputation as an artist—is entitled "The Anatomy Lesson of Dr. Nicolaes Tulp" (1632). This depicts Dr. Tulp, the renowned surgeon (he was also the mayor of Amsterdam), lecturing to members of the guild in the Anatomy Theater (the painting now hangs in the Mauritshuis in Den Haag—see p. 228).

and sold wine. This fine 1633 building has the guild's patron, St. Urban, carved above the door, plucking grapes from a vine.

Walking back up Koestraat, turn right and look across Kloveniersburgwal canal to the huge gray sandstone **Trippenhuis** on the opposite bank. Built in a classical style, its facade is broken up by Corinthian pilasters, and the chimneys are carved in the shape of huge mortars, symbolizing the armaments industry, the source of the Trip brothers' wealth. Justus Vingboons (1612–1672), architect and brother of Philips Vingboons, designed this house in 1660,

Zuiderkerk
- 🅜 Map p. 73
- ✉ Zuiderkerkhof 72
- ☎ 689-2565
- 🕐 Tower open Apr.–Sept., Mon.–Sat.
- 🚊 Tram: 4, 9, 14, 16, 24, 25

zuiderkerk amsterdam.nl

observing the brothers' request for one facade but two separate houses. Look carefully at the middle windows and you will see the dividing wall behind the glass.

On this side of the canal you'll see No. 26, known as the **Kleine Trippenhuis,** built in 1696 for the Trip brothers' coachman. The facade is a mere 10 feet (3 m) wide, but it has an ornate semicircular gable over which two sphinxes are draped—their precise significance has never been established. The diminutive house

INSIDER TIP:

A great place to take photos of Zuiderkerk tower is the Staalstraat drawbridge, which crosses the tree-lined Groenburgwal canal.

—KEITH JENKINS
travel blogger
VelvetEscape.com

resulted from the coachman's complaint that his masters were extravagant in building such a palatial mansion for their home, and that he himself would be content with a house no wider than the Trip brothers' front door. Whether he meant it or not, the Trip brothers took him at his word.

Zuiderkerk

The next bridge left down Kloveniersburgwal leads to Nieuwe Hoogstraat, with its shops specializing in vintage clothes and African and

Indonesian tribal art. The first right, Zanddwarsstraat, leads to the Zuiderkerk (Southern Church), built between 1603 and 1611 to the designs of Hendrick de Keyser, who is buried here. Zuiderkerk was the first large church in the Netherlands constructed specifically for Protestant worship, as opposed to being converted from an existing Catholic church. The distinctive church tower contains a carillon of bells built by the Hemony brothers and dominates the surrounding area. Guided tours in spring and summer offer

---

Licorice at Jacob Hooij

At Kloveniersburgwal 10–12, don't miss the photogenic Jacob Hooij herbalist shop (see p. 261). Founded at this spot more than 200 years ago, the store still sells about 400 different herbs and spices—some for cooking, others for medicinal use.

One of their best-selling lines is licorice. Once sold as a remedy for sore throats, today licorice comes in all shapes and sizes, and is the Netherlands' most popular candy, known as "drop." The Dutch spend €135 million each year on "drop," consuming 194,000 pounds (88,000 kg) each day. While you might be familiar with sweet licorice, try the genuine salt drop for a truly Dutch experience.

the opportunity to admire the sweeping views from its peak.

A pioneering structure in its day, the Zuiderkerk attracted a visit from the English architect Christopher Wren, who came to study it when tasked with rebuilding St. Paul's cathedral in London after the 1666 fire. Claude Monet immortalized the Zuiderkerk in a painting he made during a visit to Amsterdam in 1874.

The last service was held in Zuiderkerk in 1929. Years of neglect followed before the church was finally restored in the 1970s. It is now used as a venue for concerts, seminars, corporate hospitality, receptions, and parties. The church is surrounded by the Pentagon housing development (so called for the shape of the site), designed by Theo Bosch in 1983–84.

One route back to the city center lies down Zand-dwarsstraat. Bridges force you to turn right onto Raamgracht, left over the canal, left again, and right down Groenburgwal, a street with an interesting mixture of old and new canal houses, warehouses, and house-boats. Halfway down, at No. 42, is the simple 18th-century Gothic **English Episcopal Church,** built for, and still used by, the English community in Amsterdam. The next right, Staalstraat, has antique shops and the very attractive **Saaihal** (Cloth Hall) on the right. Completed in 1641 to the design of Pieter de Keyser (1590–1657), the son of Hendrick, the gables are draped in theatrical bunches of linen, carved in sandstone, in a witty reference to the building's use as the guild house of the Cloth Merchants. From here the massive bulk of the Stadhuis-Muziektheater complex, the home of the National Ballet and the Nederlands Opera, lies to the left (see p. 105), while turning right takes you via Nieuwe Doelenstraat to Rokin and the Allard Pierson Museum (see pp. 78–79). ∎

The tower clock of the Zuiderkerk has measured time through four centuries of Amsterdam history.

A Waterside Stroll

Amsterdam's first dockyards and warehouses were located just beyond the city walls, which are traced in this walk around the city's original waterfront. The route passes through an area of Amsterdam still crowded with moored vessels of all types, from houseboats to sturdy seagoing sailing ships.

Oudezijds Voorburgwal canal leading up to Sint Nicolaaskerk (St. Nicholas's Church)

With your back to Centraal Station, head left toward the NH Barbizon Palace Hotel. Next door to the hotel is the baroque **Sint Nicolaaskerk** ❶ (Church of St. Nicholas), built in 1887 as the successor to the secret attic church in the Museum Ons' Lieve Heer op Solder (see pp. 86–89). St. Nicholas is the patron saint of seafarers, and the dedication of the church reflects the fact that this was the sailors' quarter of Amsterdam.

Turning left (as you face the church), it is a short walk to **Prins Hendrikkade 84–85** ❷, called Batavia, named for the capital of Indonesia (Jakarta was once known as Batavia). Several of the firms based in this fine art deco building continue to trade with Indonesia

NOT TO BE MISSED:

Sint Nicolaaskerk • Prins Hendrikkade 84–85 • Schreierstoren • Montelbaanstoren • de Appel Arts Centre

(formerly the Dutch East Indies). Continue past this building and follow the curve of the road to reach the **Schreierstoren** ❸, an attractive drum-shaped tower built in 1482. The name is said to mean "Weepers' Tower" or "Tower of Tears," as it is from here that sailors' wives watched their menfolk depart on hazardous voyages. A plaque on the tower records that one such voyage began aboard "The Half Moon" on April 4, 1609. This expedition was led by Henry Hudson, in search of the fabled westward passage to the Spice Islands. Instead,

- See also area map pp. 72–73
- ► Centraal Station
- ⏱ 2 hours
- ↔ 1.1 mile (1.8 km)
- ► de Appel Arts Centre

Hudson and his crew stumbled across Manhattan Island and the Hudson River, and New Amsterdam would soon be on the map of the New World.

Continue to the right of the tower, down Geldersekade, where fishermen once unloaded their catch for sale in the great fish market of Nieuwmarkt. You'll come across several elegant 18th-century houses to admire at the start of the street. No. 8 exhibits a splendid frieze above the door, showing tobacco leaves spilling out of bales and barrels, while No. 16 has an exotic plant forming the central rib of the tall window above its doorway.

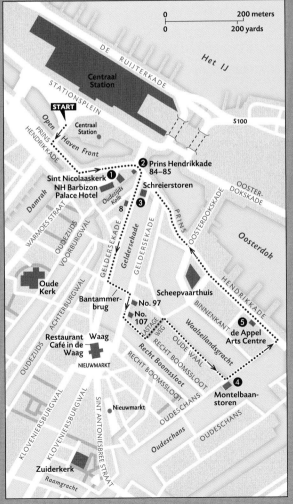

Farther down on the left is the **Bantammerbrug,** one of several art deco bridges in the area with ornate wrought-iron lamp standards at each corner. Cross the bridge and turn right, and take note of No. 97, a fine step-gabled 17th-century house with a plaque indicating that its owner was involved in the cognac trade. No. 107, to the right, built in 1634, is known as "the House with Eight Entrances," because eight different chandlers and ships' suppliers had their premises here.

Turn left down leafy Recht Boomssloot, a canal named after the 16th-century shipwright Cornelis Boom. His shipyard, on the site of Amsterdam's oldest dockyard, once occupied Lastageweg, the first street to the left.

A modern school and housing project now stand on this historic spot.

On the other side of this precinct, you emerge onto Oude Waal (Old Welling). From here there are sweeping views across the boat-filled Waalseilandsgracht to the spiky outline of the **Scheepvaarthuis,** literally "the Shipping Transport House," on the opposite bank. Built by J. M. van der Mey for a shipping company in 1916, this decorative office block is one of the earliest and finest examples of the Amsterdam School style of architecture. The maritime theme is worked into all the decorative details, from the rippling railings to the carvings of a bearded Triton over the entrance.

Turn right along Oude Waal, noting the attractive houses and warehouses lining the embankment and the variety of boats moored in the canal. At the end of the street is the **Montelbaanstoren ❹**, a tower that leans rather perilously over the edge of the Oude-schans canal. The Oudeschans—meaning "Old Rampart"—formed part of the extended city defenses constructed in 1512. Hendrick de Keyser added the attractive spire that rises from the Montelbaanstoren in 1606.

Reaching Oudeschans, look right and across the canal to the far bank, which is lined with old warehouses. Now converted into apartments, they retain their unadorned triangular gables and sail-shaped shutters painted in distinctive colors. Turn left and walk up Kalkmarkt to the Prins Hendrikkade, turning left onto this thoroughfare. Two minutes' walk will bring you to **de Appel Arts Centre ❺** at No. 142 *(tel 625-5651, closed Mon. & Tues.–Sun. a.m., $$, deappel.nl).* This little gem was founded in 1975 as a groundbreaking platform for the presenta-tion of international contemporary art and still hosts innovative exhibitions, installations, and visual arts performances. It has run an acclaimed eight-month Curatorial Programme since 1994, instructing budding curators from across the world. As well as an excellent shop, de Appel boasts an atmospheric café and res-taurant in the basement, MOES, which serves local produce garnished with herbs from the pretty back garden.

The Montelbaanstoren, on the Oudeschans canal, was built in 1516 to defend the city.

Unparalleled diversity: the parks of Plantage, Artis zoo, Rembrandt's home, the Jewish Quarter, Eastern Docklands, and Amsterdam Noord

Jodenbuurt, Plantage, Oostelijk Havengebied, & Environs

Introduction & Map   100–101

Jodenbuurt   102–109

**Experience: Attend a Free
    Lunchtime Concert**   103

**Experience: Learn to Paint
    Like a Dutch Master**   105

Feature: The Genius of Rembrandt   106–107

Plantage   110–114

Tropenmuseum   115

Exploring Plantage & Maritime
    Amsterdam   116–117

Oostelijk Havengebied   118–125

**Experience: A Good Book at the
    Openbare Library**   123

Noord   126

Hotels & Restaurants in Jodenbuurt,
    Plantage, Oostelijk Havengebied,
    & Environs   246–247

Rembrandt self-portrait outside his former home

Jodenbuurt, Plantage, Oostelijk Havengebied, & Environs

This diverse area of Amsterdam ranges from the parks and promenades of Plantage to the maze of alleys in the Jewish Quarter. It swings from the history and classic lines of the Hortus Botanicus and Hermitage to the edgy design and architecture of the regenerated Eastern and North Docklands. From flea markets and diamond factories to historical museums and science centers, there is something here for everyone.

Fleeing persecution in other parts of Europe during the 16th century, Jewish migrants settled to the east of Amsterdam, in what was then a slum beyond the medieval city walls. Still known as the Jodenbuurt (Jewish District), this area honors the history of those early settlers, with the moving Joods Historische Museum (Jewish Historical Museum; see pp. 108–109) at its heart. The chimneys of the nearby Gassan Diamond Works and lively Waterlooplein market are both tangible signs of the Jewish legacy in Amsterdam. Although they received little credit for it at the time, the Jews and Protestant dissenters who settled in this district brought with them skills and a work ethic that would help the city to blossom economically, laying the foundations for the Golden Age. Also nearby is the house where Rembrandt van Rijn painted most of his masterpieces, drawing inspiration for his bearded Old Testament prophets from the ordinary people of Jodenbuurt's streets.

Side by side with the slums of the Jodenbuurt lay the leafy suburb of Plantage (meaning "the Plantation"), originally an area of parks and gardens, with lush tea gardens, elegant theaters, and grand public promenades. The area became built-up in the 19th century, but the pleasure gardens live on in the colossal Artis zoo (see pp. 112–113), and in the ponds, palm houses, and flower beds of the Hortus Botanicus (Botanical Gardens; see pp. 110–111).

Immediately north of Plantage, in the Oostelijk Havengebied (Eastern Docklands), the scene changes even more dramatically. The former quays, harbors, maritime buildings, and wave-breaking peninsulas of the once thriving docks now house museums, concert halls, hotels, restaurants, concept stores, and homes. The iconic green hull of the NEMO science museum (see pp. 122–123) dominates this dockland seascape, its foundations laid upon the underwater IJ tunnel. Thundering through that tunnel, and on free ferries above it, traffic heads for the blossoming area of Amsterdam Noord, which blends a cultural breeding ground and contemporary urban design with rural tranquillity. ∎

NOT TO BE MISSED:

A visit to Amsterdam's Jewish Quarter 102–109

Exploring Rembrandt's house and studio 103–105

Afternoon tea in the Orangery Café at Hortus Botanicus 110–111

Seafaring history at the Dutch Maritime Museum 118–120

Learning science and having fun at NEMO 122–123

A bike ride in Noord 126

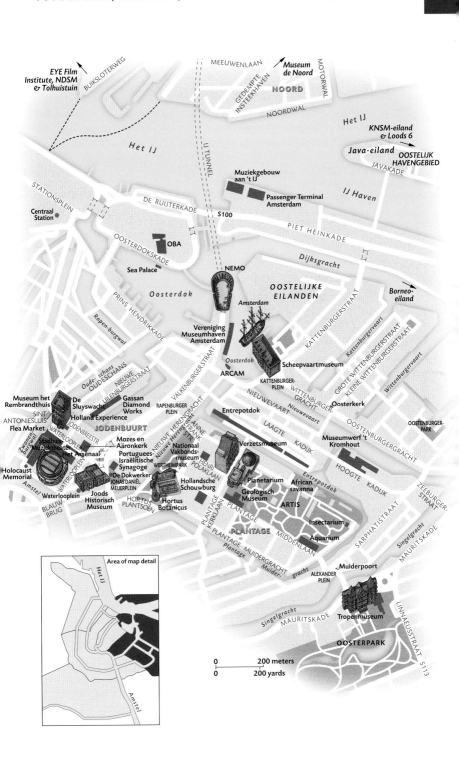

Jodenbuurt

Jewish refugees arriving in Amsterdam around 1600 were not welcomed. Denied civil rights and excluded from many trades, they struggled to survive. Despite poverty and discrimination, many became wealthy and influential citizens. The Jewish Historical Quarter reveals their story in its Jewish Historical Museum, Portuguese Synagogue, and Hollandse Schouwburg.

Groundbreaking sculpture inside the Stadhuis-Muziektheater (aka the Stopera)

Gassan Diamond Works

- 🗺 Map p. 101
- ✉ Nieuwe Uilenburger-straat 173–175
- ☎ 622-5333
- 💲 Free tours daily
- 🚊 Tram: 9, 14

gassan.com

Waterlooplein

The Waterlooplein district is dominated by the vast Stadhuis-Muziektheater complex, known to Amsterdammers as the Stopera—a portmanteau of Stadhuis and opera and an ironic reference to the 1980s "Stop the Opera" campaign, mounted by demonstrators who deemed the building expensive and elitist.

The Museum Het Rembrandt-huis (see pp. 103–105) is one of the few buildings to survive the postwar redevelopment of the Jewish quarter. It stands alongside **Sint Antoniesluis** (St. Anthony's Lock), from where there is a fine view northward down Oude-schans to the Montelbaanstoren (see p. 98). The lock mechanism survives, along with the lock-keeper's cottage, dated 1695, now a café called **De Sluyswacht.**

The tall chimney you see to the right belongs to the massive **Gassan Diamond Works.** This is one of the few industrial buildings left in central Amsterdam, a reminder that diamond cutting and polishing was introduced to Amsterdam by Jewish refugees from Antwerp in the 17th century. Take a free tour and see raw stones being turned into sparkling jewels, and learn why Amsterdam has been a center for this industry for the past 400 years.

On the opposite side of the road are the stalls of the **Waterlooplein** flea market. The large square has been Amsterdam's largest and liveliest marketplace since the 1880s, when Jews and Gentiles met here to do business. Trading ceased during the Nazi occupation but resumed in the 1950s, and today the market extends around two sides of the Stadhuis, selling everything from new and recycled clothes to jewelry and crafts.

South of the market you come to a **memorial slab** of polished black marble, set by the water's edge, commemorating the Jewish victims of World War II. Along the bank, with the barge-filled waters of the Amstel River to your right, you can enjoy extensive views that stretch from the **Blauwbrug** (Blue Bridge) in the east (see p. 188) to the distant spire of the **Munttoren** (see p. 63) in the west.

Museum Het Rembrandthuis

Rembrandt lived and worked in the building that is now the **Rembrandthuis** (Rembrandt House) for nearly 20 years (1639–1658). It was the birthplace of his son, Titus, and where his wife, Saskia, died, and it was here that he created his masterpieces, including "The Night Watch" (1642). Ultimately, the house was to ruin him. Living well beyond his means, Rembrandt was declared bankrupt. Everything was sold,

and he moved to cheap rented accommodations in the Jordaan.

In 1906, the Amsterdam council bought the house and opened it to the public in 1911. This enduringly popular museum was extended in 1998: The main house was painstakingly restored and a new wing added to house some 250 of his engravings and

Museum Het Rembrandthuis

🅰 Map p. 101
✉ Jodenbreestraat 4–6
☎ 520-0400
💲 $$$
🚊 Tram: 9, 14

rembrandthuis.nl

EXPERIENCE: Attend a Free Lunchtime Concert

Should you not be able to attend a full concert at the Stopera or Concertgebouw, you can catch a flavor of the talents hosted by both establishments during a free lunchtime concert. Every Tuesday, starting at 12:30 p.m. in the **Boekmanzaal** at the Stopera, the Dutch Philharmonic Orchestra gives an hour-long performance. Places are offered on a first-come, first-served basis, so arrive in plenty of time.

Similarly, the **Concertgebouw** (*Concertgebouwplein 2–6, tel 671-8345, concertgebouw.nl*) hosts a free lunch concert on Wednesdays at 12:30 p.m (Sept.–May). The concerts vary from open rehearsals by the Koninklijke Concertgebouworkest (Royal Concertgebouw Orchestra) to performances by conservatory ensembles, and from chamber music to recitals by new young talents. A list of concerts is posted on the Concertgebouw website a week in advance.

---

other artworks. The inventory compiled by the Secretary of the Chamber of Insolvency listed all of Rembrandt's possessions prior to their sale in 1658. This exhaustive document enabled the curators to re-create each room precisely as it was when Rembrandt lived there.

Expensive Habits: When Rembrandt and Saskia moved into the house in 1639, the artist was at the height of his fame. Nonetheless he borrowed the considerable sum of 13,000 guilders to buy the house. Unfortunately, Rembrandt had expensive tastes. He was a dealer as well as an artist, and he bought numerous paintings and engravings from his contemporaries, intending to resell them at a profit. Some of these works (mainly dramatically painted scenes from the Bible and classical mythology) have been loaned back to the Rembrandt House Museum and now hang on the walls of the downstairs rooms, which Rembrandt used as an art gallery.

Cabinet of Curiosities: Rembrandt also maintained a collection of rare and exotic objects, which has been re-created in the upstairs **Cabinet Room.** Such acquisitions of curiosities, forerunners of modern museums, were quite common among the very wealthy, but Rembrandt was a mere artist, and his collecting habits added to his financial burden. To try and make ends meet, he converted the attic into a big studio space and took in scores of pupils, sometimes passing off their work as his own. These paintings are now more accurately accredited to "School of Rembrandt." All these efforts were to no avail. Far from paying his debts, he borrowed more, until his creditors grew impatient and called in the bailiff.

The Master Engraver: Rembrandt often used the objects he collected as props in his paintings, and he frequently copied the work of artists he admired, such as Dürer, not as deliberate plagiarism, but more as a tribute from one great artist to another. He would also invite people from the streets to serve as his models, as you can see if you visit the comprehensive collection of engravings displayed in the gallery built next to his

Pigments used by Rembrandt in his studio, at the Rembrandt House Museum

EXPERIENCE: Learn to Paint Like a Dutch Master

If simply standing in the very studio in which Rembrandt painted so many of his masterpieces inspires you to put brush to canvas, why not take part in an artistic workshop at the Rembrandthuis Museum? Organized in conjunction with **De Vrije Academie** (The Free Academy), the largest educational institute for art history in the Netherlands, the Rembrandthuis runs three different workshops. These daylong classes enable you to learn how to paint, draw, or etch like Rembrandt, using the very same 17th-century techniques he adopted, and perfected. If you choose to take part in the etching workshop, for example, you will have the opportunity to handle Rembrandt's original 17th-century etching plates and put them through the printing press to make your own unique prints. You will also create your own plate, feeling the metal yield under your needle and *échoppe* and marveling at how Rembrandt achieved such softness of touch in this challenging medium.

Each workshop runs from 11 a.m. to 3:30 p.m. and includes expert tuition in your chosen discipline, all materials for the class, and a coffee. Once you have completed the workshop, you will receive a guided tour of the museum—the knowledge gleaned over the course of the day will enable you to admire Rembrandt's work in a very different light.

house. For all his spending, he was most at home depicting ordinary people—beggars, workmen, street characters—with a realism and a spontaneity that were rare in his day.

Stadhuis-Muziektheater

A short way along the riverbank toward the Blauwbrug lies the vast **Stadhuis-Muziektheater** complex. Some 60 years in the making, the curved building is probably the most controversial building in Amsterdam. From the riots that blighted the first attempts at its construction to the ongoing jibes about its ugliness, few Amsterdammers are fans.

Nontheless, the Muziektheater is the city's principal opera house and home of the Netherlands Opera, National Ballet, and Holland Symfonia. It also houses the **Boekmanzaal,**

INSIDER TIP:

Once a year, on March 9 at 8:39 a.m., the sun shines upon the grave of Saskia van Uylenburgh, Rembrandt's beloved wife, in the Oude Kerk [see p. 84–85]. A simple and moving "Sun Breakfast" service is held in her honor by her grave.

—GABRIELLA LE BRETON
National Geographic author

where free lunch concerts are held. By the exit of the Muziektheater, a display explains about the geographical datum known as **Normaal Amsterdams Peil** (N.A.P., or Normal Amsterdam Level). Because so much of the (continued on p. 108)

Stadhuis-Muziektheater
- Map p. 101
- Waterlooplein 22
- 551-8117
- Tram: 9, 14

muziektheater.nl

The Genius of Rembrandt

Of all the great artists to come out of the Netherlands during the Golden Age, Rembrandt remains one of the most enigmatic—and, at the same time, one of the most human.

Rembrandt's 17th-century artworks continue to fascinate viewers in the 21st century.

Rembrandt van Rijn was born in 1606 in Leiden, where his wealthy father owned and operated a mill on the Rhine River, which was called De Rijn. Though pushed toward a career in law, he gave up his university studies to concentrate on art. A thriving city, home to many wealthy patrons of art, Amsterdam was the place where artists could best make a living, so Rembrandt moved here in 1631.

The city's guilds and civic guards were in the habit of commissioning group portraits to hang on their clubroom walls. Rembrandt's first commission was to paint the renowned Dr. Tulp giving an anatomy lesson, observed by a group of distinguished guild surgeons. "The Anatomy Lesson of Dr. Nicolaes Tulp" (1632) now hangs in the Mauritshuis in Den Haag (see sidebar p. 93 & p. 228). The surgeons who commissioned the work wanted to be shown in a flattering light—preferably in full profile—so their poses are awkward. But the sponsors

were happy, the painting was well received, and fame and fortune followed. The artist, however, grew restless, chafing against the restraints and conventions of the time.

Rembrandt's Etchings

Even as he continued to produce portraits and large oil paintings of biblical subjects for public consumption, Rembrandt turned to engraving as a more private activity. His combination of hard line (achieved by etching the printing plate with acid) and of softer lines and shading (produced by cutting the plate directly with etching tools) marked him as a technical innovator. The Jewish quarter where he lived provided him with a constant source of subjects. He would approach passersby and ask them to model for him as he sketched out Old Testament prophets with lined faces and flowing beards. He loved to draw neighborhood characters: rat-catchers, vagabonds, beggars, organ-grinders.

Personal Tragedy

Rembrandt's engravings were eagerly sought by collectors. On canvas, too, he began to depart from convention—in ways that did not please his patrons. It's possible that events in his personal life made him less eager to please the self-important *burghermasters* (mayors) and nouveau riche merchants for whom he toiled. His wife, Saskia, and three of their four children died, leaving only the sickly Titus. In 1642, the year of Saskia's death, Rembrandt painted what many consider to be his masterwork, "The Night Watch" (see p. 195). Although now considered a masterpiece of realism, it was openly derided in its day. Among Rembrandt's transgressions, according to the critics, was letting the figures overlap so that some are partly hidden.

After this, Rembrandt received fewer commissions, prompting him to retreat into his own world. Deep in debt, he moved to a modest house in Rozengracht, in the Jordaan, where he painted as much for his own satisfaction as for public consumption. In 1665 he produced the brilliant "Jewish Bride," with its impressionistic background, and its paint applied so lavishly as to be three-dimensional. These experiments in technique, 200 years ahead of their time, help to explain the luminescence of the portrait and its intense emotional quality.

"The Jewish Bride" would be one of Rembrandt's last works. Titus died in 1667 at the age of 27, and Rembrandt followed in

less than a year. He was buried in an unmarked pauper's grave in Westerkerk (see p. 139)—an ignoble end for a towering artistic talent.

INSIDER TIP:

Don't forget to visit the Mauritshuis in Den Haag [The Hague; see p. 228]. Reopened in 2014, this small, beautiful museum features several exceptional pieces by the Dutch Masters, including some key Rembrandt paintings.

—JUSTIN KAVANAGH
National Geographic
International Editions editor

Visitors admire Rembrandt's "The Night Watch" at the recently renovated Rijksmuseum.

Netherlands lies below sea level, sea level itself cannot be used as the benchmark for establishing relative heights and depths, so N.A.P. is used instead. Beside the display, a mural shows a cross-section of north Holland, revealing just how many well-known Dutch landmarks lie below the surface level of the North Sea, which is held back by artificial dikes and natural dunes.

The huge Catholic church located near the Stadhuis-Muziektheater complex is the **Mozes en Aäronkerk,** built between 1837 and 1841.

Jewish Historical Museum

The museum is set in a complex of four Ashkenazik synagogues, built by Jewish refugees from Germany and Poland in the late 17th century. Those parts of the complex that survive in their original form are used to explain Jewish religious life and ritual. The remaining rooms and galleries document the flight of Jews from repressive Catholic regimes elsewhere in Europe, and their new lives in the Netherlands. A large room explores the shattering of so many lives when Germany invaded the Netherlands in 1940. Despite losing much of its original collection during the Nazi occupation, the museum has a wealth of art and historical objects. There is also an excellent JHM Children's Museum, run by the Hollander family, that teaches kids about Jewish traditions, music, and jokes.

Early Protestant Amsterdam grudgingly tolerated the Jews but placed many barriers in their path. Forbidden to own shops and barred from the trade guilds, the refugees slowly built their wealth as peddlers and market traders, later prospering as bankers and brokers, and bringing new crafts, including diamond processing and printing.

Once full equality arrived in 1796, when laws concerning Jewish emancipation were passed, there were no legal constraints on the entrepreneurship of the Jewish community. Local cottage industries quickly blossomed into full-blown factory enterprises, helping to lead Amsterdam into the industrial era.

The Joods Historisch Museum uses media old and new to tell the story of Amsterdam's Jewish community.

Monuments to Jewish History

The Jewish Historical Museum encourages visitors to explore the Jewish Cultural Quarter, once home to some 80,000 Jews. Leaflets from the museum shop detail a self-guided discovery tour of Jewish Amsterdam.

Opposite the entrance to the museum is **Het Arsenaal** (the Arsenal: *Nos. 6–8 Nieuwe Amstelstraat*), a 16th-century warehouse originally used to store bread, cheese, and peat, which were distributed to Amsterdam's poorest citizens. The charity was administered from the handsome pedimented building of 1654 called the **Huiszittenaalmoeze-niershuis,** around the corner to the left.

Directly opposite the museum lies the **Portugees-Israëlitische Synagoge** (Portuguese-Israelite Synagogue), dating back to 1675. At the time, this was one of the world's largest—and wealthiest—synagogues, and its 17th-century interiors are almost completely preserved. The entrance, to the left of the big brick building, faces onto the street called Mr. Visserplein, one of several local place names that commemorate prominent Jews. (Mr. Visser was the president of the Supreme Court of the Netherlands until the Nazi invasion, and he played a leading role in the Dutch resistance.) Marie Andriessen's 1952 statue **"De Dokwerker,"** a burly longshoreman, erected nearby, commemorates the 1941 general strike, led by Amsterdam's dock-workers and transport workers, in protest of Nazi treatment of the Jews. It stands on Jonas Daniël Meijerplein. Jonas Daniël Meyer (1780–1834) was the first Jew to be admitted to the Dutch legal profession, and a campaigner for Jewish civil rights.

East of the synagogue lies the Hortus Botanicus (Botanical Gardens; see pp. 110–111), at the beginning of the wealthy Plantage suburb that became home to many of the city's most prosperous Jews in the late 19th and early 20th centuries. The **Hollandsche Schouwburg** (Dutch Theater; *Plantage Middenlaan 24*) has a pediment carved

INSIDER TIP:

Don't miss the opportunity to visit the Portuguese Synagogue with its lavish original interiors— entrance is included with your Joods Historisch Museum ticket.

—LARRY PORGES
*National Geographic
Travel Books editor*

with cavorting nudes, recalling its prewar heyday as a theater. Now a roofless shell, it stands as a memorial to the many thousands of Jews who were rounded up and assembled here before being sent by train to the Westerbork internment camp, and from there to the death camps of Auschwitz and Bergen-Belsen. ■

Joods Historisch Museum

- Map p. 101
- Nieuwe Amstelstraat 1
- 531-0310
- Closed Yom Kippur
- $$$
- Tram: 9, 14

jhm.nl

Portugees-Israëlitische Synagoge

- Map p. 101
- Mr. Visserplein 3
- 624-5351
- Closed Sat., except for Sabbath Day service at 8:45 p.m.
- $$
- Tram: 9, 14, 20

Plantage

With fine museums, a zoo, and historic botanical gardens, Plantage is Amsterdam's garden of learning. Founded in 1638 as the Hortus Medicus, the Hortus Botanicus is one of Europe's oldest botanical gardens. Shoehorned into 3 acres (1.2 ha), it nonetheless provides space for 6,000 plants of some 4,000 species of tropical and desert plants in state-of-the-art conservatories.

The Arts and Crafts building designed by H. P. Berlage, home of the National Trade Unions Museum

Hortus Botanicus

- 🅰 Map p. 101
- ✉ Plantage Middenlaan 2A
- ☎ 625-9021
- 💲 $$
- 🚊 Tram: 7, 9, 14

dehortus.nl

Hortus Botanicus

As 17th-century Dutch explorers ventured farther afield, they sent back a constant supply of rare and exotic plants. This new material provided the foundation for the pioneering research of Carolus Linnaeus (1707–1778), the creator of the classification system used to name all plants. It was also economically useful: a coffee plant propagated here would help establish a worldwide coffee industry (see sidebar opposite).

Amsterdam's gardens have always been used for entertainment as well as research. City notables were once granted privileged access to the botanical gardens to marvel at curiosities like the monkey puzzle tree or the giant Amazonian water lily. A big attraction of the Palm House is the rare Cycad palm, which flowers very infrequently (one was planted 300 years ago, making it now the world's oldest potted plant). Today's visitors can enjoy the sight of beautifully patterned butterflies dancing among the nectar-bearing plants or explore the new climate-controlled greenhouses. Smaller glass houses dot the landscaped gardens, filled with rare cacti.

Elevated walkways rise above dense forest in the large **Palm House** and meander past tropical plants and pools. A walk above the forest canopy with views down over the luxuriant foliage is the perfect antidote to a cold Amsterdam day. If you want to linger longer, the **Orangery Café** is a delightfully peaceful spot for lunch or tea.

Nationaal Vakbondsmuseum

The National Trade Unions Museum, housed in a charming Arts and Crafts building designed by Amsterdam School pioneer H. P. Berlage, is worth a visit just for the interior.

In 1894, Henri Polak founded the ANDB, the General Dutch Diamond Workers Union. In 1900, the union asked the radical architect Berlage to design a new headquarters. The building, called De Burcht (The Stronghold), has survived almost untouched.

Berlage's building bristles with socialist symbolism. The castle-like battlements and tower suggest the strength of union solidarity, while inside, the stairwell is lit by a glass lantern symbolizing the light of the future. Monumental stone-carved friezes portray laborers working at heroic tasks. Simple yet elegant wooden furniture and Tiffany-style glass lamps show that Berlage also valued ideals of beauty amid the battle for working-class power.

The Nationaal Vakbonds-museum only opens once a month and you have to book in advance. Visitors should check their website *(deburcht.nl)* for opening days. Visitors to this informal museum can wander at will. Rooms still function as meeting places and research facilities for those interested in trade union history. Downstairs are a snack bar and a library of early socialist books. The walls and the staircases are lined with historic labor movement posters, many produced on the printing presses displayed in the basement. Upstairs are photographs, trade union banners, and newspaper extracts charting the rise of trade union influence in the Netherlands.

Nationaal Vakbondsmuseum

- Map p. 101
- Henri Polaklaan 9
- 624-1166
- Frequently closed: Check website (deburcht.nl) for openings
- Tram: 7, 9, 14

NOTE: Though most of the printed matter in the National Vakbondsmuseum is in Dutch, an English summary is available from the ground floor information desk.

WIC Coffee Plantations

In 1706 a coffee plant smuggled out of Ethiopia was brought to the Hortus Medicus for propagation. Cuttings were subsequently exported to Brazil, where the Dutch West India Company (WIC) was developing coffee plantations, which would go on to become the basis for the world's largest coffee industry.

The WIC also operated coffee plantations in Suriname, which was captured by the Dutch in 1667 and governed as Dutch Guiana until 1954. The country eventually achieved independence in 1975. During the 18th century, Suriname was run by the Suriname Society, which was owned by the WIC, the city of Amsterdam, and the Van Sommelsdijck family. The society negotiated the sale of Surinamese products, especially coffee and sugar, and African slaves, who were shipped to Suriname to be sold and put to work on the plantations.

Artis Zoo

The three wealthy citizens who founded Amsterdam's zoo in 1838 signaled the seriousness of their commitment to research by naming the zoo Natura Artis Magistra (Nature Is the Teacher of Art). Now known simply as Artis, this zoological garden combines numerous attractions (many of them indoors, making it the perfect place to visit on a cold or wet day).

The museum entrance is flanked by two indoor attractions. To the left is the **Planetarium,** with an exhibition of spectacular images taken by the Hubble telescope, which examines the universe and the future of space exploration. Films are shown every hour on the 6,750-square-foot (628 sq m) curved dome. Although the soundtrack is in Dutch only, program notes are available in English.

On the right of the entrance is the **Geologisch Museum,** which brings alive the interplay between geological processes and the history of life on Earth. Fossil evidence plays a major part in the displays that cover the heyday of the dinosaurs, major events such as earthquakes and volcanic eruptions, and the rise of mammals.

Outside, winding paths meander around a dense and varied landscape populated by lemurs, camels, apes, gazelles, prairie dogs, and sea lions, to name but a few. Enclosures flank the zoo's perimeters, housing reptiles, gorillas, and birds. In all, more than 900 species of animals and 200 species of trees fill the lush gardens, complemented by various sculptures and monuments.

A large area landscaped to resemble the African savanna houses zebra, antelope, and gnu. This is visible from the adjacent

Lionesses strike a pose at Artis zoo.

restaurant and can be enjoyed with some excellent French fries. A more authentic Dutch dining experience can be enjoyed in the **Pancake House** by the main entrance. Continuing around the site, you come to the **Insectarium.** Not many people pay a zoo ticket to see some creepy-crawlies, but this captivating insect house is one of the biggest in the world, and worth a visit. Here, you'll meet a Giant Prickly Stick Insect (*Extatosoma tiaratum*) with a gender twist: The females don't need a male to produce offspring. Here too, you will watch up to a hundred species of cockroaches, locusts, tarantulas, ants, and grasshoppers as they feed.

INSIDER TIP:

Don't just marvel at the animals. Also take some time to enjoy the luscious green. Artis features more than 200 species of trees and 80 different varieties of tulips.

—GABRIELLA LE BRETON
National Geographic author

To wash that image away, head over to the **Aquarium,** the oldest in the Netherlands, where fascinating displays re-create different ecosystems. One shows the countless varieties of fish that teem in the waters of the Amazon River. Another presents the richly colorful life of the coral reef.

Feeding Time at the Zoo

If you find that watching animals feed is hungry work, fear not: There is an appetizing range of dining options for humans too at Artis zoo. Homo sapiens can enjoy table service at the Restaurant Flamingoserre, which overlooks the old flamingo pond, or a filling buffet at the Restaurant de Twee Cheetahs (Two Cheetahs), while watching the animals on the savanna. You can gently swat butterflies off your cookies and ice cream in the Vlinderrestaurant (Butterfly Restaurant) or stop by a Bakfiets (Tray Bicycle) for a snack as you stroll around the grounds.

However, don't miss the opportunity to enjoy a real Dutch tradition: *poffertjes* (mini pancakes) in the Poffertjeshuis, located by the Petting Zoo. These dense, freshly cooked pancakes are served hot by the half dozen and best enjoyed drowning in butter and powdered sugar.

Equally riveting is the brick-lined tank with bits of rusting bicycle littering the floor; this mock-up of a typical Amsterdam canal has more living creatures than you might expect, including eels and carp.

The **Butterfly Pavilion** is the largest of its kind in the Netherlands, housing thousands of butterflies that flitter through the air and feed from flowers. Species include the spectacular Blue Morpho (*Papilio achilles*) and the fastest butterfly in the world, the Swallowtail (*Papilio machaon*).

If you have a burning question about any of the Artis inhabitants, check the daily program for details about zookeeper talks, which offer the opportunity to grill the keepers about their wards.

Artis Zoo
- 🅰 Map p. 101
- ✉ Plantage Kerklaan 38–40
- ☎ 0900/2784-796
- 💲 $$$
- 🚋 Tram: 9, 14
- ⛴ Artis Express boat service links the zoo to Centraal Station

artis.nl

Verzetsmuseum

Verzetsmuseum

- Map p. 101
- Plantage Kerklaan 61
- 620-2535
- $$
- Tram: 9, 14

verzetsmuseum.org

Verzetsmuseum

Nazi Germany invaded the Netherlands on May 10, 1940, and for the next five years the Dutch lived under the tyrannical rule of an oppressive foreign regime. The Verzetsmuseum (Resistance Museum) reveals the many ways in which they responded and conveys a very

Kites fly in the main hall of the Tropenmuseum.

real sense of what life was like for ordinary people living through the war.

The museum's permanent exhibition comprises authentic objects, photos and documents, and film and sound fragments that tell the history of the people who lived through the Nazi occupation. The exhibition recounts their story in chronological order, from the early 1930s to 1950,

giving an insight into the different forms of resistance: strikes, forging of documents, assisting of hideaways, underground newspapers, escape routes, armed resistance, and espionage.

Resistance at Home & Abroad: The museum brings to life the oppression and resistance to German rule that grew among the Dutch people, not only within the Netherlands but also in the Dutch colonies of Suriname, Antilles, and the Dutch East Indies.

A separate part of the exhibition focuses on the suffering experienced in the Dutch East Indies under the Japanese regime of terror. Throughout the exhibition, care is given to contextualize the environment in which the resistance took place—everyday life in a politically and denominationally segregated society, in which the church played an important role. It also explores how the experiences of the occupation continue to affect today's society in the Netherlands.

In addition to the permanent exhibition, temporary exhibitions focus on specific themes, and the adjoining Children's Museum accommodates some 16,000 schoolchildren annually.

Pick up the informative pocket booklet titled "Persecution and Resistance," published by the Resistance Museum. This 18-page booklet details a walk between the Resistance Museum and the Anne Frank House, picking out key historical landmarks, events, and sights. ■

Tropenmuseum

The Tropenmuseum (Museum of the Tropics) is one of Europe's leading ethnographic museums and, thanks to its relatively remote location, one of Amsterdam's best-kept secrets. The bright, lively, and exotic museum introduces visitors to the daily life, beliefs, and cultures of diverse peoples around the world.

Ten permanent exhibitions explore the diverse social and cultural history and environments of Africa, Latin America and the Caribbean, the Dutch East Indies, New Guinea, India, West Asia and North Africa, and Southeast Asia. The visitor is also encouraged to explore world music, relive inspirational traveling tales, and investigate the way in which man interacts with his subtropical environment.

The lively, interactive exhibitions incorporate around 175,000 artifacts collected by anthropologists working in the former Dutch colonies, ranging from fine textiles and intricate 15th-century mahogany furniture to dramatic tribal masks and headdresses. Video and sound are used to enhance the static displays. Visitors can take a stroll through an interactive re-creation of an Arabic souk (market), or take shelter from a sandstorm in the African savanna, or set sail on a virtual adventure down the Amazon.

Temporary exhibitions address current ethnographic issues and often highlight some of the global projects with which the Tropenmuseum is actively involved—collecting and preserving cultural heritage across the world; raising funds to provide accommodation, transport, and education; and countering theft and illegal trade in art and antiquities. The museum also hosts supplementary activities such as lectures, films, and exuberant live music and dance performances.

INSIDER TIP:

Add your voice to the human story in the Museum of Forgotten Songs, a part of the "World of Music" exhibit: Sing a song from your childhood, modern or traditional.

—JUSTIN KAVANAGH
*National Geographic
International Editions editor*

The Tropenmuseum Junior, founded in 1975, boasts interactive and immersive exhibitions for 6-to 13-year-olds and is a superb family attraction. There's also a shop selling ethnic art, and two restaurants, which serve a range of authentic dishes from around the world. The **Soeterijn Café** serves a generous afternoon tea (reserve ahead) and dinner as well as lunch. ∎

Tropenmuseum

- Map p. 101
- Linnaeusstraat 2
- 568-8200
- $$$
- Tram: 3, 7, 9, 10, 14. Bus: 22
- Museumboot

tropenmuseum.nl

Exploring Plantage & Maritime Amsterdam

Two adjacent districts, each with its own distinctive character, fill the space between the end of the canal belt and the eastern harbor. Plantage, with its zoo, botanical gardens, theaters, and leafy streets, was a center for entertainment in the 18th and early 19th centuries, later becoming a wealthy residential quarter. A narrow canal separates Plantage from the Eastern Docklands, where, on a hot day, warehouses still exude the scent of pepper and cloves.

A sphinx helps illuminate Wertheimpark in the Plantage.

Start at **Hortus Botanicus** (see p. 110) and turn right, crossing the road over to the entrance to **Wertheimpark,** where stone sphinxes flank the gate of the city's oldest public park (created in 1895). Turn left down Plantage Parklaan and take the first right onto Henri Polaklaan, named for the founder of the Dutch trade union movement. To see inside one of the large and elegant villas lining this street, visit the **Nationaal Vakbondsmuseum** ❶ a short way up on the left (see p. 111). On the opposite side of the road, at Nos. 6–12, a plaque with a pelican

NOT TO BE MISSED:

Artis zoo • Entrepotdok
• Scheepvaartmuseum

feeding her young indicates that this was the site of the Portuguese Jewish Hospital (the pelican is a symbol of self-sacrifice).

When you reach the entrance to **Artis** ❷ (see pp. 112–113), turn left to walk down Plantage Kerklaan. No. 61, on the left, was built in 1875 as a concert hall and is now home to the **Verzetsmuseum** ❸ (see p. 114).

At the end of the street, cross the Nijlpaardenbrug (Hippopotamus Bridge). This takes you over to the vast **Entrepotdok** warehouse complex ❹, which was built between 1708 and 1840 for entrepôt goods, stored here in transit before shipment to another country, and hence not subject to Dutch customs tariffs or import duties.

Walk along the dockside, with the boat-filled dock to the right, to an arch beside the Entrepotdok Café (after No. 63 and before No. 66). Go through the arch and turn right at the other end of the passage, then take the next left, down a footpath and cycleway, to reach Hoogte Kadijk. Turn right here and walk across the next lifting bridge (a type of drawbridge) to the **Museumwerf 't Kromhout** ❺ (Kromhout Working Museum, Hoogte Kadijk 147, tel 627-6777, machinekamer.nl), housed in the magnificent 19th-century iron sheds of the former Kromhout shipyard. The yard itself has been in operation since 1757, and the Kromhout Working Museum now specializes in the restoration of historic ships' engines, several of which are on display.

From the museum, return across the lifting bridge and, just beyond 119 Hoogte Kadijk, turn right down Overhaalsgang. Straight ahead are the three manmade Oostelijke Eilanden (Eastern Islands), created in 1658 by filling in shallow stretches of the IJ River. They were needed to provide more space for wharves when the Dutch East India Company began its rapid expansion from the mid-17th century. It was here that Tsar Peter the Great toiled in the shipyards in 1697–98, working alongside ordinary Dutch carpenters, learning the shipbuilders' craft before returning to St. Petersburg to found the Russian navy.

This area has been comprehensively redeveloped to provide modern housing, bars, restaurants, boutiques, and offices (see pp. 124–125). The 1671 **Oosterkerk** ⑥ (Eastern Church) survives, on the opposite side of the road to the lifting bridge; it has now been converted to offices and a concert hall. It was the main harbor of Amsterdam until the railroad closed it off from the IJ River.

After your visit to the church, turn left down Wittenburgergracht, a busy road that leads to the impressive sandstone building in classical style, built in 1656, that houses the nautical exhibits of the **Scheepvaartmuseum** ⑦ (Dutch Maritime Museum; see pp. 118–120).

🅐	See also area map p. 101
▶	Hortus Botanicus
🕒	3 hours
↔	1.3 miles (2 km)
▶	Scheepvaartmuseum

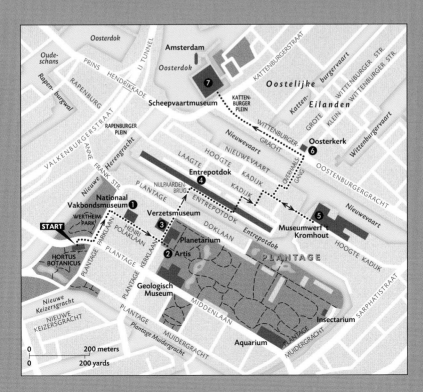

Oostelijk Havengebied

In Oostelijk Havengebied (Eastern Docklands), you'll find the ghosts of maritime history everywhere in former quays, harbors, and once-busy docks. This renewed area pulses now with museums, concert halls, hotels, and restaurants. The Scheepvaartmuseum (Dutch Maritime Museum) offers an impressive collection of artworks, charts, and model ships. Children can play pirates on a real tall-masted East Indiaman ship moored in the dock just outside the museum.

Scheepvaartmuseum (Dutch Maritime Museum), Oosterdok: the heart of maritime Amsterdam

Scheepvaart-museum

- Map p. 101
- Kattenburgerplein 1
- 523-2222
- $$$
- Bus: 22, 48

hetscheepvaart museum.nl

Scheepvaartmuseum

The building housing the museum is almost as interesting as the displays it contains. Built in 1656 to the severe classical designs of Daniel Stalpaert, as the 's Lands Zeemagazijn, it was the city's arsenal, with cannon and other munitions stockpiled in the courtyard. The vaulted cellars were used to store up to 10,600 gallons (40,000 l) of rainwater for drinking. The main building stored all the goods needed to equip the fleet of ships entrusted

with defending Dutch naval interests and with protecting Dutch harbors and merchant shipping. This task involved the Netherlands in a series of long, costly wars with rival colonial powers, most notably England. The building was of such strategic importance that it incorporated novel fireproofing precautions—sand was stored in the floor and ceiling cavities so that it would drop through the burning timbers and douse the flames in the event of a fire. The perennial problem of vermin was resolved by employing an army of cats.

Courtyard & Entrance:

The Maritime Museum's truly impressive facade does not flatter to deceive. Visitors are not disappointed once they step inside. The large inner courtyard, once used to store munitions, is now covered by a spectacular self-supporting glass ceiling constructed from thousands of pieces of glass in an intricate metal frame. From the entrance (South), a dedicated children's area (West) spans two floors and includes educational and stimulating exhibits such as "The Tale of the Whale," where kids can play inside a life-size whale model, and the interactive installation titled "See You in the Golden Age."

East: The East section also covers two floors and encompasses an impressive collection of world-class maritime artwork, from eye-wateringly precise 16th-century etchings to the moody seascapes and naval war scenes of the Dutch masters to contemporary works. It further includes displays of original ships' decorations; navigational instruments; exquisite boat models of 17th-century round-bottomed boats and contemporary racing yachts; globes marking the discovery of new territories; and beautiful silver, glass, and porcelain collections. A cozy sitting room with sofas and leather armchairs enables visitors to listen to audiotapes of maritime derring-do while leafing through photograph albums, which chronicle the lives of old seafaring families and naval crews.

North: The North section incorporates the "24/7 Amsterdam Port" installation, which highlights the comings and goings of one of the world's busiest ports, a virtual adventure at sea in the "Voyage at Sea"; the stately Christiaan Brunings steamship, which was built in an Amsterdam shipyard in 1900 and meticulously restored; and the reproduction of the 1740 Dutch East India-man ship *The Amsterdam.*

A Drink in Weepers' Tower

The Schreierstoren (Weepers' Tower) is a 15th-century defense tower located on the Amstel River. The tower is the point from which Henry Hudson set sail to discover the river in North America that would bear his name. He would also discover the island of Manhattan in 1609, where he established New Amsterdam. Many other mariners left from here, and the Schreierstoren is said to take its name from the tearful sailors' wives who watched their husbands sail off for foreign climes. Today, the tower houses the VOC (Dutch East India Company) Café, which features several nautically styled rooms, including the rustic Herenkamer (Gentlemen's Room), the cozy Terraskamer (Terrace Room), and a flower-bestrewn terrace overlooking the canal. Visit on a summer weekend and chances are you'll find a Dutch wedding party in full swing in this popular spot.

The Amsterdam

In the dock beside the museum several historic ships reside, including a full-scale reproduction of a Dutch East Indiaman—the workhorse of the Dutch East India Company, which had a fleet of 1,500 such ships. Climbing aboard *The Amsterdam*, you are welcomed by English-speaking actors who play the part of the crew and answer questions about life on board. The cramped quarters of the crew differ dramatically from the cathedral-like space of the hold, where a video (with English subtitles) explains the lucrative trade in spices and textiles. Orders for goods placed in Amsterdam typically took two years to fulfill, and the shipping companies could expect a profit of 250 percent on goods landed in the city. The downside of such trade was that up to a third of the poorly paid crew usually died on a voyage, either from disease or by drowning. It's a sobering thought that the original *Amsterdam,* launched in 1749, sank on its maiden voyage, when it was caught in a fierce storm at Hastings, England.

ARCAM

- 🗺 Map p. 101
- ✉ Prins Hendrikkade 600
- ☎ 620-4878
- 🕐 Closed mornings, Sun., Mon.
- 🚌 Bus: 22
- ⛴ Museumboot

arcam.nl

The Maritime Museum also houses an excellent shop, **The Warehouse,** which is full of maritime-related mementos. If you're hungry, stop into the museum's **Restaurant Stalpaert.** This chic restaurant sits on the water's edge and serves simple yet delicious locally sourced, organic produce. It's a perfect place to enjoy an evening meal accompanied by views of the sun setting over the harbor. The Stalpaert is equally popular with locals and museum visitors.

Back Toward the City Center

Landscaping of the Amsterdam waterfront has created an attractive pedestrian route between the museum and the city center, signposted "Route Oosterdok." As you exit the museum, turn right onto busy Prins Hendrikkade and cross over the water, looking for a ramp that leads toward the large, green, ship-shaped NEMO museum (see pp. 122–123). Before going down the ramp, take a look at the large 1641 warehouses on the opposite side of Prins Hendrikkade. These were built for the financially strapped West India Company (see p. 150), set up in 1621 to coordinate growing Dutch trade in the Americas and West Africa along the same lines as the more successful East India Company.

Going down the ramp, you will pass the modern bronze fountain featuring the sea goddess, Salacia, one of the alluring sirens in Homer's *Odyssey.* To the right, you will spot ARCAM, the Amsterdam Centre for Architecture. The compact and sculptural René van Zuuk–designed building is semi-clad in coated aluminium, which folds over the roof and right down to the ground, while the waterside is constructed entirely of glass.

ARCAM

ARCAM was established as a foundation in 1986 with the intention of enhancing the appeal of, and interest in, architecture for a broad audience in and around Amsterdam. Within the futuristic podlike building, a sleek exhibition space and information point provide visitors with varied installations about local architects, buildings, and urban developments, as well as architecture abroad. A selection of architecture books, magazines, maps, and newspaper cuttings advises travelers on Amsterdam's architectural highlights. A current affairs bulletin board carries topical news and developments in the fields of architecture, urbanism, and landscape. An essential port of call for budding architects, ARCAM is also well worth a visit for any traveler with even a passing interest in architecture.

Returning to the "Route Oosterdok" toward Centraal Station, you will pass the **Vereniging Museumhaven Amsterdam**

INSIDER TIP:

Have lunch at Bloem 36, in the superb Entrepotdok, across the water from Artis zoo. The 84 18th-century industrial storehouses at these docklands are now a calm getaway within the busy city.

—PANCRAS DIJK
National Geographic magazine in the Netherlands writer

(Amsterdam Harbor Outdoor Museum) on your right before reaching NEMO. This interesting nautical attraction is not so much a formal museum but a collection of restored and fully working historic ships moored in the Oosterdok.

Vereniging Museumhaven Amsterdam

- 🗺 Map p. 101
- ✉ Oosterdok
- 💲 $$$
- 🚌 Bus: 22

NOTE: The **Brouwerij't IJ** *(Brewery the IJ, Funenkade 7, tel 622-8325, brouwerijhetij .nl)* is located to the south of the Eastern Docklands. Your first glimpse of a towering thatched windmill reveals why it's also known as the windmill brewery. Deceptively potent beers are brewed right here in the windmill and drunk in the bar beneath it from 3p.m. to 8 p.m. daily.

The Amsterdam, **a reproduction of the 1740 Dutch East Indiaman at the Scheepvaartmuseum**

NEMO

Resembling a green-hulled ship moored in Amsterdam's harbor, NEMO (the new Metropolis Science and Technology Center) is one of the city's most striking landmarks. The NEMO houses a state-of-the-art science

reached by a sweeping flight of terraced steps, offers an unrivaled panorama over the city. **The Café DECK5** on this Mediterranean-inspired roof terrace, known as the "piazza," serves light lunches and remains open until 7 p.m. in summer, making it the ideal spot

The dramatic prow of the NEMO museum, Oosterdok

NEMO

- 🅰 Map p. 101
- ✉ Oosterdok 2
- ☎ 531-3233
- 🕐 Closed Mon. with the exception of Easter holidays
- 💲 $$$
- 🚌 Bus: 22, 48

e-nemo.nl

museum—the perfect place for inquisitive children on any day, but especially when it is cold or wet.

Designed by Genoese architect Renzo Piano (designer of the Centre Georges Pompidou, Paris, and The Shard, London), NEMO is built above the IJ tunnel, which serves as its foundation. The curve in the tunnel is reflected in the graceful curve of the building, and the pinnacle of its "hull,"

for sundowners. It also hosts open-air concerts, details of which can be found on the NEMO web-site. (The roof terrace and café can be visited without purchasing a museum ticket throughout the year, with the exception of Easter school vacations.)

Children will thrill to NEMO's interactive exhibits, which cover real-life applications of modern science and invite them to experiment, touch, and play.

NEMO's permanent exhibitions include "Chain Reactions," which involves live demonstrations of kinetic energy; "The Search for Life," where you can cycle on the moon; the fun "Teen Facts" exhibition, about what goes on in the heads, hearts, and bodies of teens going through puberty; and "A Journey Through the Mind," which tackles the complex workings of the human brain. (One experiment measures pulse rate and sweat excretion when you see a picture of a rose, a spider, or a nude.) "Amazing Constructions" is an exhibit about technical constructions, where visitors explore the effects of form, strength, and balance in architecture and experiment with wobbly skyscrapers, cables, and high-speed elevators.

Children can don a lab coat and protective glasses to conduct experiments under the watchful eye of adult lab technicians in the

INSIDER TIP:

Avoid the crowds at NEMO by arriving early [opening time is 10 a.m.]; start at the top floor and work your way down, the opposite direction taken by most visitors.

—GABRIELLA LE BRETON
National Geographic author

NEMO Wonder Lab. In summer they can cool off in the rooftop "Splashing Water Wonder" park, where 880 gallons (4,000 l) of water flow through 30 water tanks in giant cascades, diverted by the kids themselves with a system of taps and wheels. **Café Renzo Piano** on the ground floor serves drinks and food, including children's dishes. Getting the children out of the NEMO shop is likely to be your final battle of the day.

EXPERIENCE: A Good Book at the Openbare Library

You've probably tried to read this guidebook on trams and in noisy cafés. But Amsterdammers love to talk. So for a quiet read in stimulating surrounds, why not head to Europe's largest public library? Occupying more than 300,000 square feet (28,000 m sq), the **Openbare Bibliotheek Amsterdam** (OBA) is a five-minute walk from Centraal Station toward the Eastern Docklands. The strikingly modern building was conceived by Jo Coenen, Holland's former state architect, and opened in 2008. Spread over seven floors, the angular glass building received countless awards for design as well as the accolade of Most

Sustainable Public Building in Amsterdam. The OBA is open seven days a week and has a huge collection of books, magazines, music, sheet music, films, and photographs stored in bright, modern rooms. It is also home to a theater, a radio station, conference rooms, an exhibition space, study pods with computers, and a children's reading and play area.

While there, savor the OBA's groundbreaking architecture and its facilities, or engage in lively debate with the locals that you'll meet in the restaurant and café on the seventh floor. The views across Amsterdam and the docklands are superb, especially on the open terrace.

Amsterdam's impressive Muziekgebouw (Music Building) hosts concerts of every musical genre.

Muziekgebouw aan 't IJ

🅜 Map p. 101

✉ Piet Heinkade 1

☎ 620-2000

🚌 Bus: 48

muziekgebouw.nl

Passenger Terminal Amsterdam

🅜 Map p. 101

✉ Piet Heinkade 27

☎ 509-1000

🚌 Bus: 48

ptamsterdam.nl

Oost

The hip and trendy homes, shops, bars, restaurants, and offices in the regenerated Oostelijk Havengebied (Eastern Docklands) are the happy result of Amsterdam's biggest post–World War II building project. Handsome historical warehouses sit side by side with ultramodern architecture and concept stores.

The Eastern Docklands were built in the late 19th century, when increased trade with the Dutch East Indies required additional deepwater harbors. Located between the IJ Bay and the Amsterdam–Rhine Canal to the east of Centraal Station, the docklands comprise four artificial *"eilanden"* (islands): Java, KNSM, Borneo, and Sporenburg. The first was primarily a wavebreaking device, with KNSM used by the Koninklijke Nederlandse Stoomboot-Maatschappij (Royal Dutch Steamboat Company), while

the last two served as harbors. As trade declined and air transport grew, the islands were neglected until the 1990s, when the city redeveloped them as a residential and cultural zone, and succeeded in creating desirable modern neighborhoods.

On the Quayside: A key element in the docklands regeneration was the transformation of the 19th-century Piet Heinkade and Oostelijke Handelskade (Eastern Quay). Both these former quays run along the IJ, with the first linked to Java Island by the Jan Schaefer Bridge and the second close to the Verbindingsdam (Joining Dam), which links the Oostelijke Handelskade with KNSM Island.

Piet Heinkade is where cruise passengers enter Amsterdam through the **Passenger Terminal Amsterdam (PTA)**. It is also home to the striking **Muziek-gebouw aan 't IJ** (The Music Building on the IJ), a glass structure perched on the waterfront dedicated to music of all genres. The panoramic seafood restaurant **Zouthaven,** located on the ground floor with uninterrupted views across the harbor, is an ideal spot for a preconcert meal. Jazz afficionados will be happy to hear that Amsterdam's celebrated **Bimhuis** jazz club (see p. 263) is thriving in its new home—a raised "black box" jutting out from the Muziekgebouw with views over the old city and a spacious bar overlooking the IJ. It also has its own café and restaurant.

The Oostelijke Handelskade houses the infamous nightclub, restaurant, and bar **Panama** and the innovative **Lloyd Hotel** (see p. 246). This austere building was constructed in 1921 as temporary housing for emigrants to Latin America. Prior to its transformation into a hotel with 120 rooms ranging from one-star comfort to five-star luxury, it was also used as a prison.

Java & KNSM Island: This large peninsula is littered with family homes, entrepreneurial businesses, quirky bars and restaurants, and designer shops. Look out for the nine whimsical little bridges that cross Java Island's ring of canals.

The large **Loods 6** (Hangar 6) building combines offices with studios, a restaurant, and exhibition space, creating the KNSM Cultuurboulevard. The former baggage hall hosts temporary art and design exhibitions, and the grand old passenger terminal is home to the **De Kompaszaal** (The Compass Room; *KNSM-laan 311, tel 419-9596, kompaszaal.nl*) café and restaurant, with great harbor views. Also on this stretch is the **Boekhandel van Pampus** (*KNSM-laan 303, tel 419-3123, boekhandelvanpampus.nl*), a large bookstore and café located in a former coffee warehouse. **Pols Potten** (*KNSM-laan 39, tel 419-3541, polspotten.nl*) sells unusual designer glassware, earthenware, and furniture created with materials sourced from far climes, and **Sissy-Boy Homeland** (*KNSM-laan 19, 419-1559, sissy-boy.nl*) is a large concept store from the popular Dutch clothing brand, complete with a café and collection of rustic antique furniture. ∎

Loods 6

- 🗺 Map p. 101
- ✉ KNSM-laan 143
- ☎ 418-2020
- 🚌 Bus: 48

loods6.nl

Borneo Island, Sporenburg, & the Python Bridge

Extending eastward like two long fingers, Borneo Island and Sporenburg are joined at the tip by Pythonbrug (Python Bridge). The red, 295-foot-long (90 m) serpentine bridge winds across the water, bringing pedestrians from Borneo Island to Scheepstimmermanstraat (Shipwright's Street). This unusual street is famous for its 60 unique houses, which are a fine example of user participation in housing. The theory of this movement, introduced in 1961 by John Habraken, gives residents the freedom to design their own homes, thereby avoiding the lifeless lack of expression that is pervasive in much contemporary urban planning.

Noord

Likened to Brooklyn in the 1990s, Amsterdam Noord (North) is fast becoming the hot new place to be—a raw cultural breeding ground with hip urban festivals and venues and the added bonus of rural tranquillity. The arrival of the futuristic EYE Film Institute here in 2012 put Noord firmly on the Amsterdam map.

Noord
🅜 Map p. 101

EYE Film Institute Netherlands
✉ IJpromenade 1
☎ 589-1400
eyefilm.nl

Tolhuistuin
✉ Buiksloterweg 5
☎ 486-2635
tolhuistuin.nl

Museum de Noord
✉ Zamenhofstraat 28A
☎ 097-5602
🕐 Closed Fri. a.m.
💲 $
museumamsterdam noord.nl

Located north of Amsterdam and separated from it by the IJ harbor, Noord is just a five-minute (free) ferry ride from Centraal Station. However, Noord is experiencing a major regeneration, likely to be completed when the Noord-Zuid metro line links it to central Amsterdam in 2017.

EYE Film Institute Netherlands

Floating above the IJ like a giant white butterfly five minutes' walk from the Buiksloterweg ferry terminal, the EYE Film Institute building houses a cinematography museum with a renowned collection of films (entrance is free). The EYE also encompasses four film auditoriums, in which classic and art-house movies are screened, a shop, and a café.

East

The best way to explore Noord is to get a map and a bike, and take the ferry to Buiksloterweg. Stay on Buiksloterweg for the **Tolhuistuin** (Toll House Garden), a large cultural complex comprising theater and concert halls, exhibition rooms, a hip-hop school, and a children's art hall as well as a lively café and restaurant. Continue north, then turn right onto the Johan van Hasseltweg and cross the water. Head north

for Buikslotermeerplein, where lively food and flea markets are held, or pedal east to the small **Museum de Noord,** which recounts the history of the area. Continue east for the old port of Nieuwendam and enjoy a coffee by the lovely lock on the terrace of Café 't Sluisje *(Nieuwendammerdijk 297, tel 636-1712).*

INSIDER TIP:

In Noord why not stay aboard the romantic houseboat Chambre B'oot [chambreboot.nl] in Schellingwoude?

—ROBBERT VERMUE
National Geographic magazine in the Netherlands editor

West

The sprawling Nederlandse Dok en Scheepvaart Maatschappij (NDSM, Netherlands Dock and Shipping Company) area lies to the west of Buiksloterweg. An active shipyard until 1984, the site is now a hub for exhibitions, festivals, and the vast indoor Skatepark Amsterdam *(T.T. Neveritaweg 15A, tel 334-3676, skateparkamsterdam.nl).* While here, stop into the Noorderlicht café *(T.T. Neveritaweg 33, tel 492-2770, noorderlichtcafe.nl).* ∎

Probably the world's most famous canals, more than 400 years old, called home by lords, princes, emperors, and Anne Frank

Northern Canals

Introduction & Map   128–129

Grachtengordel North   130–135

Anne Frank Huis   136–138

Westerkerk   139

A Stroll Through the Jordaan   140–144

Experience: Taste Amsterdam's Best Apple Cake   144

Singel & Brouwersgracht   145–147

Feature: Brown Cafés & Dutch Gin   148–149

Haarlemmerbuurt   150–151

Experience: Eat Fresh Herring   151

Spaarndammerbuurt   152–153

Westelijke Eilanden   154–155

Westerpark   156

Hotels & Restaurants in the Northern Canals   247–249

Window detail at Café 't Smalle, a brown café in the Jordaan

Northern Canals

Of Amsterdam's 165 scenic canals (crossed by a grand total of 1,281 bridges), the three main canals of the Grachtengordel (canal belt)—Herengracht, Prinsengracht, and Keizersgracht—garner the most attention. Constructed in the 17th century, the creation of this band of concentric residential canals flanked by grand houses, with designated areas for workers and industry located nearby, was a pioneering piece of urban planning.

By the 14th century, the thriving city of Amsterdam was barely contained by its medieval walls, and by 1585, the Singel canal, which had served as a moat around the city, was dug to create more room for its burgeoning population. With immigration rising, the municipal carpenter Hendrick Staets (see p. 38) came up with a novel idea in 1609 to provide more land for housing, warehousing space, and berths for merchants' barges. He proposed tripling the size of the city by wrapping four concentric semicircular canals around the ancient heart of medieval Amsterdam, with their ends resting on the IJ Bay. Three canals would be used mainly for residential development (Herengracht, Prinsengracht, and Keizersgracht) while the fourth outer canal, Singelgracht, would be used for defense and water management.

The adjacent Jordaan district was also conceived as an integral part of the plan—an area

for factories and artisans, removed from the city's residential areas yet connected to them by canals for transporting goods.

Construction started in the north in 1613 and proceeded for some 50 years from west to east. The result communicated Amsterdam's Golden Age wealth and glory to the world: The elegant canal houses lining the Grachtengordel, most of which have survived, presented an unbroken vista of classic facades, individualized by ornate gables and fine doorways. The Grachtengordel was awarded UNESCO World Heritage status in 2010, when it was described as "a masterpiece in hydraulic engineering, town planning, construction, and architectural know-how."

Amsterdammers continually seek out living and recreational space. In keeping with Staets's innovative approach, they have transformed the industrial Westelijke Eilanden into a neighborhood and turned Westergasfabriek, a former gasworks, into a cultural park. Residents now benefit from the Amsterdam School's vision for social housing in Spaarndammerbuurt. ■

NOT TO BE MISSED:

Popping into a *hofje*
on Prinsengracht **135**

Remembering Anne Frank **136–138**

Hearing the same bells of
Westerkerk heard by Anne **139**

The leafy Brouwersgracht **146–147**

Admiring Amsterdam
School architecture in
Spaarndammerbuurt **152–153**

Drinks at sundown in the
Westelijke Eilanden **154–155**

0   200 meters
0   200 yards

TASMANSTRAAT
NOVAZEMBLASTRAAT
SUIKER-PLEIN
V. Noordtgracht
SPAARNDAMMERSTRAAT
POLANENSTRAAT
ZAANSTRAAT
WESTERPARK
Haarlemmervaart
HAARLEMMERWEG
← Haarlem
NASSAU-PLEIN
F.D.N. Statue
WESTER-PARK
WESTERKANAAL BRUG
HAARLEMMER-PLEIN
HOUTMANKADE
Westerkanaal
HOUTMANKADE
VAN DIEMENSTRAAT
ROGGEVEENSTRAAT
BARENTSZ-PLEIN
BARENTSZSTRAAT
Zoutkeetsgracht
De Gouden Reael
REALENEILAND
REALENGRACHT
ZANDHOEKS-BRUG
DRIEHARINGENBRUG
WESTELIJKE EILANDEN
SLOTERDIJKBRUG
De Dierencapel
GALGENSTR.
Haarlemmer-poort
PRINSEN-EILAND
Beelden Bickerseiland
BICKERS-EILAND
ZANDHOEK
Westerdok
WESTERDOKSDIJK
BICKERSGRACHT
BICKERSSTR.
G.

HAARLEMMER HOUTTUINEN
HAARLEMMERDIJK
BUITEN-ORANJESTR.
WESTERDOKS-KADE
NIEUWE WESTERDOKSTRAAT
DE RUIJTERKADE
Het IJ
S100
Singelgracht
MARNIXSTRAAT
LIJNBAANSGRACHT
BROUWERSGRACHT
Brouwers-gracht
PALM-GRACHT
PALMSTRAAT
WILLEMSSTRAAT
HAARLEMMER-BUURT
EENHOORNSLUIS
GOUDSBLOEMSTRAAT
Theo Thissen Monument
Posthoorn-kerk
No. 60
LEMMERSTR.
West Indische Huis
HAARLEMMERSLUIS BRUG
STROMARKT
LINDENGRACHT
LINDENGRACHT
Noorder-kerk
NOORDER-MARKT
Sports Center
Groenland Pakhuizen
HAAR
Brouwers-
HEREN-MARKT
HERENGRACHT
gracht
Singel
NIEUWEN-DIJK
De Zeevrugt
Ronde Lutherse Kerk
De Silveren Spiegel
KATTENGAT
Lijnbaansgracht
Huys Zitten Weduwen Hofje
LINDENSTRAAT
BOOMSTRAAT
WESTERSTRAAT
JORDAAN
ANJELIERSSTRAAT
TUINSTRAAT
Café de Tuin
Café 't Smalle
Claes Claesz Hofje
Van Brienenhofje
Zonshofje
HERENSTR.
Blauwburgwal
Huis Multatuli
Het Oude Veerhuis
NIEUWEZIJDS VOORBURGWAL
SPUISTRAAT
Prinsengracht
KEIZERSGRACHT
KEIZERSGRACHT
Het Huis met de Hoofden
Architectura et Natura
Singel
Anne Frank Huis
Egelantiers-gracht
Sint Andrieshof
MARNIXSTRAAT
LIJNBAANSGRACHT
BLOEMGRACHT
Bloem-gracht
BLOEMGRACHT
Westerkerk
Anne Frank Statue
Homomonument
Nos. 174–176
LELIEGRACHT
Huis Bartolotti
E.D.D. Statue
TOREN-SLUIS
ROZENGRACHT
RAADHUISSTRAAT
Nieuwe Kerk

Grachtengordel North

The northern part of Amsterdam's canal belt, from Brouwersgracht to Raadhuisstraat, is a blend of patrician houses, almshouses, houseboats, cafés, and shops. The area's three canals show subtle differences in architectural style and social status. Traditionally, the Herengracht (Lord's Canal), nearest the city center, housed the wealthiest citizens; the Keizersgracht (Emperor's Canal) the merchant class; and the Prinsengracht (Prince's Canal) combined warehouses and modest houses.

The Bloemgracht, in the Jordaan district, is one of the city's most beautiful canals.

One of the finest examples of an aristocratic Golden Age house is the **Huis Bartolotti,** at Herengracht 170 (see sidebar opposite). The house was built for the wealthy Guillelmo Bartolotti, whose brother-in-law built an equally flamboyant house— **Het Huis met de Hoofden** (The House with the Heads)— nearby on Keizersgracht (named after the Holy Roman Emperor). To find it, continue down Herengracht, and turn right onto Leliegracht. Along this short canal are several good antique shops and one of Amsterdam's best specialist bookshops—**Architectura et Natura**—at No. 22. Those with an interest in architecture, gardening, or natural history should stop for a browse in the 75-year-old store, which has a large selection of English-language books.

Towering over its neighbors at the end of the street is an unusually tall building, **Keizersgracht 174–176,** built in art nouveau style, with a mosaic high up in the corner tower. It depicts a child watched over by a guardian angel, the symbol of the insurance company for whom the building was constructed in 1905.

Renaissance Houses

The House with the Heads lies a short way down on the right, at **Keizersgracht 123.** Canal-boat tours all stop here to look, for this is one of Amsterdam's most celebrated Dutch Renaissance houses. Built in 1622, it has a very fine elevated neck gable (shaped like the neck of a wine bottle) rising from a facade enlivened by blank niches and columns of painted sandstone, contrasting with the delicate brickwork. The name of the house refers to the six heads set in the facade, which depict the classical deities Apollo, Ceres, Mars, Pallas Athene, Bacchus, and Diana.

That, at least, is the official explanation. A more colorful theory holds that the heads were placed there to commemorate the bravery of a servant girl who beheaded six burglars with an ax when they tried to rob the house in the owner's absence. The architect is unknown, but the house bears a strong resemblance to the style of Hendrick de Keyser (see sidebar p. 133); it may have been the work of his son, Pieter.

Side Streets & Radial Canals

Off Keizersgracht lies **Herenstraat,** a fascinating shop-lined side street with tempting cafés and artful window displays. Here you can browse for antiques,

books, crafts, cut flowers, jewelry, clothes, and toys. Several shops specialize in art deco and art nouveau goods, while others offer various oriental crafts and antiquities.

Back on Keizersgracht, look across the canal to see the way that some of the houses lean at precarious angles. That is usually a sign that the pile foundations were inadequate or that they have rotted or broken. Amsterdam's subsoil is soft and unstable, so deep piles were driven through the upper layers of peat, clay, and thin sand to the more solid sand bed that lies between 16 and 23 feet (5 and 7 m) below ground level. The piles, made of pine or birch, were used to support a platform of oak plates, atop which the brick walls were built.

Skimping on the house's foundations—by using too few

Architectura et Natura

- ⓘ Map p. 129
- ✉ Leliegracht 22
- ☎ 623-6186
- 🕐 Closed Sun.
- 🚊 Tram: 13, 14, 17

architectura.nl

Historic Huis Bartolotti

Huis Bartolotti (Bartolotti House; *Herengracht 170*) was built circa 1617 for Willem van den Heuvel tot Beichlingen. Van den Heuvel was one of the wealthiest Amsterdammers of his time, thanks largely to an inheritance left to him by his childless, unmarried uncle, Giovanni Battista Bartolotti, a salesman from Bologna.

Willem van den Heuvel changed his name to Guillelmo Bartolotti in honor of his uncle. This was subsequently reflected in the name of his house. With money no object, Bartolotti commissioned Hendrick de Keyser, the city's leading architect, to design the house. De Keyser's flamboyant style, rich in urns, niches, scrolls, and masks, earned the building its other nickname, Het Bonte Huis (The Gaudy House).

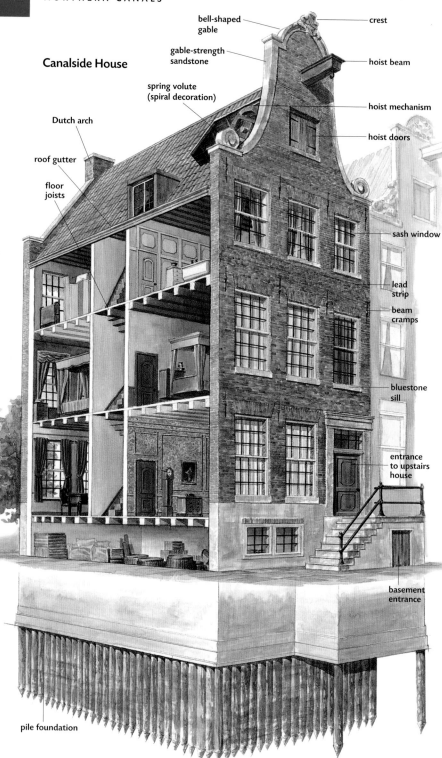

Canalside House

bell-shaped gable

crest

gable-strength sandstone

hoist beam

spring volute (spiral decoration)

hoist mechanism

Dutch arch

hoist doors

roof gutter

floor joists

sash window

lead strip

beam cramps

bluestone sill

entrance to upstairs house

basement entrance

pile foundation

piles, by driving the piles in at an angle rather than vertically, or by making the piles too short—usually resulted in subsidence. Rotting, too, can cause houses to sink. Hence, piles are now made of reinforced concrete.

You may notice that all the houses on the left-hand side of the canal—from No. 90 all the way down to No. 46—have facades of equal width. This is because housing plots along the canal belt were initially sold with precisely 98 feet (30 m) of frontage. Developers frequently subdivided these into three narrower plots. Occasionally the plots were divided into two; less often, the whole plot would be used to accommodate a single palatial town house. Local taxes were levied on houses according to the width of their facade, so only the very wealthy could afford to build and live in the largest houses.

Warehouses

Nearly all of these houses were built for merchants, hence the hoisting beams that project from the gables, from which a pulley and tackle could be hung for lifting goods up to the roof space. The gable windows, through which the goods were hoisted, differ in size and shape from those in the lower facade (furniture is still winched through the windows because the staircases in most canalside houses are narrow and steep).

The canals themselves were used heavily. Each of the three Grachtengordel canals is 82 feet (25 m) wide, broad enough to accommodate four lanes of shallow-drafted barges or lighters (the boats used to unload larger ships docked in Amsterdam harbor and convey goods to the houses of merchants). Up to 4,000 ships could be, and often were, berthed in the canal circle, and the wide quays, now sadly used as parking lots, once bustled with porters delivering goods by sled, cart, or wheelbarrow.

Trees have always been a feature of the canals—though many of the big elms of old have succumbed to disease and have since been replaced by tougher, younger trees.

Some of the buildings nearest to the port were built exclusively as warehouses. As you continue down Keizersgracht, note the three **Groenland Pakhuizen** (Greenland Warehouses) at Nos. 40–44 (on the opposite bank), which once contained huge tanks used for the storage of whale oil. Built in 1621 by the

Hendrick de Keyser

Hendrick de Keyser (1565–1621), a sculptor from Utrecht, was put in charge of municipal building projects in Amsterdam in 1595. He designed the city's three great 17th-century churches, pioneering a new Protestant style for the Zuiderkerk (1614), the Noorderkerk (1620), and the Westerkerk (1621). De Keyser's style—widely considered the pinnacle of Dutch Renaissance architecture—is unmistakable. His facades have been likened to the tiers of a wedding cake, with one story piled on top of another, and each one slightly smaller than the layer below it.

Greenland Whaling Company, the step-gabled buildings fell out of use when whale hunting ended in 1819 and have since been converted to housing. A short way farther down the street is an unusually large building, formerly a

INSIDER TIP:

For a dose of genuine Amsterdam life, visit De Twee Zwaantjes [The Two Swans] at Prinsengracht 114. This tiny pub hosts sing-along nights on Mondays and the atmosphere is unbeatable.

—GABRIELLA LE BRETON
National Geographic author

Jesuit church, now a sports center. This church was built in 1835 on the site of an earlier clandestine church, and its classical exterior respects the style of surrounding buildings, though it once had the kind of highly ornate, statue-filled interior more normally associated with Jesuit churches.

Prinsengracht

At the northern end of Keizersgracht, turn left onto Pastoorsbrug to walk along Brouwersgracht (see pp. 146–147), and then turn left up the eastern bank of Prinsengracht (named after Prince Willem of Orange). There is a good view across the canal to the Jordaan district and its fine church, the

Noorderkerk, designed by Hendrick de Keyser in 1620 (see sidebar p. 133). On this side are the well-restored houses at Nos. 1A, 3, and 5, bearing gable stones carved with reliefs of St. Peter, St. Paul, and the Apostles who met the resurrected Jesus on the road to Emmaus. No. 1A has a neck gable with carved sandstone side cheeks, a style that was current from 1640 to the 1770s. Slightly later in date are the bell gables of Nos. 3, 5, and 7, a style introduced about 1660 and lasting until the 1790s. Most houses along this bank have flat cornices, however, a style that came from France in the late 17th century and became popular up until the 19th century.

Gables were one way to give your house individuality and to distinguish it from houses of similar size and materials on either side. The number and the disposition of the windows was another. Many of these houses have very large windows because, although glass was expensive, it helped to cut down the weight of the facade, making the house less liable to subsidence. Doors, fanlights, and railings all add to the variety, and most of the houses along this stretch have basements, so that the ground floors begin about 5 feet (1.5 m) above street level. The entrance is reached via a flight of steps, or *stoop*, with cast-iron balusters and handrails. The basements were used for storage or as servants' accommodation, and have a separate hatch or low door to provide access.

Almshouses: The rhythm of equal-size houses is broken by Nos. 89–133 Prinsengracht, a block with high windowless walls.

You can push open the small door to enter the peaceful courtyard of the **Van Brienenhofje,** an almshouse built in 1804 by Arnout Jan van Brienen on the site of the former Star Brewery. This is still often referred to by locals as the Star Hofje. Legend has it that Van Brienen founded the almshouse after he accidentally locked himself inside the strong room of his house *(Herengracht 182).* In danger of suffocating, he knelt and prayed, promising to devote his life to the needy if he was rescued from his predicament—which, in due course, he was.

A short way up the canal you'll come across more almshouses, these built on a more modest scale. Nos. 159–171 are known as **Zonshofje** (Sun Court) and consist of houses originally built for elderly members of the Mennonite religious community in 1765. You can go into the *hofje (closed Sat. & Sun.),* and enter the quiet courtyard with its clock and a depiction of Noah's Ark and a large sun with a smiling face. "The Sun" and "Noah's Ark" were names given to clandestine Catholic churches that stood on this site before the almshouses were built.

If you continue up Prinsengracht from here, the next building of note you will reach is the **Anne Frank Huis** (see pp. 136–138); beyond that lies the **Westerkerk** (see p. 139).

You can then return to the city center by turning left at the church and going back to Dam Square via Raadhuisstraat. ∎

High windows fill the interior of Noorderkerk with natural light.

Anne Frank Huis

What is it that makes an almost empty house on Prinsengracht one of Amsterdam's most visited attractions? It is, of course, the compelling story of the family who hid there during the Nazi occupation of the Netherlands, and the tragic story of young Anne Frank, whose dreams of becoming a writer ended with her death, aged 15, in the Bergen-Belsen concentration camp.

Anne Frank Huis

- Map p. 129
- Prinsengracht 263
- 556-7100
- Closed Yom Kippur
- Tram: 13, 14, 17, 20
- Museumboot

annefrank.nl

Looking at the long lines that build up outside the Anne Frank House during peak holidays, you'll find it hard to believe that there were plans to demolish it in the 1950s. At that time, the name of Anne Frank was almost unknown, yet today few people in the world can be unfamiliar with the story of the girl who hid in the secret annex at the back of the house, from July 1942 to August 1944.

The Achterhuis

Like many houses in Amsterdam, Prinsengracht 263 has a front part and a rear annex, the *achterhuis*. Otto Frank used the front of the house as the base for his company, which specialized in spices, food additives, and flavorings. He had fled from Frankfurt to Amsterdam with his family in 1933, when Hitler's National Socialist Party came to power. However, now trapped in Nazi-occupied Amsterdam, Otto, his wife, Edith, and their daughters, Margot and Anne, went into hiding in the achterhuis on July 6, 1942. They were joined by the Van Pels family, Hermann and Auguste, with their son, Peter, and later by another refugee, Fritz Pfeffer.

A wooden bookcase was all that separated them from discovery. That and the dedication of the trusted friends and employees who supplied them with food and fuel, at great risk to themselves, during the two years and thirty days they spent in hiding.

The Diary

Throughout that time, Anne Frank kept a diary, filling three separate volumes with her thoughts and feelings. After hearing an appeal on the radio for people's accounts of the war, she rewrote large parts of her original entries, in the hope her diary might be published once she and her family were free. However, someone—never identified—reported the Franks' hiding place to the Nazis; the fateful knock on the door came on August 4, 1944. The family was separated—Anne was taken to Bergen-Belsen, where she died of typhus in March 1945, days before the British arrived to liberate the camp on April 15.

Soon afterward, Otto returned to Amsterdam, desperate to be reunited with his two daughters. He was, however, the sole survivor of the group that had hidden in the annex. Miep Gies, one of the Frank family's loyal helpers, had found Anne's diary in the annex following their arrest and returned it to Otto. Inspired by his daughter's literary ambitions, he offered the diary to various publishers after the war. Eventually a small Dutch publishing house

Anne Frank's bedroom (shared with Fritz Pfeffer)

offices

offices

fices

Hermann and Auguste van Pels's room

Peter van Pels's room

Otto, Edith, and Margot Frank's bedroom

bookcase doorway

Anne Frank poured her soul into a secret diary during the Occupation.

printed the first edition in 1947. It was published in English in 1952, before being turned into a Broadway play in 1955 and a movie in 1959. Today, Anne's diary is an international best seller, translated into more than 60 languages, and her manuscripts are listed on the UNESCO World Documentary Heritage List.

Making the Museum

After his return to Amsterdam, Otto Frank devoted his life to working for human rights, answering thousands of letters from readers of Anne's diary and overseeing the establishment of the Anne Frank Huis museum. This opened in 1960 and has hosted countless hard-hitting exhibitions, addressing issues of anti-Semitism, racism, and discrimination.

The wartime appearance of the front of the house has been restored. However, once you climb the steep staircase that leads to a replica of the bookcase that hid the cramped annex, you'll find it largely bare—a somber reflection on how it was when Otto returned.

INSIDER TIP:

Skip the long lines for the Anne Frank House by buying your tickets online. Bring your print-outs and avoid the wait!

—PANCRAS DIJK
National Geographic *magazine in the Netherlands writer*

A few salvaged documents and objects remain on display, such as the pictures Anne cut from Hollywood movie magazines and pasted on the walls. Plasma screens show touching interviews with some of the friends who helped the hideaways.

The canal house next to the Franks' house, **265 Prinsengracht,** has now been appropriated by the museum and houses Anne's original diaries and other writings; temporary exhibitions; the interactive Free2Choose exhibition, encouraging visitors to contemplate the importance of democracy and human rights; and a museum café and bookshop. ■

Take a Tour of Anne's Amsterdam

Created by the Anne Frank House, the Anne's Amsterdam app offers an insightful tour of the city, on foot or bicycle. The app leads the user to some 30 places dotted around Amsterdam and related to Anne's life, supplemented with videos, photographs, and interviews. You'll walk around places where Anne loved to play, and to her former school, where you can listen to her friends recount stories of her adventurous spirit. As you walk along the streets she once walked, you hear the roar of German tanks as they rumbled into Amsterdam and see prewar photographs of the very spot on which you're standing.

Westerkerk

In her diary, Anne Frank noted the companionship of the bells that rang out the quarter hours from the Westerkerk (Western Church), which lies a short way up Prinsengracht from her home. The bells still ring out—often with recognizable melodies—every 15 minutes.

Designed by the ubiquitous Hendrick de Keyser, the church was begun in 1620 and completed in 1638. It was the largest Protestant church in Amsterdam, with the city's tallest tower looming 278 feet (85m) above the Prinsengracht. The tower's golden crown is modeled on that of the Holy Roman Emperor, Maximilian I, who granted the city the right to use the crown in its coat of arms in 1489 in thanks for loans received from local bankers.

INSIDER TIP:

Attending an organ recital is the best way to soak up the rich interiors of the Westerkerk. The nearby Pianola Museum [Westerstraat 106, tel 627-9624, pianola.nl] also holds vintage player-piano concerts.

—JEREMY GRAY
National Geographic author

Westerkerk was the last resting place of Rembrandt (see pp. 106–107), who was buried in an unmarked pauper's grave.

To the south of the church stands a small **statue of Anne Frank** (erected in 1977) by Marie Andriessen. Two pink granite

The golden-crowned tower of Westerkerk (Western Church)

triangles at the eastern end of the square on which the church stands, facing onto Keizersgracht, form part of the **Homomonument** (1987), a memorial to persecuted homosexuals (the pink triangle was worn by homosexual victims of the Nazi holocaust). A third triangle sits on a terrace by the canal, usually strewn with flowers left by friends and relatives of AIDS victims. On the northern side of the church, the house at Westermarkt 6 has a plaque recording that the French philosopher René Descartes (1596–1650) lived here in 1634. As he wrote: "Where else in the world could one choose a place where all life's commodities and all the curiosities one could wish for are so easy to find as here?" ■

Westerkerk

- Map p. 129
- Prinsengracht 281
- 624-7766
- Open 11 a.m.– 3 p.m. except Sundays
- $ Tower
- Tram: 13, 14, 17

westerkerk.nl

A Stroll Through the Jordaan

The Jordaan lies on the western fringe of the canal belt, stretching for 1.5 miles (2.4 km) from north to south and divided into a maze of tiny streets named after trees and flowers. Because of this, the French-speaking refugees who settled there in the 17th century called it Le Jardin—The Garden—a name later corrupted to Jordaan.

De Kaaskamer, a traditional cheese shop in the Nine Streets area

Start at **Palmgracht,** the northernmost street of the Jordaan district. The black facade of Nos. 28–38 has a gable stone depicting a turnip. The Dutch word for turnip is *raep,* and it's a pictorial pun on the name of Pieter Adriaenszoon Raep, who founded this **almshouse** in 1648, and whose coat of arms is proudly displayed above. This is one of the city's earliest *hofjes* (courtyards), so called because the almshouses were built, in the style of a religious cloister, around a communal courtyard.

Most hofjes were founded by wealthy citizens to house sick or elderly employees and their widows and orphans. There are dozens packed into the Jordaan, many with attractive gardens. Their existence is not publicized, because of the nuisance that intrusive visitors can cause residents. If you go for a closer look, respect the privacy of the occupants (most hofjes close from 6 p.m. to 9 a.m.).

Walk to the end of Palmgracht, noting the many gable stones on the houses on both sides of the street. Turn left on Lijnbaansgracht. This street runs alongside boat-filled **Lijnbaansgracht ❶**, the canal that marked the outer edge of the city from 1660 until the mid-1900s. As you walk, note how many of the streets are named after plants: Palmgracht itself (Palm

	See also area map p. 129
►	Palmgracht
⊕	2 hours
↔	2.2 miles (3.6 km)
►	Westerkerk

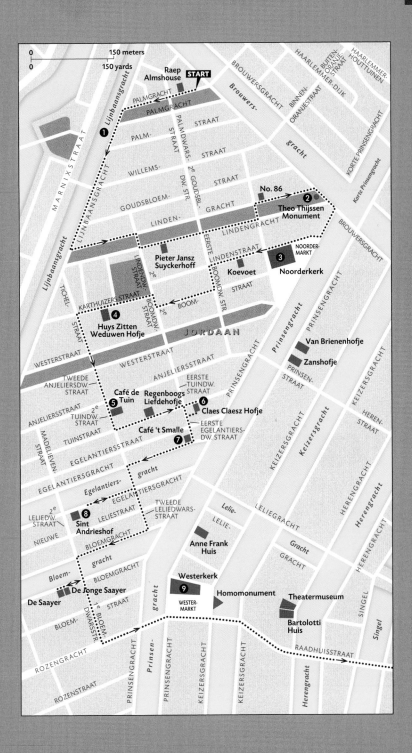

Canal—now filled in), followed by Palmstraat (Palm Street), Goudsbloemstraat (Marigold Street), and Lindengracht (Lime Tree Canal).

On leafy **Lindengracht,** cross the road to No. 167, where a gable stone depicting De Drie Linden (The Three Limes) records the restoration of this fine neck-gabled house in 1982. Next to it, the inscription above the entrance of Nos. 163–149 reveals that this is the **Pieter Jansz Suyckerhoff** (*hoff* is an archaic form of *hofje*), founded in 1670. Push open the door to enter the courtyard. The pleasant gardens were originally used for drying laundry and laying out cloth to bleach in the sun. Able-bodied *hofje* residents worked for the owners as cloth finishers, seamstresses, or laundresses.

Leaving the hofje, turn right and check out the secondhand clothes shops, cafés, and bars as you walk down the street, watching for unusual gable stones. **No. 86,** on the opposite side of the road, has a Dutch barge in full sail. At Nos. 55–57 you can see an amusing plaque showing a fish sailing through the branches of a tree, the date 1672 upside down, and an unpronounceable name: THCARGNEDNIL.

NOT TO BE MISSED:

Noorderkerk • Claes Claesz Hofje • Café 't Smalle • Westerkerk

Look carefully: This is LINDENGRACHT spelled backward—the gable stone represents the trees of Lindengracht reflected in the waters of the (now filled-in) canal.

At the end of Lindengracht stands a **monument ❷** to Theo Thijssen (1879–1943), the teacher and educational reformer who did much to try to improve living conditions for the poor of the Jordaan, having been raised here himself.

Turn right, then immediately right again into **Noordermarkt,** the market square that was laid out in 1620 in front of the magnificent **Noorderkerk ❸** (Northern Church), the last work of the great Dutch Renaissance architect Hendrick de Keyser (1565–1621). On Mondays you can pick up textiles of all descriptions at the Lapjesmarkt (Cloth Market) held here,

Frits Sieger's statue of Multatuli's "Woutertje Pieterse en Femke" at the Noordermarkt

while on Saturdays the Boerenmarkt (Farmers Market) is held. Here, vendors sell organic eggs, cheese, vegetables, bread, and much more from their stalls.

The gables of the row of houses to the right of the church (on the northern side of Noordermarkt) reveal the goods that were once sold here. No. 15 (with a pair of cloth shears) and No. 16 (with bales of cloth), indicating a tailor and a cloth merchant, stand alongside the butchers' houses (sporting a cow, a cock, and a lamb) and a freight carrier's (with a barge).

Continue up Lindenstraat, past No. 4, a house with a gable stone depicting King David and his harp, and No. 17, once a brown café (see pp. 148–149), but now an intimate and popular Italian restaurant called the Koevoet and run by Sicilian owners. Turn left onto Eerste Boomdwarsstraat, and right onto Boomstraat (Tree Street), noting the different architectural styles: No. 61 is a recent house built in traditional style with a step gable and incorporating the gable stone of its predecessor, the Crowned Star; the contemporary No. 68, opposite, faced in aluminum whose colors (the three primaries, plus black and white) owe much to the works of the Dutch artist Pieter Cornelis Mondriaan (1872–1944).

Take the next right, Tweede Boomdwarsstraat. All the streets running at right angles to the main streets are called *dwars straaten* (cross streets). They are numbered from east to west—*eerste* (first) and *tweede* (second)—followed by the name of the street they intersect. Hence Tweede Boomdwarsstraat literally translates as "Second Tree Cross Street."

Take the next left, onto **Karthuizersstraat,** named after the medieval Carthusian monastery that once stood where the school playground is now located, on the right. Opposite, at Nos. 11–19, a row of five houses, dated 1737, bears the names of the Four Seasons (here Lent, Summer, Harvest, and Winter) under pictorial gable stones.

Next comes a long facade with wooden drying racks outside every window; this is the **Huys Zitten Weduwen Hofje** ❹ (Almshouse of the Elderly Widows) of 1650, and the drying racks show that the residents were expected to work for their accommodations. Go in through the main entrance to look at the courtyard with its garden and graceful water pumps. The Amsterdam coat of arms features on one of the courtyard's classical pediments, with a trading ship on the other.

INSIDER TIP:

Pop into Oogst Sieraden [Harvest Jewelry], the jewelry store of Lotte Porrio and Ellen Philippen. Located at Tweede Tuindwarsstraat 8, the designers sell their one-of-a-kind pieces inspired by nature and handmade here in the Jordaan.

—GABRIELLA LE BRETON
National Geographic author

Coming out of the hofje, turn left, then left again onto **Tichelstraat,** looking for the gable stones at No. 33 (Batavia—the old Dutch name for Jakarta, capital of Indonesia) and No. 53 (a basket of coiled rope). Note, too, the excellent view of **Westerkerk** tower, leaning to the right, at the end of the street. Continue in the direction of the church, crossing wide Westerstraat onto Tweede Anjeliersdwarsstraat. This marks the start of the Jordaan's main shopping street, where secondhand shops sit side by side with craft shops and small boutiques run by design cooperatives. **Café de Tuin** ❺ (*Tweede Tuindwarsstraat 13, tel 624 4559*), on the left in the next section of the street, is a good place to soak up the local atmosphere along with your coffee and apple cake.

Take the next left, onto Tuinstraat, passing another almshouse, **Regenboogs Liefdehofje** (Rainbow Love almshouse) on the left. At the next junction—Eerste Egelantiersdwarsstraat—look to your left for a gable stone showing the hand of God appearing from a cloud and wielding a hammer (the sign of a goldsmith); next to it a stone depicts a baker utilizing a long-handled shovel to put loaves into his oven.

Cross over to the other side of Tuinstraat and continue down the street to the first house on the right, whose gable stone shows an organist and the words **Claes Claesz Hofje** ⑥. Go back and turn left onto Eerste Egelantiersdwarsstraat to see the narrow entrance to this delightful hofje, restored in 1971. The atmosphere of this hidden hofje is enhanced by the strains of violin music echoing around the court, or the sounds of an operatic soprano in full flow, for these days it provides accommodations for music students studying at Amsterdam's prestigious Conservatoire.

Turn left out of the hofje, and walk up to the atmospheric **Café 't Smalle** ⑦ (*Egelantiersgracht 12, tel 623 9617*) on the next corner on the right. Founded in 1780 as the outlet for a gin distillery, this is one of the city's oldest traditional cafés, and it retains its 18th-century interior. It overlooks the Egelantiersgracht, which is lined with attractive 17th- and 18th-century houses. Among the finest are No. 50, on the right, with its gable stone of a bee flying toward a wild rose; No. 63, on the opposite bank, with

a hooded falcon; No. 69, with a dove; and No. 87, with its two leather workers. Across the next junction lies the **Sint Andrieshof** ⑧, which is entered through a passageway lined with old Delft tiles. The courtyard is a tranquil haven, with a statue of Christ on the wall to the left.

Turning right out of the hofje, take the next right, Tweede Leliedwarsstraat, cross Nieuwe Leliestraat, and turn right on Bloemgracht, appropriately nicknamed the Herengracht (Gentlemen's Canal) of the Jordaan, because of its large and dignified houses. Cross the next bridge, then turn right, to see the step-gabled building at Nos. 87–91, designed by Hendrick de Keyser and known as The Three Hendricks. Next on the left is No. 81, called **De Jonge Saayer** (The Young Sower), depicting a child scattering grain across the newly plowed soil, perhaps built by the son of the owner of No. 77, **De Saayer** (The Sower).

Retrace your steps and take the next right, onto Eerste Bloemdwarsstraat, and head straight up to busy Rozengracht, then turn left up toward **Westerkerk** ⑨ (see p. 139). This sudden return to traffic-filled streets highlights just how peaceful the Jordaan is. To get back to central Amsterdam, walk past Westerkerk and continue all the way up Raadhuisstraat, eventually bringing you to Nieuwezijds Voorburgwal.

EXPERIENCE: Taste Amsterdam's Best Apple Cake

Enjoy a true Amsterdam tradition: Stock up on artisanal, organic food at **Noordermarkt**'s Saturday-morning farmers market, or on vintage textiles at Monday's **Lapjesmarkt** (Cloth Market), and then indulge in a slab of appel taart (deep-dish apple cake) at **Winkel Café** (*Noordermarkt 43, tel 420-8545, winkel43 .nl*). Easily spotted on the southwestern corner of Noordermarkt with its green-and-white striped awning—and the orderly lines that build up outside

it—Winkel bakes what is largely held to be Amsterdam's best apple cake. Dutch apple cake, which is served warm and under a cloud of whipped cream, differs from its American and English cousins predominantly by the addition of lemon and cinnamon, and generally features larger chunks of apple. Testament to the undisputed deliciousness of Winkel's cake, the tiny café sells 100 cakes (600 slices) on market days and a further 150 cakes during the week.

Singel & Brouwersgracht

The name Singel probably derives from *cingel*, meaning "belt." This canal marks the line of the 15th-century city wall, and it loops around to join the Amstel River, in the south, to form a moat encircling the medieval city. At the northern end of Singel is Brouwersgracht (Brewers' Canal), dug between 1585 and 1612 and one of the prettiest of the city's 165 canals.

The Singel canal traces the city's medieval wall and delights modern-day travelers with its leafy banks.

Singel

The lovely district of Singel was once lined with merchants' warehouses, but it gained its residential character in the 17th century, when the canal circle was dug. A good place to take in the views up and down this canal is the **Torensluis** (Tower Lock), a wide bridge to the west of Nieuwe Kerk (see pp. 57–59), where locals and visitors come to sit and enjoy the sunshine. The great width of the bridge (138 feet/42 m) is due to the presence of a tower that served as a military prison until it was

demolished in 1829; prisoners were also kept in cells underneath the bridge.

A large **statue** of Eduard Douwes Dekker (1820–1887), a local government official who wrote plays, novels, and poetry under the pen name of Multatuli (Latin for "I have suffered greatly"), now occupies the site of the tower. Multatuli's radical (and often humorous) novels about life in Amsterdam and in the Dutch colonies made him a great influence on Dutch social reformers. A small **museum** (see sidebar p. 147) devoted to his

Singel & Brouwersgracht

Map p. 129

life and work is tucked inside the nearby house where he was born.

Singel has the appearance of being frozen in time, but the view is a constantly changing one. The most recent addition can be seen at **Blauwburgwal,** Amsterdam's shortest canal, to the north: Looking across the canal to the right you will see No. 109, with its prominent postmodernist facade, built in 1994. The bridge itself was constructed in 1652 to replace an earlier ferry, which explains why the house at Nos. 83–85, decorated with Ionic pilasters and swags, is known as **Het Oude Veerhuis** (The Old Ferryhuis).

INSIDER TIP:

If you're an art deco fan, don't miss a screening at Amsterdam's oldest cinema house, The Movies [themovies.nl] at Haarlemmerdijk 161. Soak up the magnificent interiors, which date back to 1912, over pre-show drinks and dinner.

—PANCRAS DIJK
National Geographic *magazine in the Netherlands writer*

Across the bridge is No. 64, with its gable dated 1637, in contrast to the 19th-century neo-Renaissance house with step gables at No. 62 and the early 20th-century house in art deco style at Nos. 46–48. More elegant than all of these is No. 36, the building known as **De Zeevrugt** (Produce of the Sea). Built in 1736 for a ship broker, the cornice above the tall door depicts a ship, and the Louis XV–style roof cornice depicts Mercury, the god of trade.

Brouwersgracht

Many bridges cross Brouwersgracht due to the fact that the city's four main canals—Singel, Herengracht, Keizersgracht, and Prinsengracht—all flow into this canal. Brouwersgracht acts as a busy terminus for the various watercraft that still use the canals, principally the glass-topped tourist boats.

Originally this was an industrial canal, lined with numerous factories and warehouses, all of which benefited from their proximity to the port. Local brewers didn't draw their water from the canal—it was too foul with discharges from the breweries themselves, and from other nearby businesses involved in drying fish, curing leather, rendering whale blubber into oil, and manufacturing soap. Instead, water barges brought in fresh water from outside the city limits.

Today Brouwersgracht is a desirable, quiet, and tree-shaded residential street that is close to the city center. Some of its houses still bear evidence of their earlier use: No. 48 has two huge fish carved on either side of the gable, and No. 52 has the gable stone of a chairmaker. To the right is **Herenmarkt** (Lord's Market), with its children's playground backing onto the **West Indische**

The Multatuli Huis Museum

The Multatuli Huis *(Korsjespoortssteeg 20, tel 638-1938, closed Mon. & Wed.–Fri., multatuli-museum.nl, $)* is a small yet intriguing museum located in the birthplace of Eduard Douwes Dekker.

During his time working as a civil servant in the Dutch colonies, Douwes Dekker was appalled by the many abuses of the colonial system. Voicing his disapproval loudly, he was forced to resign and returned to Amsterdam, determined to expose what he had seen. Adopting the name of Multatuli, he wrote the novel *Max Havelaar,* which was read widely throughout Europe and spawned international discussion about the morality of colonialism.

Douwes Dekker went on to write other literary and political works, and was a favored author of Sigmund Freud, topping his list of "ten good books." In addition to giving an insight into the daily life of Douwes Dekker, the museum offers an exhibition of his furniture, notebooks, and personal effects. It's a must for anyone interested in Dutch colonial history.

Huis, the former headquarters of the Dutch West India Company (see p. 150).

Singel Back to Centraal

Back on Singel, the **Haarlemmersluis bridge** (see p. 150) leads across to the eastern bank of the canal. The *sluis* (lock) beside this bridge at one time controlled the water level in the entire canal system by holding the water back when the tide went out. Now that the IJ River is dammed, and no longer subject to the rhythm of the tides, the lock remains permanently open.

To the right of the bridge is **Stromarkt,** once the site of the city's Straw Market, where thatching materials and animal bedding were sold.

If you walk up Singel a short way you will pass No. 7, which is often said to be the smallest house in Amsterdam because the facade is only as wide as the door (in fact, this is the back entrance to a much bigger building on Jeroensteeg). Just beyond is the huge bulk of the **Ronde Lutherse Kerk** (Round Lutheran Church), a splendid building of 1668 designed by Adriaan Dortsman. Known locally as the Knitting Basket, because of its green copper dome, it's an unusual feature in a city of towers and spires. The church burned down several times and was rebuilt in the mid-1990s exactly as before. Now it's used as a conference center and concert hall, operated by a hotel.

Next door to the church on Kattengat are two of the city's most interesting buildings, **De Gouden Spiegel** (The Golden Mirror) and **De Silveren Spiegel** (The Silver Mirror). Built in 1614 by Hendrick de Keyser, they both have step gables, a style introduced around 1600, which continued to be popular until the 1670s. The buildings now house a restaurant, De Silveren Spiegel. From here it's a short walk up Kattengat and then left down Hekelveld to return to Centraal Station. ■

Brown Cafés & Dutch Gin

You are never far from a *bruin* (brown) café in Amsterdam, so called because of the dark wood paneling and the caramel patina of the tobacco-stained walls and ceilings. Neither are you likely to be far from a *proeflokaal* (tasting place), where freshly distilled gin was sampled before it was bought. A visit to both is essential while in the city.

Café 't Smalle, perhaps Amsterdam's most famous brown café

Brown Cafés

Brown cafés are an Amsterdam institution and are to locals what English pubs are to Londoners. They function like the old village water pump—the place where people from the immediate neighborhood gather after work and on weekends to gossip, read the papers, and discuss the latest news. A genuine bruin café is *gezellig* (cozy) and full of quirky old collectibles and flickering candles.

On the whole, Amsterdammers are loyal to one or two cafés, although some have come to attract a particular clientele—some are popular with artists, writers, or students; and others are

known for their blues nights, their beer selection, their home-brewed *jenever* (Dutch gin), or their home-baked apple cake. They are virtually all small, with tables tucked into every available nook and cranny and, once the sun comes out, spilling out onto the sidewalk. Exotic woven rugs cover the tables of the older cafés to soak up spills, a tradition dating back to the Golden Age, as depicted in paintings of tavern scenes in the Rijksmuseum (see pp. 192–197).

Most cafés serve at least three different beers on tap: a *pils* (lager), which usually hails from the Amstel or Heineken breweries, a blond, and either a *donker* (dark) or *bruin* (brown) brew, both of which are stronger and typically Belgian. Beers are served in a relatively small, 8.5 fluid ounce (25 cl) glass known as a *vaasje* (small vase). Hence, a typical order is for *"een biertje"* (a small beer), as opposed to *"een grote bier"* (a large beer, or pint).

To accompany the drinks, *hapjes* (little bites) are served, such as *bitterballen, croquetten, frik-adellen,* and blocks of Gouda dipped in mustard (see pp. 24–25). Depending on the café, and particularly in an *eetcafé* (eating café), more sub-stantial *broodjes* (sandwiches), soups, pastries, and the classic Dutch café dessert of a*ppelgebak* (apple cake) might also be available.

Dutch Gin

The traditional drink of bruin café patrons is jenever, which has been brewed in Amsterdam since the 17th century and has a pronounced juniper and citrus flavor. As the quality of jenever was somewhat unpredictable in those early centuries, distilleries typically had a *proeflo-kaal* (tasting place), where clients could sample a batch before having their bottle filled. There are two types of jenever—*jonge* (young) and *oude* (old). The first is sweeter and creamier than the latter, which is mellowed for several years in oak barrels. Both are delicious.

INSIDER TIP:

If you find yourself with locals celebrating an AFC Ajax or Netherlands soccer victory, the protocol is to knock back your short, ice-cold glass of *jenever* [Dutch gin], followed by a glass of lager. This combo is known colloquially as a *kopstoot* [head butt]. You have been warned!

—JUSTIN KAVANAGH
*National Geographic
International Editions editor*

Amsterdam's Best Bruin Cafés & Proeflokaals

Arendsnest *(Herengracht 90, tel 421-2057)* prides itself on serving only Dutch beers, and manager Peter van der Arend has tracked down some 100 of them, 30 of which he offers on tap.

Café Hoppe *(Spuistraat 18–20, tel 420-4420)* is one of the city's oldest cafés, founded in 1670 in Oude Zijde. Head straight for the back bar on the right of the building, which retains much of its original interior and atmosphere.

Café 't Smalle *(Egelantiersgracht 12, tel 623-9617)* in the Jordaan is an Amster-dam institution. Pieter Hoppe founded a distillery on the pretty canal in 1780, with an adjoining *proeflokaal* (tasting place), which serves as a café today. Look out for the original tap, once used to fill custom-ers' bottles, that still takes pride of place.

Café de Still *(Spuistraat 326, tel 620-1349)* is a tiny vintage bar that serves hundreds of the world's oldest and rarest whiskeys in the heart of Oude Zijde. This small, cozy *bruin* (brown) café is a real whiskey-drinker's treasure trove.

Café de Twee Zaantjes *(Prinsengracht 114, tel 625-2729)* in the Northern Canals is the epitome of a bruin café and has popular sing-along nights on Mondays.

De Wildeman *(Kolsteeg 3)* in Nieuwe Zijde has 18 different beers on tap and 250 bottled brews, served among old wooden barrels and tiled floors.

Proeflokaal Wijnand Fockink *(Pijlsteeg 31, tel 639-2695)* in Oude Zijde is a former distillery, founded in 1679. Its original tasting room is lined with beautiful antique hand-painted bottles.

Haarlemmerbuurt

Haarlemmerbuurt is the name of the former working-class district that lies on either side of the old road leading out of Amsterdam to the neighboring town of Haarlem. Today it is lined by quirky small shops and restaurants, offering a relaxed village atmosphere.

To get to Haarlemmerbuurt from the railroad station, head west up Nieuwendijk. Don't be too discouraged by the somewhat unsalubrious nature of this pedestrian-only street with its string of uninviting businesses: It will eventually bring you to **Haarlemmersluis Brug** (Haarlem Lock Bridge).

The Old Road to Haarlem

Haarlemmerstraat begins on the other side of Haarlemmersluis bridge. If you followed the road for 10 miles (16 km), you would reach Haarlem itself (see pp. 222–223), the capital of North Holland province. Livestock were once brought into the city along this road, but the cattle markets and slaughterhouses were swept away in the late 19th century. Several shops retain decorative facades from that period. **No. 60,** a short way up on the right, has art nouveau tiles advertising the sale of *koffie*, *thee*, and *cacao*.

Opposite No. 60 is the much earlier **West Indische Huis,** built in 1617. This building was used as the headquarters of the Dutch West India Company from 1623. The company was granted a monopoly on Dutch trade with the Americas and West Africa but was never as successful as its sister company, the Dutch East India Company. For a brief period, the WIC controlled Manhattan Island in the United States, which it called Nieuw Amsterdam (New Amsterdam). The trading colony prospered under the governorship of Pieter Stuyvesant until English soldiers captured the island in 1664 and renamed it New York.

Coffee shop on Haarlemmerdijk

A variety of boutiques, interspersed with galleries, delis, and bakeries, lines the next stretch of Haarlemmerstraat, voted by the Dutch as the most popular street in the Netherlands. Set back a little from the street is the gaunt **Posthoornkerk** (Post Horn Church) of 1860–1863, built by P. J. H. Cuypers. The name of this striking building, a major landmark in the city, comes from a clandestine church where Catholics met for secret worship above the stables belonging to the Amsterdam–Haarlem mail coach.

The Eenhoornsluis

The next bridge, **Eenhoornsluis,** crosses Prinsengracht. This is the only canal in the Grachtengordel that drains directly into the IJ River. Every barge entering the canal belt had to come through this point of entry, and the lock was deliberately built narrow as a defensive measure to limit the size of the boats allowed into the heart of the city.

On the other side of the bridge, the former canal becomes the **Haarlemmerdijk.** On the left, No. 39 is decorated with art nouveau tiles depicting an octopus and a seal, advertising the sale of seafood. No. 43, a tea and coffee shop, has a ship's figurehead carved in the shape of a Tahitian maiden and a gable stone showing a ship at anchor— both represent the faraway and exotic origins of the products formerly sold here. This may also explain the symbolism of the porpoise on the gable stone of No. 45.

EXPERIENCE:
Eat Fresh Herring

Amsterdammers love to stop for a portion of raw herring, chopped onions, and gherkins from the stand in the middle of the **Haarlemmersluis Brug.** So join in and eat it the local way, by holding the herring up by its tail, tipping back the heads, and taking great bites. You can also cut the herring into bite-size portions or enjoy it in a *broodje haring* (bread roll). The most sought-after herring is Nieuwe Hollandse (New Dutch), caught between late May and late June. Vlaggetjesdag (Little Flags Day) celebrates the opening of the herring season in Scheveningen (see p. 229) with great fanfare. Hundreds of fishing boats sail from the harbor. The first boat to return is greeted rapturously, and its first barrel of herring is auctioned for charity.

The Haarlem Gate

At the end of the street is busy **Haarlemmerplein,** with its bulky triumphal arch, known as the Haarlemmerpoort (Haarlem Gate) to locals. Its official name is Willemspoort (William's Gate), as it was built for the coronation of King Willem II of the Netherlands in 1840.

Another three-quarters of a mile (1.25 km) away you will come to Spaarndammerbuurt (see pp. 152–153); or you can explore the Westelijke Eilanden (Western Islands; see pp. 154–155) or the Jordaan (see pp. 140–144), or head back to the city center along pretty Brouwersgracht, the canal that runs parallel to the Haarlemmerdijk, two blocks south. Once lined by breweries, this canal has many fine bridges. ∎

Spaarndammerbuurt

Spaarndammerbuurt (Spaarndam District) is the location for an Arts and Crafts housing complex built by the pioneering architects of the Amsterdam School. Postcards depicting buildings on the complex are sold throughout the city, though few visitors take the trouble to see the real thing, because it is relatively far from the center—but the effort of getting there is rewarded by a glimpse of a different side of Amsterdam.

Spaarndammerbuurt complex, designed by Michel de Klerk

local nickname, in this case Het Schip (The Ship). This reflects the building's streamlined shape with a broad "stern," tapering toward a narrow "prow."

Forming a triangular block bounded by Oostzaanstraat, Hembrugstraat, and Zaanstraat, Het Schip is still used for its original purpose: "a palace for workers," or, in other words, subsidized public housing. The architects of the Amsterdam School who worked on the project from 1911–1923 under the leadership of the innovative Michel de Klerk firmly believed that the souls of the working class should be stimulated by architecture of aesthetic beauty.

Zaanhof & Museum Het Schip

Het Schip's former post office now serves as the main entrance to the building complex. As you approach the curiously shaped **tower** that marks the prow of the ship looming above you, take some time to appreciate the decorative detail lavished upon the building's exterior: the barrel-shaped **oriel window,** which bulges on the corner of Hembrugstraat and Zaanstraat; the way the redbrick walls billow and bulge and fold and curl in a

Spaarndammer-buurt

 Map pp. 128–129

From Centraal Station, board a number 22 bus, in the direction of Spaarndammerbuurt, to the last stop, Zaanstraat. This will deposit you directly in front of the Spaarndammerbuurt housing project. The block's official name is Zaanhof, but, like many Amsterdam landmarks, it has long gone by its popular way that lends the structure fluidity and plasticity; **the waves** that are carved into beams beneath the **projecting windows** and worked into the facade brickwork; and the dramatically carved **brick bird and lion heads**. This wealth of whimsical detail reflects Michel de Klerk's inventive and experimental style and his ability to treat this functional building as if it were a sculpture. By stark contrast, the post office, which is the only part of the building to retain its original interiors, is almost disappointingly plain and utilitarian.

Museum Het Schip incorporates three separate parts of the Zaanhof complex: the post office; an apartment restored to represent a 1920s worker's home, which also provides access to the turret; and a small yet growing exhibition space, café, and garden decorated with original street design furniture, located in a neighboring block called Spaarndammerplantsoen.

INSIDER TIP:

Informative, 45-minute guided tours of Museum Het Schip, usually in English, start every hour on the hour from the exhibition space in Spaarndammerplantsoen.

—GABRIELLA LE BRETON
National Geographic author

This adjacent block was also designed by Michel de Klerk.

Plans are currently afoot to expand the museum by appropriating De Catamaran (The Catamaran) schoolhouse, which is located within Het Schip.

If you plan to visit the Spaarndammerbuurt complex on a Saturday afternoon, extended guided tours of the surrounding neighborhood are available. Reservations must be made well in advance ■

Museum Het Schip

✉ Spaarndammer-plantsoen 140
☎ 418-2885
🕐 Closed Mon.
$ $$
🚌 Bus: 22

hetschip.nl

GETTING AROUND: Bus No. 22 provides a fast link from here back to Centraal Station. Alternatively, you can return to Haarlemmerplein to explore the Western Islands (see pp. 154–155) or the Jordaan (see pp. 140–144).

The Amsterdam School of Architecture

The architects of the Amsterdam School, which flourished as an informal grouping of like-minded architects from 1912 to 1940, were often criticized for their obsessive attention to decorative detail, which added greatly to the cost of buildings that were commissioned by the city and intended as dignified but low-cost dwellings for the city's poor.

In many respects, the Amsterdam School had much in common with other Arts and Crafts movements, especially in their appreciation of the skills of the humble bricklayer, carpenter, and metalworker. Evidence of this can be seen in Spaarndammerbuurt's playfully elegant

shapes of the porches, staircases, doors, number plates, and window frames of this block, all of which display consummate craftsmanship.

If you're inspired to learn more about the Amsterdam School of architecture, visit Spaarndammerbuurt's sister property, De Dageraad (The Dawn), which is located in De Pijp (see p. 209). The Bezoekerscentrum (Visitors Center) houses an exhibition on the development of Amsterdam Zuid (South) and the role the Amsterdam School played in its creation. It is also the starting point for guided walking and cycling tours of the housing complex and area.

Westelijke Eilanden

Construction of the three Western Islands of Prinseneiland, Realeneiland, and Bickerseiland began in 1621. As a place where inflammable tar—used for sealing the hulls of wooden boats—could be made and stored, it was set away from central Amsterdam. Once bustling with forges, shipyards, noxious fish-smoking houses, and shipbuilders' wharves, the area is now gentrified with converted warehouses providing stylish homes, artists' studios, and cafés.

Houses and houseboats at Prinseneiland (Prince's Island)

Westelijke Eilanden
Map p. 129

A railroad, built up on a high embankment, was constructed along the harbor in 1870, cutting off the three Western Islands from the rest of the city. Hidden behind the high viaduct, the islands seem to belong to a different world, with their own tranquil, village-like atmosphere.

To reach them, follow the old Haarlem road through Haarlemmerbuurt (see pp. 150–151) to **Haarlemmerplein,** turning right to pass under the railroad tracks.

Prinseneiland

Turn right just after the railroad bridge takes you down Sloterdijkstraat and across narrow Sloterdijkbrug, with views of houseboats and rusting ships' hulls awaiting restoration, and then over to **Prinseneiland,** where working timber yards sit side by side with chic warehouse apartments displaying sail-shaped shutters. Ahead lies Galgenstraat (Gallows Street), a grim reminder that the gallows on the opposite side of the IJ River were once visible from this spot. Turn left, past a warehouse block, then right, passing a boat-builders' yard, then turn left to cross pretty Drieharingenbrug (Three Herrings Bridge).

Realeneiland

The bridge takes you over to **Realeneiland.** Turn right on Realeneiland, and down Realengracht, whose modern houses show how close the islands came to wholesale redevelopment in the 1960s. The Dutch author Jan Mens (1897–1967) led a campaign to conserve the islands' character. One of his novels, *De Gouden Reael (The Golden Real,* 1940), was set here, in what was then a gritty dockworkers' district.

At the end of Realengracht, turn left into **Zandhoek** (Sand Corner). Sailing boats are usually moored in Westerdok, where the sand barges that gave their name to Zandhoek once unloaded to supply the construction industry.

The houses on the left-hand side of Zandhoek have been beautifully restored. The two rows date from 1660, their lower facades built of timber, the fashion at the time. The houses have different gable designs, from the simple spout gables of Nos. 8–14 and the step gable of No. 6 to various bell gables and the slightly later cornice at No. 2 (probably an 18th-century replacement for the original gable).

Several houses retain their original gable stones. In Amsterdam, these stones often provide a pictorial reference to the name of the house—hence the Golden Lion, the White Horse, Noah's Ark, St. Peter, and St. John. No. 14 is called De Gouden Reael, and the gable stone depicts the Spanish real coin, a pun on the name of Laurens Jacob Reaal, the wealthy landowner after whom Realeneiland is named. The building now houses a great café specializing in French provincial food (see pp. 248–249).

INSIDER TIP:

Dine at Restaurant Pont 13 *[Haparandam, tel 770-2722, pont13.nl]* in the Westelijke Houthavens [Western Lumber Ports]. It's a restored ferry moored in the old harbor serving seasonal food.

—ROBBERT VERMUE
National Geographic *magazine in the Netherlands editor*

Bickerseiland

Across Zandhoeksbrug lies **Bickerseiland** (named after 17th-century shipyard owner Jan Bicker). Take the first right, and follow cobbled Bickersgracht as it turns left past the popular **De Dierencapel,** a children's farm, where kids can feed the geese, ducks, rabbits, and goats. Take the second street on the left, Minnemoerstraat, then turn right onto Grote Bickersstraat. Stop here for refreshments at 't Blauwe Hoofd Café, a popular spot with locals. Emerging from the underpass, walk up Buitenoranjestraat to return to Haarlemmerdijk. ■

De Dierencapel

- Map p. 129
- Corner of Bickersgracht & Bickersstraat
- Free (donations welcome)
- Bus: 18, 22

Westerpark

Travelers seeking a relaxed, culturally diverse Amsterdam vibe should hop a tram or bus to this rejuvenated park on the site of Amsterdam's former gasworks. Here, you can enjoy a stroll, a visit to Westerpark's Culture Park, tea on a sunny terrace, or a film in the Ketelhuis cinema.

De Bakkerswinkel bakery and café is located in the former Regulateurshuis (Regulator's House).

Westerpark

- 🅰 Map p. 129
- 🚊 Tram: 10
  Bus: 21

westergasfabriek.nl

The Westergasfabriek (Western Gasworks) was constructed in 1883 by the British Imperial Continental Gas Association, mainly to power public lighting. The majority of the redbrick buildings were designed by Isaac Gosschalk, in a variation on the Dutch Renaissance style. After the discovery of natural gas in the 1960s, some of the buildings were demolished. Thanks in part to squatters who prevented the remaining buildings from being knocked down, they were recognized as industrial heritage monuments in 1989, and Westerpark was opened as a "culture park" in 2003.

The term "culture park" denotes the coexistence of a large, tranquil parkland with a pond, petting zoo, swimming pool, tennis courts, and surprisingly attractive industrial buildings and monuments, several of which now house cafés, galleries, event spaces, bars, and restaurants, as well as a quirky cinema and theater. Music festivals, markets, photography exhibits, art installations, and dance performances are all held in the park.

Be sure to stop at **De Bakkerswinkel** (Polonceaukade 1, tel 688-0632, debakkerswinkel.nl), Westerpark's bakery and café. While locals buy freshly baked bread for breakfast, you can stock up for lunch by the drawbridge. The restaurant **Raïnaraï** (Polonceaukade 40, tel 486-7109, rainarai. nl) serves Algerian dishes on the quayside, while **Westergasterras** (Klönneplein 4–6, tel 684-8496, westergasterras.nl) is a popular spot for afternoon drinks by the pond. The **Pacific Parc** (Polonceaukade 23, tel 488-7778, pacificparc.nl) rock-and-roll café has a bohemian feel by day; at night live bands and DJs liven things up. After dinner, catch a movie at the **Ketelhuis** (Passanistraat 4, tel 684-0090, ketelhuis.nl), which shows films in Dutch and English and regularly hosts international guests for seminars and premieres. ■

Elegant canals echoing with Golden Age glory; the Nine Streets, Leidseplein, and Rembrandtplein reflecting Amsterdam old and new

Southern Canals

Introduction & Map 158–159

Southern Singel & Spuistraat 160–161

Grachtengordel South 162–167

Experience: Revel in the
    Canal Festival 165

Experience: Drink "High Wine" at
    the Dylan 166

Leidsegracht 168–169

Koningsplein & Leidseplein 170–173

Spiegelkwartier 174–175

Gouden Bocht 176–179

Rembrandtplein &
    Thorbeckeplein 180–181

Canal House Museums 182–183

Hermitage Amsterdam 184

Feature: Houseboats 185

A Walk Along the Amstel River 186–188

Hotels & Restaurants in the
    Southern Canals 249–251

Magere Brug (Skinny Bridge)
on the Amstel River

Southern Canals

The southern part of the Grachtengordel stretches from Raadhuisstraat around to the Amstel River. Constructed after the northern section, purchasers of plots here were often the wealthy heirs of merchants, manufacturers, and bankers. They built exceptionally grand houses, and this part of the canal belt became known as the Gouden Bocht (Golden Bend).

The residential tranquillity of the area was shattered in the mid-19th century, when new thoroughfares were driven through the Gouden Bocht, linking the city center with suburbs developing around the Museum Quarter and Vondelpark (see pp. 204–205). As a result, the area has seen more recent redevelopment than the northern stretch and has a greater mixture of buildings. Here you find not just elegant houses, antique shops, and galleries, but also churches, theaters, brothels, hotels, and university housing,

NOT TO BE MISSED:

Strolling around De Negen Straatjes (The Nine Streets) 163

Fun at the Canal Festival 165

Taking "High Wine" at the Dylan Hotel 166

Coffee at Café Americain in Leidseplein 172–173

Browsing for antiques in the Spiegelkwartier 174–175

The Golden Age magnificence of the Gouden Bocht 176–179

A taste of Russia in Holland at the Hermitage Amsterdam 184

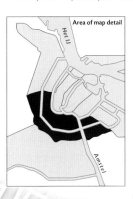

Area of map detail

as well as the lively nightlife hubs of Leidseplein and Rembrandtplein. Toward the Amstel River, upon which the Hermitage Amsterdam (see p. 184) sits, the character of the canal belt changes yet again. The river, alive with the bustle of barges and spanned by elegant bridges, provides a wide-open vista to contrast with the enclosed world of the Gouden Bocht. ∎

Southern Singel & Spuistraat

Slums and rotting warehouses along the southern stretch of the Singel canal were swept away during 19th-century redevelopment, and more would have been demolished during the 1980s were it not for the activities of squatters, who defied the authorities and won the day. As a result, this corner of Amsterdam is a kaleidoscope of architectural styles from several centuries.

**Singel &
Spuistraat**

Map p. 158

Raadhuisstraat was cut through the canal belt in the 1890s to create a tram route linking the city center and the western outskirts. Where the street crosses the Singel canal, you can look back for a fine view of the rear of the Koninklijk Paleis

Magna Plaza, Amsterdam's former main post office, now houses one of the city's most luxurious department stores.

(Royal Palace; see pp. 54–57). To the left lies the flamboyant **Magna Plaza,** built by Cornelis Hendrik Peters in 1889 in the eclectic style, borrowing architectural elements from the Romanesque, Gothic, and Renaissance periods. Originally built as the city's main post office, this fine building is now a shopping center with a splendidly arcaded atrium.

In the other direction, running around the southern curve of Raadhuisstraat, is an art nouveau **shopping arcade,** built in 1898 by the Van Gendt firm of architects, its canopy decorated with crocodiles and dragons.

Southern Singel

Turning down Singel, the first building you'll come to on the left after Paleisstraat is the eight-story **Bungehuis** *(Singel 239),* constructed of gray limestone in the 1930s for the Bunge Trading Company. The main entrance around the corner on Spuistraat is a splendid example of art deco design.

A short way farther down Spuistraat, Nos. 214–216 have a vibrant painted facade, a monument to the squatters' movement of the 1970s and 1980s, when many young people moved into empty properties to protest against the lack of affordable housing then available in Amsterdam.

Back on Singel, the innocuous-looking No. 295 housed the city's most expensive brothel, **Yab Yum,** for more than 30 years. Today it's an equally expensive "private members club."

Spuistraat

Farther down Singel is an area of small shops specializing in postage stamps, coins, and antiquarian books. The alleys running off to the left lead to the cafés of **Spuistraat,** a popular spot for Amsterdammers to socialize after work.

This stretch of Singel used to house the city's fruit market. Look for No. 367 where Adam and Eve and the serpent in the Garden of Eden, the symbol of the Fruitsellers' Guild, are carved on the gable stone. The existence of the market might explain the names of the adjacent **Vliegensteeg** (Fly Alley) and its venerable restaurant, **d'Vijff Vlieghen** (The Five Flies; see p. 250), which also likes to call itself a "culinary museum."

Farther along the opposite bank, at No. 446, looms the Jesuit church of **St. Francis Xavier,** built in 1883. Known as **De Krijtberg** (The Chalk Hill) after a chalk warehouse that once stood on the site—and that doubled as a clandestine Catholic church in the 18th century—this house of worship is well worth a look. Inside, check out the ornate Gothic-revival rood screen and stained-glass east window.

From the church, there is a good view across Singel to the simple **Oude Lutherse Kerk** (Old Lutheran Church; see p. 62), now part of the University of Amsterdam library. Farther down, the grand double-fronted building you see is the former **Doelen** building, radically altered in 1773 but originally constructed to allow members of the city militias to practice shooting with their longbows and crossbows. Next to the Doelen, you'll find the **Stadts Magazijn** (City Arsenal), which retains its original 1605

INSIDER TIP:

Join locals for a beer at Café Hoppe [Spuistraat 18–20]. The original distillery and tasting room was housed at No. 18 Spuistraat and still has many of its original interior decorations.

—GABRIELLA LE BRETON
National Geographic author

facade, with its wide, flat-topped gable decorated with scrollwork. This edifice was originally built for the storage of weapons used by Amsterdam's militias. All of these buildings, from the Arsenal up to the church, have now been converted into a library for the University of Amsterdam. ∎

Grachtengordel South

Walking around the charming part of the canal belt that stretches from Raadhuisstraaat to Leidsegracht, you'll run across scores of interesting architectural details to see and savor. The grand houses here are far from cheap to buy or rent—many have been turned into offices for advertising, design, or fashion companies—but the overall character remains residential.

A wander through De Negen Straatjes (the Nine Streets) offers the traveler many aspects of Amsterdam.

Nine Streets
🅰 Map p. 158

When the canal belt was built, shops and workshops were deliberately restricted to the short cross streets linking the radial canals. Wolvenstraat, two blocks south of Raadhuisstraat and one block over from the Singel canal (see pp. 160–161), is a typical example. It can be reached down Oude Spiegel-straat (named after Pieter

Spiegel de Oude, who owned land in this area in the 17th century). Continue across the next bridge toward Wolven-straat, looking over to the right as you go, across to **Herengracht No. 284.** This has a splendid sandstone facade dating from 1728. If you walk down for a closer look, you will see that the central bay has window frames heavily ornamented with acanthus leaf carvings, and an ornate crest rises from the roof cornice. The architect is not known, but the obsession with symmetry is apparent in the way the off-center front door has been made very plain so as not to distract from the central axis.

De Negen Straatjes

Beyond No. 284 lies Wolven-straat, whose name means "Wolf Street." All the cross streets to the north and south of here have names associated with the fur and tanning trades: Reestraat and Hartenstraat (Roe Deer and Harts), Berenstraat (Bears), Huidenstraat (Hides), and Runstraat (Bark, used in tanning). This was once an area that thrived on the furs and hides trade, though the furriers' shops have now been replaced by a medley of charming cafés and restaurants, quirky specialty shops, and art galleries. The area is known collectively as De Negen Straatjes (Nine Streets; see sidebar below).

Crossing the next bridge, note the buildings on the left, Nos. 314–316, as you reach the western bank of Keizersgracht. You might date this elegant building to the middle of the 17th century because of its step gable, small-paned sash windows, and fine brickwork. Actually, it was only constructed in 1935 by A. A. Kok, an architect who believed in using the traditional idiom for new buildings constructed in the historic city center. It's a perfect example of architectural good manners, not observed by every architect whose work is found along the Grachtengordel.

As you turn right down Keizersgracht, you come to Nos. 298–300, a glass-and-concrete building of 1955 that was regarded as revolutionary in its time but now just looks jaded and incongruous. The debate about

The Nine Streets: The Essence of Amsterdam

De Negen Straatjes (The Nine Streets; *de9straatjes.nl*) encompasses a lattice of nine intersecting side streets of the Prinsengracht, Keizersgracht, Heren-gracht, and Singel canals. These house a delightful collection of one-off boutiques dedicated to cutting-edge clothing, shoes, handbags, and jewelry, and diverse cafés and restaurants. From the Prinsengracht toward the Singel and beginning with the northernmost streets, the streets are Reestraat (Roe Deer Street), Hartenstraat (Harts Street), Gasthuismolensteeg (Inn Mill Alley), Berenstraat (Bear Street),

Wolvenstraat (Wolf Street), Oude Spiegelstraat (named after Pieter Spiegel de Oude), Runstraat (Bark Street), Huidenstraat (Hides Street), and Wijde Heisteeg (Wide Heath Street).

Work up a shopping-induced appetite and visit the Wijnsalon De Apotheek (Pharmacy Wine Salon; *Reestraat 8, tel 523-5225, hotelpulitzeramsterdam.nl/ wijnsalon*). Housed in a former pharmacy with interiors dating back to 1800, the intimate venue serves multicourse dinners, each of which is accompanied by a different wine.

A welcoming interior at the Houseboat Museum on Prinsengracht

new architecture in the canal belt continues among architects, critics, and city council planners, and is renewed every time a site comes up for development.

Keizersgracht

Among the older buildings on Keizersgracht are Nos. 292–294, a pair of 1730 houses with elongated neck gables and side pieces decorated with seashells and marine motifs. Farther down Keizersgracht, Nos. 242–252 form a group of buildings that were squatted in during the late 1970s and were the scene of violent battles when riot police attempted to evict the occupants. In the end, the city council agreed to restore the buildings and rent them to the former squatters at a subsidized price. Needless to

say, such a policy enraged some Amsterdammers, who resented the fact that law-breaking squatters ended up living cheaply in palatial and prestigious canal houses that are beyond the means of many ordinary and law-abiding citizens.

Reestraat

Shop-lined **Reestraat** is a good place to stop for a coffee—perhaps in the upscale Pulitzer Café on the corner with Keizersgracht. The café is part of the **Pulitzer Hotel** (see p. 249), which occupies a whole block of 17th- and 18th-century canal-side houses and warehouses running from Keizersgracht to Prinsengracht. Peter Pulitzer, grandson of the newspaper publisher who founded the annual Pulitzer Prizes for journalism, literature, music, and drama, founded the hotel in 1968. All of the rooms and public areas have works of art on the walls, and sculptures dot the fine courtyard gardens (much of the art is for sale).

Turn left down Prinsengracht and note the medallions set high in the facade of Nos. 357–359, showing the deer trademark of the former **Red Hart Brewery,** which occupied these premises from around 1612 to 1841. Brewers in Amsterdam dealt in fresh water as well as beer. In the days before drinking water was supplied by tap, they imported fresh water by barge both for their own use and for sale to the public. Farther down the street, the plain building at No. 415 was the home of Johannes Commenius (1592–1670), the Moravian priest who wrote a pioneering treatise on educational theory, *Didactica Magna,* and who was the first to advocate the use of pictures (today's "visual aids") as a learning tool.

Berenstraat & the Houseboat Museum

The next left is Berenstraat, another shop-lined cross street, with the **Houseboat Museum** (see p. 185) on the opposite bank. At the end of Berenstraat, you have a view across Keizersgracht to No. 317, another relatively plain house with a distinguished former resident: Peter the Great, the tsar of Russia, quite literally turned up on the doorstep in December 1716.

The owner of the house was Christoffel van Brants, a merchant who had spent much of his early life in Russia, where he became a friend of the young tsar (they were both fascinated by shipbuilding). When Peter set off on his tour of Europe, traveling incognito, he called on his old friend without any prior warning. Reminiscing about

EXPERIENCE: Revel in the Canal Festival

If you love classical music, you'll want to visit Amsterdam in August, when the city's waterways resound with music during the ten-day **Grachtenfestival** (Canal Festival; *grachtenfestival.nl*).

Throughout this festive period, you can choose from a host of performances in locations dotted around the canal belt and in Amsterdam Noord. The setting for each musical event is chosen with great care, typically reflecting the history or content of the piece being played, and ranges from private canal houses and gardens to boats and rooftop terraces. However, you won't know the exact location until the morning of the performance, when ticket holders receive a text message with the address. You'll hear the talents of internationally renowned artists and young, homegrown Dutch talent. To catch the grand finale of the Canal Festival head to the floating platform outside the Pulitzer Hotel.

the past, Peter is said to have drunk a great deal of beer before falling asleep on the hard floor of Brants's bedroom. Once the city council heard that the tsar was in town, it hastily prepared a reception for the ruler and persuaded him to move into the Herengracht house of the Russian ambassador (see p. 177).

EXPERIENCE: Drink "High Wine" at the Dylan

If you've had your fill of Dutch tea, step into the **Dylan Hotel** (*Keizersgracht 384, tel 530-2010, dylanamsterdam.com*) for High Wine, a vinous take on traditional afternoon, or high, tea. Located on the prestigious Keizersgracht, the hotel is built on the site of a 16th-century Roman Catholic almshouse and orphanage, which was subsequently turned into a 17th-century theater before being transformed into one of Amsterdam's most glamorous hotels. With the Michelin-starred Vinkeles restaurant located in the former almshouse bakery, the Dylan rates high on Amsterdam's foodie destination list. High Wine provides the opportunity to sample some of the Dylan's Dutch-inspired light bites accompanied by a specially selected flight of wines in the hotel's chic bar.

Bijbels Museum

- 🅐 Map p. 158
- ✉ Herengracht 366–368
- ☎ 624-2436
- 🕐 Closed Sun. a.m.
- 🚊 Tram: 1, 2, 5
- ⛴ Museumboot

bijbelsmuseum.nl

Felix Meritis Building

On this side of the canal, at No. 324, is another building with Russian connections: The **Felix Meritis Building** was used as the headquarters of the Dutch Communist Party from 1945 until 1968. This was just one episode in the building's varied history. It was built in 1787 for the Felix Meritis society (whose name, meaning "Happiness Through Merit," is carved beneath the pediment). This institution was set up to nurture interest in the arts and sciences.

Behind the building's well-proportioned classical facade was an auditorium where the society's lectures took place. Upper rooms in the building were designed for use as artists' studios, and an astronomical observatory on the roof offered scientists the chance to look at the stars.

Intellectual Amsterdammers were proud of their Temple of Enlightenment, but others were less impressed. Napoléon was brought here for a reception after his grand entry into the city in 1811, but he had hardly set foot through the door before he beat a hasty exit, complaining that the auditorium stank of tobacco smoke. On another occasion, Brahms conducted a performance of his Third Symphony in the building and departed with the stinging criticism that his hosts were "good people but bad musicians." It was Brahms's musical rebuke that spurred the city to build the Concertgebouw (see p. 262) and to set up a permanent professional orchestra.

Fire destroyed the interior of the Felix Meritis Building in 1932, and in its rebuilt form, it housed the Communist Party until 1968. The building then became the Shaffy Theater, named after the actor Ramses Shaffy, but its program of avant-garde and experimental drama failed to attract audiences, and the Shaffy closed in 1989. The building was rescued by the Felix Meritis Foundation, which now runs it as a theater for the promotion of European arts—dance, music, and drama—with a lively summer school. There is a café to the left of the entrance, a popular meeting point for young arts enthusiasts and a relaxing place to gather your thoughts.

Bijbels Museum

At the next junction after the
the Felix Meritis Building, turn
left across the bridge and walk
down Huidenstraat, then turn
right onto Herengracht. A
short way down is the **Bijbels
Museum** (Biblical Museum).

The museum's sandstone
buildings are identifiable as
the work of Philips Vingboons
because of the ornate neck
gables. This group of buildings dates from 1660, and his
client was Jacob Cromhout, a
merchant whose trademark,
a crooked stick, appears on a
plaque on the facade. The building combines classical elements
(the pedimented windows) with
baroque (the garlanded oxeye
windows in the attic story).

The interior retains its stately
period details and ceiling paintings by the celebrated Jacob de
Wit, a stunning elliptical English
staircase, the best preserved
17th-century kitchens in Holland, and a lovely back garden
with terraces and pools.

The museum dates back to
1851, when Reverend Leendert
Schouten put his now famous
model of the Tabernacle on
display. This is now complemented by some 1,000 Bibles,
telling the story of the holy
book's origins with the aid
of interactive touch screens,
archaeological finds, and
Egyptian antiquities.

Just beyond the museum is
another decorative building,
Nos. 380–382, built between
1888 and 1891 for a tobacco
millionaire. The facade borrows
its style from that of the French
Renaissance châteaux of the Loire
Valley in France. This building now
houses the **Nederlands Instituut
voor Oorlogsdocumentatie**
(NIOD, Dutch Institute for War
Documentation). The NIOD is
worth visiting for its opulent
neo-Renaissance interiors. ∎

NIOD

- Map p. 158
- Herengracht 380–382
- 523-3800
- Closed Sat.–Mon. a.m.

niod.knaw.nl

The stairwell in the Bijbels Museum

Leidsegracht

Leidsegracht is an unusual canal in that it cuts across the canal belt. In fact, it marks the end of the first section of the Grachtengordel, constructed from 1609 to 1660, and the beginning of the second phase of 1660 onward. The name "Leiden canal" indicates that this was where boats traveling the inland waterways between Amsterdam and Leiden once moored.

The intersection of Leidsegracht and Keizersgracht canals

Leidsegracht
Map p. 158

The buildings that line the canal include several large warehouses where goods that were essential to the functioning of the city were unloaded. No. 88, the **Archangelsk Pakhuizen** (Archangel Pakhuis), is named after the Russian port with which the warehouse owner, Egbert Thesingh, carried out his trade. He imported timber for shipbuilding, including ships' masts, and in turn Thesingh

exported luxurious fabrics to the Russian Imperial Court. At No. 108 is the city stonemasons' yard. It was here, on the edge of 17th-century Amsterdam, that the stone and bricks used for constructing municipal buildings were unloaded, stored, and worked.

The adjacent bridge takes you across to the south bank of the canal with a view to the right of the massive former dairy, now the famous **Melkweg** arts center. In the bad old days, according to local folklore, unscrupulous milkmen delivering milk by barge would adulterate it by adding canal water to the churns. So widespread was this practice that a new market in guaranteed fresh milk was created. The farmers would lead their cows to your door and milk the beasts before your eyes! Today's Melkweg has evolved from being a hippie center in the 1970s into a valuable multimedia arts center, offering a diverse program of performing arts, music, film, and photography.

Cornelis Lely

On the other side of the canal from the Melkweg is **No. 39,** a simple spout-gabled building where Cornelis Lely was born in 1854. Lely was the engineer who transformed the Netherlands by planning and supervising the construction of the Afsluitdijk (Enclosing Dam), which was completed in 1932, three years after his death. The dam cut the shallow tidal Zuiderzee off from the North Sea. With the dam in place, the Zuiderzee became a freshwater lake (now called the IJsselmeer), parts of which have been reclaimed to create some 70 square miles (1,800 sq km) of new land. Much of this forms the new Dutch province of Flevoland, whose capital— Lelystad—was named to honor the engineer.

Farther along the street, there are good views, especially at night, when the arches of the bridges are outlined by strings of white lights. Look at the side cheeks of the neck gable at No. 11, decorated with a carving of intertwined snakes and lizards. The motif is unique in Amsterdam. Some say the snakes symbolize the financial entanglements of the first owner, a silversmith, who got himself deeply into debt.

INSIDER TIP:

Melkweg [melkweg.nl] is the place to be on King's Eve [see p. 19], with live bands playing through the night of April 26 into King's Day. Book tickets well in advance to secure your place at the party.

—JUSTIN KAVANAGH
*National Geographic
International Editions editor*

The Golden Bend

Where Leidsegracht joins the Herengracht you will see a pretty pair of identical late 17th-century houses, Nos. 396 and 398, known as the **Twee Zusjes** (Two Sisters). No. 402 is a fine sandstone house, in the style of Philips Vingboons, with an ornate curving *stoop* (the name is the same in English) dating from 1750. In similar style, No. 408 has a fine fanlight over the door, while No. 412 is the work of Vingboons himself, who built it in 1667. These and the houses opposite are in the grander style of the so-called Golden Bend (see pp. 176–179). ∎

Melkweg

🅰 Map p. 158
✉ Lijnbaansgracht 243a
☎ 531-8199
🚊 Tram: 1, 2, 5, 6, 7, 10

melkweg.nl

Koningsplein & Leidseplein

Narrow Leidsestraat is one of Amsterdam's main shopping streets. In places the street is so narrow that trams have to line up to pass, while pedestrians and bicycles dodge each other along the crowded sidewalks. The square of Leidseplein is one of Amsterdam's main nightlife centers, located on the crossroads of the Weteringschans, the Marnixstraat, and the Leidsestraat.

The Bloemenmarkt (Flower Market) on Singel is a horticulturalist's wonderland.

Koningsplein

Map p. 158

Koningsplein

Leidsestraat starts at the Bloemenmarkt (Flower Market; see p. 63), the world's only floating flower market, supplying Amsterdammers with blooms since 1862.

Standing at the market and looking back toward the city center, you can see the **AMRO Bank,** an attractive Arts and Crafts building in the style of the Amsterdam School, with owls and stylized human faces carved on the facade. Also on the opposite bank stands the huge brick complex of 1896–1897, which comprises the city's defunct indoor swimming baths and the former public records office; it is now a shopping mall.

Heading away from the center are the big, late 19th-century stores, many of them with corner towers or domes, a feature of Koningsplein and of its southwestern continuation, Leidsestraat.

A good example of early shop design at the point where the street crosses Herengracht is the art nouveau clothing store that has an almost unbroken wall of plate glass running around the first three stories, thanks to the innovative use of iron framing, a relatively new technique when the store was built in 1901.

INSIDER TIP:

Housed in a converted church, about a minute's walk from Leidseplein, Paradiso [Weteringschans 6–8, tel 626-4521, paradiso .nl] is one of Amsterdam's best, and quirkiest, venues for live music.

—GABRIELLA LE BRETON
National Geographic author

Metz & Co. Building

Just before the next bridge, on the right, is another pioneering commercial building. Now an Abercrombie & Fitch store, this beautiful building formerly housed Amsterdam's famous textiles, furnishings, and clothing store, Metz & Co. It was built for the New York Life Insurance Company, which wanted an exact copy of its office in Vienna, hence its Viennese appearance. Metz & Co., founded in 1740, celebrated its 150th birthday by moving into the building in 1890. It was a progressive company, selling the designs of artists and small artisan businesses, rather than mass-produced products. In 1933, it commissioned the radical Dutch architect Gerrit Rietveld (1888–1964) to design a glass and metal rooftop showroom for the store. Rietveld was a leading member of the group of artists known as De Stijl (The Style), who espoused simple geometric designs in bold primary colors, a style that greatly influenced the Bauhaus and modernist movements. Rietveld's cupola survives today, and although it's no longer accessible, you can easily see it from the street—look for the "METZ" sign, which was also designed by Rietveld.

Farther along Leidsestraat is **Dikker & Thijs Fenice Hotel,** a hotel and restaurant on the right at the corner of Prinsengracht. Mr. A. W. Dikker opened a delicatessen here in 1895, to be joined by Henri Thijs, fresh from Paris in 1915. Although they moved to new premises, the property always retained its gourmet heritage. To the right, running down Prinsengracht to Leidsegracht, stands the former **Paleis van Justitie** (Palace of Justice). It was built between 1825 and 1829, replacing the city orphanage. Farther down Leidsestraat, No. 88, on the right, has a tile portrait of Christiaan Huygens (1629–1693), the scientist who invented the first pendulum clock.

Leidseplein

Leidsestraat leads into the open expanse of Leidseplein, one of Amsterdam's main tourist and

Metz & Co. Building
- Map p. 158
- Leidsestraat 34–36

Dikker & Thijs Fenice Hotel
- Map p. 158
- Prinsengracht 444
- 620-1212

dtfh.nl

Leidseplein
- Map p. 158

Stadsschouwburg

- Map p. 158
- Leidseplein 26
- 624-2311
- Tram: 1, 2, 5, 7, 10

stadsschouwburg
amsterdam.nl

Finding the Leidsebos Zagertje

If you look hard enough in the dense plane trees in the Leidsebos park, just across from the Leidseplein, you will find Het Zagertje (The Little Sawyer). A favorite "communal" artwork of many Amsterdammers, it is an endearingly small sculpture of a man sawing off the branch he's standing on. The piece was installed in 1989 under cover of night by an unknown "guerrilla" artist, who is attributed with similar sculptures and pieces of art across the city.

---

nightlife locations. In winter a skating rink is set up in the square, while in summer tables spill out onto the sidewalks from the restaurants lining the square and nearby side streets. These range from inexpensive but well-regarded places, such as the **Tandoor,** at No. 19, to gourmet temples, such as **'t Swarte Schaep** (The Black Sheep; see pp. 250–251). There are plenty of fast-food outlets, but probably not enough to justify the square's nickname, La Place de la Mayonnaise.

Neon lights advertising discos, cinemas, and nightclubs add to the square's variety. Culture vultures come for the various plays and ballets put on at the **Stadsschouwburg** (City Theater)

on the right, built in 1894. The theater hosts Dutch and international groups and is a key venue in many festivals, including the Holland Festival. Others come for the two renowned rock and world-music venues, Melkweg and Paradiso (see p. 264).

The American Hotel

Beyond the Stadsschouwburg is the American Hotel. There are few more atmospheric places for coffee or afternoon tea in Amsterdam than the hotel's splendid Tiffany-style **Café Americain** (Leidsekade 97, tel 556-3000). Built in 1904, the

INSIDER TIP:

The Café Americain [cafeamericain.nl] is a great place for a mellow Sunday brunch to the strains of a live jazz band. It also hosts regular musical recitals. Check the website for forthcoming events.

—JUSTIN KAVANAGH
National Geographic International Editions editor

hotel has been progressively stripped of its art nouveau style by successive modernizations, but the café survives in all its glory, complete with stained-glass windows and delicate chandeliers. While the café is the haunt of Amsterdam's literati, the Bar Américain is the place to while away an Amsterdam hour or two sipping cocktails, trying out the local gins, and maybe even spotting the occasional celebrity doing likewise.

Across the road stands the **Leidsekadebrug** with its art deco granite columns carved as sea monsters and its wrought ironwork, suggestive of waves. This bridge marks the edge of the pre-19th-century city, and the water to the right formed a defensive moat around Amsterdam until parts began to be filled in the 1860s.

Chess & Culture

A boardwalk on the left of the Leidsekadebrug runs along the waterside skirting the glass walls of the Holland Casino. This walk-way leads to the **Max Euweplein,** a public space named after Max Euwe, the celebrated Dutch chess player who was world champion from 1935 to 1937. A giant chess set in the square never fails to attract an interested crowd as local and visiting players publically pit their wits against each other. Beside the chess set, a water rill gives off the soothing sound of cascading water.

Various other sculptural works are dotted around the plaza, and if you walk through the adjacent shopping center, you will come to the columned entrance, where the classical pediment bears the beautifully lettered Latin inscription: *"Homo Sapiens non Urinat in Ventum."* This fun bit of epigrammatic Latin affirms optimistically that humankind does not piss in the wind. This reminder that we do not strive entirely in vain could

apply to the artists, authors, and activists who come to give talks at the **Café de Balie.** Established in 1982 as a platform for debates, seminars, film showings, and live music, this cultural center is enduringly popular. Its iconic Grand Café is a wonderful place to enjoy coffee served with intellectual conversation and music recitals. ∎

Café de Balie

- Map p. 158
- Kleine Gartman-plantsoen 10
- 553-5100
- Tram: 1, 2, 5, 7, 10

debalie.nl

The Café Américain in Leidseplein

Spiegelkwartier

The Spiegelkwartier (Spiegel Quarter) is named after the little Spiegelgracht, which, literally translated, means "Mirror Canal." However, the name has nothing to do with reflections: Hendrik Spiegel was mayor of Amsterdam at the time the canal was dug in 1660, and it was named for him. Today, the Spiegelkwartier is renowned for its antique shops and art galleries, selling everything from rare 17th-century maps and tribal art to ultramodern paintings.

Delftware dominates the window of an antique shop in Nieuwe Spiegelstraat in the Spiegelkwartier.

Spiegelkwartier
Map p. 158

The shop windows along Spiegelgracht (and its continuation, Nieuwe Spiegelstraat) are filled with artistically arranged displays of nautical instruments, Louis XVI furniture, art nouveau lamps, and Roman statuettes. The area developed as the antiques sector of Amsterdam in the 1880s, shortly after the nearby Rijksmuseum (see pp. 192–197) opened to the public. The street's proximity to the museum meant it was frequently used by art lovers walking from the city center to the Museum Quarter (see pp. 190–205). Gradually, Amsterdam's antique dealers gravitated to this street to take advantage of the passing trade.

If you are passionate about antiques or Asian and African arts and crafts, make your way slowly down Spiegelgracht, where every shop window is like a museum display, and even the cafés possess a nostalgic dose of antique charm. Across Prinsengracht, on Nieuwe Spiegelstraat, the many temptations include antique jewelry, Delftware, clocks and globes, Golden Age furnishings, paintings, and silverware. The prices are high, but you will also find attractive, reasonably priced botanical prints or old navigational maps.

On Spiegelgracht, **Heinen** (No. 13) specializes in hand-painted Delftware, while **Hoog-kamp** (No. 27) and **Spiegeling Art** (No. 26) sell paintings and Old Master prints.

In Nieuwe Spiegelstraat, the bright colors of the Amazonian artifacts on offer at **Tribal Design** (No. 52) interrupt the cozy patina of wood and canvas.

The **Amsterdam Antiques Gallery** (No. 34) has numerous eclectic dealers under one roof, while **Eduard Kramer** (No. 64) specializes in antique painted tiles.

On the right, the **Spiegelhof** is a modern arcade sheltering several more upscale antique shops. The **Galerie Lieve Hemel** (No. 3) has intriguing displays of paintings, sculpture, silverware, and jewelry by modern artists and artisans. Its quirky name, "Good Heavens Gallery," harks back to the low ceilings of the apartment that housed the owners' first gallery in 1968. The story goes that on first entering, visitors would invariably exclaim, "Good Heavens, mind your head!"

If the high prices in the Spiegelkwartier exceed the limits of your travel budget, take a stroll along Kerkstraat, which cuts across Nieuwe Spiegelstraat, where you will find shops selling crafts and pictures at somewhat more affordable prices.

Today, the stretch that runs east from Nieuwe Spiegelstraat up to Leidsestraat is home to several gay bars, hotels, and shops. Westward, Kerkstraat runs all the way round to Plantage, dotted with a mix of squats, low-cost housing, small neighborhood stores, budget hotels, and inexpensive cafés. ∎

Amsterdam Antiques Gallery

- ✉ Nieuwe Spiegelstraat 34
- 🚊 Tram: 6, 7, 10
- 🚢 Museumboot & Canal Bus

New Views of the Old City: Dinner Cruises on the Canal

An evening canal cruise offers a different perspective on Amsterdam, with canal houses illuminated by soft lights and candles, and bridges lined with hundreds of tiny fairy lights. The Canal Company (Weteringschans 26–1hg, tel 217-0500, canal.nl) offers a wealth of choice in evening cruises, from the Cocktail Cruise, which departs at 9 p.m. and includes cocktails and nibbles, to the Pizza Cruise, Candlelight Cruise, and the popular Dinner Cruise. This last option includes a four-course dinner, cooked fresh onboard, served during a 2.5-hour-long voyage along the canals with wine.

Alternatively, you can really push the boat out with Vinkeles on the Water: Guests staying at the Dylan Hotel (Keizersgracht 384, tel 530-2010, dylan amsterdam.com) can enjoy an intimate dinner (maximum eight guests) prepared by Michelin-starred chef Dennis Kuipers and served onboard a beautifully restored canal boat.

Gouden Bocht

The Gouden Bocht (Golden Bend) earned its name from the magnificence of its houses, which are larger than elsewhere on the canal belt. Adding to their grandeur is the use of sandstone instead of humble brick for the frontages. In style they are classical with elegant pillars, cornices, and pediments replacing the more traditional neck and bell gables.

The sandstone facade of a 17th-century Golden Bend building

Starting on the northern bank of the Herengracht, No. 475 is one of the canal belt's finest 18th-century houses. Built in 1733, it has a richly decorated central bay carved with volutes and foliage rising to a crest. On one side of this sits a female figure representing Plenty; on the other side, two children shake apples from a tree. Although previously attributed to the French Protestant refugee designer Daniel Marot

(1661–1752), who introduced the baroque Louis XV style to Amsterdam, historians now believe the building was constructed by another architect, based on Marot's published engravings.

Golden Age Wonder

Walking south along the canal, you will see **Herengracht 466** on the opposite bank, on the corner of Nieuwe Spiegelstraat and Herengracht. A good example of the Gouden Bocht's classical style, the house was built between 1669 and 1671 by Philips Vingboons and known as the Eagle because of the bird carved on its pediment. Next door, No. 468 and its neighbor, No. 470, built for brothers-in-law in 1665–1669, once shared a common facade. The buildings were thoroughly overhauled in 1949, when No. 470 was converted into the **Goethe Instituut** *(Herengracht 470, tel 531-2900).*

No. 474 (1666) is unusual in that it is the only single-width house on this stretch of the canal, providing a scale against which the grandiose proportions of the surrounding properties can be measured. Its neighbor, No. 476 (1667), has an opulent brick facade broken up by stone Corinthian pilasters, reflecting the owner's passion for the architecture of Andrea Palladio.

Cryptic Inscription

Back on the northern bank of Herengracht, **No. 495** is unusual in having a balcony above the front door, whose brasswork contains an inscribed quotation from the Roman writer and historian Sallust (86–34 B.C.): *"Omnia Orta Occidunt"* (All Creation Passes Away). The letters of the inscription also contain the date of the building (MDC-CVII—1707) in cryptic form.

No. 507 is a pleasing building built in 1666 with Corinthian pilasters, making its neighbor, **No. 505,** look rather antiquated with its old-fashioned bell gable. **No. 497** houses the unusual and idiosyncratic **KattenKabinet,** a gallery devoted to art with a feline theme. Cats are immortalized in every medium here, from Golden Age oils and Ancient Egyptian sculptures to contemporary lithographs, prints, and photographs, displayed in a number of beautifully restored rooms. Regardless of whether you are a cat lover or not, the KattenKabinet offers you an opportunity to admire the interiors of a grand canal house.

Peter the Great & Napoléon

Follow the Herengracht across Vijzelstraat, a broad and busy thoroughfare, to **No. 527,** which boasts a fine facade in Louis XVI style, with fluted Ionic pilasters rising to a pediment carved with an imperial eagle. This was once the Russian embassy, and it was here that Peter the Great, tsar of Russia, stayed during his visits to Amsterdam to study shipbuilding. Famous for his alcoholic excesses, the tsar had to pay a large sum of money for repairs to the house following his visit, during which the wall paintings were vandalized. A later visitor, Napoléon Bonaparte, displayed greater decorum when he came by in 1811.

On the far bank of the canal is **No. 520,** the official residence of Amsterdam's mayor, flying a flag with the Amsterdam coat of arms on it. To the left, you will see that **Nos. 504–510** form a group of four neck-gabled houses with boldly carved sidepieces. They depict, in turn, rampant heraldic dogs holding the owners' coats of arms, scrolls ending in a lion's

INSIDER TIP:

If you visit the Rijksmuseum [see pp. 192–197], seek out Gerrit Berckheyde's painting "The Bend in the Herengracht near the Nieuwe Spiegelstraat in Amsterdam" [1671–1672] to see how little this stretch of the Lord's Canal has changed.

—BARBARA A. NOE
*National Geographic Travel Books
Senior Editor*

foot motif, tritons cavorting in the waves and blowing their trumpets, and Neptune riding a dolphin while brandishing his trident.

KattenKabinet

- Map p. 158
- Herengracht 497
- 626-9040
- Closed Sat. & Sun. a.m.
- $
- Tram: 1, 2, 5, 16, 24, 25

kattenkabinet.nl

Tassenmuseum

- Map p. 159
- Herengracht 573
- 524-6452
- Closed Sat. & Sun. a.m.
- $$
- Tram: 4, 16, 24, 25

tassenmuseum.nl

Similar nautical motifs also appear on this side of the canal, at **No. 535,** which has art nouveau seahorses forming a frieze around the door, and at **No. 539,** with its sea gods reclining on the roof cornice and its caryatids supporting the first-floor balcony.

Confusion At the Moor's

On the opposite bank, **No. 514** is known as In de Mooriaantjes (At the Moor's) because of the black marble busts that flank the balcony above the entrance. The busts have often caused misunderstanding. The house was built for the Salm brothers as the headquarters of their insurance company, and the busts are 18th-century Italian, but their presence has led many to believe that the house was that of a slave trader. The hero of *La Chute (The Fall),* Albert Camus's 1950 novel, makes this assumption when he passes the house. Political radicals opposed to what they perceive as symbols of repression have repeatedly threatened to smash the sculptures. Farther down, at **No. 526,** is another building with a neck gable flanked by monstrous fish. At this point, the canal is interrupted by leafy Thorbeckeplein (see pp. 180–181), from where you can either continue along Herengracht or walk up Thorbeckeplein.

Handbags & Purses

Continuing along the Herengracht will bring you first to the quirky **Tassenmuseum** (Museum of Handbags and Purses; see sidebar above) at No. 573. Beyond this, you will cross

Visit the Tassenmuseum

It's a handbag-lover's heaven: Some 500 years of handbag history await your discovery in a beautiful canal house on Herengracht.

The Tassenmuseum (Museum of Bags and Purses, now located at Herengracht 573) was started by Hendrikje Ivo, who collected bags and purses for more than 35 years and invited fellow fans to admire them in her home.

Today, her daughter Sigrid Ivo curates the museum, which has grown into the world's largest handbag and purse collection and moved to premises large enough to accommodate it.

Utretchtsestraat, a lively street peppered with Indonesian restaurants, designer boutiques, music stores, and unusual interior design shops. Continuing along Herengracht, you will reach **No. 619,** which was built for Jan Six (1618–1700), the son of a wealthy merchant family who served as mayor of Amsterdam in 1691 and became a leading cultural figure in the Dutch Golden Age.

A devotee of the arts, Six was a friend and patron of Rembrandt's and built up an extraordinary collection of paintings, drawings, etchings, furniture, and artifacts, including a celebrated portrait of himself painted by Rembrandt.

His collection, known today as the **Collectie Six** (Six Collection), has been handed down through ten generations of the Six family and is one of the last great European family art legacies, incorporating works by Michelangelo, Vermeer, and Frans Hals. While many of the collection's prized pieces are on loan to Dutch and international museums, it is possible to view the remaining works in the palatial Six family home at Amstel 218 (only two minutes' walk from Herengracht 619). Visits are possible on weekdays from 10 a.m. to noon but granted exclusively upon request made via the website (*collectiesix.nl*).

Servants' Quarters

For a change from Herengracht, walk up Thorbeckeplein and turn left onto the colorful Reguliersdwarsstraat, a street lined with good restaurants, gay bars, and shops. Several of the properties on the left-hand side of the street as you walk west are housed in low two-story buildings, which are the coach houses of the grand houses on Herengracht.

Where Reguliersdwarsstraat emerges onto busy Vijzelstraat you will see the **NH Carlton Hotel** on the right, which dates from 1929. In its day, this was the most luxurious hotel in the Netherlands. Its construction marked the start of a scheme to widen and develop Vijzelstraat to form a wide avenue linking central Amsterdam to the southern suburbs. This controversial scheme, which would have involved the demolition of several fine buildings, was abandoned during the 1930s Depression. But fate took a hand in 1943 when a British Halifax bomber crashed at the back of the hotel, its bombs and fuel causing fires that destroyed many nearby buildings. That explains the presence of the bulky and unfriendly office block on concrete stilts, built in 1964, to the rear of the Carlton Hotel. ∎

Longing looks at the Tassenmuseum

Rembrandtplein & Thorbeckeplein

Rembrandtplein and Thorbeckeplein are two adjoining squares ringed by sidewalk cafés. Both are frequented by tourists and night owls—and the tacky neon-lit trappings that often accompany them.

The Rain Restaurant, a lively café at Rembrandtplein 44

Tuschinski Theater

🅰 Map p. 158

✉ Reguliersbree-straat 26–28

☎ 0900-1458

🚋 Tram: 4, 9, 16, 24, 25

pathe.nl

Rembrandtplein

Originally a gateway through the medieval defensive walls of Amsterdam, Rembrandtplein became the site of the city's Botermarkt, or butter market, at some point around the middle of the 17th-century. The market continued to operate here until 1876, when a statue of Rembrandt van Rijn, who had lived nearby, was erected in the center of the square, which was thereafter named after him.

An impressive cluster of bronze-cast sculptures now gathers at the base of Rembrandt's statue, in a lifelike representation of the artist's famous painting "The Night Watch." The **Tuschinski Theater** (see p. 262) lies to the west of the square on Reguliersbreestraat. This twin-towered building bristles with wrought-iron decorations, looking like a palace of entertainment in the futuristic city created by Fritz Lang for his 1926 film *Metropolis.* Founded by Abram Tuschinski (a Polish Jew who died at Auschwitz), the movie theater opened in 1921, and the glitzy art deco furnishings have been restored to their original glory.

Thorbeckeplein

To the south of Rembrandtplein is another small square ringed by bars and nightclubs. Originally known as Kaasplein (Cheese Square), because it was once the site of the city's cheese market, it was renamed **Thorbeckeplein** in 1876 in honor of Johan Thorbecke (1798–1872), the reforming politician elected first prime minister of the Netherlands in 1848.

Thorbecke's statue, at the southern end of the square, looks up **Reguliersgracht.** The name of this canal refers to the Reguliers, a monastic order whose monastery here burned down in 1532. Plans to fill in the canal to create a tramway were opposed at the start of the 20th century, thus preserving what is arguably the most picturesque stretch of canal in Amsterdam.

The canal is at its most photogenic at the junction with Keizersgracht, a spot known as the Seven Bridges because of the number of humpbacked bridges in the view—three of them on the junction itself. At night the outlines of the bridges are illuminated by strings of white lights, making the view even more attractive.

All the houses surrounding the junction lean in a pronounced manner. These tilting facades are a deliberate feature of buildings that had warehouse storage space in their lofts. The facades were built "in flight"—tilting forward, so that goods being winched up to the loft had sufficient clearance, and would not bang or drag against the front.

The **Museum Van Loon** (see p. 183) lies on the opposite bank of Keizersgracht. Continuing up the canal brings you to the start of the Amstel walk

INSIDER TIP:

Door 74 [Reguliers-dwarsstraat 74] is like a secret speakeasy cocktail bar. Phone 0634/04-5122 on the day you want to visit to make a reservation, leave a message, and you'll receive a text message advising you when to arrive.

—PAUL RÖMER
Managing Editor,
National Geographic Traveler
magazine in the Netherlands

(see pp. 186–188) and will lead you to Reguliersgracht Nos. 57 and 63, on the left. Both are built in the style known as "Carpenter's Gothic," so called because they were built by carpenters in order to show off their skills in decorative woodwork. ∎

Canal House Museums

A cluster of museums in old canal houses re-create Amsterdam's Golden Age: Het Grachtenhuis Museum recounts the history of the development of the canal belt; the Museum Van Loon and the Museum Willet-Holthuysen provide a more personal account of their previous owners.

The enchanting gardens of the Museum Van Loon

Het Grachtenhuis

- Map p. 158
- Herengracht 386
- 523-1822
- Closed Mon.
- $$$ (discounts if bought online)
- Tram: 1, 2, 5

hetgrachtenhuis.nl

Het Grachtenhuis Museum

Designed by the ubiquitous Philips Vingboons for the wealthy merchant Karel Gerards in 1667, Herengracht 386 has always been a prestigious house. Several important bankers and politicians have called it home, including American president John Adams. It was here too that Dutch loans given by the Amsterdam banker Jan Willink to the United States government were signed in the 18th century.

Today, thanks to the endeavors of a Dutch industrialist who purchased the house in 2009 and transformed it into a museum, it should be the first stop for anyone seeking to understand the 400-year history of the canal belt, recognized by UNESCO as a World Heritage site in 2010.

A 40-minute audio tour and interactive exhibits lead you through the ages, sitting in on 17th-century town planning meetings with the visionary Hendrick Staets and peering through the windows of a model canal house (built in the tradition of the Golden Age doll house), enriched with holograms of its past and current residents.

Museum Van Loon

The imposing **Museum Van Loon,** the former house of the regent Van Loon family, is at No. 672 Keizersgracht. Both this house and No. 674 were owned by a wealthy merchant, Jeremias van Raey, who commissioned the celebrated architect Adriaan Dortsman to design them. Van Raey rented No. 672 to the painter Ferdinand Bol (1616–1680), a pupil of Rembrandt's. The Van Loon connection dates from 1884, when Jonkheer van Loon, the wealthy descendant of a founder of the Dutch East India Company, bought the house as a wedding present for his son. The family still own the property.

Today's museum is a Golden Age time capsule, filled with 17th-century interior details such as ornate period furniture, precious silver and Delftware, and Van Loon family portraits, which stud the walls. The property also boasts a beautiful garden laid out in formal style and bordered by the classical facade of the restored Coach House, which houses many original Van Loon family carriages, harnesses, and livery as well as temporary exhibitions.

Museum Willet-Holthuysen

Built in 1685, Herengracht 605 was redesigned in 1739 to feature its fashionable Louis XIV facade. Contemporary visitors enter through the basement kitchens, where elaborate meals were once prepared for the wealthy guests of the owners, Abraham Willet and Sandrina Holthuysen. Willet was an avid collector of art, and his marriage to the wealthy Holthuysen allowed him to refurbish the house as a showcase for his glass, silver, and porcelain collections. Mrs. Willet-Holthuysen bequeathed the house to the city in 1895 as a museum.

The museum has several splendid rooms, including a magnificent ballroom and a lavish dining room set with silver and crystal. ■

Museum Van Loon
- Map p. 158
- Keizersgracht 672
- 624-5255
- Closed Tues.
- $$
- Tram: 16, 24, 25

museumvanloon.nl

Museum Willet-Holthuysen
- Map p. 159
- Herengracht 605
- 523-1822
- $$
- Tram: 4, 9, 14

willetholthuysen.nl

The Foam Photography Museum

The Foam Photography Museum *(Keizersgracht 609, tel 551-6500, $$, foam.org)* is an internationally recognized museum exhibiting all genres of photography, including fine art, documentary, applied, historical, and contemporary. The museum issues its own international photography magazine *(Foam Magazine)* and organizes special guided tours, lectures and discussions, films, and other events, while Foam Editions sells limited-edition prints from both well-known and up-and-coming photographers.

Photographs are displayed in a number of galleries throughout the museum, including the large, bright Tuinzalen (Garden Halls), which overlook Foam's attactive garden courtyard; the windowless Fodorzalen (Fodor Halls), in which the museum's headline shows are typically displayed; and the contemplative Voorzalen (Front Halls), which retain many of the old canal house's original features. The museum offers free guided tours on Thursdays at 7:30 p.m. and regularly runs photography workshops.

Hermitage Amsterdam

Located on the banks of the Amstel River in a classically proportioned building dating back to 1681, the Hermitage Amsterdam is western Europe's sole independently managed branch of St Petersburg's State Hermitage Museum. Hermitage Amsterdam stages two large-scale, temporary exhibitions each year, drawing on the collections and scholarship of Russia's museums.

Hermitage Amsterdam

- 🅰 Map p. 159
- ✉ Amstel 51
- ☎ 530-7488
- 💲 $$$
- 🚋 Tram: 9

hermitage.nl

From his youth, Tsar Peter the Great collected art, a passion that led him to found Russia's first museum, planting the seed for St. Petersburg's Hermitage. He also had a special affinity for Amsterdam, having lived in the city for several years. Relations between the two nations have endured through the centuries, culminating in the launch of the Hermitage Amsterdam in 2009.

INSIDER TIP:

Back in St. Petersburg, the original Hermitage once enticed visitors with a free shot of vodka. No such policy applies here, but the café Neva is open to all, even if you don't have a ticket for the museum.

—GABRIELLA LE BRETON
National Geographic author

The building in which the Hermitage Amsterdam is housed was built in 1681 as the Amstelhof, a nursing home for elderly women. At that time, the Amstelhof's classical facade was the city's longest, extending 335 feet (102 m) along the River Amstel. Today, visitors enter the building by way of the large **Ossenpoort** (Oxen Gate), the former tradesman's entrance, and walk through the large open courtyard to the reception. The wings that once provided shelter for the women are now hung with priceless artworks, with rotating exhibitions that range from vast canvases by Monet and Gauguin and the works of the Prophets of the Avant-Garde, such as Bonnard and Denis, to glittering displays of Peter the Great's jewels, paintings, and personal effects. In echoes of the tsar's palaces, long wings of small rooms, painted in rich colors, are connected by open doorways in an almost dizzying lesson in perspective. While the exhibition space is relatively small, the quality of works on display is exceptional.

The Hermitage Amsterdam hosts concerts and lectures in the restored **Church Hall.** It also boasts a large retail store, well-stocked with art books, Russian literature, music, and films, as well as select pieces relating to current exhibitions, and a contemporary café/restaurant, Neva. The Hermitage for Children, housed in the adjoining Neerlandia building on Nieuwe Herengracht, offers five workshops, two classrooms, a canteen, and a gift shop, and is an entertaining place for children to discover and develop their creative talent. ∎

Houseboats

Some 2,200 licensed houseboats ride at anchor inside Amsterdam's boundaries, of which about 700 are tethered within the city center. This aquatic lifestyle came about through the happy confluence of two factors: the postwar housing shortage and the modernization of the Dutch cargo fleet, the latter of which made available a number of surplus ships.

The 1960s and '70s saw a boom in houseboat living as hippies and political activists embraced this inexpensive, alternative way of life. Walking up Prinsengracht, you'll quickly discern that the section of the canal belt from Raadhuisstraat to Leidsegracht boasts an unusually high number of houseboats. These range in style from beautifully restored seagoing barges to ramshackle sheds. In theory, if rarely in practice, no houseboat exceeds 50 feet (15m) in length or rises higher than 8 feet (2.5m) above the waterline.

Rising Costs

Living on a houseboat is no longer cheap. The cost of mooring licenses soared when the city council stopped issuing new permits in the 1980s. A sound boat will cost you dearly, although an ark—a houseboat built on a hull not constructed to sail—is cheaper. Concrete hulls are low maintenance, but owners of steel- or iron-hulled boats must check for signs of corrosion every three to four

A cozy houseboat moored along a sunny Amsterdam canal

years; this typically results in an expensive trip to the shipyard. As well as maintenance and annual premiums, there is also the cost of paying for a connection to the city sewage system.

Given all these expenses—not to mention property tax and diesel fuel, plus standard costs such as running water, electricity, telephone, and cable TV—living on a boat is no cheaper than buying an apartment. Why, then, would anyone bother? The answer has more to do with the heart than the head. Some people just won't have it any other way: They love their boats and everything related with life afloat.

Houseboat Museum

To learn more about this waterborne way of life, the best place to start is the Houseboat Museum, moored opposite Prinsengracht 296 (tel 427-0750, houseboatmuseum.nl, closed Mon. in summer, Mon.–Thurs. in winter, tram: 13, 14, 17). The Hendrika Maria was built in 1914 and still has her original skipper's cupboard bed, as well as museum photos, memorabilia, and model ships.

A Walk Along the Amstel River

This last section of the Grachtengordel, abutting the western bank of the wide Amstel River, leads to the edge of the canal belt. Construction here came to a halt in the 17th century. This explains why many of the buildings on the opposite bank of the Amstel are of relatively recent vintage; they date from the mid-19th century, when the semicircular belt of canals enclosing the medieval core of Amsterdam was finally completed.

The Magere Brug (Skinny Bridge) on the Amstel River opens for barges headed to the IJ River.

Start at the big, windy square called **Amstelveld** (Amstel Field). Dominating Amstelveld is the 1669 **Amstelkerk,** looking like a New England church, with its white-painted clapboard construction. It was built as a "preaching barn" and was intended to be temporary, pending the construction of a new brick and stone church. A century later, the church had still not been built, and the "barn" had acquired the appearance of a permanent structure, with ancillary buildings up against its walls, providing homes for the verger and bailiff. By the 19th century, it became obvious that no new church would

NOT TO BE MISSED:

Magere Brug • Museum Willet-Holthuysen • Blauwbrug

be built, and the congregation paid for the remodeling of the interior, which is now largely used for musical recitals. Café Nel stands up against the sunny south-facing wall of the church—a popular spot with parents who bring their children to play in the adjacent playground.

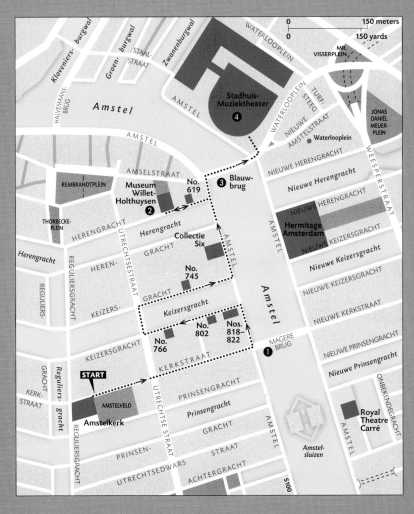

0   150 meters
0   150 yards

Kloveniers- burgwal
Groen- burgwal
STAAL-STRAAT
Zwanenburgwal
WATERLOOPLEIN
MR. VISSERPLEIN
HALVEMANS-BRUG
Amstel
AMSTEL
Stadhuis-Muziektheater ❹
WATERLOOPLEIN
NIEUWE
TURFSTEEG
JONAS DANIËL MEIJER-PLEIN
AMSTEL
AMSTELSTRAAT
Waterlooplein
AMSTELSTRAAT
NIEUWE HERENGRACHT
WEESPERSTRAAT
REMBRANDTPLEIN
Museum Willet-Holthuysen ❷
No. 619
❸ Blauw-brug
Nieuwe Herengracht
NIEUWE HERENGRACHT
THORBECKE-PLEIN
HERENGRACHT
Herengracht
Collectie Six
Hermitage Amsterdam
NIEUWE KEIZERSGRACHT
Herengracht
HEREN-GRACHT
GRACHT
No. 745
Amstel
Nieuwe Keizersgracht
UTRECHTSESTRAAT
NIEUWE KEIZERSGRACHT
REGULIERSGRACHT
KEIZERS-
GRACHT
Keizersgracht
No. 802
Nos. 818–822
Amstel
NIEUWE KERKSTRAAT
Herengracht
REGULIERSGRACHT
KEIZERSGRACHT
No. 766
KERKSTRAAT
MAGERE BRUG
❶
NIEUWE PRINSENGRACHT
Nieuwe Prinsengracht
ONBEKENDEGRACHT
GRACHT
Reguliers- gracht
START
AMSTELVELD
PRINSENGRACHT
KERK-STRAAT
UTRECHTSE STRAAT
Prinsengracht
AMSTEL
Royal Theatre Carré
Amstelkerk
REGULIERSGRACHT
PRINSEN-
GRACHT
STRAAT
Amstel-sluizen
UTRECHTSEDWARS
ACHTERGRACHT
S100

Walk east, down Kerkstraat, with its boutiques and art galleries, to the **Magere Brug** ❶, one of Amsterdam's most famous landmarks (outlined by white lights at night and floodlit in summer). The name is often translated as "Skinny Bridge," but a more faithful translation would be "Meager Bridge," a reference to the disproportionate fragility of its timber construction in relation to the might of the Amstel River, which it crosses. Originally built in the 17th century, it was almost entirely rebuilt after World War II—desperate Amsterdammers

⚑ See also area map p. 159
▶ Amstelveld
🕐 2 hours
↔ 0.9 mile (1.4 km)
▶ Stadhuis–Muziektheater

used the timbers as firewood during the final winter of the war. The bridge was operated manually until 1994. Large barges pass through, since this branch of the Amstel provides a link from the IJ River to the inland waterways system of the southern Netherlands.

Looking across the river, you will see the **Royal Theater Carré** *(Amstel 115–125, tel 524-9455)* to the right, with its ballooning green roof. Built in 1887 as a permanent tent for the Oscar Carré Circus, the theater still stages circus shows, as well as concerts, plays, musicals, and comedy performances.

At the Magere Brug, turn left down the Amstel and left again down **Keizersgracht. No. 802** is a late 19th-century former dairy (built for the Plancius company, which prided itself on supplying milk untainted by drowned cats, rats, or mice!), while the highly ornate **No. 766,** with its art deco windows and balcony, was once the premises of a baker. In the early days of the canal belt, such a commercial site would have been relegated to the side streets, but here it occupies a prime canalside position.

Turn right at Utrechtsestraat and right again to return down the opposite bank of the Keizersgracht. Halfway down, at **No. 745,** is a unique sight: a house with a garage. The garage door once led to a coach house and stable block in the garden to the rear of the house. For 300 years the passage of horses,

coaches, and carriages, and latterly of motor cars and vans, was the cause of constant disputes between the owners and their neighbors. The owners voluntarily gave up the use of the garage in the 1970s, but for three centuries it enjoyed the unique status of being the only canalside property in Amsterdam with vehicular access.

Head on to the beautiful ornate doorcase of the **Museum Willet-Holthuysen** ❷ (see p. 183). On the opposite bank to the museum, Nos. 568 and 570 have gables featuring giant polar bears and lizards, a splendidly exotic piece of decoration.

Return to the Amstel and turn left for a view of the **Blauwbrug** ❸ (Blue Bridge). The name derives from the fact that its timber predecessor was painted blue, with bridge lamps topped by imperial crowns and set on granite columns clasped by ships' prows. Built in 1884, the Blue Bridge draws its inspiration from the Pont Alexandre III in Paris. Straight ahead lies the bulky **Stadhuis– Muziektheater** ❹ (see p. 105), clad in the white marble that has given rise to its local nickname: "the set of dentures."

Potted flowers and the ubiquitous Amsterdam bicycle set the scene along Keizersgracht canal.

World-class art museums and the Concertgebouw; Vondelpark, Amsterdam's green lung; and the multicultural De Pijp district

The Museum Quarter, Vondelpark, & De Pijp

Introduction & Map   190–191

Rijksmuseum   192–197

Experience: The World of the Dutch Masters   195

Van Gogh Museum   198–200

Feature: Vincent van Gogh   201

Stedelijk Museum   202–203

A Walk Around the Museum Quarter & Vondelpark   204–205

De Pijp   206–207

Experience: Wake Up to Coffee & Auntie's Cake   207

Experience: Enjoying the Local Parks   208

More Places to Visit in the Museum Quarter, Vondelpark, & De Pijp   209–210

Hotels & Restaurants in the Museum Quarter, Vondelpark, & De Pijp   251–253

"Allow Us to Introduce Ourselves" by Pieter Pietersz at the Rijksmuseum

The Museum Quarter, Vondelpark, & De Pijp

After the construction bonanza of the Golden Age, Amsterdam's expansion ground to a virtual halt. However, as the city began to flourish once more during the second half of the 19th century, the architect H. P. Berlage was commissioned in 1900 to design an expansion scheme, leading to the development of Amsterdam Zuid (Amsterdam South).

Berlage's initial plan for the underdeveloped area south of Amsterdam between the Amstel and Schinkel rivers envisioned traditional winding streets and was rejected by the city council. Berlage's second plan, submitted in 1914 for four new districts (Nieuwe Pijp, Stadionbuurt, Apollobuurt, and Rivierenbuurt) with small side streets intersected by straight, wide streets and punctuated by squares, was approved, and building commenced in 1917.

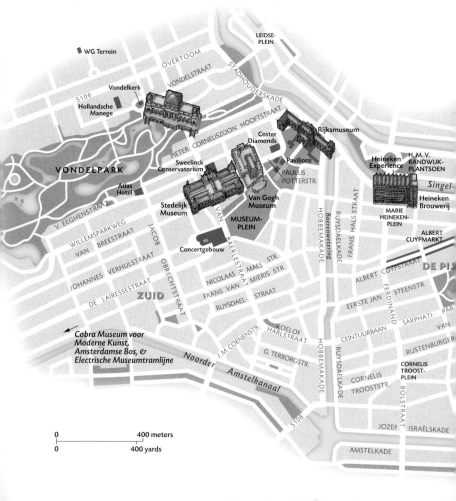

By this time, Amsterdam Zuid already incorporated the new Rijksmuseum, Stedelijk Museum, and Concertgebouw, which were clustered around Museumplein. Since 2013, these two museums and the Van Gogh Museum have been repositioned to open onto the Museumplein, as per the original plan.

While many of the grand houses in this blossoming Museum Quarter were built in the Arts and Crafts style, Berlage was a pioneer of social equality and favored large social housing blocks built in the groundbreaking architectural style of the Amsterdam School, such as De Dageraad (see p. 209), over private homes.

Within strolling distance from Museumplein are the expansive green spaces of Vondelpark, much loved by Amsterdammers for jogging, dog-walking, tai chi, skating, and weekend picnics. The park is also the venue for festivals and national celebrations such as King's Day (April 27).

NOT TO BE MISSED:

Exploring the magnificent rooms of the Rijksmuseum   192–197

Enjoying a Rijksmuseum canal cruise   195

Getting acquainted with Vincent van Gogh   198–201

Love it or hate it? Deciding about the Stedelijk   202–203

A picnic in Vondelpark 204–205

Multicultural De Pijp   206–207

The hustle and bustle of the Albert Cuypmarkt   206–207

Enjoying an ice-cold glass of Holland's favorite beer at the Heineken Experience   210

Farther south and east from Museumplein, De Pijp has developed over recent years into a vibrant, multicultural dining and nightlife hot spot. The boisterous Albert Cuypmarkt dates back to 1905 and bursts with delicacies, clothing, and knickknacks from across the world, while the streets surrounding it abound with quirky restaurants, cafés, bars, and boutiques. ■

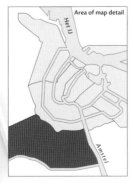

Area of map detail

Rijksmuseum

From a small core of paintings belonging to the Dutch royal family in the 18th century, the Rijksmuseum has developed into one of the world's most comprehensive collections, open to an admiring public 365 days a year.

The Rijksmuseum at the Museumplein, reopened in 2013, once more the cultural heart of Amsterdam

Rijksmuseum
- Map p. 190
- Museumstraat 1
- 674-7000
- $$$
- Tram: 2, 5, 7, 10, 12
- Museumboot

rijksmuseum.nl

In addition to spending time admiring Rembrandt's masterpieces, visitors to the Rijksmuseum can experience 800 years of Dutch history through some 8,000 artworks and artifacts presented in a total of 80 galleries.

In April 2013, the Rijksmuseum emerged from an intensive, ten-year process of renovation, rebuilding, and restoration. To the relief of the Dutch, the transformation left the magnificent exterior of Pierre Cuypers's building untouched, with its combination of Gothic and Renaissance elements and rich decorations as striking now as they were at the time of the building's construction in 1876.

Spanish Influence

However, the interior of the 19th-century building was transformed by Spanish architects Cruz y Ortiz, who were given the truly Herculean task of implementing the renovation.

The concepts for the restoration were in keeping with the clear layout originally conceived by Cuypers. Many of the architectural additions made through the 20th century have been removed, stripping the building back to its former glory.

A wonderfully large, bright **atrium** ushers visitors in from the Museumplein, with a glass roof and pale polished Portuguese stone floors. The area was created by revealing two original inner courtyards, sinking the floor to below ground level, and connecting them via an underground zone beneath the original passageway that ran through the building. The **passageway** features glass walls through which to admire the courtyards. The museum's high-ceilinged, late-19th-century galleries have also been restored to their former glory, revealing the original richly decorated walls and ceilings, yet are complemented by state-of-the-art lighting and climate-control features. Cuypers's signature style is best preserved in the **library,** where his original design and ornaments remain virtually untouched.

Return of the Masters

The Rijksmuseum's famous collection is presented in a chronological sequence spanning 800 years (1200 to 2000)

of Dutch art and history, set in an international context. It draws visitors effortlessly through its impressive array of galleries spread across four floors. The bright, spacious rooms are filled with objects of interest and beauty: Exquisite paintings, prints, photographs, sculptures, silver, porcelain, Delftware, furnishings, jewelry, costumes, and other artifacts.

More than 30 galleries are dedicated to the glory of the Golden Age, with Gerrit Berckheyde's magically detailed paintings of Amsterdam, Haarlem, and The Hague showing how little many of those cities streets have changed in the intervening centuries. At the heart of this section is the breathtaking **Gallery of Honour,** which presents the most prized pieces of the collection from illustrious masters including Rembrandt, Vermeer, Jan Steen, and Frans Hals.

THE RIJKMUSEUM'S CYCLE PATH: To celebrate the spirit of the ordinary Amsterdammer, take a cycle ride along this storied bicycle path. Plans for the Rijksmuseum's renovation were stalled (at considerable cost) when it emerged that they involved the destruction of the old bicycle "tunnel" that ran through the museum grounds.

Despite the protestations of the Rijksmuseum's curators and architects, Amsterdam's cyclists won the battle: The plans were redrawn and the shortcut reopened shortly after the museum did, with hundreds of cyclists turning out to pedal through the beautiful arched tunnel in celebration, ringing their bells triumphantly.

With its vaulted ceilings and intricately painted arches, the Gallery of Honour sets the scene well for the vistor. Every painting here seems specially chosen to reveal Dutch art in

The Great Hall of the Rijksmuseum: a work of art in itself

all its vibrancy and variety—from religious pictures, portraits, and still lifes to morality tales, tavern and winter scenes, and sea battles. Johannes Vermeer (1632–1675) shows scenes from everyday life—"The Milkmaid," "Woman in Blue Reading a Letter," and "The Little Street"—yet they are painted with such an assured feeling for the effects of light that they seem to glow with luminescence. The artist Abraham van den Tempel (1622–1672) depicts "David Leeuw with His Family" as the epitome of marital unity and happy family life by showing them making harmonious music. Alongside, "The Merry Family" by Jan Steen (1626–1679) depicts the same subject, but there is an underlying sinister parody of harmony, with everyone, including the children, engaged in a drunken tavern song. If the moral isn't obvious, the artist has inscribed the title in Dutch—"Soo De Oude Songen, Soo Pijpen De Jonge" ("As the Old Sing, So the Young Chirp")—so beware of setting a bad example.

However, it is the work of Rembrandt that steals the show here in the Gallery of Honour, with a remarkable collection of his paintings on display. "The Syndics of the Drapers' Guild" is a brilliant and compelling work that shows Rembrandt's ability to transform a commonplace subject into a work of genius. "The Jewish Bride" is notable not so much as a study in bourgeois complacency but for the technique that Rembrandt employed to emphasize the profligate extravagance of their gold-encrusted clothes: The thickly layered slabs of red and yellow paint give a striking three-dimensional quality to the man's sleeve.

EXPERIENCE: The World of the Dutch Masters

In conjunction with the **Blue Boat Company** *(Stadhouderskade 30, tel 679-1370, blueboat.nl)*, the Rijksmuseum offers a waterborne art history tour, which brings to life the places and people featured in the museum. As you cruise along Amsterdam's canals, your personal audio tour will not only provide an informative, historical tour of the city but will also point out places and houses depicted in paintings exhibited in the Rijksmuseum, as well as locations where artists such as Rembrandt and Vermeer lived and painted. A souvenir booklet contains copies of the art works mentioned in your tour as well as priority entry to the Rijksmuseum.

It is worth extending your ticket to include entrance to the Museum Het Rembrandthuis (see pp. 103–104) and discounted entry to Het Grachtenhuis Museum (see p. 182).

The Night Watch: The most famous work of art in the Rijksmuseum is probably Rembrandt's "Night Watch," although it is more correctly known as "The Militia Company of Captain Frans Banning Cocq and Lieutenant Willem van Ruytenburch." The colossal painting was the only piece in the Rijksmuseum to be returned to its original place following the renovation, in its dedicated **Night Watch Gallery.** In 2013, watched closely by hundreds of Amsterdammers, the monumental work was wheeled from its temporary home in the Philips Wing and winched through a specially cut hole in the ceiling of the museum to its original spot.

A clue to Rembrandt's true intention with this monumental work is the spotlit figure of the girl in the center of the painting. What is she doing here, with her golden dress, her moneybag, and a dead cockerel hanging from her waist? She seems to be laughing at the posing pretensions of the militiamen, and the cockerel could be a pun on the name of Captain Cocq.

20th-Century Galleries

The Rijksmuseum presents a fascinating group of galleries focused on the 20th century, with numerous paintings, furniture,

Model of a 74-gun Dutch battleship, now on display at the Rijksmuseum

Rijksmuseum: Two Hundred Years in the Making

It could well be argued that it took over two centuries for the Rijksmuseum to really find its feet. The collection first opened to the public as De Nationale Kunst-Galerij (National Art Gallery) in 1800. It moved several times before being established in Amsterdam as Het Koninklijke Museum (The Royal Museum) by decree of the King of the Netherlands, Louis Bonaparte, in 1808. Seven years later, in 1815, King Willem I gave the collection its current name, Het Rijksmuseum (The State Museum). However, only in 1885 did the Rijksmuseum move to its current building, which emerged from a ten-year refurbishment in 2013.

photography, posters, film, and the oldest existing authentic Dutch airplane (1918), conjuring a vivid picture of Dutch culture in the past century.

These 20th-century collections enable visitors to enjoy famous and unexpected objects from the fields of design, the applied arts, science, and national history. The scope of the eclectic exhibitions ranges from a rare white Rietveld chair (1923) to the legendary "Mondrian" dress (1965/1966), created by celebrated French fashion designer Yves Saint Laurent and based on the work of the Dutch artist, to the powerful painting entitled "The Square Man" (1951) by one of the founders of CoBrA, Karel Appel, and a relief by Zero artist Jan Schoonhoven (1963).

Asian Pavilion

In addition to its collection of Dutch art and artifacts, the Rijksmuseum houses a rich collection of Asian art, beautifully presented in the Asian Pavilion. Situated facing the Museumplein in the garden to the south of the Rijksmuseum, the irregularly shaped, two-story pavilion is surrounded by water. With its walls faced in pale Portugese stone and glass, it stands out well against the warm redbrick walls of the Rijksmuseum to which it is linked by an underground passageway.

The Asian Pavilion showcases objects and works of art from China, Japan, Indonesia, India, Vietnam, and Thailand, dating from 2000 B.C. to A.D. 2000. Keep an eye out for the beautiful 12th-century bronze figure of the Dancing Shiva (Chola dynasty, southern India), the Hindu deity whose nature combines the opposites of creation and destruction, visibility and invisibility, and masculine and feminine.

The Garden

Based on a 1901 design by Pierre Cuypers, the Rijkmuseum's extensive gardens favor the traditional formal style, liberally dotted with restored statues and fragments of ancient buildings. These pieces are complemented each summer, when the museum hosts its annual international sculpture exhibitions. If you are traveling with young children, they will enjoy the time spent around the fountain, pond, greenhouse, and the children's garden.

The Rijksmuseum's multi-disciplinary education center is also located in the garden, in the historic Teekenschool (Drawing School). This sensitively restored building, conceived by Cuypers, was first opened in 1892 as a drawing school, a forerunner of the Gerrit Rietveld Academy. Today it is an engaging and inspiring center of art education, with three modern studios accommodating a diverse range of workshops and activities for visitors of all ages.

INSIDER TIP:

If the museum isn't too busy, lie briefly on the floor to admire British artist Richard Wright's bewitching network of black stars on the ceiling of the room adjacent to "The Night Watch."

—JUSTIN KAVANAGH
National Geographic
International Editions editor

Philips Wing

Used during the refurbishment of the Rijksmuseum, the Philips Wing is itself undergoing extensive renovations in the aftermath of the museum's reopening. The wing is to become a new home for temporary exhibitions and features a new café and restaurant. ■

"The Merry Family" by Jan Steen at the Rijksmuseum

Van Gogh Museum

Standing out from the grand neo-Gothic villas lining Paulus Potterstraat is a building of stark simplicity. The white concrete cube, designed in 1963 by Dutch modernist Gerrit Rietveld and complemented in 1999 by an elliptical extension designed by Kisho Kurokawa, serves as the perfect foil for the vibrant works of Van Gogh and his contemporaries.

The master's work beguiles visitors at the Van Gogh Museum.

Van Gogh Museum

- 🗺 Map p. 190
- ✉ Paulus Potterstraat 7
- ☎ 570-5200
- 💲 $$$
- 🚊 Tram: 2, 3, 5, 12, 16
- ⛴ Museumboot

vangoghmuseum .com

The Van Gogh Museum boasts the world's largest collection of the artist's work, and its popularity means you should book your tickets online and arrive early or late in the day to enjoy it in relative quiet. It remains open until 10 p.m. on Friday nights, lending it a lively, inclusive atmosphere. The museum is an exploration of Van Gogh in the context of the art and culture of his time, featuring works by contemporaries such as Monet, Gauguin, and Seurat.

The Museum

Upon Vincent van Gogh's death in 1890, his unsold works were left to his brother, Theo, who in turn left the collection to his wife, Johanna van Gogh-Bonger. While Johanna sold many of Vincent's paintings, she kept a private collection of his works, which was inherited by her son Vincent Willem van Gogh in 1925. Loaned to the Stedelijk Museum Amsterdam for many years, it found its current home in the Van Gogh Museum on Museumplein in 1973.

Celebrating its 40th anniversary by reopening in 2013 after a major renovation, the most recent improvement for the Van Gogh Museum is the new entrance building. Designed by the firm of the late architect Kisho Kurokawa, who designed the museum's exhibition wing, the modern glass entrance provides greater harmony not only between the main building and extension, but also with the neighboring Stedelijk Museum and Rijksmuseum, reorienting all three attractions to open out onto the Museumplein.

The Collection

The four-story Rietveld building houses the permanent collection, café, and shop. The Kurokawa wing, accessed from the Rietveld building via an underground tunnel called "The Node," is used for major temporary exhibitions.

The Rietveld building features a chronological display of the works of Van Gogh from 1880 to 1890. During this time, Van Gogh was astonishingly productive: The 200 or so major works in this museum were produced in the space of a decade, during which time he also made more than 800 paintings, 1,000 drawings, and untold numbers of sketches and watercolors.

Passing through the museum, you appreciate Van Gogh's rapid development from his early works, such as "View of the Sea at Scheveningen" (1882) and "Cottages" (1883), to "The Potato Eaters" (1885), his first large-scale painting. Moving to Paris, Van Gogh embraced new techniques inspired by the Impressionists and Japanese paintings, as reflected in "The Courtesan" and "The Bridge

After Rain" (1887). Too poor to afford a model, Van Gogh made several "Self Portraits" that reflect his nascent style of powerful colors and strong lines.

Provençal Inspiration: It was in 1888, when Van Gogh moved to Arles, that he found his true style. The light, warmth, and rich colors of Provence set him alight, and he poured out works that first year in celebration: "The White Orchard," "The Pink Peach Tree," "Wheatfield,"

Skip the Lines

Avoid the lengthy ticket queues for the Van Gogh Museum by popping into Coster Diamonds (adjacent to the museum at Paulus Potterstraat 2), where you can buy tickets at the same price and walk straight to the front of lines. While you're there, consider taking a Coster Diamonds tour, which will inform you of the history and processes behind the diamond industry. You can also book tickets ahead of time online at *vangogh museum.globalticket.nl/*.

and "The Harvest." The artist abandoned his former realism and somber tones for simple subjects, which he imbued with emotive force through the use of warm, vibrant colors. The predominant colors of his palette were yellow, orange, ocher, and green, as reflected in his 1889 paintings "The Yellow House,"

"The Bedroom," "Gauguin's Chair," and one of five paintings of "Sunflowers" that he made at this time. Eager to establish an artists' colony in Arles, Van Gogh encouraged Paul Gauguin to join him there. However, they quarreled frequently, and in the aftermath of a row, Van Gogh attempted to cut off his own ear, sending Gauguin fleeing back to Paris. Van Gogh

INSIDER TIP:

If you're keen to learn more about Van Gogh, the excellent website *vangoghletters.org* features all the letters written by and to him.

—GABRIELLA LE BRETON
National Geographic author

admitted himself to a mental health clinic in St. Rémy, where he was forbidden to paint until he recovered. The work he produced after his recuperation includes some of his lightest, best-known pieces, such as "Irises" and "Almond Blossom," as well as the dark, brooding "Undergrowth" and "Pietà."

In May 1890, Van Gogh moved to Auvers, an artists' village near Paris. He produced a great number of paintings of the local surroundings and people, several of which have been interpreted as reflections of his deepening depression, such as "Tree Roots" and "Wheatfields Under Thunderclouds." His

letters home offer few clues to the reason for his imminent suicide, though they do voice his concern about his lack of commercial success; he felt guilt that he was a financial burden on his brother. Vincent van Gogh tragically shot himself in the chest on July 27, 1890, and died two days later from his wounds.

Getting to Know Van Gogh

In addition to admiring Van Gogh's artwork, visitors are encouraged to learn more about his life, artistic identity, development, and unique techniques. Several of his personal effects are found in the museum, such as original sketchbooks, paint tubes, his only surviving palette, and items he used in his still-life paintings.

As visitors view the collection highlights in chronological order —"Self-portrait," "Irises," "Almond Blossom," "The Yellow House," and "Sunflowers"—they will gain a sense of the context of the life from which these masterpieces emerged. The museum showcases paintings, drawings, objects, and many of Van Gogh's letters to set the scene for each work.

Considerable attention is also devoted to Van Gogh's contemporaries. You will not only discover who inspired Van Gogh, but also learn how Van Gogh has remained an inspiration to many artists, some of them surprising, right up to the present.

Finally, workshops, painting lessons, guided tours, and seminars are available at the museum for visitors age six and up. ■

Vincent van Gogh

One of the great ironies of Vincent van Gogh's life is that the artist whose work now attracts global veneration and commands world-record prices at auction scarcely sold a painting in his own short and troubled lifetime (1853–1890).

Van Gogh's artistic career began in 1880, when he was rejected as a trainee minister, and ended with his suicide in 1890. Within those ten short years, he produced 2,000 works of art—an average of one every two days. Some of them were dashed off in a moment of inspiration; others were the result of meticulous studies and preliminary sketches. No matter how they were composed, each represented an astonishing achievement for a man who did not begin to paint until he was 27 years old and was largely self-taught.

Self-portrait of the artist at work, Van Gogh Museum

Art & Commerce

Van Gogh's interest in art started early in life, with three of his uncles working as art dealers. Together with his brother, he joined the international art dealers firm Groupil & Cie in July 1869. His apprenticeship took him to The Hague, Brussels, London, and Paris at a time of inspirational artistic ferment, yet he was fired in 1876, inspiring him to retrain as a clergyman. Fortunately for Van Gogh, his brother, Theo, was promoted to manager of Groupil's Montmartre branch, enabling him to provide Vincent with financial support for the rest of his life.

The Life of an Aesthete

Van Gogh was far from extravagant with money. What little he had, he spent on paint, brushes, and canvas—and on candles, which he wore around the brim of his hat so he could continue to work at night. Food was not a priority—his diet largely consisted of stale bread, coffee, and alcohol. It is likely his resulting undernourishment precipitated his predisposition to depression. A failed attempt to set up an artistic colony in Arles

and a quarrel with the one artist who joined him there, Paul Gauguin, reinforced this depression, making Van Gogh's suicide in July 1890, age 37, sadly unsurprising.

Recognition

Van Gogh perceived himself as a misfit and a failure. Yet in the year he died, his paintings were exhibited in Paris and Brussels, and reviewers praised the intense emotional quality of his palette. In September 1890, Theo—who had inherited all of his brother's artwork—mounted a memorial exhibition in his Parisian apartment, only to die himself four months later. Vincent's legacy remained with the Van Gogh family, and largely thanks to the efforts of Theo's widow and son, an extensive collection of his work remains intact today at the Van Gogh Museum.

Stedelijk Museum

With a huge collection of international modern art to its name, the Stedelijk is more art gallery than museum, with ever-changing displays of cutting-edge works. Following its renovation, the Stedelijk is once more the hub of Amsterdam's creative avant-garde social and debating scene.

Built in 1895, the Stedelijk Museum is the largest museum of modern and contemporary art and design in the Netherlands. Reopening in 2013 after a nine-year closure and extensive renovation, the original building has gained a giant, futuristic white carbon-fiber extension aptly named De Badkuip (The Bathtub) and a redesigned basement for additional exhibition space, as well as a slick restaurant and shop.

The Bathtub

Once you pass through the Stedelijk's glass entrance doors on Museumplein, you find yourself in a large entrance hall. Pale-gray stone floor below you, the white bottom of the bathtub is visible overhead, while the neo-Renaissance facade of the original Stedelijk building is framed as an interior wall.

Above, two hallways extend from the Bathtub to join with the old museum on the second floor. To your left lie the museum shop and restaurant, whose rear wall features a black-and-white textile by Petra Blaisse. The basement, accessed by cantilevered stairs, holds a library and Amsterdam's largest open exhibition space, measuring some 12,000 square feet (1,100 sq m).

The galleries in the original building and extension are similar enough to ensure cohesion between old and new. Seemingly floating white walls (created with recessed baseboards) and large

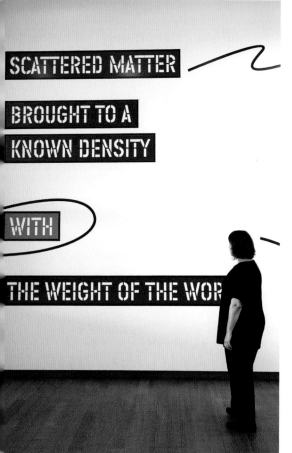

The writing on the wall at the Stedelijk Museum

The Stedelijk "Bathtub" Extension

Designed by the Amsterdam-based Benthem Crouwel Architects, the Stedelijk's Badkuip (Bathtub) extension has been a controversial addition, receiving mixed reviews from locals and architecture buffs since it was unveiled in 2012. Some argue that the futuristic porcelaneous tub perfectly reflects the cutting-edge collection of works housed within the Stedelijk, while others regard it as a monstrosity that only denigrates the original neo-Renaissance building.

Michael Kimmelman of the *New York Times* wrote: "Entering an oversize plumbing fixture to commune with classic modern art is like hearing Bach played by a man wearing a clown suit."

Controversial architecture apart, the extension does serve to provide the Stedelijk with nearly 100,000 square feet (10,000 sq m) of additional exhibition space, enabling it to show a far greater proportion of its vast collection than ever before.

windows mean the bright, airy rooms provide a neutral backdrop for the powerful images and installations on display. Start your visit by following the development of modern art with pieces from its pioneers—Cézanne (1839–1906), Piet Mondrian (1872–1944), Kasimir Malevich (1878–1935), Pablo Picasso (1881–1973), and Georges Braque (1882–1963). The museum has a rich collection of work by Malevich, presented along with quotations from his unpublished essays, as an example of one artist's personal pilgrimage from representational art to pure abstraction. Other key works in the Stedelijk's vast collection include "The Beanery" by Edward Kienholz and pieces by Wassily Kandinsky, Marc Chagall, Andy Warhol, Matisse, and Jackson Pollock.

Stedelijk Stairs

Once you have explored the ground floor, climb the museum's famous grand staircase. Its four long handrails were the only objects left untouched in the Stedelijk's refurbishment, deemed worth keeping as they have been touched by so many celebrated artists. As a journalist wrote in 1969: "An artist who has never fallen down these stairs doesn't count in the history of the avant-garde." The stairs lead you up to a luminously white second floor, which is further illuminated by red, yellow, and blue neon light installations by American artist Dan Flavin. Rooms leading off from the stairs house many contemporary, and controversial, pieces and installations, such as a portrait of Osama bin Laden from 2010 by Marlene Dumas.

Children

The Stedelijk caters well to children, with the Family Lab providing ample drawing and painting materials to encourage creativity, as well as a tiny cinema showing educational films. The complimentary "Family Trail" pack contains leaflets that lead families through the museum, suggesting children question the art they see, try to re-create it, and discuss it with their parents. ∎

Stedelijk Museum

🅰 Map p. 190
✉ Museumplein 10
☎ 573-2911
💲 $$$
🚋 Tram: 2, 3, 5, 12, 16
🚢 Museumboot

stedelijk.nl

A Walk Around the Museum Quarter & Vondelpark

The Museum Quarter has undergone a transformation in recent years with the reorientation of Museumplein, the construction of bold new buildings, and the restoration of some old favorites. In addition, the area has a fine park and offers great shopping.

Walking on Museumplein

NOT TO BE MISSED:

Shops on Pieter Corneliszoon Hooftstraat • Houses on Roemer Visscherstraat • Vondelpark

Begin your walk at the **Rijksmuseum** (see pp. 192–197), whose gardens give way to **Museumplein ❶**. The large glass plaza is dotted with cafés and surrounded by glorious museums. In summer it fills every day with locals and tourists.

Across the Museumplein you will see the **Concertgebouw** (see pp. 44 & 262), the classical building with the golden lyre on its pediment, home to the world-famous Royal Concertgebouw Orchestra.

Turning right from the Rijksmuseum onto Paulus Potterstraat, the eclectic-style building you see on the right-hand side of the street, with its corner turrets topped with witches-cap roofs, is home to **Coster Diamonds ❷** *(Paulus Potterstraat 2–6, tel 305-5555)*. Stop in to take a free tour and see demonstrations of diamond cutting. Beyond this lies the cubist **Van Gogh Museum ❸** (see pp. 198–200) and the red-brick, neo-Gothic **Stedelijk Museum ❹** (see pp. 202–203), with its "Bathtub" extension.

At the end of Paulus Potterstraat, turn right along Van Baerlestraat, with the **Conservatorium** on the right. This building once housed Amsterdam's highly regarded music school and is now a stylish hotel. The next right, onto Jan Luijkenstraat, takes you past numerous late-19th-century buildings with art nouveau balconies (No. 102) and door surrounds (Nos. 92 and 94), stained glass (No. 64), and tile pictures of *Aesop's Fables* (No. 60).

Turn left here and left again onto Pieter Corneliszoon Hooftstraat to indulge in a spot of window-shopping on Amsterdam's most upscale shopping street. Back on Van Baerlestraat, turn right and cross a bridge that doesn't have a canal running underneath: Instead you look down on a footpath leading to leafy Vondelpark (see p. 208). Take the first right, onto Roemer Visscherstraat, to see a charming group of houses (Nos. 20–30) built in 1894 in the national styles of the Netherlands, England, Russia, Italy, Spain, France, and Germany.

Turn left onto Tesselschadestraat and left again onto Vondelstraat, passing more grand 19th-century houses, now converted to hotels or Amsterdam University faculty housing. Cross Eerste Constantijn Huygensstraat and continue down Vondelstraat toward the **Vondelkerk ❺**, which lies straight ahead. Inspired by German Gothic church architecture and completed in

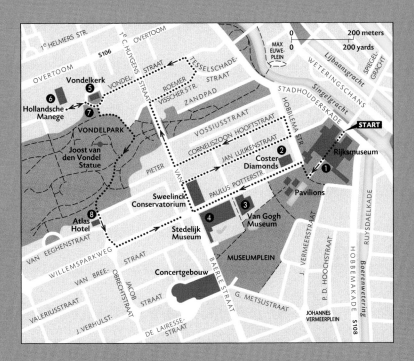

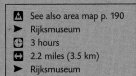

See also area map p. 190
► Rijksmuseum
🕐 3 hours
↔ 2.2 miles (3.5 km)
► Rijksmuseum

1880, this romantic church (now converted to offices) is the work of Rijksmuseum and Centraal Station architect P. J. H. Cuypers (1827–1921). Many architecture buffs regard Vondelkerk as his finest work. Continue past the church and you will see the Arts and Crafts-style house on the left (Nos. 77–79) that Cuypers built for his own use in 1899.

A little farther along a surprising sight (and smell) greets your senses: At No. 40, on the right, an ordinary domestic-looking facade disguises the entrance to the **Hollandsche Manege ⑥** (*Vondelstraat 140, tel 618-0942, dehollandschemanege.nl*). Built in 1882, the oldest riding school in the Netherlands still runs classes for all ages and abilities.

Returning toward the church, enter the gate beside Cuypers's house that leads you into the wonderful expanses of **Vondelpark ⑦**. This 112-acre (45 ha) green lung stretches for a mile (1.5 km) westward and is the city of Amsterdam's year-round playground, thronging with joggers, skaters, cyclists, and dog-walkers. On the right as you continue along the main path you'll come across a statue of the poet and playwright Joost van den Vondel (1582–1674), dubbed the Shakespeare of the Netherlands, after whom Vondelpark is named. Keep the ponds and statue to your right as you bear away from the city center, take the next path left, and you'll leave the park to join Jacob Obrechtstraat. Pass the **Atlas Hotel ⑧**, with its decorative art nouveau tiles. Similarly fanciful houses line Willemsparkweg (the third street on the left after you emerge from the park). This leads you back to Paulus Potterstraat, from where you can easily make your way back to the Museumplein and to the Rijksmuseum.

De Pijp

Originally built to accommodate the working-class and migrant population overflowing from the Jordaan neighborhood in 19th-century Amsterdam, De Pijp (The Pipe) has become a vibrant, multicultural haunt of artists, students, and locals of all nationalities. Despite its dense concentration of restaurants, bars, and boutiques, De Pijp remains true to its gritty roots.

An outdoor café on Helstraat, in De Pijp

De Pijp

⛰ Map p. 190

Albert Cuypmarkt

⛰ Map p. 190

✉ Albert Cuypstraat

🕐 Closed Sun.

🚊 Tram: 4, 16, 24, 25

albertcuypmarkt.nl

The origin of De Pijp's name is no longer known, although it is alleged to derive from the area's long, straight streets reminiscent of pipes. The longer established De Oude Pijp (The Old Pipe) lies north of the attractive Sarphatipark, while De Nieuwe Pijp (The New Pipe) lies south of it. Named after Samuel Sarphati (1813–1866), a physician and city planner who fought tirelessly to advance hygiene and waste management in 19th-century Amsterdam in an attempt to help the poor, the park was initially meant to be a railway station linking De Oude and Nieuwe Pijp.

De Cuyp

The hub of De Pijp is the Albert Cuypmarkt (Albert Cuyp Market), named after the Golden Age landscape artist. Dating back to 1905, and known as De Cuyp to locals, it is said to be Europe's biggest street market. There is enough to exhaust the most avid shopper in this mile-long (1.6 km) market, with exotic fruit, vegetables, spices, olives and nuts, fish of all kinds, poultry, flowers, cheeses, and household goods for sale, all at bargain prices, not to mention street performers. Between the market stalls and the shops that line the street, you can buy everything from bicycles to wedding dresses to sexy underwear.

Eating & Drinking

De Pijp has long been an area of great culinary diversity, thanks to the influence of its international inhabitants, the presence of the Albert Cuypmarkt, and the fact that it is the home of one of Holland's best-known exports: Heineken beer. The first Heineken brewery opened in 1863 on a square now called the Marie Heinekenplein (Marie Heineken Square). As demand for beer exceeded, however, the brewery's capacity, it was closed and largely demolished in 1988. One of the 1930s buildings survives in the form of the interactive Heineken Experience museum (see p. 210).

The streets surrounding the Albert Cuypmarkt are lined with quirky cafés, restaurants, bars, and shops. You can feast on virtually any kind of global cuisine from North African tagines served in a former Reformed church at Bazar (Albert Cuypstraat 182, tel 675-0544, bazaramsterdam .nl) to classical French food at Le Restaurant (Tweede Jan Steenstraat 3, tel 379-2207, lerestaurant.nl) and American-style burgers at The Butcher (Albert Cuypstraat 129, tel 470-7875, the-butcher.com). The bars in De Pijp, and on the lively Eerste van der Helststraat, include Chocolate, the Kingfisher, the Hotel Okura's Twenty Third cocktail bar, and Café Flamingo Bar.

De Badcuyp

The transformation of the music venue called De Badcuyp is a great example of the development of De Pijp from its simple, working-class roots to today's cultural scene.

The name is a play on words, combining the building's original use as a public bathhouse (badkuip is a bathtub), a crucial local amenity as many of the social housing units did not have private bathing facilities, and the surname of Albert Cuyp. However, for over 20 years now, the Badcuyp has served as an intimate live music venue, specializing in jazz. Musicians from across the world perform on the small stage, which has replaced the old bath and shower facilities with audiences enjoying light bites and drinks as the bands play. ∎

De Badcuyp

Map p. 191

Eerste Sweelinckstraat 10

675-9669

Tram: 4, 16, 24, 25

badcuyp.org

EXPERIENCE: Wake Up to Coffee & Auntie's Cake

Siemon de Jong and Noam Offer are the dynamic duo behind **De Taart van m'n Tante** (My Auntie's Cake; Ferdinand Bolstraat 10, tel 776-4600, detaart.com). This legendary "cake parlor" and bespoke cake bakery is located in De Pijp, where De Jong and Offer have been making delicious and imaginative baked goodies since 1989.

Their flamboyant creations have been exhibited (and eaten) at the Rijksmuseum, Stedelijk Museum, and Van Gogh Museum and appeared on national television and in international films, ensuring their fame has spread from De Pijp across the Netherlands and around the world. The cake parlor, or café, is an eye-poppingly kitsch collection of brightly colored furniture, mismatched crockery,

doilies, and over-the-top decorations. Oversize cakes tower above customers, who stream into the cozy spot throughout the day, either to indulge in a slab of cake with tea or to buy an entire mountain of it as a gift. Bespoke cakes are created following meetings with dedicated cake designers and feature everything from edible flowers and clothing to exotic flavors and toys.

In 2004, the pair opened a bed & breakfast located above their café, **Cake Under My Pillow** (see p. 252; cakeunder mypillow.nl). There are just three bedrooms, each prettily decorated in surprisingly traditional and low-key style. The bonus of staying here, of course, is starting the day with breakfast prepared by the master bakers of Amsterdam.

EXPERIENCE: Enjoying the Local Parks

Despite the city being so densely populated, there are more than 30 parks in Amsterdam, including Vondelpark, which attracts some nine million people every year. With the vast majority of Amsterdammers living in small apartments, they invariably grab a book, a picnic, and some friends and head for the park when the sun comes out. The best way to commune with the locals—as well as with nature—is, therefore, to explore their parks.

Whether you stretch your legs in the Amsterdamse Bos (Amsterdam Wood, see p. 209), have tea by the drawbridge in Westerpark (see p. 156), attend an open-air theater performance in Vondelpark (see pp. 204–205), or sleep off lunch by the fountain in Sarphatipark, there's an Amsterdam park out there for you (*amsterdam .info/parks*).

Amstelpark (*Arent Janszoon Ernststraat 1*): An expansive park in southern Amsterdam with flower gardens, a playground, and a petting zoo. The Glazen Huis (Glass House) and Orangery regularly host art exhibits.

INSIDER TIP:

At the Oosterpark join in a game of soccer, or reflect a moment at sculptures acknowledging Dutch slavery and the slain movie director Theo van Gogh.

—PANCRAS DIJK
National Geographic *maga-zine in the Netherlands* writer

Oosterpark (*Oosterpark*): An extensive park located to the east of the city by the Tropenmuseum (see p. 115), dotted with ponds, streams, meandering paths, and a children's wading pool. Oosterpark hosts several summer festivals, including Amsterdam's largest music event, the Roots Festival in June. Expect to hear outspoken views at the Spreeksteen (Speaker's Stone) on Sundays at 1 p.m.

Park Frankendael (*Middenweg 72*): Amsterdam's sole remaining 17th-century country estate, located in the city's southeast. A romantic park, with a period garden, landscaped grounds, the grand Huize Frankendael (Frankendael House) where cultural events are held, and two excellent restaurants, Merkelbach and De Kas (see p. 246).

Rembrandtpark (*Orteliuskade 57*): A delightful family park in western Amsterdam, with the city's oldest petting zoo, De Uylenburg, and various playgrounds, ponds, and picnic spots.

Vondelpark (*hetvondel park.net*): Amsterdam's most popular park, with an abundance of roses, lakes, restaurants, cafés, buskers, skate parks, storks, and walks. Locals flock to the sunny garden of Groot Melkhuis (Great Milk House), by the pond in the center of the park, for postwork beers and weekend brunch.

Vondelpark provides an idyllic setting for a relaxing afternoon.

More Places to Visit in the Museum Quarter, Vondelpark, & De Pijp

Amsterdamse Bos & the Electrische Museumtramlijn

The Amsterdamse Bos (Amsterdam Wood) is a giant park on the city's southwestern outskirts, carved out of an area of agricultural land as part of a job-creation scheme in the 1930s. More than 5,000 unemployed people worked to create the woodlands, boating lakes, and an artificial hill used for winter sports. The small visitor center, the Bezoekerscentrum het Bosmuseum (*Koenenkade 56, tel 676-2152, closed Mon.*), has displays on the park's history and wildlife.

A popular way to get to the park is on the antique tramcars of the **Electrische Museumtramlijn** (Electric Tramline Museum). Trams operate between Haarlemmermeerstation and Amstelveen, a 20-minute trip with various stops along the way. A variety of rolling stock from all over Europe is used, dating from 1908 to 1958. Other trams and streetcars are displayed at the Haarlemmermeerstation, itself a historic building. The tramline skirts the Amsterdamse Bos, with good views of the Olympic Stadium, built for the 1928 games. *museumtramlijn.org.* Map pp. 190 Haarlemmermeerstation, Amstelveenseweg 264 673-7538, museumtramlijn.org $ Tram: 16. Bus: 170, 171, 172; trams run only Sun. Easter–end Oct.

Cobra Museum

The Cobra Museum of Modern Art (*cobra -museum.nl*) is located in the southern suburb of Amstelveen, about half an hour's tram ride from Centraal Station. The museum focuses on artworks and documentary material from the CoBrA movement, a name derived from the initial letters of the cities of Copenhagen, Brussels, and Amsterdam and formed in 1948 in the Café Notre-Dame by Karel Appel, Constant, Corneille, Christian Dotremont, Asger Jorn, and Joseph Noiret. The artists' aim was to achieve total freedom of color and form, resulting in abstract and figurative work depicting dreamlike figures or demons from mythology, or bright abstract images drawn in bold primary colors. *cobra-museum.nl* Map p. 190 Sandbergplein 1, Amstelveen 547-5050 Closed Mon. $$ Tram: 5. Metro: 51. Bus: 170, 171, 172.

INSIDER TIP:

After visiting the museums, stroll to Zuidermarkt, the organic market at Jacob Obrechtplein by Vondelpark. Filled with flowers, bread, meat, and vegetables, this is a great place to pick up picnic supplies.

—ROBBERT VERMUE
National Geographic *magazine in the Netherlands editor*

De Dageraad

In keeping with H. P. Berlage's intentions to make De Pijp an area rich in social housing, and his passion for the architecture of the Amsterdam School, the district is home to a number of important buildings of that era. These are predominantly centered around Pieter Lodewijk Takstraat, with the **De Dageraad (The Dawn)** at its heart. A monumental housing complex designed by Michel de Klerk and Piet Kramer in similar style to Spaarndammerbuurt (see pp. 152–153), De Dageraad was completed in 1923 and makes adventurous use of bricks and tiles to create projecting windows, turrets, and clock towers. *hetschip.nl.* Map p. 191 Burgemeester Tellegenstraat 128 418-2885; Tram: 4, 12, 25

The Heineken Experience: brewing history on tap

Heineken Experience

Heineken is Amsterdam's native brew—or was until the brewery closed in 1988, a victim of its own success. This inner-city brewery couldn't produce enough beer to satisfy the city's thirst, not to mention international demand. The main operations moved to Zoeterwoude, close to Leiden, to the relief of Amsterdammers, who complained about the smell.

The old brewery has been given a new lease on life as a visitor attraction, one of the most popular in Amsterdam, due in no small part to the free samples. The exhibitions take in the history of brewing, from ancient Assyrian origins to today. Interactive displays explain the brewing process and the unique Heineken recipe, which was developed by **Gerard Adriaan Heineken** when he acquired the brewery in 1864. An important ingredient in the brew is the yeast, developed for the firm by one of Louis Pasteur's students, whose formula remains a closely guarded secret. There is no doubting the beer's popularity: Heineken's factories in the Netherlands produce more than one million bottles a day just to satisfy the thirst of the Dutch. Annual global production exceeds

4.5 billion gallons (171 million hectolitres), making it the world's third-largest producer. *heinekenexperience.com*

🅰 Map p. 190 ✉ Stadhouderskade 78
☎ 523-9435; 🕐 Closed Mon. 💲 $$$
🚊 Tram: 7, 10, 16, 24, 25

WG Terrein

Few Amsterdammers are familiar with the **Wilhelmina Gasthuis Terrein** (Wilhelmina Hospice Estate; *wg-terrein.nl*), a sizable complex discretely tucked away five minutes' walk north of Vondelpark (see pp. 204–205). The first building of the complex was constructed in 1634 as a Pesthuys, or hospital for infectious and terminal patients, far from the city center in open landscape. In 1893, the thirteen-year-old queen-in-waiting Wilhelmina laid the first stone in works to extend the complex, creating a number of small redbrick buildings with large windows and plenty of parkland between them, for the well-being of the patients.

The now renamed Wilhelmina Gasthuis and hospital was a leading medical center until 1983, when all units were moved to a newly built Academic Medical Centre on the new outskirts of Amsterdam. The derelict buildings fell foul of squatters and vandals until the pioneering Stichting Beheer WG-Terrein (WG-Terrein Management Foundation) bought up several buildings to preserve them in 1985. Spaces in these were then offered rent free to politically or socially disadvantaged individuals and start-up companies, artists, and designers, with the stipulation that they pay for essential repairs and running costs and spend one to two days a week assisting in the upkeep of the property. The innovative concept proved successful, not only in regenerating the estate but in nurturing a strong community spirit and launching several successful companies. Today, the secluded estate still comprises residential apartments, offices, artists' studios, and a café and restaurant, creating its own urban village.

🅰 Map p. 190 ✉ Ketelhuisplein 41
🚊 Tram: 1, 17

Endless bulb fields, windmills and polders, Delft's delicate porcelain, Leiden's ancient university, and Rotterdam's ultramodern architecture

Excursions

Introduction & Map   212–213

Biking in Waterland   214–217

**Experience: Take a Wetlands
    Canoe Safari**   216

Enkhuizen   218–221

Haarlem   222–223

**Experience: Bike to the Zandvoort
    Beach**   223

A Drive Through the Bulb Fields of
    Haarlem   224–225

Leiden   226–227

Den Haag   228–229

Delft   230–231

**Experience: Create Your Own
    Delft Pottery**   231

Rotterdam   232–234

**Experience: Enjoy Romance in
    the Euromast**   233

Hotels & Restaurants
    for Excursions   253–255

The detail on this old Delft porcelain plate shows boaters on a river.

Excursions

Rent a bike from Centraal Station and you could be cycling through gentle Dutch countryside in less than 20 minutes. Take a train from Centraal Station and you could be at the heart of Haarlem in about the same time. The Netherlands is a very small country, and the integrated transportation system offers frequent and reliable train and bus services. This makes it very easy to get out of Amsterdam and explore the Dutch countryside, or visit cities that have played such an important part in European history.

Tall houses line the Oude West canal, Leiden.

inextricably linked with the concepts of peace and humanity, thanks to the establishment here of the United Nations International Court of Justice (1946) and the International Criminal Court (2002).

But these cities are far more than just famous names. They are all very distinctive and attractive places, with a vibrant cosmopolitan mix of shopping centers and art-filled museums, clubs and bars, and quiet leafy canals—something for everyone to enjoy. Only Rotterdam, bombed into submission by the Nazis at the outbreak of World War II, has lost its historic city center, though it has compensated by encouraging modern architects to create some of the most daring and innovative buildings anywhere in the world. ∎

Within an hour's travel from Amsterdam are the great cities of Utrecht, Rotterdam, Leiden, Haarlem, Delft, and Den Haag (The Hague)—all places with resonant names, all players on the great stage of world history. The Treaty of Utrecht, signed in 1579, ended a hundred years of warfare and ushered in the Golden Age of European prosperity. Rotterdam is the port from which the Pilgrims set sail in 1620 on their historic voyage to the New World. Settlers from Haarlem gave their name to what is now the New York neighborhood, and Delft is renowned for distinctive blue-and-white pottery produced in the town since the 17th century. The name of The Hague is

NOT TO BE MISSED:

A bicycle ride through rural
   Holland   214–217

Traveling to Enkhuizen by steam
   train and boat   218–221

Haarlem, the picturesque home
   of Frans Hals   222–223

The elegant charms of
   Den Haag   228–229

Experiencing the beauty of
   Vermeer's Delft   230–231

Manhattan on the Maas—
   Rotterdam's ultramodern
   architecture   232–234

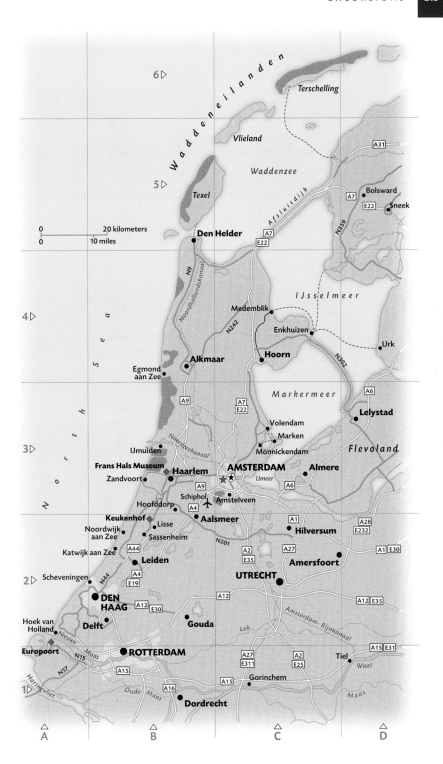

Biking in Waterland

This bike ride shows how easy it is to get out of Amsterdam and experience the Dutch countryside. The route covers 22.5 miles (36.5 km), with a 5-mile (8 km) optional extension to Marken. There are cafés and shops providing refreshment stops, but it's advisable to carry your own water. (For details on renting bikes, see p. 238.)

Wipe your feet before entering the spotless village of Broek in Waterland.

Passing numerous small dairy farms, you will reach **Broek in Waterland ❶** after 15 minutes. This village is famous as the place where Napoléon was forced to take his boots off when he came to see the mayor in 1811. The villagers were obsessed with cleanliness because they didn't want alien bacteria to

From the rear of **Centraal Station** (see pp. 48–49) take the free ferry that crosses the IJ River. On the northern bank, follow the canal towpath that lies straight ahead. When you reach the first lock, you will see the first of a series of fingerposts marked with a hexagonal ANWB cycleway symbol. These are placed at every junction you come to. Follow the signs for Broek in Waterland.

Continue along the canal, past boats, anglers, and colorfully painted houses. After five minutes, a sign directs you across a bridge to the opposite (right-hand) bank of the canal. For a short time, the canal and bike path run parallel to a busy main road, but another ten minutes on, at **Het Schouw,** bear right to pass under the road and leave the main Noordhollands Kanaal to follow the Broekvaart, a smaller side canal.

- ⬛ See also area map p. 213 C3
- ► Centraal Station
- 🕓 8 hours
- ↔ 27.5 miles (44.5 km) with optional excursion to Marken
- ► Centraal Station

NOT TO BE MISSED:

**Broek in Waterland • Zeedijk
Marken • Ransdorp**

infect the culture they used for making cheeses. Today it remains pristine, a village of beautiful timber houses, some in pastel hues, others painted gray in token of mourning for those who lost their lives and livelihoods following the disastrous floods in 1825. The beautiful village church, founded in 1573, is worth a quick look for its splendid woodwork and stained glass. If biking has made you hungry, stop at De Witte Swaen (The White Swan), a café set in a lovely 1596 house at the point where you enter the village, offering 40 different varieties of pancakes.

From the café, follow signs to Zuiderwoude, passing beneath the main road through a tunnel. Cross the next canal bridge, and 200 yards (220 m) farther on, having crossed the next bridge, turn right following signs to Zuiderdorp. At the junction follow the Zuiderdorp sign left, then at the next junction, go left, following the green hexagonal signs that say "Aeën en Dieën."

The track leads straight to the village of **Zuiderwoude ②**, little more than a waterside

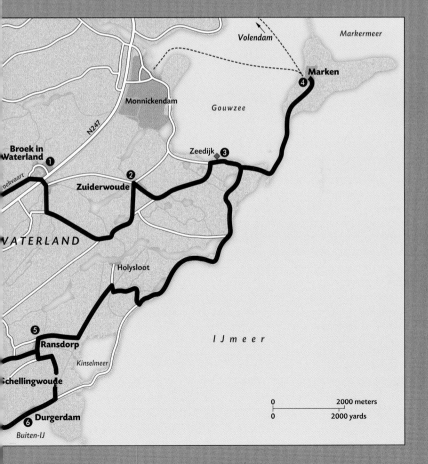

EXPERIENCE: Take a Wetlands Canoe Safari

Get up close and personal with rural Holland during a canoe safari of Amsterdam's wetlands, or *achtertuin* (back garden). Meet your guide at Centraal Station, and just a short time later, you will be paddling a canoe through a quintessentially Dutch landscape, little changed since the 17th century. As you pass small villages, fields of grazing cows, and ancient windmills turning languorously in the breeze, you will find yourself in the midst of countryside that inspired great Golden Age painters, such as Rembrandt and Van Ruysdael.

Throughout the trip, your English-speaking guide will point out the flora and fauna that make up the wetlands: Tall reeds, richly scented waterplants,

and meadows provide sanctuary for native wildlife such as moorhens and black-tailed godwits. In addition to paddling through the wetlands, you can walk through them and—weather permitting—swim as well. Drinks are served before and after the tour, and you will also enjoy a tasty picnic lunch of locally made produce.

Wetlands Safari *(P.O. Box 11273, 1001 GG Amsterdam, tel 06/5355-2669, wetlandssafari.nl)* runs daily guided canoe safaris from mid-April to mid-September. The meeting point is the bus station behind Amsterdam's Centraal Station (IJzijde) at 9:30 a.m. Mon.–Sat. and at 10 a.m. on Sundays. The tours last 5.5 hours and are not suitable for children under the age of seven.

church and a cluster of houses around the main square, reached in 25 minutes from Broek. You might like to stop for ice cream at the candy store just before the bridge leading into this tiny village. Another 25 minutes of cycling take you to the **Zeedijk** (Sea Dike) ❸, which is all that stops Waterland from being flooded by the IJmeer. Climb the dike to look out over the boat-filled expanse of water. Away to the right is the village of Marken, reached by a long causeway. If time is a consideration, you may wish to start the return journey; otherwise it is worth the ride along the causeway to this historic village.

Marken ❹ was an island until 1959, and the inhabitants built their wooden houses on artificial mounds called *werven*. Space on the mounds was limited, so the timber houses, painted black and green, are attractively crowded together. Because it is such a tourist attraction, you will find older ladies of the village posing for photographs in traditional costume in front of their houses, which double as souvenir shops. Plenty of cafés cluster

around the small harbor, serving mussels and pancakes. An express boat service departs from the harbor every 30 to 45 minutes for the equally attractive fishing villages of **Volendam** and **Monnickendam,** which lie farther north on the shores of the IJsselmeer (the last boat back is at 5:30 p.m.; you can take your bike for a small extra fee).

Back on the mainland, the route back to Amsterdam simply involves following the dike-top path. After ten minutes or so the "Aeën en Dieën" path will take you off the dike and inland toward Holysloot. You do not want to go to the village, though; instead, take the first left turn you come to, signposted **Ransdorp** ❺. Take the next turn right, also signposted Ransdorp, and head for the church when you reach the village. This stands opposite the attractive 1652 town hall. The 105-foot (32 m) Gothic brick church tower, built when the villlage was thriving through maritime trade in the 15th century, is well worth climbing for expansive views across the polder to Amsterdam *(Open mid-April–end Sept., 11 a.m.–5 p.m.*

Sat. & Sun., and daily, except Mon., in July & Aug.).

The easiest way to get back to Amsterdam now is to continue past the church and go right across the drawbridge when you reach the end of the village. Follow signs to **Schellingwoude** until the path reaches the banks of the IJ, then turn right along the river bank following signs for Centrum, until you return to the IJ ferry. As you leave Ransdorp, you will see the village of **Durgerdam** ⑥ in the distance to the left. If you still have energy, you might like to visit this pretty village of waterside houses, then continue around the dike-top path to return to the main route at Schellingwoude.

Whichever route you take, you will bike through land rich in wildlife. The ditches that drain the agricultural land are full of snipe, shelducks, and mallard, not to mention the numerous heron. Depending on the season, there are yellow flags and purple loosestrife in flower among the stands of reed mace and water reed. The song of the lark will accompany you, as well as the haunting cries of oystercatchers and curlews.

If you get bitten by the cycling bug, re-member that there are some 22,000 miles

INSIDER TIP:

The west and north coasts offer superb cycling paths through much of the Netherlands' dune reserves. Hire a bike and get maps and information on routes in the visitor center in Overveen, just west of Haarlem, or visit *dutchcycling.nl*.

—JUSTIN KAVANAGH
*National Geographic
International Editions editor*

(35,000 km) of *fietspaden* (cycle paths) to explore in the Netherlands, creating a network that will take you to all sorts of places that cars cannot go. Every VVV tourist information center in the Netherlands sells maps and guides detailing local routes, and ANWB, the Dutch motoring organization, produces numerous guidebooks detailing cycling routes. You can also visit *holland.com* or *dutchcycling.nl* for suggestions of routes of varying lengths.

The flat Waterland countryside is ideal for leisurely cycling.

Enkhuizen

The fascinating Zuiderzeemuseum in Enkhuizen is a living history museum that covers 3,000 years in the life of the village, from Bronze Age settlement to a prosperous herring port. Getting to the museum is an adventure in itself, traveling backward in time from modern railroad to steam train and then to paddle steamer.

All aboard: the steam train that travels between Hoorn and Medemblik

Enkhuizen

Map p. 213 C4

Visitor Information

Tussen Twee Havens 1

0228/313-164

vvvenkhuizen.nl

Although you can go straight to Enkhuizen by train (see side panel p. 219), it's much more fun, especially if you're traveling with children, to take the normal train service from Centraal Station to Hoorn, then join the steam train service that goes from Hoorn to Medemblik, where you continue your journey by paddle steamer. Make sure you arrive in Hoorn in plenty of time to catch the 11 a.m. steam train, or the occasional 10 a.m. departure. This departs from the **Museumstoomtram** (Steam Train Museum), and you can buy an all-inclusive ticket at the museum covering the rest of the journey, including entry into Enkhuizen's Zuiderzeemuseum.

As the sturdy antique steam train meanders through the West Frisian countryside, you get an intimate view of neat and productive suburban gardens, open countryside, apple and pear orchards, dairy farms, and fields full of colorful blooms. Depending on the season, these flowers, grown for the cut-flower trade, might include daffodils, tulips, roses, carnations, or chrysanthemums. The journey to **Medemblik** takes 75 minutes, leaving plenty of time to explore the town before the paddle-wheel boats depart at 1:30 p.m. The journey to Enkhuizen takes 90 minutes, offering views of small coastal towns and hundreds of leisure craft darting about the surface of the IJsselmeer.

The IJsselmeer

Until 1932, the IJsselmeer was known as the **Zuiderzee** (Southern Sea). For centuries it provided the people of Holland with an outlet to the North Sea for fishing and trade. Continual silting meant that it was too shallow for modern shipping, so the Noordzeekanaal was dug to provide a more direct route from Amsterdam to the North Sea and opened in 1876. High tides always brought the risk of flooding to the regions bordering the Zuiderzee, and a particularly destructive flood in 1916 led to the revival of an idea, first proposed by Cornelis Lely in 1891, of closing off the Zuiderzee altogether. This led to the construction of the **Afsluitdijk**, the Enclosing Dike, built by sinking rafts of woven willow laden with stones and concrete. The final section of the dike was completed in 1932, beginning the slow transformation of the saltwater Zuiderzee into today's freshwater lake.

Villages around the Zuiderzee flew flags at half-mast when the dike was officially opened, mourning the loss of access to the sea and their long-established maritime and fishing industries. All have since adapted to the new conditions: Leisure boats now fill the harbors, and visitors flock in summer to enjoy the unspoiled character of these former fishing towns, with their numerous seafood restaurants.

Museumstoom-tram, Hoorn
- ✉ Van Dedemstraat 8
- ☎ 0229/214-862
- ⏱ Closed Dec.–Feb.

museumstoomtram.nl

ENKHUIZEN DIRECT: If time is limited, you can take the train directly to Enkhuizen. Trains leave daily from Centraal Station at 9 and 39 minutes past the hour from 6 a.m. to 12:39 a.m. the next day, and the journey takes 57 minutes.

The Enclosing Dike

The Afsluitdijk (Enclosing Dike) is a 20-mile-long (32 km) causeway in the Netherlands, constructed between 1927 and 1933. The bridge provides a road link between the North Holland province and Friesland, and is a fundamental part of the larger Zuiderzee Works, which dammed off the Zuider Zee, a saltwater inlet of the North Sea, and turned it into the freshwater lake of the IJsselmeer.

The dam was the site of an intense World War II battle in May 1940, as the Germans tried to seize the Afsluitdijk as a means of invading the Netherlands from the north. Lead by Captain Christiaan Boers, the Dutch army inflicted considerable damage on the German forces, surprising them by sneaking in antiaircraft weaponry under cover of night and firing from the sloop HNLMS *Johan Maurits van Nassau*, anchored 11 miles (18 km) away in the Wadden Sea. The Dutch held Fort Kornwerderzand until their surrender on May 15, 1940.

Zuiderzeemuseum, Enkhuizen

✉ Wierdijk 12–22

☎ 0228/351-111

💲 $$$ (including travel)

zuiderzeemuseum.nl

Enkhuizen

Enkhuizen has prospered more than most by virtue of the **Zuiderzeemuseum,** which attracts thousands of visitors every year. There is a **Binnen-museum** (Indoor Museum) and **Buitenmuseum** (Open-air Museum). The steamer docks alongside the entrance to the latter so that you step straight into a village frozen in time. Historic buildings—cottages, churches, shops, farms, and barns—have been rescued from all over the Netherlands and reconstructed here to form a complete community, with costumed guides to explain life as it was prior to the enclosure of the Zuiderzee.

It takes a couple of hours to see the Open-air Museum, but leave some time for the Indoor Museum, housed in the **Peper-huis,** an imposing Renaissance building dating from 1625 that was once used for storing spices from Indonesia. The displays here cover the history of the whaling and herring fishing industries, and the constant struggle the Dutch have faced to control the water that surrounds them and threat-ens to encroach upon them.

Hoorn

The ten-minute walk back to Enkhuizen's railroad station is clearly signposted. On your way back to Amsterdam (or in the morning, if you have time)

Mending nets in the fishermen village of the open-air Zuiderzeemuseum, Enkhuizen

Hoorn's Heritage

Founded in 716, Hoorn grew to become a major harbor town, serving as a hub for the Dutch East India Company (VOC) during the Golden Age. The Hoorn fleet plied the oceans, returning laden with precious commodities, and its sailors established the town's name far and wide: Jan Pieterszoon Coen (1587–1629) founded the city of Batavia in 1619 (now Jakarta), and Willem IJsbrantszoon Bontekoe (1587–1657) immortalized a journey he undertook in 1618 in a journal published in 1646. The book's title was *Journal, or memorable description, of the East-Indian voyage of Willem Ysbrantz Bontekoe of Hoorn, comprising many wondrous and dangerous things experienced by him.*

In 1616, the explorer Willem Corneliszoon Schouten braved storms to round the southernmost tip of South America, which he named Kaap Hoorn (Cape Horn) in honor of his hometown.

INSIDER TIP:

In summer, don't miss the Thursday cheese market in Hoorn. This hour-long re-creation of the town's ancient cheese market features farmers, horse-drawn carts, and cheese maids. Grab a seat at the Waag café for the best views.

—GABRIELLA LE BRETON
National Geographic author

it is worth stopping in **Hoorn** for a taste of Dutch provincial life. The little fishing town has two distinct centers—the main square and the harbor.

The main square is dominated by the splendid **Westfries Museum,** with its flamboyant facade, dating back to 1632 and flanked by larger-than-life stone lions and Hoorn's coat of arms. A museum since 1881, it boasts a remarkable collection of more than 30,000 statues, sculptures, artworks, and pieces of furniture from the Golden Age, displayed in a number of period rooms.

South of the square, residential streets lined with patrician houses of the 17th and 18th centuries give way to a series of inner harbors with warehouses whose names—Appelhaven, Bierkade, Korenmarkt (apple, beer, and corn)—give an idea of the commodities once shipped and stored here. The main harbor is marked by a leaning tower, known as the **Hoofdtoren,** which was built in 1532 as a defensive tower but is now topped by a pretty bell tower. Two ship boys cast in bronze and clambering up the sea wall commemorate Willem IJsbrantszoon Bontekoe, who was born in a nearby house and who wrote a best-selling diary in 1646 describing a voyage to the East Indies.

From the harbor, look for a route marked with arrows set in the sidewalk. The route takes you back to the main square round the eastern side of the town, past some fine 17th-century houses, several containing art galleries and antique shops. ■

Hoorn

🅰 Map p. 213 C4

Visitor Information

✉ Veemarkt 4

☎ 0229/218-343

vvvhoorn.nl

Westfries Museum, Hoorn

✉ Rode Steen 1

☎ 0229/280-022

🕐 Closed Sat. & Sun. a.m., 3rd Mon. in Aug.

💲 $

westfriesmuseum .nl

Haarlem

Although located just minutes away from Amsterdam, Haarlem is a world away in atmosphere. Virtually unchanged since the 17th century, the city center is a maze of traffic-free streets lined with bookstores, galleries, antique shops, and old-fashioned cheesemongers, lending it the title of the Netherlands' best shopping city. A visit to the Frans Hals Museum is a must.

A café in Grote Markt Square is a good place to observe Haarlem life.

Haarlem
🗺 Map p. 213 B3
Visitor Information
✉ Verwulft 11
☎ 0900/616-1600
vvhaarlem.nl

Grote Kerk
✉ Grote Markt
☎ 023/532-2040
🕐 Closed Sun.
💲 Free
bavo.nl

Five minutes on a train from Amsterdam's Centraal Station brings you to Haarlem, whose art nouveau railway station is a ten-minute stroll from the city center. Follow signs for Grote Markt (Large Market) and you will soon find yourself stepping straight into a Golden Age painting. All that has been added since the 17th century is a mass of busy sidewalk cafés, turning this leafy square into one large open-air dining room. The statue in the middle of the square depicts Laurens Coster, the Haarlem man who is considered by many Dutch to be the inventor of the printing press.

Bavo

To the west of the square is the elaborately gabled **Renaissance Stadhuis** (Town Hall) while the **Grote Kerk** (also known as Sint-Bavokerk, or Bavo, after its patron saint) lies to the southeast. This aptly named Gothic Large Church (built between 1400 and 1550) boasts an interior rich in woodwork and brass, and the flamboyant organ is one that Handel played in 1738, and Mozart in 1766. Recitals offer the opportunity to hear why Mozart shouted for joy on trying it out.

Next to the church is the extravagantly decorated

Verweyhal, named after the artist Kees Verwey, whose gabled dormer windows project from a roof bristling with pinnacles, baroque scrolls, and lion masks. This 19th-century building was linked to the 17th-century Vleeshal (Meat Hall) and Vishal (Fish Hall), where markets were held, and given the joint name **De Hallen** (The Halls).

Frans Hals Museum

Today, De Hallen are part of the world-class Frans Hals Museum and used to display contemporary art. The classical collection of the museum is located south of Grote Markt in Haarlem's former Oudemannenhuis (Old Mens' Almshouse), founded in 1609. The home was governed by five regents, whose portraits were painted by Frans Hals in 1664 and are on display in the museum. Born in Antwerp in 1581, Hals moved to Haarlem shortly afterward and remained there for the rest of his life. Although one of the greatest artists of his age, Hals lived to nearly 86—so long that his painting style became outdated and he died in poverty.

Teylers Museum

Haarlem's other museum of note is the Teylers Museum, which bridges the gap between science and art. Founded in 1779 by merchant Pieter Teyler van der Hulst (1702–1778), the museum is the oldest in the country and has an outstanding collection of early scientific instruments and drawings, including rare works by Rembrandt, Dürer, and Michelangelo.

Hofjes

Haarlem is home to 21 *hofjes*, almshouses clustered around a central courtyard. Those worth visiting include **Teylers Hofje** *(Koudenhorn 64a),* **Hofje van Bakenes** *(founded in 1395, Wijde Appelaarsteeg 11),* and **Hofje van Noblet** *(New Canal 2).* ∎

De Hallen
- ✉ Grote Markt 16
- ☎ 023/511-5775
- 🕐 Closed Sun. a.m.
- 💲 $$ (cheaper if you buy a combined ticket for this & the Frans Hals Museum)

dehallenhaarlem.nl

Frans Hals Museum
- ✉ Groot Heiligland 62
- ☎ 023/511-5775
- 🕐 Closed Sun a.m.
- 💲 $$

franshalsmuseum.nl

Teylers Museum
- ✉ Spaarne 16
- ☎ 023/516-0960
- 🕐 Closed Mon.
- 💲 $$

teylersmuseum.nl

EXPERIENCE: Bike to the Zandvoort Beach

Zandvoort is Amsterdam's nearest beach resort and receives thousands of visitors each time the sun comes out on a summer's day. Fortunately, it is big enough to cope, with more than 5.5 miles (9 km) of sand bordered by dunes. Much of this sandy strip is flanked by brightly painted pavilions containing cafés, restaurants, bars, and nightclubs, as well as sailing and windsurfing clubs. The farther end is a designated nude bathing area. Behind the beach, the 15-square-mile (38 sq km) **Nationaal Park Zuid-Kennemerland** (South Kennemerland National Park) has varied habitats—lakes, woods, and heath, as well as extensive dune systems—that are home to more than a hundred species of birds, various types of native deer, rabbits, and foxes, as well as Highland cattle, Shetland ponies, and European bison.

To reach Zandvoort, you can rent bicycles in Amsterdam (simply put your bike on the train at Amsterdam's Centraal Station; see p. 238) or pick them up once you reach Haarlem (Bike Planet; *Gierstraat 55–57, tel 023/534-1502, bikeplanet.nl*). From there, it's just over 4 miles (7 km)—a gentle cycle ride to the beach through woods, polders, and sand dunes.

A Drive Through the Bulb Fields of Haarlem

From late January through mid-May, the fields south of Haarlem are striped with the bold colors of crocuses and tulips, gladioli and lilies, grown for the bulb market and the cut-flower trade. Driving through this region, you can admire the vivid patchwork of colors created by this industry and visit the superb show gardens at Keukenhof.

The colored bands of flowers reflect market tastes in these bulb fields of Haarlem.

It takes about 40 minutes to drive from Amsterdam to Lisse, following signs for the A4/E19 road south toward Haarlem. Take exit 1 (Oude Wettening) for Lisse.

Lisse ❶ is an attractive town in the middle of the Bloembollenstreek, the bulb-growing district, whose flat, multicolored fields stretch for nearly 20 miles (30 km) from Haarlem in the north to Leiden in the south. Within the town, the small **Museum de Zwarte Tulp** (Black Tulip Museum; *Grachtweg 2A, tel 025/241-7900, museumdezwartetulp.nl, closed Mon., $*) is devoted to the fascinating history of the tulip, introduced to the Netherlands from Turkey in the 1550s and so highly prized that small fortunes were once paid for prize blooms, including that of the elusive and legendary Black Tulip—a pure black bloom desired by all collectors, though no one had ever produced one, despite fraudsters persuading gullible

NOT TO BE MISSED:

Lisse • Keukenhof • Noordwijk aan Zee

customers to pay large sums of money for bulbs they claimed were black.

Just to the north of the town is the entrance to **Keukenhof ❷** *(tel 025/246-5555, keukenhof.nl, spring garden open mid-March–mid-May, summer garden Aug., $$$),* the 80-acre (32 ha) park that has served as a showcase for the Dutch flower industry for 65 years. Spectacular color effects (and heady scents) are the theme of this park, where more than 7 million bulbs are planted in layers to ensure a continuous show of color from March to May, complemented by the blooms of cherry trees and numerous sculptures. Some of the gardens are themed—natural gardens, water gardens, secret gardens, historical gardens, and mazes. In addition, there are pavilions with displays of photographs, works of art, and specialist plants such as orchids. During the summer, when the bulbs are dormant, there is an equally vivid display of perennial and bedding plants and flowering shrubs.

If you don't have a car, you can visit Keukenhof gardens by organized tour or by public transportation *(Bus no. 858 leaves from Schiphol Airport., tel 0900/9292 for travel information).*

From Keukenhof, turn right to follow the N208 southward through the bulb fields to **Sassenheim ❸**. On the western edge of the town is the pretty **Kasteel Teylingen,** an

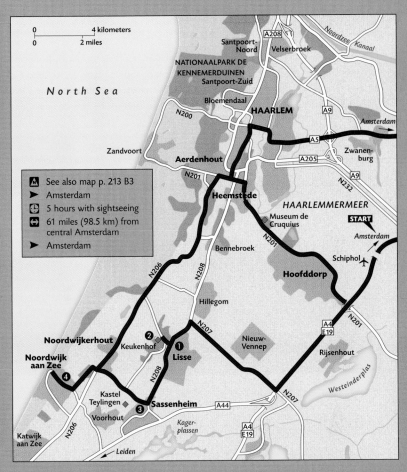

0   4 kilometers
0   2 miles

North Sea

NATIONAALPARK DE KENNEMERDUINEN

Santpoort-Noord   Velserbroek

A208

Noordzee Kanaal

Santpoort-Zuid

Bloemendaal

N200   **HAARLEM**   A9

Amsterdam

A5

Zandvoort

Aerdenhout

Zwanenburg

A205

N201

A9

N232

Heemstede

HAARLEMMERMEER

Museum de Cruquius

START

Amsterdam

Bennebroek

N201

Schiphol

N206

N208

Hoofddorp

Hillegom

Nieuw-Vennep

N207

A4 E19

N201

Noordwijkerhout

2 Keukenhof

1 **Lisse**

Rijsenhout

Westeinderplas

Noordwijk aan Zee

4

N208

Kastel Teylingen

3 **Sassenheim**

A44

N207

Voorhout

Kager-plassen

Katwijk aan Zee

N206

Leiden

A4 E19

- See also map p. 213 B3
- ► Amsterdam
- 🕐 5 hours with sightseeing
- ↔ 61 miles (98.5 km) from central Amsterdam
- ► Amsterdam

11th-century castle. Follow the N208 as it bends westward to meet the N206 near **Noordwijk aan Zee ④**. This is a seaside town where you'll find miles of glorious sand backed by dunes and perfect conditions for windsurfing.

The N206 will take you north to Haarlem through some of the bulb districts' most intensively colored fields. As you approach Haarlem, you can stop off for a visit to the city (see pp. 222–223), afterward returning to Amsterdam on the A5; or stay on the N206 and N201 and visit Zandvoort, returning to Amsterdam on the N201 via Hoofddorp.

If you return via Hoofddorp, you will pass the **Museum de Cruquius** (*Cruquiusdijk 27, tel 023/528-5704, closed Nov.–late Feb., $*), which shows how the bulb fields were created in the mid-19th century by draining the shallow Haarlemmermeer (Haarlem's Lake). The museum is housed in one of the pumping stations used for this mammoth task, and it is named after Nicolas Cruquius (1678–1754), the engineer who devised the drainage scheme in 1750, although it was not implemented until 1852. One of the exhibits shows the waterways of the Netherlands and the truly astonishing amount of land that has been reclaimed by the Dutch through drainage.

Leiden

Leiden is a university town with a long and honorable history and lively student life. Rembrandt (born in Leiden in 1606) was a law student here before he abandoned his degree to take up art. Highlights of the charming town include 12 excellent museums, lush botanical gardens, lively street markets, 35 picturesque hofjes, and countless cafés and antiquarian bookstores.

The Molenmuseum de Valk (Falcon Mill Museum), Leiden

Leiden

⬛ Map p. 213 B2

Visitor Information

✉ Stationsweg 41

☎ 071/516-6000

vvvleiden.nl

Molenmuseum de Valk

✉ 2e Binnenvest-gracht

☎ 071/516-5353

🕐 Closed Mon. & Sun. a.m.

💲 $

molendevalk.leiden.nl

Leiden is 30 minutes from Amsterdam by train. Its railroad station (home to the tourist office) stands just outside the historic city defenses, with three attractions located nearby. These are the seven-story **Molen-museum de Valk** (Falcon Mill Museum), built in 1743 and now the city's last surviving mill; the **Museum Volkenkunde** (National Anthropological Museum), which was founded in 1837 and is one of the world's oldest anthropological museums yet bursts with color, noise, and vitality; and, slightly farther into the city, the **Museum de Lakenhal** (Cloth Hall Museum). This last museum houses masterpieces by Rembrandt, Jan Steen, and Lucas van Leyden as well as a prized bronze cauldron, acquired by the starving people of Leiden in 1574 after the defeat of the Spanish soldiers who had held their city to a yearlong siege during the Revolt of the Netherlands (see p. 29). The Dutch traditionally cook a *hutspot* (hotchpotch stew) every October 3 to commemorate the siege, the recipe based on remnants found in the cauldron of the departing soldiers.

Courage & Learning

The citizens of Leiden withstood starvation and disease long enough for Willem of Orange, leader of the Dutch army, to inflict a decisive blow against the enemy. In gratitude, Willem founded the first university in the Netherlands here in 1575. Several of the classical buildings you pass on your way into the city housed the university's early faculty.

Leiden was one of Europe's first universities to have a botanical garden, planted in 1587. The entrance to the **Hortus Botanicus** lies halfway down Rapenburg, and you can see the original garden. It was named in honor of Carolus Clusius, Leiden's first professor of botany—the man who introduced the tulip to the Netherlands.

Opposite the garden entrance, Kloksteeg alley leads to Pieterskerk, a rose-pink brick Gothic church dating back to 1121, where John Robinson (1575–1625), leader of the Pilgrims, lies buried. Robinson was one of many Protestant refugees who found asylum in Leiden in the 17th century, and his preaching inspired the Pilgrims to set sail for the New World, although he fell ill and was unable to join them. Learn more about the pilgrims at the Leiden American Pilgrim Museum (*Beschuitsteeg 9, tel*

071/512-2413, closed Sun.–Tues., $), which is located in a beautifully preserved 14th-century house near the Hooglandskerk clock tower.

Cobbled lanes and antiquarian bookstores surround Pieterskerk, while two blocks north is the **Rijksmuseum van Oudheden** (National Museum of Antiquities). The museum houses a world-class collection of Egyptian artifacts, mummies, sarcophagi, a genuine Egyptian temple, and an exhibition on Dutch archaeology.

Shops & Cafés

Leiden's commercial heart lies farther to the east, at the confluence of two Rhine channels—the Oude Rijn and the Nieuwe Rijn (Old and New Rhine). The Nieuwe Rijn is crossed by the elegant Korenbeursbrug (Corn Exchange Bridge), a covered timber bridge dating from 1825 when it was built to provide shelter for the grain traders' stands. On Wednesdays and Saturdays, Leiden's street market continues a 900-year-old tradition, selling everything from local cheese and flowers to exotic herbs and spices. ∎

Museum Volkenkunde
- ✉ Steenstraat 1
- ☎ 071/516-8800
- 🕐 Closed Mon. & Oct. 3
- 💲 $$

volkenkunde.nl

Museum de Lakenhal
- ✉ Oude Singel 28–32
- ☎ 071/516-5360
- 🕐 Closed Sat. & Sun. a.m., Oct. 3.
- 💲 $$

lakenhal.nl

Hortus Botanicus Leiden
- ✉ Rapenburg 73
- ☎ 071/527-5144
- 🕐 Closed Oct. 3 & Mon. Nov.–Mar.
- 💲 $

hortusleiden.nl

Rijksmuseum van Oudheden
- ✉ Rapenburg 28
- ☎ 071/516-3163
- 🕐 Closed Mon. & Oct. 3
- 💲 $$

www.rmo.nl

Leiden's Floating Restaurants

Leiden has several "floating restaurants"—eateries that serve meals on prettily decorated barges tethered on the city's canals. There's something deeply pleasing about enjoying your lunch on the water, as ducks paddle past you—effortlessly outstripping the red-faced tourists in their hired rowing boats—and cyclists cross the ancient stone bridges that pass over the canals. The local's favorite is Annie's Verjaardag (*Hoogstraat 1a, tel 071/512-5737, annies .nu*), located in the heart of town at the confluence of three canals. Annie's serves brunch, lunch, afternoon tea, dinner, and various snacks.

Den Haag

Den Haag (The Hague) is the political capital of the Netherlands, chosen as a neutral meeting point by the leaders of the seven provinces that came together to form the Netherlands in 1586. The city was then no more than a hunting lodge owned by the counts of Holland surrounded by woods. Today it is an elegant city of palaces, public buildings, parks, shops, and diverse museums, with the vibrant seaside town of Scheveningen a short step away.

The Binnenhof (Dutch Parliament) and Hof Vijver (Court Lake) in The Hague

Den Haag
🅐 Map p. 213 B2
Visitor Information

✉ Spui 68
☎ 0900/340-3505

vvvdenhaag.nl

Mauritshuis
✉ Korte Vijverberg 8
☎ 070/302-3456
🕐 Closed Mon.
💲 $$$

mauritshuis.nl

ProDemos Visitors Centre
✉ Hofweg 1
☎ 070/364-6144
💲 $$

prodemos.nl

Den Haag Centraal Station is a 35-minute train ride from Amsterdam. From there, it is a short walk to Hof Vijver, the little lake that marks the historic center of the city. This tranquil stretch of water is all that remains of the medieval moat that protected the early city.

Reflected in the Vijver's calm surface are the noble facades of the parliament buildings and the beautiful **Mauritshuis,** built in 1644 as a private mansion for Count Johan Maurits when he retired from his post as governor of Brazil. The house was bequeathed to the state on his death and now makes an elegant home for the small but choice collection of paintings making

up the Royal Collection. On just three floors you will find some of the finest works ever produced by Carel Fabritius ("The Goldfinch," 1654), Vermeer ("Girl with a Pearl Earring," 1665), and Rembrandt ("The Anatomy Lesson of Dr. Nicolaes Tulp," 1632).

The fine courtyards of the Binnenhof, home to the Dutch parliament, are best appreciated during a guided tour, provided for a nominal fee by the **ProDemos Visitors Centre,** located on the other side of the Binnenhof from the Mauritshuis. These informative tours include a visit to the turreted, 13th-century Ridderzaal (Knights' Hall) at the heart of the complex. This was the dining hall of the original hunting lodge around which The Hague has grown. You can trace the story of the city's development in old paintings, furnished rooms, and period dollhouses in the adjacent **Haags Historisch Museum.**

Urban Delights

If you enjoy shopping, head for the pedestrian-only streets west of the Binnenhof, which are lined with chic boutiques, antique shops, art galleries, cafés, and upscale restaurants. Don't miss De Passage, an elegant covered arcade with beautiful stores. Noordeinde, the main shopping street, takes you north to a circular building housing the **Panorama Mesdag,** a vast and astonishingly realistic painting of the North Sea coast, which lines the inside wall and was created in 1881 by members of the Dutch Impressionist School, led by H. W. Mesdag (1831–1915).

The **Gemeentemuseum Den Haag** is a leading contemporary art museum, with the world's largest collection of works by Piet Mondrian (1872–1944), as well as pieces by Picasso, Klee, and Appel. It also hosts regular temporary exhibitions, which focus on modern design, fashion, and art.

A cruise aboard a small, traditional wooden boat with De Ooievaart (*Bierkade 18B, tel 070/445-1869, ooievaart.nl*) is the ideal way to explore Den Haag, with the option to hop on and off at key sights. There are also extended High Tea cruises, which whisk you to Delft and back with a generous teatime meal.

Farther Afield

Children always have fun at **Madurodam,** an interactive open-air park of miniature Dutch cities, towns, land- and waterscapes, and monuments, all of which are modeled with astonishing accuracy at a scale of 1:25. Also popular is the seaside town of Scheveningen, just a short tram ride from Den Haag (Tram: 1, 7, 8, 9). The seafront promenade looks out to long stretches of golden sand, liberally peppered with cafés and bars. Outdoor terraces are sheltered

INSIDER TIP:

If you're mad about nuts, visit de Notenkoning [The Nut King; *Grote Halstraat 16*]. This emporium sells every kind of nut imaginable, as well as freshly ground nut butters.

—LARRY PORGES
National Geographic Travel Books editor

from wind by glass walls, enabling hardy types to sit outside virtually year-round. The palatial Kurhaus was used for spa cures during Scheveningen's heyday as a 19th-century resort and now houses a luxury hotel and casino. Other attractions include the action-packed **Sea Life Scheveningen** aquarium and **Muzee Scheveningen,** which recounts the town's evolution from fishing port to spa destination. ∎

Haags Historisch Museum

✉ Korte Vijverberg 7
☎ 070/364-6940
🕐 Closed Mon.
💲 $$$

haagshistorisch
.museum.nl

Panorama Mesdag

✉ Zeestraat 65
☎ 070/310-6665
🕐 Closed Sun. a.m.
💲 $$$

panorama-mesdag
.com

Gemeentemuseum Den Haag

✉ Stadhouderslaan 41
☎ 070/338-1111
🕐 Closed Mon.
💲 $$$

gemeentemuseum.nl

Madurodam

✉ George Maduroplein 1
☎ 070/416-2400
💲 $$$$

madurodam.nl

Sea Life Scheveningen

✉ Strandweg 13
☎ 070/354-2100
💲 $$$

visitsealife.com

Muzee Scheveningen

✉ Neptunusstraat 92
☎ 070/350-0830
🕐 Closed Mon.
💲 $

Delft

When Dutch East India ships returned from Asia bearing Chinese porcelain, Delft potters quickly copied the exotic new style, albeit decorating their pieces with scenes from daily Dutch life. Thus the Delftware industry was born in the 17th century, and soon no Dutch home was without its blue-and-white-painted tiles, jugs, and tulip jars. Today, the town still bristles with shops selling new and antique pottery and proudly bears the legacy of both Prince Willem of Orange (1533–1584), who died here, and Johannes Vermeer (1632–1675), who lived here.

Delft pottery has brought this small town global recognition.

Delft is an hour's direct train trip from Amsterdam. The historic center lies just a few minutes' walk from the railway station—head straight until you reach the Oude Delft canal. Shaded by lime trees and crossed by a series of humpbacked bridges, it is a quintessentially Dutch canal, lined with venerable old buildings, including Oostindische Huis at No. 39, the 17th-century Delft headquarters of the Dutch East India Company.

Prinsenhof

Turning left along Oudeschans you come to **Museum Het Prinsenhof,** a cluster of old buildings in the shadow of the Oude Kerk tower. Originally the Convent of St. Agatha, the Prinsenhof was renamed in honor of Prince Willem of Orange, who used the convent as his campaign base during the Dutch Revolt. Fighting a long drawn-out war of attrition against the Spanish Catholic rulers, he led the Dutch army to victory. Desperate to break Dutch morale, the Spanish trained one Balthazar Gerards to assassinate Prince Willem, which he did in the Prinsenhof's Moordzaal (Murder Hall). Visitors to the museum can see the holes in the wall made by

Gerards's bullets as well as displays of Delftware, paintings, tapestries, and other decorative arts.

Crossing Oude Delft to the Gothic Oude Kerk (Old Church), you can see the tombs of Vermeer and two more heroic Dutch military leaders: Admiral Maarten Tromp (1598–1653), who defeated the English fleet in 1652, and Admiral Piet Heyn (1577–1629), who captured the Spanish silver fleet in 1628. Willem of Orange was buried in nearby Nieuwe Kerk (New Church) at the head of Delft's main square, with its 320-foot (100 m) tower, added in 1872. Here lies his richly decorated mausoleum, designed in 1614 by Hendrick de Keyser.

De Keyser also designed Delft's Renaissance-style Stadhuis (Town Hall) on the opposite side of the long market square as you leave the church. Completed in 1618, it survived an explosion that devastated much of the town in October 1645, when the National Arsenal caught fire.

Vermeer

The painter Johannes Vermeer was born in Delft, and he lived, worked, and died here. The **Vermeer Centrum Delft** is housed on the site of the former St Lucas guild, where he was dean for many years. The center re-creates Vermeer's world. It also studies his revolutionary painting techniques, shows many of his original pieces, and hosts exhibits that explore his global impact. On Sundays, entrance tickets include a walking tour of Delft (at 10:30 a.m.). Ask at the tourist office about ticket combinations that include entry to the Vermeer Center, Prinsenhof, Old and New Churches, Royal Delft Experience, and a canal cruise.

In Pursuit of Porcelain

Delft's streets are lined with shops selling new and antique Delftware, and several local factories offer tours. Of these, **De Porceleyne Fles** (The Porcelain Flask) stands out as the oldest, founded in 1653. ∎

Delft
🅰 Map p. 213 B2
Visitor Information
✉ Kerkstraat 3
☎ 015/215-4051
vvvdelft.nl

Museum Het Prinsenhof
✉ St. Agathaplein 1
☎ 015/260-2358
🕐 Closed Mon.
💲 $
prinsenhof-delft.nl

Vermeer Centrum Delft
✉ Voldersgracht 21
☎ 015/213-8588
💲 $$
vermeerdelft.nl

De Porceleyne Fles
✉ Rotterdamseweg 196
☎ 015/215-2030
🕐 Closed Sun.
💲 Tour: $$
royaldelftexperience.nl

EXPERIENCE: Create Your Own Delft Pottery

De Porceleyne Fles (*Rotterdamseweg 196, tel 015/251-2030, $$$$$, royaldelftexperience.nl*) offers various two-and-a-half-hour-long, hands-on workshops that teach the basic skills of earthenware painting in classic Delft Blue style. After coffee and apple cake, you will enjoy a guided tour of the pottery before settling down to work, with experienced professionals on hand to talk you through the creation of your blue-and-white masterpiece. You could decorate a Dutch tile with old-fashioned windmills, animal motifs, nautical or biblical scenes, or make your own design. For a special gift, a group of friends can create a tile tableau by painting individual tiles in the same theme. Alternatively, try your hand at painting a decorative plate, vase, or medallion, which comes complete with a leather chain and eyelet to make a pleasing gift, or a festive porcelain bauble or bell for Christmas. Prebooking these popular workshops is essential.

Rotterdam

First founded as a dam on the Rotte River in 1270, Rotterdam bloomed in the Golden Age, only for much of the city to be flattened during World War II. Rotterdam is now a city of modern architecture, its striking skyline punctuated with iconic structures such as the Erasmus Bridge.

Cube houses by architect Piet Blom, in Rotterdam

Rotterdam

⚑ Map p. 213 B1

Visitor Information

✉ Binnenwegplein, Coolsingel 195–197

☎ 010/790-0185

🕐 Closed Sun. Oct.–end March

rotterdam.info

Museum Boijmans van Beuningen

✉ Museumpark 18–20

☎ 010/441-9400

🕐 Closed Mon.

💲 $$

boijmans.nl

Dutch pragmatism is apparent in the way Rotterdammers viewed the destruction of their city during World War II as an opportunity to rebuild it in a more efficient, workable way. Thanks to its strategic location at the Rhine-Meuse-Scheldt delta on the North Sea, Rotterdam was a key shipping hub servicing Holland, England, and Germany as early as 1350, growing in importance over the centuries to become the major international commercial center it is today. Locals regard it as a no-nonsense workers' city, saying: "Money is earned in Rotterdam, divided in The Hague, and spent in Amsterdam."

Rotterdam Welcome

The train trip from Amsterdam to Rotterdam takes one hour. Follow signposts for the tourist office, a 15-minute walk from the railway station. Here you can buy a Rotterdam Welcome Card, which, like the I amsterdam City Card, is available for 24, 48, or 72 hours and gives unlimited use of public transport, free or discounted entry to over 50 museums and attractions, and discounts in restaurants, shops, and bars.

Visit the **Museumpark** next, with its landscaped gardens and outdoor sculptures flanked by exhibition venues such as the **Museum Boijmans van**

Beuningen. A world-class gallery containing works by Pieter Brueghel, Dürer, Jan van Eyck, and Rembrandt among the Old Masters, Boijmans also houses a large modern art collection, with works by surrealist artists Dalí and Magritte. Other institutions on the Museumpark include the **Kunsthal** (Hall of Culture), which holds a rolling program of eclectic exhibitions; the fascinating **Natuurmuseum** (Nature Museum) with its exhibitions of fossils, skeletons, insects, and stuffed birds and animals; the **Chabot Museum,** dedicated to the work of Expressionist artist Henk Chabot; and the **Nederlands Architectuurinstituut (NAI),** an archive, museum, library, and cultural podium, which also houses one of the world's largest architecture collections.

Keep walking west to Het Park (The Park), a popular park over which towers the **Euromast** (see sidebar below). Built in 1960, the tower has restaurants and a viewing gallery 328 feet (100 m)

up, the ideal spot from which to get your bearings. Reach 607 feet (185 m) by taking the rotating glass elevator up the Space Tower.

Delfshaven

From the Euromast, there are extensive views of the Europoort, the world's second-largest container port after Shanghai, stretching 25 miles (40 km) along the banks of the Maas and Rijn (Rhine) to the North Sea. Also visible are the last traces of Old Rotterdam—Delfshaven (Delft Harbor) and Oude Haven (Old Harbor), waterways filled with leisure boats. The Delfshaven Oude Kerk (known as the Pilgrim Fathers' Church) marks the spot where the Pilgrims embarked the *Speedwell* in 1620 to meet their sister ship, the *Mayflower,* in Southampton. Across the city, Oude Haven combines old warehouses with modern architecture, such as Piet Blom's Kubus houses. Built in 1984, these cube-shaped apartments

Kunsthal
- ✉ Westzeedijk 341
- ☎ 010/440-0300
- 🕐 Closed Mon.
- 💲 $$

kunsthal.nl

Natuurmuseum
- ✉ Westzeedijk 345
- ☎ 010/436-4222
- 🕐 Closed Mon.
- 💲 $

nmr.nl

Chabot Museum
- ✉ Museumpark 11
- ☎ 010/436-3713
- 🕐 Closed Mon.

chabotmuseum.nl

Nederlands Architectuurinstituut
- ✉ Museumpark 25
- ☎ 010/440-1200
- 🕐 Closed Mon.
- 💲 $$$

nai.nl

EXPERIENCE: Enjoy Romance in the Euromast

Located over 330 feet (112 m) above Rotterdam in the **Euromast** (see p. 254; *Parkhaven, tel 010/436-4811, euromast.nl*) are two of the city's most sought-after suites: Heaven and Stars. These two contemporary suites are both semi-circular, taking up half of the mast each, feature the organic shapes of the 1960s, when the Euromast was built, and offer unparalleled views. Heaven is situated on the south side of the Euromast, overlooking the Maas and the harbor, while Stars is located on the north side, with glittering city views and an indulgent jacuzzi bathtub. Each evening from 10 p.m. until 10 a.m. the following morning, guests have exclusive access to the upper platforms of the Euromast, ensuring total privacy and the highest and largest balcony in Rotterdam, upon which to enjoy a complimentary bottle of champagne. Breakfast can be enjoyed in the comfort of the suite or in the brasserie below.

Euromast

✉ Parkhaven 20
☎ 010/436-4811
$ $$$

euromast.nl

Kijk-Kubus

✉ Overblaak 70
☎ 010/414-2285
$ $

kubuswoning.nl

Maritiem Museum Rotterdam

✉ Leuvehaven 1
☎ 010/413-2680
🕐 Closed Mon.
$ $$$

maritiemmuseum.nl

are tipped at dizzying angles, forming a crystalline structure standing on top of stalklike towers. Taste life in a cube by visiting the fully furnished **Kijk-Kubus** "Show Cube" or spend a night in one at the Stayokay Hostel Rotterdam (Overblaak 85–87, tel. 010/436-5763, stayokay.com).

INSIDER TIP:

Drop by the New York Hotel [hotelnewyork.nl] opposite the Erasmus Bridge for a taste of old America. Built in 1872 as the head office of the Holland-America Line, it's lost in time with original furnishings, and includes a restaurant, café, and barber shop.

—GABRIELLA LE BRETON
National Geographic author

The Bibliotheek van Rotterdam (public library) is known to locals as the "glass waterfall" for its striking glass exterior. Attracting some 3.5 million visitors annually, it offers an extraordinary collection of books, music, and films as well as seminars, live theater, and music performances.

Maritime Rotterdam

Along Leuvehaven, there are three museums devoted to local and Dutch maritime history and tradition, notably the excellent **Maritiem Museum**

Rotterdam (Maritime Museum Rotterdam). Take a ride aboard an amphibious Splashtours bus (Willem Buytewechstraat 45, tel 010/436-9494, $$$, splashtours.nl) to see the modern port. Departing from the Maritime Museum, the bus makes a scenic city tour before plunging into the Maas River to cruise around the port.

City Center

North of the port, the city center reveals the modern, multicultural, and vibrant metropolis that Rotterdam has become, with diverse restaurants, bars, clubs, galleries, and stores. While Delfshaven is peppered with antique stores and the trendy Witte de Withstraat abounds with cutting-edge fashion boutiques, international fashion chains and department stores line the area around Lijnbaan and Beursplein. The Beurstraverse shopping mall runs below street level here, lending it the local nickname De Koopgoot (The Shopping Gutter). East of the major thoroughfare Coolsingel, Meent boasts interesting fashion and design concept stores, while Nieuwemarkt and Pannekoekstraat offer a more bohemian, arty feel.

On Tuesdays and Saturdays a large general market takes over the Binnenrotte area, while an antiques and bric-a-brac market takes place on Sundays among the mini-Manhattan architecture on Schiedamsedijk, by Leuvehaven. Here, you'll see why Rotterdam is often referred to as "Manhattan on the Maas." ■

Travelwise

Planning Your Trip   236

How to Get to Amsterdam   236–237

Getting Around   237–238

Practical Advice   238–240

Emergencies   240–241

Further Reading   241

Hotels & Restaurants   242–255

Shopping   256–261

Entertainment & Activities   262–264

Trams are a convenient and scenic way to get around Amsterdam.

TRAVELWISE

PLANNING YOUR TRIP

When to Go

Amsterdam is what you make of it, but some seasons here are particularly good for particular interests, be it traditional events, gardens, festivals, or weather.

January & February

Although somber weather generally prevails at this time of year, it is a good time to seize on good value accommodation, relatively empty restaurants and museums, and sales bargains.

March & April

Visiting Amsterdam in spring guarantees you a blaze of glorious bulbs, daffodils, and crocuses. A visit to Keukenhof and a drive or cycle ride through the bulb fields make for an unforgettable spring. Easter, which may fall in March or April, brings age-old Dutch traditions and spellbinding music in Amsterdam's churches. On April 27, Amsterdam goes orange to celebrate King's Day with a carnival atmosphere consuming the entire city (see p. 19).

May & June

Amsterdam joins the rest of the Netherlands on May 4 when its citizens pay their respects to the fallen soldiers of World War II and more recent military conflicts and peacekeeping operations on Herdenkingsdag (Remembrance Day). Then it's time for a national party on May 5, as crowds take to the streets to celebrate their freedom on Bevrijdingsdag (Liberation Day). The Holland Festival of performing arts runs through most of June, and Open Tuinen Dagen (Open Garden Days) takes place the third weekend of June, enabling you to gain access to private homes and gardens.

July & August

Come July in Amsterdam, summer is in full swing: The city beaches host dance music events, the Amsterdam International Fashion Week struts its stuff, the Robeco Summer Concert Series returns to the Concertgebouw, and festival season starts in earnest. August kicks off with Gay Pride before ceding into the classical music Grachtenfestival (Canal Festival) and the multi-event Uitmarkt.

September & October

Clinging to the last rays of sunshine in September, Amsterdam still offers plenty in the way of festivals, such as the Dutch Theater Festival and accompanying Fringe Festival, and the Valtifest music event in Noord. This can be a delightful month to visit, with fewer tourists and crisp autumnal days. As the nights draw in come October, events head indoors, such as the Cinekid Festival and Amsterdam Dance Event (ADE), the world's biggest club festival.

November & December

These winter months are when Dutch *gezelligheid* comes into its own, with long, cold days made bearable by hunkering down in cozy, candlelit cafés and beautifully decorated shops and hotels. With the hotly anticipated Sinterklaas celebration on December 5, Christmas, and New Year's Eve just around the corner, this is the time to embrace Amsterdam's age-old traditions: chocolate letters, gifts from Zwarte Piet (Black Peter), *pepernoten* and *speculaas*, mulled wine, Christmas markets, ice-skating, and holiday concerts and plays.

Climate

In Amsterdam they say that the weather has only three states: If it's not already raining, then it has either just stopped or is just about to start. In truth, it doesn't rain quite so much, but the city's maritime climate does result in many overcast days. Those cloudy Dutch skies were an inspiration to Golden Age landscape painters, but to modern travelers, they are a warning not to travel without a waterproof coat or an umbrella.

Spirits soar perceptibly during summer, when temperatures can rise to the 80s°F (high 20s°C) and Amsterdammers become Mediterranean, making the most of the fair weather by eating and drinking outdoors as much as possible. Fall can also be delightful, with blue skies and fluffy clouds and a riot of autumnal foliage along the canals. Winter can bring freezing sea fog that hangs over the city for days at a time. As soon as the wind changes to an easterly direction, the fog blows away and is replaced by cold blue skies. Snow and deep frost are now rare, because the city has such a warm microclimate.

Passports & Visas

Visitors from the U.S., Canada, Australia, New Zealand, and most European nations can visit the Netherlands for up to three months with a valid passport and no visa.

HOW TO GET TO AMSTERDAM

By Airplane

Amsterdam's Schiphol Airport is one of the busiest hub airports in the world and is also consistently voted one of its best. Myriad shops, bars, cafés, and restaurants are complemented by a mini branch of the Rijksmuseum, a spa, hotel, and casino (airport inquiries tel 0900/0141, schiphol.nl).

Located just 12 miles (20 km) from Amsterdam, Schiphol is served by its own railroad station, underneath the airport itself, with direct services to Centraal Station (Amsterdam CS) every 15 minutes. Train tickets are available from the yellow ticket machines and in the ticket offices near the platforms at Schiphol Plaza. Direct journeys to Centraal Station take about 20 minutes and cost no more than €4 ($5) one-way (national rail inquiries tel 0900/20-21163, ns.nl).

Connexxion Schiphol Hotel Shuttle buses travel frequently to and from Schiphol Plaza and the center of Amsterdam (Leidseplein), taking only about 30 minutes. Tickets cost €10 ($13) round trip (tel 038/339-4741, airport hotelshuttle.nl).

Taxis are considerably dearer than public transportation (approximately €40/$50), so worth considering if you're traveling in a group of four or more people. The official stand is just outside the main exit. Don't take rides from casual drivers soliciting within the airport. Allow 20 to 30 minutes from the airport to your hotel—more if you arrive during rush hour.

By Cruise Ship & Ferry

Increasing numbers of visitors arrive in Amsterdam by cruise ship, sailing right into the heart of the city to arrive at the striking **Passenger Terminal Amsterdam** (PTA; tel 509-1000, ptamster dam.nl), with its undulating waveline roof. From here, it's a pleasant 15-minute walk along the waterside to Centraal Station. Or take Tram 26 from opposite the Muziekgebouw aan 't IJ (just to the right of the PTA) or Tram 25, located to the left of the PTA.

The following companies offer car and foot passenger ferry services across the North Sea between England and the Netherlands: **DFDS Seaways** (tel 0871/522-9955, dfdsseaways.co.uk). Two ferries sail daily from Newcastle to the Felison Terminal at the port of IJmuiden, on the outskirts of Amsterdam. From IJmuiden, it is a 35-minute drive to central Amsterdam by car or regular DFDS Seaways-operated coach service. Alternatively, take the **Fast Flying Ferry** (tel 0900/266-6399, fff.nl) hydrofoil service directly to Centraal Station. **Stenaline** (tel 08705/707-070, stenaline.com). Twice daily (day and overnight service) from Harwich to Hoek van Holland. It is a one-hour-and-20-minute drive from Hoek van Holland to Amsterdam or one hour and 45 minutes by train, with regular departures from the port. **P&O North Sea Ferries** (tel 087/1664-2121, poferries.com). A nightly service between Hull and Rotterdam's Europoort. It is 90 minutes' drive from Rotterdam to Amsterdam. P&O operates a coach service from the Europoort to Rotterdam Centraal Station (tickets need to be prebooked at the reservations department), from where it is about one hour to Amsterdam Centraal Station. A Eurolines bus service also goes from Europoort to Amsterdam Centraal Station.

By Train

Amsterdam is easily reached by fast, modern trains from all parts of continental Europe, with several services a day from Paris, Brussels, Berlin, Cologne, Frankfurt, Luxembourg, and beyond (for details of international rail services see the Dutch national website, ns.nl). They all arrive right in the heart of Amsterdam, at Centraal Station. From London,

Eurostar provides a seven-hour passenger service to Amsterdam via Brussels (tel 08432/186-186 or 0044/1233-617-575 from outside the UK, eurostar.com).

By Car

Each year, about a million tourists arrive in Amsterdam by car. At the hub of several trans-European motorways, the city is easily reached by road from continental Europe. However, the inner city is something of a maze with very limited car parking. It is thus recommended that drivers make use of the parking garages and park-and-ride facilities located just outside of the central area. These offer excellent public transport connections, and many also incorporate bicycle hire in the cost of parking. Visit iamsterdam.com for further details. Drivers from the U.K. can bring their car using the ferry services (see above), or the Eurotunnel shuttle service linking Folkestone to the French terminus at Calais (tel 0443/353-535, eurotunnel.com).

GETTING AROUND
By Tram, Bus, & Metro

Amsterdam has a fully integrated transportation system, incorporating trams, buses, metro, and ferries, which link up to provide seamless transitions. OV-chipkaart (PT Smart Card) tickets are valid for all forms of transportation and can be topped up with a single journey or credit in euros, or for one- to seven-day unlimited use tickets. The I amsterdam City Card also provides unlimited access to public transportation for 24, 48, or 72 hours (see p. 10). Most important, as you will be reminded while riding public transport, don't forget to check in and check out. When you start each journey, hold your card up to the reader until a green light appears. A bleeping sound will indicate that your card has been read. If you change to another bus/tram/metro, you have to check out (by scanning your card at the machine again), and check in again at your next stop. If you forget to check out, the card will no longer be valid and you risk a fine. Visit www.en.gvb.nl for further information about Amsterdam's public transportation.

The hub of the city's public transport system is Amsterdam Centraal Station (Central Station), from where buses and trams depart for all parts of the city. There is also a metro station here and a ferry terminus (for free ferries to Amsterdam Noord). To the left of the metro entrance (next to the VVV tourist office) is the office of GVB, the authority that runs Amsterdam's public transportation, where you can buy tickets, travel cards, excursion packages, and route maps. Essentially, trams provide a comprehensive service within the city center and are best suited to tourists, while buses are the best link to the suburbs, and the metro is really intended for commuters, serving predominantly residential areas ringing the city.

By Water

Trams will take you to your destination fast, but if you want a more leisurely ride, you can take to the water (see p. 68). Canal boat services are a more romantic way of getting around, although they are not part of the public transportation system and are relatively expensive. However, an I amsterdam City Card includes one free canal cruise, and buying a ticket with the major cruise operators will give you discounted entry to some museums.

Canal Bus (tel 623-9886, canal.nl) and **Lovers** (tel 530-090,

lovers.nl) both offer 24-hour hop-on/hop-off tickets (Canal Bus also has a 48-hour option), which build in discounts on admission to various museums.

Water Taxi (tel 535-6363, water-taxi.nl) is a rigid inflatable boat that accommodates up to eight passengers and charges by the minute for inner-city journeys.

By Taxi

Traveling by taxi isn't generally necessary in Amsterdam, unless you're carrying lots of luggage or running late. Taxi regulations have been significantly tightened up recently, with the introduction of official, monitored taxi stands (you are not supposed to hail taxis in the street) and licensed cabs with regulated meters ensuring more consistent fares. Reserve a taxi through **Taxicentrale Amsterdam (TCA)** by telephone or online (tel 777-7777, tcataxi.nl). If time is not of the essence, consider calling a **Tuk Tuk** sightseeing taxi (tel 06/2020-9294) or bicycle taxi (tel 06/1859-5153).

By Bicycle

Thanks to its compact size and extensive network of bike paths, Amsterdam is the perfect city to explore on two wheels, making bicycle rental an appealing option. However, for the uninitiated, the sheer numbers of cyclists on the roads, the labyrinth of bicycle paths, and backpedal brakes take some getting used to. Before you hit the city streets, take a few minutes to familiarize yourself with your bike and the rules of the road—MacBike offers a free, multilingual leaflet on how to cycle safely through Amsterdam. Also be sure to follow instructions the vendor will give you on how to park and lock the bike in authorized locations, always securing it to a

fixed, immovable object such as a lamppost. Failure to do so will incur the loss of your deposit, regardless of whether you have taken out insurance against the event of theft. To rent a bike, you will be asked to leave a blank credit card slip, or your passport and a cash deposit. MacBike has a wide range of bicycles and outlets at Centraal Station, Leidseplein, Waterlooplein, and Marnixstraat (tel 620-0985, macbike.nl).

If you are nervous about cycling on your own, several companies offer guided bicycle tours of Amsterdam and the surrounding countryside, including **Yellow Bike** (Nieuwezijds Kolk 29, tel 620-6940, yellowbike.nl), **Mike's Bikes** (Kerkstraat 134, tel 622-7970, mikesbiketoursamsterdam.com), and **Orange Bike** (Oudezijds Voorburgwal 147, tel 528-9990, orange-bike.nl).

PRACTICAL ADVICE

Currency

The euro currency is used in the Netherlands: 100 euro cents make one euro. Coins are in denominations of 1c, 2c, 5c, 10c, 20c, 50c, €1, and €2. Notes are in €5, €10, €20, €50, €100, €200, and €500.

Credit cards are not used as widely as in most other European countries and are not accepted in major supermarkets or most smaller cafés, restaurants, and bars.

Electricity

Dutch sockets are of the Continental two-pin type, so you need a converter to use equipment with U.S. or U.K. plugs. The voltage (220V, 50HZ) is fine for U.K. equipment, but to use lower-voltage U.S. equipment you need a transformer.

Liquor & Narcotics

Individuals can legally buy and consume alcohol from the age of

16. Supermarkets and shops can sell beer and wine or alcoholic beverages only with an upper alcohol limit of 13 percent. Spirits are sold only in liquor stores.

Dutch law distinguishes between "soft drugs" (namely cannabis, excluding hallucinogenic mushrooms) and "hard drugs," allowing the personal use of the former by adults aged 18 and over in a limited, controlled way in designated coffee shops. These coffee shops are permitted to stock a maximum of 17.5 ounces (500g) of cannabis at any time and can sell a maximum of 0.17 ounces (5g) to any adult. It is not legal to smoke cannabis outside of a designated coffee shop. The possession, use, and sale of hard drugs such as heroin, LSD, ecstasy, and cocaine are illegal.

Media
You can buy the world's leading newspapers and magazines from the **Athenaeum Nieuwscentrum** (Spui 14), **Waterstone's** (Kalverstraat 152), or the **American Book Center** (Kalverstraat 185). The Dutch read De Telegraaf (conservative) and De Volkskrant (progressive). As you will hear if you take a taxi, most people listen to 3FM, the public pop and chat channel (91.5 FM). More serious talk radio and news is broadcast (in Dutch) on Radio 1 (88.5 FM).

Museum Card
If you intend on visiting plenty of museums during your visit to Amsterdam, it is worth considering an **I amsterdam City Card,** which gives access to some 40 attractions for 24, 48, or 72 hours (see p. 10). Alternatively, and particularly if you are able to spend a week or more in the city and plan to visit other Dutch cities, consider purchasing a **Museumkaart (Museum Card).** Valid for a year, these cards cost

€45 ($58) per adult and €22.50 ($29) for under 18s, and give unlimited access to some 400 museums across the Netherlands, including the key attractions in Amsterdam (tel 0900/4040-910, museumkaart.nl).

Opening Hours
Shops are open from Monday to Saturday, 9 a.m. to 6 p.m. (Saturday until 5 p.m. and Thursday evenings until 9 p.m.) and Sundays 12 p.m. to 5 p.m. Some supermarkets stay open until 8 p.m. or 10 p.m. on weeknights. Most businesses operate Monday to Friday, 8:30 a.m. to 5 p.m. Banks are open weekdays only, between 9 a.m. and 4 p.m.

Post Offices
Post offices are generally open weekdays only, between 9 a.m. and 5 p.m. However, Amsterdam's main post office, located in the basement of Singel 250 (tel 556-3311), to the rear of the Royal Palace, has longer opening hours (7.30 a.m.–6.30 p.m. Mon.– Fri.; 7.30 a.m.–5 p.m. on Sat.; closed Sun.).

Public Holidays
Very little closes in Amsterdam except on the three big occasions of New Year's Day, King's Day (April 27), and Christmas Day. In addition, the following are public holidays; some dates vary from year to year according to the liturgical calendar:
Easter Sunday and Monday (April or March)
Liberation Day (May 5)—official holiday every five years from 2015
Ascension Day (May or June)
Pentecost Monday and Sunday (May or June)
Sinterklaas (December 5)—not an official public holiday but often taken as a holiday by the Dutch
Boxing Day (December 26)

Restrooms
Men are well provided for, with Parisian-style pissoirs located all around the city center. Streetside public conveniences are otherwise rare—people use café restrooms, but these are for customers only, so you should buy a drink before using the facilities. Museums and public buildings have clean, modern facilities, some of which ask for a 20c or 50c tip for use.

Smoking
While smoking is officially banned in all bars, pubs, restaurants, and other public places, you will find that the Dutch still light up in some bars and clubs.

Telephones
The city dialing code for Amsterdam is 020, which is not required when making calls within Amsterdam but only when you're outside the city. To make a local call from a public telephone in Amsterdam, you will need a telephone card, available from post offices, newsagents, and several tourist offices. The international access code to call abroad from the Netherlands is 00, plus the code of the country you wish to call. When calling Amsterdam from abroad, dial 0031 (for the Netherlands) and 20 (for Amsterdam). In the Netherlands, toll phone numbers are preceded by the code 0800; premium rate lines by the code 0900; and cell phones by 06.

Useful Telephone Numbers
International directory inquiries 0900-8418
International and national operator 0800-0410
National directory inquiries 0900-8008

Time Differences

The Netherlands observes Central European Time (CET), one hour ahead of Greenwich Mean Time (GMT).

Tipping

Value added tax and service charges are included in hotel, restaurant, and shopping bills and taxi fares. Tips for extra service are not necessary in cafés or bars unless you feel the service was outstanding. In restaurants, a tip of 5 to 10 percent is always appreciated but not necessary: Pay the waiter directly by rounding up the bill. Tipping taxi drivers is rare, unless you get a particularly friendly one or receive assistance with luggage from him, in which case you can tip up to about 10 percent of the fare.

Tourist Information

Tourist information services are provided by the VVV (pronounced Fay Fay Fay in Dutch). There are branches dotted across the city, but the flagship office is located in the cream-painted timber **Noord-Zuid Hollandsch Koffiehuis** building on the waterfront opposite Centraal Station (Stationsplein 10, tel 702-6000). It is open Mon.–Sat. 9 a.m.– 6 p.m., and Sun. 10 a.m.–5 p.m. Other sizable tourist offices are found at Schiphol Airport and Leidseplein. You can book accommodation, excursions, boat trips, concert tickets, guided tours, and I amsterdam City Cards in person at these tourist offices or online at iamsterdam.com.

Useful Websites

artsholland.com for culture lovers
iamsterdam.com a mine of information from the tourist office covering everything from the city's hotels and events to its history and last-minute deals

and details of the I amsterdam City Card
dutchnews.nl Dutch news in English
holland.com the official tourism website of the Netherlands
lastminuteticketshop.nl sells official tickets to concerts, theater performances, and other events in Amsterdam for half the regular price when bought on the day
ns.nl the national railway inquiries website
petitepassport.com/category/amsterdam an informative and entertaining blog by a resident Amsterdammer
9292.nl general public transport advice

EMERGENCIES
Police, Fire, & Ambulance

To summon any of these services, dial 112 from any telephone, free of charge. The emergency services operator will speak English. Tell them the address where the incident has taken place and the nearest landmark, crossroads, or house number; also tell them precisely where you are.

To report a theft to the police, or if you have other queries, dial 0900-8844.

There are police stations in central Amsterdam at Beursstraat 33 (just off Damrak), Nieuwezijds Voorburgwal 104, Marnixstraat 148, and also Elandsgracht 117.

Embassies/Consulates
American Consulate
Museumplein 19, Amsterdam
(tel 575-5309)
British Consulate
Koningslaan 44, Amsterdam
(tel 676-4343)
Canadian Embassy
Sophialaan 7, The Hague
(tel 070/311-1600)
For a full list of all embassies and consulates in Amsterdam, visit government.nl.

Health Precautions

There are no inherent health risks involved in visiting Amsterdam. If you do need a doctor or dentist during your visit, ask your hotel reception for advice. If the problem is minor, go to the nearest chemist (pharmacy) and speak to the pharmacist.

Useful telephone numbers:
Ambulance 112
24-hour doctor 0800-0030-600
24-hour pharmacy information line 592-3315
(Dutch-speaking, no guarantee of English, can advise on which outlets are nearest to you and open at the time of your call)

Public hospitals in Amsterdam with 24-hour emergency departments include:

OLVG Hospital, Eerste Oosterparkstraat 279 (tel 599-9111)

Sint Lucas Hospital, Jan Tooropstraat 164 (tel 510-8160)

Many drugs freely available in the U.S. cannot be bought over the counter at an apotheek (pharmacy) in the Netherlands. Be sure to bring sufficient supplies of medicines from home. If more are needed, take the packaging with a full printed description of its contents to the chemist for advice on buying the nearest equivalent. Pharmacies are usually open Monday through Friday, from 9 a.m. to 5.30 p.m.

Apotheek Leidsestraat is open seven days a week from 8:30 a.m. until 11 p.m. (Leidsestraat 74–76, tel 422-0210).

Lost or Stolen Credit Cards

Report any loss or theft immediately to your credit card company, so cards can be stopped, and to the local police station. Also phone your bank.

Lost Property

Always inform the police if you lose something of value, to validate insurance claims. Report a lost passport to your embassy (and carry a separate photocopy of the information pages so a replacement can be expedited).

Luggage lost on a train should be reported at the desk to the left of luggage lockers in Centraal Station. Objects found on trains are stored centrally in Utrecht, so you might have to go there to retrieve your items. For items found elsewhere in the city, contact the **Bureau Gevonden Voorwerpen** (Office of Lost Property; Stephensonstraat 18, tel 559-3005), located a little way out of town, near Amstel station.

Sensible Precautions

Keep valuables locked in the hotel safe. Note, and preferably photocopy, any important information on passports, tickets, and credit cards, and keep this information safe in a separate place.

Keep only a small amount of money with you; put the rest in the hotel safe. Keep the documents and money in a closed bag when you carry them. Do not leave your bag unattended, or on the floor of a restaurant, theater, or cinema. Do not travel alone at night, unless in a licensed taxi or along well-lit streets and in buses with other people. Avoid parks at night.

FURTHER READING

Amsterdam: A Brief Life of the City, by Geert Mak. This entertaining and intelligent history of the city was written by one of Amsterdam's best-known journalists and social commentators.

Building Amsterdam, by Herman Janse. All you need to know to understand the architecture of Amsterdam, with meticulously hand-drawn sections to explain the different parts of a typical canalside house.

The Diary of Anne Frank: The Critical Edition, edited by David Barnouw and Gerrold van der Stroom. There are numerous editions of the famous wartime diary of Anne Frank, but this is the best because it provides the complete text of the diaries, including material that was cut from many editions because it was considered too personal.

The Embarrassment of Riches, by Simon Schama. Some would say that Simon Schama's prose is itself embarrassingly prolix, but there are many who enjoy reading his speculative and highly subjective account of Dutch cultural history.

Girl with a Pearl Earring, by Tracy Chevalier. This historical novel is set in the 1660s and concerns a 16-year-old girl called Griet who is hired as a servant in the household of the Dutch painter Johannes Vermeer. The story is full of information about the life and work of the artist.

The Holland Handbook, edited by Stephanie Dijkstra. Described as the indispensable reference book for the expatriate, this is full of practical information for anyone intending to live in the Netherlands, whether for a few weeks or several years. It covers everything from starting your own business to getting your children into a Dutch school.

Love in Amsterdam, by Nicolas Freeling. One of numerous detective stories set in Amsterdam in which Detective Van der Valk probes a mystery and comes up with an unexpected result.

Rembrandt's Eyes, by Simon Schama. Another mammoth tome full of psychological speculation about the life and mind of the great Dutch artist and an insight into the wider meanings of his works.

Tulip Fever, by Deborah Moggach. Another historical novel set in 17th-century Amsterdam, this riotous book concerns the antics of painter Jan van Loos against the background of the speculative market for rare tulips.

The UnDutchables, by Colin White and Laurie Boucke. Written by Americans who lived and worked in Amsterdam for many years, this humorous account of the Dutch and their culture explains what they really think about sex and drugs and rock-and-roll, how to behave on your birthday (a very important celebration for the Dutch), and how to haggle in flea markets.

Hotels & Restaurants

Amsterdam is one of Europe's most popular weekend break destinations, and the small city barely has enough hotel rooms to meet the demand. So it is essential to reserve accommodation well in advance of your visit, not only to secure yourself a bed but to avoid paying too much for a room. Once there, you'll find no shortage of international cuisine to enjoy in this cosmopolitan city.

HOTELS

Fully aware of the fact that demand outstrips supply for its hotel rooms, Amsterdam has been experiencing a much-needed hotel revolution in recent years, with new properties springing up across the city. Crucially, a disproportionately large number of these new additions are not large chain hotels but chic boutique hotels and B&Bs. Remaining true to Amsterdam's heritage and inimitable style, hotels like the Canal House, JL No. 76, and the Conservatorium have given historic buildings a new lease on life, dressing ancient sloping walls with modern Dutch art, placing rolltop baths by tall windows overlooking the canals, and commissioning handmade wallpaper based on traditional embroidered artworks.

By no means limited to making old look good, Amsterdam's hip hotel scene also includes cutting-edge properties like The Exchange, which features rooms designed by students of the Amsterdam Fashion Institute (AMFI). The Lloyd Hotel, located in the Eastern Docklands, pioneered the concept of providing rooms ranging in quality (and price) from one- to five-star, while the College Hotel is staffed by students of the Amsterdam Hotel Management School. Stay in a delightfully bijou B&B like the canalside Kamer 01 or Cake Under My Pillow in trendy De Pijp, blow the budget in the palatial Hotel Amstel, or spend the night on a houseboat or in a former water tower.

In the throes of this very exciting revolution, Amsterdam offers unparalleled choice in accommodation, so it's well worth taking some time to consider your priorities when booking your base. Given how compact the city is, location need not have too much bearing on your choice, although there is something magical about waking up to a view of ducks paddling down a tree-lined canal. Staying in an established hotel brings the benefits of a concierge, greater choice of amenities, and the ease of in-hotel dining, while a small B&B will offer more personalized service and an insight into local life. The Amsterdam Tourist Office (iamsterdam.com) has access to an extensive directory of properties across the city, also available online, and can advise on which might be best for you, if there is availability, and if there are any strong deals on particular properties.

Visitors with disabilities or particular needs in comfort, services, or anything else should bear in mind that smaller hotels located in historical buildings don't always have elevators or similar amenities, so check before you book.

Finally, don't rule out hotels in neighboring towns such as Den Haag, Haarlem, Delft, and Utrecht. There are some charming properties in these atmospheric spots, which are invariably less expensive than Amsterdam and only a short train ride from the capital.

RESTAURANTS

Just as Amsterdam's hotel revolution is leaving its mark on the city, so is its quiet food revolution making itself felt. Dutch cuisine is unlikely to take the culinary world by storm, and Amsterdam's restaurant scene isn't on a par with London's or New York's, but things have improved significantly in recent years. Innovative, talented Dutch chefs are returning from leading restaurants across the world to open their own establishments, such as Proef, Marius, Lastage, and De Kas, which focus on local produce and tap into Holland's colonial heritage. Amsterdam now boasts nine Michelin-starred restaurants (two of which have two stars), in addition to a host of ethnic restaurants, which enable visitors to sample a colossal range of different cuisines, from Cantonese and Moroccan to French and Japanese, with a particularly strong contribution from the

PRICES

HOTELS

An indication of the cost of a double room in the high season is given by $ signs.

$$$$$	Over $450
$$$$	$350–$450
$$$	$250–$350
$$	$120–$250
$	Under $120

RESTAURANTS

An indication of the cost of a three-course meal without drinks is given by $ signs.

$$$$$	Over $80
$$$$	$55–$80
$$$	$40–$55
$$	$25–$40
$	Under $25

---

former Dutch colonies of Indonesia and Suriname. Vegetarians are well catered to—almost every restaurant and café has meat-free dishes on the menu, although beware of the classic Dutch *groentesoep* (vegetable soup), which has meatballs in it.

Where Amsterdam's restaurant scene really differs from that of New York or London is in its informality—even in the smartest establishments, the dress code is invariably informal. By and large, restaurants are small and intimate, with seating for no more than 40 or so customers. Amsterdammers enjoy dining out, particularly on Fridays and Saturdays; so if you have your heart set on a particular restaurant, always reserve a table in advance. You must remember to ask for the bill at the end of the meal: It is considered rude for the server to bring the bill before you are ready to pay. Service in Dutch restaurants is often regarded as slow, but locals don't seem bothered by it—eating out is seen as a social activity, with as much emphasis on drinking and chatting as on eating.

Finally, many of Amsterdam's informal *eetcafés* (literally translated as an eating café, reflecting the fact that they serve more substantial food than merely pastries and snacks) close at 6 or 7 p.m. Thus, while not officially open for dinner, early diners can still enjoy a light—and very affordable—evening meal, should they wish.

Abbreviations

L = lunch
D = dinner
AE=American Express, DC=Diners Club, MC=Mastercard, V=Visa.

In the following selection, hotels are listed under each location by price, then in alphabetical order, followed by restaurants also by price and alphabetical order.

▓ NIEUWE ZIJDE

HOTELS

🏨 HOTEL DE L'EUROPE
🍽 $$$$$
NIEUWE DOELENSTRAAT 2–14, 1012 CP
TEL 531-1777
leurope.nl
Built in the grand style of 1896, Hotel de l'Europe stands on the site of a medieval bastion at the junction of several canals, almost entirely surrounded by water. The new Dutch Masters Wing has spacious, well-appointed suites. The waterside setting can be enjoyed from spacious balconied rooms and the popular **Het Terras** café. The gourmet **Bord'eau Restaurant** counts among Amsterdam's best, and **Freddy's Bar** (named after former regular Alfred Heineken) oozes atmosphere.
🛈 111 🚊 Tram: Muntplein
🅾 All major cards

🏨 NH GRAND HOTEL KRASNAPOLSKY
$$$$$
DAM 9, 1012 JS
TEL 554-9111
nh-hotels.com
A rather faded glory, the Krasnapolsky nonetheless boasts a prime location on Dam Square, with views of the copper-domed Royal Palace and the square. The 35 furnished apartments, in restored historic houses, are good for families.
🛈 468 🚊 Tram: Dam
🅾 All major cards

🏨 DIE PORT VAN CLEVE
🍽 $$$$
NIEUWEZIJDS VOORBURGWAL 176–180, 1012 SJ
TEL 714-2000
dieportvancleve.nl
An Amsterdam stalwart,

located by the Magna Plaza shopping center, Die Port van Cleve comprises three 18th-century houses and revels in Amsterdam's rich history, with lavish, traditional interiors. The **Brasserie De Poort** and the blue-tiled **Bodega De Blauwe Parade** serve traditional Dutch food: Try authentic *erwtensoep* (split pea soup with ham hock) and delicious Zeeland mussels.
🛈 122 🚊 Tram: Dam
🅾 All major cards

🏨 THE EXCHANGE
$$$
DAMRAK 50, 1012 LL
TEL 523-0080
exchangeamsterdam.com
The rooms of the innovative Exchange have been designed by students of the Amsterdam Fashion Institute (AMFI) in suitably quirky style. The "fashion hotel" allots rooms one- to five-star status, depending on their size, views, and amenities, but each is unique. A short distance from the Red Light District, it's at the heart of Old Amsterdam and popular with young visiting designers and fashionistas.
🛈 61 🚊 Tram: Dam
🅾 All major cards

🏨 HOTEL BROUWER
$$$
SINGEL 83, 1012 VE
TEL 624-6358
hotelbrouwer.nl
A traditional hotel decorated in the style of Dutch masters, which has been family-owned for more than 90 years. Brouwer's location on the Singel means most rooms have canal views and it's within a stone's throw from the main sights.
🛈 8 🚊 Tram: Nieuwezijds Kolk 🅾 All major cards

🛗 Elevator 🚭 Nonsmoking ❄ Air-conditioning 💪 Health Club 🅾 Credit Cards

RESTAURANTS

🍴 SUPPERCLUB
$$$$
JONGE ROELENSTEEG 21
TEL 344-6400
supperclub.nl
The now global supperclub started at this establishment in Amsterdam, its concept of combining dinner with music, dance, art, and general theater having proved hugely popular. There are no tables; you dine barefoot on oversize white beds, and you can expect to dance and be entertained by performers, artists, light shows, and DJs as you eat.
🚊 Tram: Dam 🕐 Closed L
🃏 All major cards

SOMETHING SPECIAL

🍴 LUCIUS
$$$
SPUISTRAAT 247C
TEL 624-1831
lucius.nl
Deliberately frugal, Lucius is one of the best places to eat fish in Amsterdam, and has been for more than 35 years. The white-tiled walls are bare except for the blackboards that tell you what is freshest and best that day—if in doubt, go for the gargantuan seafood platter and work your way through an exotic plateful of shellfish and crustaceans. Smart-suited business executives come here as well as families with children.
🚊 Tram: Dam/Spui
🕐 Closed L 🃏 All major cards

🍴 1E KLAS
$–$$$
CENTRAAL STATION,
STATIONSPLEIN 15
TEL 625-0131
restaurant1eklas.nl
Also known as Eerste Klas, this atmospheric restaurant occupies the former first-class waiting room on Platform 2b of Amsterdam's Centraal Station. Aproned waiters serve everything from tasty burgers to classic Dutch and French dishes beneath the high ceilings and frescoed walls of this fine building. A good spot for coffee and cake.
🚊 Tram: Centraal Station
🃏 All major cards

🍴 CAFÉ LUXEMBOURG
$$
SPUISTRAAT 22–24
TEL 620-6264
luxembourg.nl
Re-creating the atmosphere of the Parisian Left Bank, this popular bar-cum-brasserie is the meeting place for Amsterdam university students and lecturers, artists, and media types. Browse international magazines and newspapers as you sample what the owners claim to be "officially" Amsterdam's best *bitterballen* (deep-fried veal ragout balls), tasty prawn croquettes, or mussels and fries.
🚊 Tram: Spui 🃏 All major cards

🍴 GARTINE
$$
TAKSTEEG 7
TEL 320-4132
gartine.nl
Tucked away in an alley between Rokin and busy Kalverstraat, Gartine is an oasis of calm and a shrine to slow food. The owners grow their own fruit and vegetables in an allotment and feature regional delicacies from the official list of protected Dutch heritage products—the Slow Food's Ark of Taste. It's the perfect spot for hearty, delicious breakfast, lunch, or high tea, served on vintage crockery.
🚊 Tram: Spui/Rokin 🕐 Closed Mon., Tues. & D 🃏 No credit cards

🍴 HAESJE CLAES
$$
SPUISTRAAT 273–275
TEL 624-9998
haesjeclaes.nl
With its old wood paneling and Delft tiles, Haesje Claes is everyone's idea of the cozy Amsterdam of an Old Master painting. Although sometimes overpopulated by tourists, Amsterdammers come here too, proving the quality of the traditional Dutch dishes that are hard to find in other restaurants. Go for classics like *gerookte paling* (smoked eel) and *hutspot* (a tasty and filling "hodgepodge" of meatballs, sausage, carrots, cabbage, and mashed potatoes).
🚊 Tram: Spui 🃏 All major cards

■ OUDE ZIJDE

HOTELS

🏨 GRAND HOTEL AMRÂTH AMSTERDAM
$$$$$
PRINS HENDRIKKADE 108,
1011 AK
TEL 552-0000
amrathamsterdam.com
The original art deco details of this former shipping house have been meticulously preserved, but the guestrooms are spacious, with a modern take on art nouveau style. Located on the IJ River, with sweeping views of the city, the hotel celebrated its centenary in 2013 yet offers guests contemporary treats like coffee machines in each room and free entrance to its beautiful spa.
🛏 165 🚊 Tram: Dam
🃏 All major cards

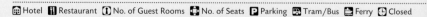

🏨 Hotel 🍴 Restaurant 🛏 No. of Guest Rooms 🍽 No. of Seats 🅿 Parking 🚊 Tram/Bus ⛴ Ferry 🕐 Closed

SOFITEL LEGEND AMSTERDAM THE GRAND
$$$$$
OUDEZIJDS VOORBURGWAL 197, 1012 EX
TEL 555-3111
sofitel.com
First a royal residence, then the City Hall, and later the Admiralty from where Holland's powerful navy was controlled, history comes as standard in the magnificent rooms of The Grand. More traditional than Amsterdam's clutch of new hotels, The Grand is walking distance from popular sights and has a pretty garden and good spa.
177 Tram: Dam
All major cards

MISC
$$$
KLOVENIERSBURGWAL 20, 1012 CV
TEL 330-6241
misceatdrinksleep.com
An excellent find in Oude Zijde, the boutique Misc features six guestrooms in a restored 17th-century canal house, which look out across the canal or the peaceful rear garden. Ranging from modern to baroque, the rooms cater to all tastes, and the owners and their guests invariably end up chatting about their day at the little cocktail bar or in the garden.
6 Tram: Centraal Station
All major cards

RESTAURANTS

SOMETHING SPECIAL

RESTAURANT LASTAGE
$$$$$
GELDERSKADE 29
restaurantlastage.nl
Situated in a beautiful historic canal house just outside the Red Light District, this Michelin-starred restaurant is the brainchild of Chef Rogier van Dam. Van Dam claims his signature style is simple and traditional Dutch cooking, with a hint of French influence. Nonetheless, the talented chef injects his sublime cuisine with flair and innovation, as reflected in dishes like poached pig cheek with langoustine, and sea bass marinated in Dutch gin.
Tram: Centraal Station
Closed Mon. & Tues., L on request All major cards

NEW KING
$$$
ZEEDIJK 115–117
TEL 625-2180
newking.nl
Giving Chinatown's well-established Nam Kee a run for its money, this Mandarin Chinese restaurant is worth the wait invariably required to secure a table. Portions are generous, and the house speciality of roasted duck is delicious served with a fragrant broth. The dim sum are also recommended.
Tram: Centraal Station
MC, V

RESTAURANT ANNA
$$$
WARMOESTRAAT 111
TEL 428-1111
restaurantanna.nl
The aim of this sleek, open-plan kitchen and restaurant in the medieval heart of Amsterdam is "to provide dinner at a very high level for an extremely reasonable price in a relaxed, informal atmosphere." It does more than achieve this, serving elegant and delicious cuisine and providing a tranquil place from which to admire Oude Kerk.
Tram: Centraal Station
All major cards

NAM KEE
$$
ZEEDIJK 111
TEL 624-3470
&
GELDERSEKADE 117
TEL 639-2848
namkee.net
Nam Kee's Zeedijk branch is almost synonymous with Amsterdam's Chinatown—there is even a novel named after it (*The Oysters of Nam Kee* by Kees van Beijnum). The Geldersekade branch, around the corner, is less frenetic and slightly more upscale. The service can be brusque, but that doesn't stop people flocking for some of the best and cheapest food in town, including *ma pa tofu* (bean curd with black bean and garlic sauce) and sizzling scallops.
Tram: Centraal Station
MC, V

PANNENKOEKENHUIS "UPSTAIRS"
$$
GRIMBURGWAL 2
TEL 626-5603
upstairspannenkoeken.nl
Situated in a 16th-century canal house, this charming pancake house lays claim to being Europe's smallest restaurant, with just four tables. A steep climb is required to reach Arno and Ali's pancake emporium, which is decorated with over 100 teapots, portraits of the Dutch royal family, and old paintings of Amsterdam. Expect classic Dutch pancakes, both savory and sweet, cooked with local organic produce, and be prepared to wait for a table. But the fare is worth waiting for.
Tram: Spui Closed D
No credit cards

🍴 POCO LOCO
$$

NIEUWMARKT 24
TEL 624-2937
diningcity.nl/pocoloco
This lively spot overlooking
Nieuwmarkt, with its retro,
1970s decor, is open all day
serving tasty tapas, huge sand-
wiches, fajitas, and meat skew-
ers. Mulled wine is served as
well as a host of Dutch beers.
There's dancing on "Freaking
Fridays," when the place really
does go *un poco loco.*
🚊 Tram: Nieuwmarkt 🚫 No
credit cards

🍴 VAN KERKWIJK
$$

NES 41
TEL 620-3316
caferestaurantvankerkwijk.nl
Although unprepossessing at
first sight, nestled into the Nes
alley that runs south of Dam
Square, Van Kerkwijk attracts
crowds of locals who jostle for
a table for its consistently good
food. There's no menu as such;
your waiter will run through
what's available, which can
range from steak and pâté to
tagine and curry.
🚊 Tram: Dam 🚫 No credit
cards

■ JODENBUURT, PLANTAGE, OOSTELIJK HAVENGEBIED, & ENVIRONS

HOTELS

🏨 LLOYD HOTEL & CULTURAL EMBASSY
🍴 **$$–$$$$$**

OOSTELIJKE HANDELSKADE 34,
1019 BN
TEL 561-3608
lloydhotel.com
Housed in a large, industrial-
age building that previously
served as an immigrant hotel
and prison, the Lloyd Hotel
is pioneering in many ways.
Although the affable, efficient
service is uniform, guest
rooms are rated from one- to
five-star, ensuring visitors of
all budgets can benefit from
its innovative design, popular
restaurant, inclusive walking
tours, and splendid location in
the Eastern Docklands.
🛏 117 🚊 Tram: Rietlandpark
🃏 All major cards

🏨 HOTEL REMBRANDT
$$$

PLANTAGE MIDDENLAAN 17,
1018 DA
TEL 627-2714
hotelrembrandt.nl
Close to Artis Zoo and well
located for the Tropenmu-
suem and Waterlooplein area,
this small, quirky hotel has
an impressive breakfast room
with mock medieval wall
hangings, and some large and
airy family rooms, decorated
in colonial style. Small doubles
are tight and the largest rooms
are at the front, where noise
from trams might disturb light
sleepers—ask for a back room
overlooking the garden.
🛏 17 🚊 Trams: Artis, Plantage
Kerklaan 🃏 All major cards

🏨 CASA WATERLOO
$$

WATERLOOPLEIN 177, 1011 PG
casawaterloo.nl
A minimalist, bright, airy, and
spotlessly clean apartment
available to rent on Water-
looplein. With a large double
bedroom, shower and bath,
open-plan kitchen and dining
area, and a little balcony, this is
a great self-catered option.
🛏 1 🚊 Tram: Waterlooplein
🃏 MC, V

RESTAURANTS

SOMETHING SPECIAL

🍴 DE KAS
$$$$

KAMERLINGH ONNESLAAN 3
TEL 462-4562
restaurantdekas.nl
One of Amsterdam's best, and
most unusual, restaurants. As
its name—The Greenhouse—
implies, owner Gert Jan Hage-
man's restaurant is housed in a
beautiful 1920s greenhouse in
the pretty Frankendael Park in
southeastern Amsterdam. Half
of the area is given over to the
intimate dining area while the
other half is used to grow the
produce on your plate. The
result is organic, healthy, fresh
food prepared using classic
techniques and served with
unpretentious flair.
🚊 Train: Hogeway ⏰ Closed
Sun. & L Sat. 🃏 All major cards

🏨 Hotel 🍴 Restaurant 🛏 No. of Guest Rooms 🪑 No. of Seats 🅿 Parking 🚊 Tram/Bus ⛴ Ferry ⏰ Closed

🍴 MOES
$$
PRINS HENDRIKKADE 142
TEL 623-5477
totmoes.nl
Located in the basement of
De Appel arts center, this
cute little café and restaurant
is decorated in suitably con-
temporary, artistic style. In an
effort to reduce the distance
from farm to fork, herbs are
grown in the back garden
(also a delightful spot to sit in
summer) and other produce
is sourced locally. The menu
is vegetarian once a month,
and even the building itself
was constructed using recycled
materials.
🚋 Tram: Centraal Station
🕐 Closed Mon., D 🚫 No
credit cards

🍴 STORK RESTAURANT
$$
BEDRIJVENTERREIN DE OVER-
KANT, GEDEMPT HAMERKANAAL
T/O 96
TEL 634-4000
restaurantstork.nl
Housed in the cavernous hall
of a former aircraft manufacturing facility, this large
seafood restaurant and grand
café is located on the banks of
the IJ in Amsterdam Noord,
in De Overkant industrial park.
Fish, oysters, and shellfish are
served up in the restau-
rant's vast, yet surprisingly
atmospheric, hall. The large
open kitchen and bar, vast
windows, glass partition near
the entrance, and revealed
piping all reflect the building's
industrial heritage.
⛴ Ferry: Buiksloterweg
🚫 All major cards

🍴 VAPIANO
$$
OOSTERDOKSKADE 145
TEL 420-1825
vapiano.com
This international chain of
Italian restaurants delivers

consistently good food in
bright, cheery surroundings.
The branch in the Eastern
Docklands is often bustling
with students after a session at
the nearby OBA public library.
🚋 Tram: Centraal Station
🚫 All major cards

🍴 WILDE ZWIJNEN
$$
JAVAPLEIN 23
TEL 463-3043
wildezwijnen.com
The name of this unusual
restaurant—Wild Boars—gives
an indication of its strength:
Carnivores flock to the trendy,
gritty property in the Eastern
Docklands, with its wall of
building materials, old stable
doors for tables, and concrete
floor, for imaginative dishes
featuring fresh, locally sourced
game. Expect wild boar stew
and grilled hanger steak but
also oysters and brill fillet.
🚋 Tram: Javaplein 🕐 Closed L
Mon.–Thurs. 🚫 DC, MC

🍴 DE SLUYSWACHT
$
JODENBREESTRAAT 1
TEL 625-7611
sluyswacht.nl
Located in a picturesque black-
painted building overlooking
the Amstel and St. Antoniesluis (St. Anthony sluice), this
cute café is the ideal spot to
while away a sunny afternoon.
The building dates back to
1695, when it was built as the
sluice master's house, and
faces Rembrandt's house. The
pub/café food isn't gourmet,
but the terrace is hard to beat.
🚋 Tram: Nieuwmarkt/Mr.
Visserplein 🚫 MC, V

◼ NORTHERN CANALS

HOTELS

🏨 ANDAZ AMSTERDAM
🍴 $$$$$
PRINSENGRACHT 587, 1016 HT
TEL 523-1234
andaz.com
Quirky Amsterdam designer
Marcel Wanders has created a
hip yet relaxed sanctuary in the
Andaz, a former public library
on the Prinsengracht. Modern
rooms feature decorative
references to Amsterdam's
history, and "standard" Andaz
amenities include compli-
mentary nonalcoholic drinks
and snacks from the mini bar
and free local calls and wire-
less. There's also a gourmet
restaurant, **Bluespoon,** and
excellent spa.
🛏 122 🚋 Tram: Keizersgracht/
Prinsengracht 🚫 All major
cards

🏨 CANAL HOUSE
$$$$$
KEIZERSGRACHT 148–152,
1015 CX
TEL 709-6992
canalhouse.nl
An indulgent and seriously
sexy property spread across
three delightful canal houses
with a delightful garden.
Guestrooms range in size and
price from "good" to "exceptional," but all boast plush
interiors, original artworks,
and treats like rolltop baths
and rain showers. Green-
fingered guests will enjoy
the two ground-floor garden
rooms, one of which has a
private terrace. Rates include a
generous buffet breakfast.
🛏 23 🚋 Tram: Westermarkt
🚫 All major cards

🏨 THE TOREN
$$$$
KEIZERSGRACHT 164, 1015 CZ

TEL 622-6352
thetoren.nl
A classic boutique Amsterdam hotel, with individual rooms that vary from bright and modern to exotic and intimate and include the Garden Cottage, which comes with its own steam shower cabin. The wood-paneled bar is a popular place for an apéritif before you stroll along the canals to dinner.

🚹 38 🚋 Tram: Westermarkt 💳 All major cards

🏨 SUNHEAD OF 1617
$$$
HERENGRACHT 152, 1016 BN
TEL 626-1809
sunhead.com
A well-established B&B located in a beautifully restored 17th-century canal house in the heart of the canal belt. The two rooms, Tulip and Narcissus, are tastefully decorated, and both feature en suite bathrooms and Nespresso coffee machines. Tulip has canal views. Host and former restaurateur Carlos makes a fantastic breakfast.

🚹 2 🚋 Tram: Westermarkt 💳 MC, V

🏨 HOTEL DE WINDKETEL
$$
WATERTORENPLEIN 8-C, 1051 PA
windketel.nl
This unusual property is located in Westerpark's car-free Eco-District, where all buildings are constructed in accordance with ecological principles and surrounded by gardens. The Windketelge-bouw (air chamber building) is a small, three-story octagonal turret, which formed part of a handful of buildings built in the early 1900s by the Municipal Water Company. Local residents bought the tower and turned it into a mini "hotel," featuring a stylish kitchen, sitting room, and en-suite double bedroom surrounded by a small garden.

🚹 1 🚋 Tram/bus: Van Hall-straat 💳 No credit cards

RESTAURANTS

🍴 CHRISTOPHE
$$$$$
LELIEGRACHT 46
TEL 625-0807
restaurantchristophe.nl
The eponymous restaurant of Chef Christophe Royer, this Amsterdam gourmet stalwart is now run by Chef Jean-Joel Bonsens. Bonsens has continued its tradition of sublime, classic French cuisine with experimental Mediterranean spices and ingredients.

🚋 Tram: Westermarkt ⏰ Closed Sun. & Mon., L on request 💳 All major cards

🍴 GROENE LANTEERNE
$$$$
HAARLEMMERSTRAAT 43
TEL 624-1952
An intimate restaurant that beckons its guests in by the gentle light of a green lantern after which it takes its name, Groene Lanteerne serves top-quality French cuisine and is the ideal spot for a romantic dinner. For such a tiny place, it boasts a very impressive wine cellar, albeit overly tilted in favor of expensive bottles.

🚋 Tram: Singel ⏰ Closed L & Sun. 💳 All major cards

🍴 MARIUS
$$$$
BARENTSZSTRAAT 173
TEL 422-7880
deworst.nl
Marius's unassuming, convivial setting in the Westelijke Eilanden (Western Islands) belies the excellent cuisine of this delightful table d'hôte. From the Parisian sidewalk terrace to the rustic vibe inside, the essence of the restaurant is "refined country kitchen," with a four-course menu devised daily according to what leading Dutch chef Kees Elfring finds fresh from local producers.

🚌 Bus: Barentszplein ⏰ Closed Sun. & Mon. 💳 All major cards

SOMETHING SPECIAL

🍴 PROEF
$$$$
GOSSCHALKLAAN 12
TEL 682-2656
proefamsterdam.nl
Located in the up-and-coming Westerpark area, Proef is the psychedelic brainchild of "food designer" Marije Vogelzan, and one of Amsterdam's most innovative dining experiences. Each of Vogelzan's dishes are small pieces of art, such as her asparagus soup, served in a glass jar with bunches of cotton wool sprouting herbs that you cut yourself with scissors. The herbs are cultivated in the large vegetable, herb, and edible flower garden out back, which Vogelzan also uses in her fabulous cocktails. Proef typically closes in winter, so save this treat for a summer visit to Amsterdam.

🚌 Bus: Van Hallstraat (Haar-lemmerweg) ⏰ Closed D, all winter 💳 MC, V

🍴 DE GOUDEN REAEL
$$$
ZANDHOEK 14
TEL 623-3883
goudenreael.nl
Located in a 17th-century former warehouse in the Westelijke Eilanden (Western Islands), overlooking the water and picturesque Pete Mayen-burg bridge, the Gouden Reael feels a million miles from the center of Amsterdam. Food here is modern French with influences from North Africa, Spain, and Italy, with dishes like duck confit and lamb tagine. Despite feeling remote, it's

very popular, so reservations
are advised.

🚌 Bus: Barentszplein/Buiten
Oranjestraat 🕐 Closed L
💳 All major cards

🍽 NOORDWEST
$$$
NOORDERMARKT 42
624-3689
restaurantnoordwest.nl
This hugely popular restaurant
is named to reflect its two
entrances: one onto the
Noordermarkt square and
the other onto Westerstraat.
The slick, modern interiors
appeal to the young, hip
crowd who flock here for
uncomplicated yet excellent
food—vast salads, unctuous
risottos, and succulent steaks.
Saturday brunch on the sunny
terrace after a stroll around
the Noordermarkt farmer's
market is a local tradition. The
restaurant's owner also runs
the neighbouring Winkel Café
(see p. 144), which makes
Amsterdam's best apple cake.
🚊 Tram: Nieuwezijds Kolk
💳 All major cards

🍽 MAZZO
$$
ROZENGRACHT 114
TEL 344-6402
mazzoamsterdam.nl
The thinking behind this
industrial-chic restaurant is to
provide Jordaan locals with a
modern, welcoming hangout
where they can enjoy authentic Italian coffee and food all
day long. Sip cappuccino on a
Chesterfield sofa as you watch
the chefs knead fresh pasta
and delve into their open
kitchen larder for inspiration.
The Pizza Mazzo, layered with
lardo and truffle, is a particular
favorite.
🚊 Tram: Rozengracht 💳 All
major cards

■ SOUTHERN CANALS

HOTELS

🏨 AMSTEL INTERCONTINENTAL
🍽 $$$$$
PROFESSOR TULPPLEIN 1,
1018 GX
TEL 622-6060
amsterdam.intercontinental
.com
The Amstel's slogan says it
all: "The choice of Royalty,
Nobility & Celebrities since
1867." This prestigious hotel,
set slightly apart from the
bustle of Amsterdam on the
river Amstel, prides itself on
indulging its wealthy guests
with attentive service, palatial
rooms, twinkling chandeliers,
antique furnishings, romantic
riverside views, and Michelin-
starred food in its Restaurant
La Rive.
ℹ 79 🚊 Tram: Oosteinde
💳 All major cards

🏨 THE DYLAN HOTEL
🍽 $$$$$
KEIZERSGRACHT 384, 1016 GB
TEL 530-2010
dylanamsterdam.com
A tastefully and glamorously
decorated historic canalside
property built on the site of
a 17th-century theater, which
later became a Catholic almshouse and orphanage. Guestrooms feature original beams,
ceilings, and fireplaces; bold,
contemporary fabrics; and
high-tech amenities. A tranquil
courtyard lies in the center of
the hotel, the Michelin-starred
restaurant Vinkeles is found
in the ancient bakery, and the
bar is popular for High Wine—
wine flights accompanied by
light Dutch bites.
ℹ 40 🚊 Tram: Spui 💳 All
major cards

🏨 PULITZER HOTEL
🍽 $$$$$
PRINSENGRACHT 315–331,
1016 GZ
TEL 523-5235
pulitzeramsterdam.com
The brainchild of art-loving
Peter Pulitzer, grandson of
the newspaper publisher who
founded the annual Pulitzer
prizes, the Pulitzer Hotel
comprises 25 restored 17th-
and 18th-century canal houses.
The entire hotel is decorated
with original artworks and
antiques, and its gardens are
delightful to stroll around and
take afternoon tea in. There's
a good restaurant and entertaining De Apotheek wine
salon, which is situated in a
former pharmacy.
ℹ 230 🚊 Tram: Westermarkt
💳 All major cards

🏨 KAMER 01
$$$$
SINGEL 416, 1016 AK
TEL 625-6627
kamer01.nl
Another classy B&B in a
superb canalside location, with
views of the flower market.
The 16th-century house features a typically steep, narrow
Amsterdam staircase, which
brings you to two modern,
stylish bedrooms—Red and
Blue. Owners Peter and
Wolter will treat you to a delicious organic breakfast in your
room or in the dining room.
ℹ 2 🚊 Tram: Spui 💳 MC, V

🏨 SEVEN ONE SEVEN
$$$$
PRINSENGRACHT 717, 1017 JW
TEL 427-0717
717hotel.nl
No. 717 Prinsengracht was
the home of a wealthy 19th-
century sugar trader, but since
1997, it has been the site of
an opulent yet discreet hotel.
Nine rooms and decadent
suites are found here, with
antique brass beds, marble

floors, and Annick Goutal bathing goodies. There's a cozy library and peaceful terrace, where you can enjoy afternoon tea (included in your room rate, together with house wines). Breakfast is served in your room, artfully delivered in a wicker hamper.

🛏 11 🚊 Tram: Prinsengracht 💳 All major cards

🏨 MIAUW SUITES
$$$

HARTENSTRAAT 34, 1016 CC
TEL 893-2933
miauw.com

Located within two old houses and part of a complex incorporating pop-up design and fashion shops and studios, Miauw Suites are luxurious apartments in the heart of the Negen Straatjes. Each stylish suite features a bedroom, bathroom, living room, and kitchen, as well as all modern conveniences and toiletries.

🛏 4 🚊 Tram: Westermarkt 💳 All major cards

🏨 SEVEN BRIDGES HOTEL
$$$

REGULIERSGRACHT 31, 1017 LK
TEL 623-1329
sevenbridgeshotel.nl

A charming small hotel with a prime location reflected in its name—the point where the Reguliersgracht and Keizersgracht canals meet and you can see seven arched bridges. The property is an antique-lover's delight, with a 15th-century oak staircase, Louis XVI furniture, and baroque commodes mixing with Biedermeier and art deco pieces. There are no public rooms, so enjoy guilt-free breakfast in bed every day.

🛏 11 🚊 Tram: Rembrandt-plein 💳 All major cards

RESTAURANTS

🍴 BEDDINGTON'S
$$$$

UTRECHTSEDWARSSTRAAT 141
TEL 620-7393
beddington.nl

This chic restaurant is named after its British chef and owner, Jean Beddington. Since opening her first restaurant in Amsterdam in 1983, Beddington has developed a signature experimental style, which blends her British roots with Asian influences and a dose of contemporary Dutch cuisine. The menu is limited but will treat you to unusual dishes like venison with crushed walnut and dark chocolate garnish.

🚊 Tram: Prinsengracht ⏱ Closed L; Mon. & Sun. 💳 All major cards

🍴 DE OESTERBAR
$$$$

LEIDSEPLEIN 10
TEL 623-2988
oesterbar.nl

This long-established little restaurant just off Leidseplein delivers consistently fresh and delicious seafood. Popular with theatergoers and tourists, the oyster platters are unashamedly generous, and the Dover sole is superb.

🚊 Tram: Koningsplein/Keizersgracht 💳 All major cards

SOMETHING SPECIAL

🍴 D'VIJFF VLIEGHEN
$$$$

SPUISTRAAT 294–302
TEL 530-4060
vijffvlieghen.nl

Yes, it's touristy, but Restaurant d'Vijff Vlieghen (Five Flies) does capture the splendor of the Dutch Golden Age with its lavish decor, which includes authentic Rembrandt etchings, rare 17th-century handmade glassware and tiles, and armor from the Eighty

Years War. The old fruit market (which perhaps gave rise to the restaurant's Five Flies name) is long gone, but the restaurant still uses predominantly organic ingredients in its mix of Dutch and international dishes. Over 150 gins and liquors are available with which you can wash down your duck, veal, or suckling pig.

🚊 Tram: Spui ⏱ Closed L 💳 All major cards

🍴 'T SWARTE SCHAEP
$$$$

KORTE LEIDSEDWARSSTRAAT 24
TEL 622-3021

A bastion of quality in the otherwise fast-food desert of Leidseplein, the Black Sheep (named after a legendary black sheep that was said to roam the area in the 17th century) manages to remain aloof from the nightlife bustle outside its antique-decorated walls. The darkened beams of this 17th-century Dutch home have seen international movie stars and Dutch royalty dine on its classic French cuisine.

🚊 Tram: Leidseplein
🕐 Closed L 💳 All major cards

🍴 CASA DI DAVID

$$$

SINGEL 426
TEL 624-5093
casadidavid.com

The House of David is a genuine Italian restaurant with handsome and flamboyant waiters, serving traditional pizza cooked in a wood-fired oven, as well as a full range of classic Italian meat and pasta dishes. The restaurant also hosts wine tastings and dinner and opera cruises throughout the year; check the website for details.

🚊 Tram: Spui 🕐 Closed L
💳 All major cards

🍴 SLUIZER RESTAURANTS

$$$

UTRECHTSESTRAAT 43–45
TEL 622-6376 / 622-6557
sluizer.nl

The two Sluizer restaurants are long-established Amsterdam favorites. The traditional, dark wood-paneled Restaurant Sluizer, with its walls hung with original Dutch artworks, serves typical Dutch cuisine while burstingly fresh seafood is served in the neighboring property, Visrestaurant Sluizer, with its Jugendstil decor and marble-topped tables.

🚊 Tram: Keizersgracht (Utrechtsestraat) 🕐 Closed L
💳 All major cards

🍴 TEMPO DOELOE

$$$

UTRECHTSESTRAAT 75
TEL 625-6718
tempodoeloerestaurant.nl

Ask any Amsterdammer which restaurant serves the best Indonesian food, and Tempo Doeloe is likely to crop up. Going strong now for 30 years, it combines authentic dishes with polished service—everyone feels like royalty when served with one of the restaurant's legendary rijsttafel banquets, consisting of 12 or 24 little dishes, contrasting in taste and texture (they also serve a vegetarian version).

🚊 Tram: Keizersgracht (Utrechtsestraat) 🕐 Closed L
💳 MC, V

🍴 EETCAFÉ SINGEL 404

$

SINGEL 404
TEL 428-0154

This busy spot serves enormous and well-priced *broodjes* (sandwiches), available both hot and cold, hearty soups, fresh smoothies, and man-size cakes. Enduringly popular, the snug café and its tables lining the canal outside fill up from late morning through to mid-afternoon, so you need patience to secure one. The wait is worth it, with imaginative and generous sandwich fillings ranging from a traditional Dutch Uitsmijter (a fried egg sandwich) with slow-cooked ham and cheese to smoked chicken with avocado, brie, and sun-dried tomatoes served on a wide choice of home-baked breads.

🚊 Tram: Spui 🕐 Closed D
💳 No credit cards

▓ THE MUSEUM QUARTER, VONDELPARK, & DE PIJP

HOTELS

🏨 CONSERVATORIUM HOTEL

🍴 $$$$$

VAN BAERLESTRAAT 27, 1071 AN

TEL 570-0000
conservatoriumhotel.com

Next door to the Stedelijk Museum, adjacent to the Concertgebouw, and a stone's throw from the Rijksmuseum, the Conservatorium occupies one of the best locations of any hotel in Amsterdam. Originally built as a bank, then taken over by the Amsterdam University's Sweelinck Conservatorium of Music, it received a designer hotel makeover from Italian architect and interior designer Piero Lissoni, combining cutting-edge design with imaginative elements like the trees planted in the basement, whose tips emerge at ground level by the bar. The result is a slick, buzzing, and justifiably popular cosmopolitan hotel.

💳 All major cards

🏨 OKURA

🍴 $$$$$

FERDINAND BOLSTRAAT 333, 1072 LH
TEL 678-7111
okura.nl

Given its size, proximity to Schiphol Airport and the RAI Conference Center, and four excellent restaurants (including two Japanese restaurants), Okura is understandably popular with business travelers. Guest rooms are well appointed but not as individual as many of Amsterdam's smaller properties. The top-floor **Ciel Bleu** restaurant, one of Amsterdam's Michelin-starred restaurants, and the trendy **Twenty Third Bar** offer mesmerizing views across the city.

🛏 300 🚊 Tram: Cornelis Troostplein/Scheldstraat
💳 All major cards

🏨 COLLEGE HOTEL

🍴 $$$$

ROELOF HARTSTRAAT 1, 1017 VE
TEL 571-1511
thecollegehotel.com

⬆ Elevator 🚭 Nonsmoking ❄ Air-conditioning 🏋 Health Club 💳 Credit Cards

Located in a late-19th-century school building, College Hotel still plays an educational role—its staff are students of the Amsterdam Hotel Management School, overseen by a team of professionals from the Nedstede Hotel Group. Classrooms have been transformed into sensuous, black-painted and antique-littered guest rooms, the former gym houses an excellent restaurant, and locals go glamorous to sip cocktails in the sultry bar.

ⓘ 40 🚊 Tram: Roelof Hartplein 💳 All major cards

🏨 JL NO. 76
$$$

JAN LUIJKENSTRAAT 76, 1071 CT

TEL 515-0453

vondelhotels.com

Located down the road from the Rijksmuseum and around the corner from the popular PC Hooftstraat and Cornelis Schuytstraat shopping streets, this is an understated, urban-chic hotel. The hospitable owner, Arjen van den Hof, invites guests to enjoy his art collection, use the honor bar, and pick his brains for local tips.

ⓘ 39 🚊 Tram: Van Baerlerstraat 💳 All major cards

🏨 SANDTON HOTEL DE FILOSOOF
$$$

ANNA VAN DEN VONDELSTRAAT 6, 1056 GZ

TEL 683-3013

sandton.eu

Located close to Amsterdam's major art museums and Vondelpark, De Filosoof (The Philosopher) offers good value accommodation. Run by the Sandton hotel group, the well-established hotel has benefited from the introduction of five new suites located across the road from the main building, which adhere to the original concept of commemorating

a different philosopher or philosophical movement.

ⓘ 38 🚊 Tram: J. P. Heijestraat 💳 All major cards

🏨 CAKE UNDER MY
🍴 PILLOW
$$

FERDINAND BOLSTRAAT 10, 1072 LH

TEL 776-4600

cakeundermypillow.nl

Run by Amsterdam's celebrated cake bakers Siemon de Jong and Noam Offer, this three-bedroom B&B is located above their "cake parlor," **De Taart van m'n Tante,** in De Pijp. The rooms are quiet, prettily decorated, and come with the bonus of breakfast prepared by the city's best bakers.

ⓘ 3 🚊 Tram: Stadhouderskade 💳 All major cards

RESTAURANTS

🍴 LE GARAGE
$$$$$

RUYSDAELSTRAAT 54–56

TEL 679-7176

Flamboyant restaurateur and TV celebrity Joop Braakhekke struck gold when he launched Le Garage in 1990. Still beloved by celebrities today, the bistro/brasserie is unashamedly glamorous, with red vinyl banquettes, glittering mirrors, and black lacquered chairs. Cuisine is sophisticated, international, and creative, and the kitchen stays open until late. Braakhekke recently opened the "streetfood/lounge bar" **En Pluche** next door to Le Garage, with equally hip interiors, a lively bar, and imaginative finger food.

🚊 Tram: Ruysdaelstraat/Roelof Hartplein 🕐 Closed L, Sat. & Sun. 💳 All major cards

SOMETHING SPECIAL

🍴 RESTAURANT GREETJE
$$$$

PEPERSTRAAT 23–25

TEL 779-7450

restaurantgreetje.nl

Decorated like a traditional Dutch dining room, complete with Delft blue porcelain, candles, fresh flowers, and a picture of Greetje, the owner's mother, this restaurant oozes homeliness. The food, organic and free of additives, is equally comforting, and although based on age-old Dutch dishes, it is executed with stylish, haute cuisine panache, such as the traditional Friesland sugar bread with duck liver pâté and homemade apple syrup.

🚊 Tram: Mr. Visserplein 🕐 Closed L 💳 MC, V

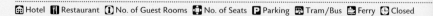

🏨 Hotel   🍴 Restaurant   ⓘ No. of Guest Rooms   🛏 No. of Seats   🅿 Parking   🚊 Tram/Bus   ⛴ Ferry   🕐 Closed

VIS AAN DE SCHELDE
$$$$
SCHELDEPLEIN 4
TEL 675-1583
visaandeschelde.nl
The owner of this well-established restaurant, Chef Michiel Deenik, lives by two mantras: "A day without good food is a day lost" and "Fish and season," reflecting his dedication to featuring only fresh, seasonal food on his ever-changing menus. Located in Amsterdam-Zuid, across from the RAI Exhibition and Congress Centre, the freshly refurbished seafood restaurant attracts business types but also well-heeled locals, who recognize it as one of the city's best.
Tram/Metro: RAI Closed L, Sat. & Sun. All major cards

DISTRICT V
$$$
VAN DER HELSTPLEIN 17
TEL 770-0884
district5.nl
Despite being located on the leafy, quintessentially Dutch Van der Helstplein square in De Pijp, District V is a little nugget of Italy. Run by a charming Italian couple, with Italian chef Emiliano Covelli in the kitchen, and frequented by Italians, the acclaimed restaurant serves honest, authentic food and wines from small-scale Italian vineyards.
Tram: Tweede van der Helststraat/Cornelis Troostplein Closed L & Tues. MC, V

LAB 111
$$$
ARIE BIEMONDSTRAAT 111
TEL 616-9994
lab111.nl
Part of the artists' platform SMART Project Space in the Oud-West part of Amsterdam (north of Vondelpark), Lab 111 serves fusion food to the tunes of live DJs, surrounded by original art by young students. A stainless-steel bar and old operation lamps above the apple green reading table create a suitably avant-garde environment for the bohemian local crowd who come here, often staying until weekend closing time at 3 a.m.
Tram: Ten Katestraat All major cards

BAZAR
$$
ALBERT CUYPSTRAAT 182
TEL 675-0544
bazaramsterdam.nl
Behind the facade of a former Reformed church lies Bazar, a fairy-tale Aladdin's cave with exotic lamps, vibrant textiles, and vividly painted ceramics. The food is North African and Middle Eastern, with an extensive menu of rich tagines, Algerian honey pancakes, kebabs, falafels, vast couscous dishes, and baklava. The kitchen stays open until late, ideal for postdrink bites in this lively part of De Pijp.
Tram: Albert Cuypstraat All major cards

DE KOFFIE SALON
$
EERSTE CONSTANTIJN HUYGENSSTRAAT 82
TEL 612-4079
dekoffiesalon.nl
With three outlets dotted around Amsterdam, De Koffie Salon's coffee is consistently rated as the city's best. If you agree, you can buy fresh coffee beans to bring home. They also serve freshly baked pastries, cakes, and sandwiches. The café near Vondelpark (Eerste Constantijn Huygensstraat) is located in a beautifully refurbished old building with original art deco stained glass.
Tram: Eerste Constantijn Huygensstraat MC, V

EXCURSIONS

DELFT

HOTEL

HOTEL DE PLATAAN
$$$
DOELENPLEIN 10–11, 2611 BP, DELFT
TEL 015/212-6046
hoteldeplataan.nl
This town house hotel is situated in the heart of the old historic center of Delft, close to the museum and marketplace. The bright airy rooms have Scandinavian-style furnishings, and several include a small yet well-equipped kitchen. The hotel café is lively and has a charming outdoor terrace.
All major cards

RESTAURANT

KLEYWEG'S KOFFIEHUIS
$
OUDE DELFT 133
TEL 015/212-4625
stads-koffyhuis.nl
This canalside café is a popular choice for lunch because of its location alongside the city's principal waterway and for its delicious *broodjes* (filled rolls) and pancakes.
Closed Sun. MC, V

HAARLEM

HOTEL

AMRÂTH GRAND HOTEL FRANS HALS
$$$
DAMSTRAAT 10, 2011 HA, HAARLEM
TEL 023/518-1818
amrathhotels.nl

Ideally located in the center of Haarlem, this chic hotel makes a comfortable base from which to explore the city. Guest rooms are spacious and well appointed, many with views across the church towers and canals of Haarlem.

🛏 82   💳 All major cards

RESTAURANT

SOMETHING SPECIAL

🍴 SPECKTAKEL
$$$
SPECKSTRAAT 4, HAARLEM
TEL 023/523-3841
specktakel.nl
This imaginative eatery takes ingredients and techniques from across the world to create unpretentious global cuisine. Sitting in the quintessentially Dutch town of Haarlem, you can enjoy the authentic tastes of Malaysia, India, Japan, and Australia, joined by the many locals who flock here.

💳 All major cards

DEN HAAG (THE HAGUE)

HOTEL

🏨 HAAGSCHE SUITES
$$$$$
LAAN VAN MEERDERVOORT 155, 2517 AX, DEN HAAG
TEL 070/364-7879
haagschesuites.nl
With just three suites, this sought-after B&B offers the luxury, amenities, style, and service of a five-star hotel with the intimacy of a private home. Each vast suite occupies an entire floor of a beautiful old house, with views over the large and immaculate back garden.

🛏 3   💳 All major cards

RESTAURANTS

🍴 SAUR
$$$$
LANGE VOORHOUT 51, 2514 EC, DEN HAAG
TEL 070/361-7070
saur.nl
A classic Den Haag restaurant, established on one of the city's most prestigious streets since 1928, Saur looks better than ever after an extensive refurbishment. The kitchen excels at seafood: Expect platters piled high with oysters, lobster, scallops, and crab, as well as some choice meat dishes.

🕐 Closed Sun.   💳 All major cards

🍴 DE BAKKERSWINKEL
$
TORENSTRAAT 142, 2513 BW, DEN HAAG
TEL 070/302-0756
debakkerswinkel.nl
Located in the Hofkwartier (Court Quarter), within walking distance of the Peace Palace and parliament offices, this lively, 1930s-style bakery and café is an ideal place for a freshly made, inexpensive breakfast, brunch, or lunch.

💳 All major cards

LEIDEN

HOTEL

🏨 DE BEUKENHOF
🍴 $$$$
TERWEEWEG 2-4, 2341 CR, OEGSTGEEST
TEL 071/517-3188
debeukenhof.nl
This charming property is located about ten minutes' drive from Leiden Centraal Station. Dating back to 1926, when two friends bought a plot of land to start a tea shop, De Beukenhof (The Beech Garden) became a restaurant in 1948, which went on to

become one of Holland's finest. It has subsequently been complemented by a boutique hotel with nine individual suites, ranging from the romantic Bestede Suite, with its original 18th-century box beds, to the palatial Hay Loft Suite.

🛏 9   💳 All major cards

RESTAURANT

🍴 LUNDI
$$
TURFMARKT 6, 2312 CE, LEIDEN
TEL 071/566-5466
restaurantlundi.nl
Combining lunch and dinner, LUNDI is a small, cozy restaurant serving French-inspired cuisine in the heart of Leiden. In summer, you can dine on a floating terrace on the canal, adding to the delightful atmosphere of this popular, welcoming spot.

🕐 Closed Mon.   💳 MC, V

ROTTERDAM

HOTELS

 EUROMAST
$$$$$
PARKHAVEN 20, 3016 GM,
ROTTERDAM
TEL 010/436-4811
euromast.nl
Push the boat out and stay in
one of Rotterdam's two most
sought-after suites, Heaven
and Stars (see sidebar p. 233).
Located 330 feet (112 metres)
above Rotterdam and taking
up half of the mast each, they
offer unparalleled views, and
each evening from 10 p.m.
until 10 a.m. the following
morning, guests have exclusive
access to the upper platforms
of the Euromast.
🛗 2 💳 All major cards

 BREITNER
$$
BREITNERSTRAAT 23, 3015 XA,
ROTTERDAM
TEL 010/436-0262
hotelbreitner.nl
This comfortable and friendly
central hotel is close to the
railway station, Euromast, the
museums, and the Delfshaven
harbor, making it a good base
for exploring Rotterdam's
many attractions. The rooms
are simple but clean and
well appointed, and there
is a pretty terrace garden.
🛗 36 💳 All major cards

RESTAURANTS

🍴 **PARKHEUVEL**
$$$$$
HEUVELLAAN 21, 3016 GL,
ROTTERDAM
TEL 010/436-0530
parkheuvel.nl
Rotterdam's premier restau-
rant has two Michelin stars

under the culinary leadership
of Erik van Loo. Located
on the edge of Het Park,
overlooking the Nieuwe Maas
River and near the Euromast,
the *heuvel* is no mere hovel,
but a round Bauhaus structure
with glass walls and elegant
new interiors. Van Loo's cui-
sine is primarily classic French,
with a focus on seasonal pro-
duce, which you can savor in a
number of multicourse tasting
menus as well as à la carte.
🕐 Closed Sun. & L. Sat.
💳 All major cards

🍴 **ZEEZOUT**
$$$
WESTERKADE 11B, 3016 CL,
ROTTERDAM
TEL 010/436-5049
restaurantzeezout.nl
As residents of a port city,
Rotterdammers are connois-
seurs of seafood, and their
favorite establishment is the
renowned Zeezout restaurant,
brainchild of Dutch celebrity
chef Patrick 't Hart. Menus
change daily, depending on
what's fresh and seasonal,
and range from a classic
bouillabaisse to seabream
in salt crust with risotto.
🕐 Closed Mon. & L. Sun.
💳 All major cards

Shopping

Shopping in its most concentrated form is to be found along the three-quarter-mile (1.2 km) strip from Centraal Station south to Muntplein, via Nieuwendijk, Dam Square, and Kalverstraat. These traffic-free streets are lined by shops of all kinds: department stores and designer boutiques, brash commercial outlets and old-fashioned shops of character, homegrown names and international brands.

However, as Amsterdam cements its position as one of Europe's hottest shopping destinations, with concept stores, designer boutiques, and slick interior design emporiums opening every day, don't forget to head off the beaten track. Unusual and specialist shops are found in De Negen Straatjes (see p. 163), Haarlemmerbuurt (see pp. 150–151), and along Utrechtsestraat, where you will find florists, textile merchants, vintage clothing outlets, and art dealers, as well as various specialists in Australian Aboriginal art, 1930s and 1950s antiques, antiquarian books—a potpourri of small shops with compelling window displays, staffed by knowledgeable enthusiasts.

P.C. Hooftstraat, in the Museum Quarter, is the place for designer fashion and all that is stylish in home interiors, while the streets nearby (namely De Lairessestraat, Cornelis Schuytstraat, and Jacob Obrechtstraat) offer more vintage, boho fashions in pint-size boutiques. The nearby Spiegelkwartier has expensive art and antique shops selling museum-quality works. Just north of Vondelpark, in Oud-West, unusual furniture and interior design shops are popping up on Overtoom street, and a number of trendy shoe stores and quirky boutiques are to be found on the Bilderdijkstraat, the Eerste Constantijn Huygenstraat, and Jan Pieter Heijestraat. At the other end of the scale, there are plenty of great bargains to be tracked down—and haggled down—at Amsterdam's numerous markets. You'll also find some good bargains in the young and friendly boutiques of the Jordaan, whose main shopping street runs from Tichelstraat to Eerste Leliedwarsstraat.

Pick up a free, detailed "Shopping in Amsterdam" guide from any of the VVV tourist offices for more information.

Opening Hours

While most stores are open Monday to Friday from 9 a.m. to 6 p.m. (to 9 p.m. on Thursday) and from 10 a.m. to 5 p.m. on Saturday, smaller specialist shops tend to open later (around 11 a.m.) and close later (6 p.m.), while those in the popular commercial areas will open on Sunday as well.

Art & Antiques

Kunst & Antiekcentrum De Looier

Elandsgracht 109
antiekcentrumamsterdam.nl
The Dutch love of a bargain is nowhere more apparent than at this covered market, with some 80 or so makeshift stands. Ostensibly an "art and antiques" market, some of the "collectibles" on sale here are really just other people's throwaways, but if you are into retro-chic, you can have fun looking for secondhand clothes, cocktail shakers, or a 1950s-style clock—just be sure not to pay a lot for what can be little more than a glorified rummage sale.

Spiegelkwartier

spiegelkwartier.nl
Just across the bridge from the Rijksmuseum, you will find more than 70 art and antique dealers trading from premises along Spiegelgracht, Nieuwe Spiegelstraat, and the adjacent streets. It is a pleasure just to walk down these streets and look at the window displays; the quality of much of the material on sale here—from Greek, Roman, and pre-Columbian antiquities to contemporary art—is as good as anything you will see in a museum. The range of antiques and collectibles on sale is very wide, from Amazonian and Aboriginal art to toys, watches, and scientific instruments. Blink and you might miss Eduard Kramer Antique Tiles (*Nieuwe Spiegelstraat 64, tel 623-0832; antique-tileshop.nl*), which is packed with beautiful antique tiles dating back to the 13th century.

Thorbeckeplein Art Market

Local artists display and sell their work every Sunday (10.30 a.m.– 6 p.m.) at this open-air market in Thorbeckeplein, a leafy square north of Rembrandtplein.

Books

The triangular plaza opposite the Amsterdam Museum on Nieuwezijds Voorburgwal has a coin, postcard, and postage stamp market on Wednesday and Sunday, and the narrow side streets (particularly toward the Spui end) have numerous small shops selling antiquarian books and prints, as well as stamps and coins. Another concentration of antiquarian booksellers is found in the Oudemanhuispoort covered passageway at the southern end of Kloveniersburgwal and Oudezijds

Achterburgwal. In both cases, the stock is mainly Dutch, but you will find beautifully made books with attractive pictorial bindings.

A detailed map of antiquarians and secondhand bookstores can be purchased for a nominal fee from the VVV tourist offices, bookshops across the city, and atnwa.nl.

American Book Center
Kalverstraat 185
tel 625-5537
abc.nl
This large discount book-store is typically packed with people catching a free read of international newspapers and magazines on the first floor and sifting through heaps of bargain books and best sellers. The two floors above are more tranquil and feature a vast range of books covering an array of subjects.

Antiquariaat Brinkman
Singel 319
tel 623-8353
antiquariaatbrinkman.nl
Established in the 1950s, this beautiful shop sells sought-after books, atlases, maps, and documents ranging from medical to musical.

Athenaeum
Spui 14–16
tel 514-1460
athenaeum.nl
Around the corner from its Kalverstraat rivals, the Athenaeum serves the university and so has a good stock of academic books in many languages, as well as a news center selling international newspapers and magazines.

The Book Exchange
Kloveniersburgwal 58
tel 626-6266
bookexchange.nl
Unload your unwanted books here for cash or in part exchange for secondhand novels, travel guides, or classic literature.

The English Bookshop
Lauriersgracht 71
tel 626-4230
englishbookshop.nl
A delightful community bookstore in the Jordaan, where you can buy quality classics and new releases, enjoy a drink in the café, and enroll in a writing workshop.

Galerie Lambiek
Kerkstraat 78
tel 626-7543
lambiek.nl
If you are into comics, you'll already know this famous establishment: Europe's first antiquarian comic shop, which dates back to 1968, sells new and secondhand comics from Europe, Canada, and the U.S., plus related toys.

Jacob van Wijngaarden
Overtoom 97
tel 612-1901
A fascinating specialist shop near Vondelpark packed with maps and guides to just about anywhere in the world, including route maps that are essential for anyone heading off to explore the Netherlands on foot or by bike.

Vrolijk Gay & Lesbian Bookshop
Paleisstraat 135
tel 623-5142
vrolijk.nu
Comprehensive stock of literature—from classic to erotic—plus travel guides, films, postcards, calendars, and posters, and a useful notice board for finding out what's on about town.

Waterstones
Kalverstraat 152
tel 638-3821
waterstones.com
A stone's throw from the American Book Center, Waterstones has a vast stock over several floors, and is the place to come if you prefer the higher production values

(and, admittedly, higher prices) of books published in the U.K. There is a good travel section with a comprehensive range of books on Amsterdam and the Netherlands.

Department Stores & Malls

De Bijenkorf
Dam 1
tel 621-8080
bijenkorf.nl
Upscale and trendy at the same time, De Bijenkorf maintains its position as Amsterdam's leading department store by stocking a comprehensive range of clothing, cosmetics and accessories, furniture, works of art, household goods, toys, and children's wear. It also owns HEMA, a national chain of stores selling more basic but still high-quality home goods, clothing, and food.

Magna Plaza
Nieuwezijds Voorburgwal 182
magnaplaza.nl
The four floors of shopping and cafés in this stunning conversion of the city's palatial former main post office are worth a look for the architectural grandiloquence and sleek branded international fashion and beauty stores. Open seven days a week.

Maison de Bonneterie
Rokin 140–142
tel 531-3400
debonneterie.nl
As old-fashioned as the name suggests, this sumptuous establishment enjoys royal patronage and sells top-end designer-label clothing and accessories—as well as sportswear, golf accessories, household goods, bed linens, and luxurious towels and bathrobes. If you want a relaxing break, visit the café-restaurant.

Design & Interiors

Capsicum
Oude Hoogstraat 1
tel 623-1016
capsicum.nl
Dutch colonial history is encapsulated in this fabric shop, which not only sells Belgian linen and lace, but takes you to the hot and colorful world of the tropics with its Indonesian ikats, gorgeous natural Thai silks, vintage Japanese kimonos, and printed Indian cottons.

Droog
Staalstraat 7b
tel 523-5059
droog.com
A pioneering collective founded in 1993, which introduced the Dutch design movement to the world, Droog also runs a must-see shop and gallery.

De Kasstoor
Rozengracht 204–210
tel 521-8112
dekasstoor.nl
You've been to the museums and seen the revolutionary furniture designs of Le Corbusier, Gerrit Rietveld, and the De Stijl movement, so this is where you come to buy copies of their now-classic designs, or new work by the radical young furniture designers of today.

Friday Next
Overtoom 31
tel 612-3292
fridaynext.com
Set up by two ambitious interior designers, this large concept store contains an intriguing mix of vintage furniture, modern Dutch design, and trendy fashion accessories, as well as a popular café.

Frozen Fountain
Prinsengracht 645
tel 622-9375
frozenfountain.nl
A two-story shop from which celebrated designers Cok de Rooy and Dick Dankers sell old favorites, like Piet Hein Eek's repurposed wood tables, and newfound objects that catch their discriminating eye in an eclectic mix of furniture, ceramics, tea towels, and glassware.

Maison NL
Utrechtsestraat 118
tel 428-5183
maisonnl.com
An approachably modern interior design store, which maintains a homely feel. Pieces are handpicked by the two engaging owners, who can tell you the story behind each one, such as the tiny Albanian pottery that produces their ceramics.

Pols Potten
KNSM-laan 39
tel 419-3541
polspotten.nl
The flagship store of this innovative Dutch company is housed in a former warehouse in the Eastern Docklands. The design emporium contains unique pieces of furniture, tableware, earthenware, and accessories sourced locally and from exotic climes.

Store Without a Home
Haarlemmerdijk 26
tel 474-3062
storewithoutahome.com
Having roamed Amsterdam looking for a permanent location for his pop-up stores, interior designer Janwillem Sanderse finally found one on Haarlemmerdijk. Here, he sells unusual one-off designs and furnishings.

Fashion

Buise
Cornelis Schuytstraat 12
tel 670-4904
buise.nl
Benefit from owner Michelle Buise's impeccable taste in the form of her select collection of designer fashion from names such as Joseph, Antik Batik, and Marlene Birger.

Carmacoma
Nieuwe Spiegelstraat 7B
tel 427-2912
carmacoma.com
An exclusive minimalist boutique in the Spiegelkwartier featuring women's clothing by edgy, chic designers such as Azzedine Alaïa, Balmain, and Gareth Pugh. The menswear store is next door, with collections by Dries Van Noten, as well as gadgets, furniture, and artwork.

Charlie + Mary
Gerard Doustraat 84
tel 662-8281
charliemary.com
Named after owners Charlotte and Marieke, this small concept store in De Pijp focuses on fashionable yet sustainable and ecological men's and women's clothing and accessories. They sell their own designs as well as other brands, inlcuding l'Herbe Rouge, MLY, and Monkee Genes.

OntFront
Haarlemmerdijk 121
tel 778-4518
ontfront.nl
The first brand store of hot Dutch designers Tomas Overtoom and Liza Koifman, OntFront is located on trendy Haarlemmerdijk and features pieces by emerging Dutch designers. Often in the store themselves, the duo happily offer shoppers invaluable styling tips.

Laura Dols
Wolvenstrat 7
tel 624-9066
lauradols.nl
Ever set your heart on a Dior number but shrank at the cost? Your luck might be in at this boutique packed with vintage clothes with an emphasis on sparkly, lacy, and little black things from the cocktail party era.

Luuks

Jacob Obrechtstraat 12
tel 670-4538
luuks.nl
A good spot for unusual, fashion-able men's and women's shoes.

Nukuhiva

Haarlemmerstraat 36
tel 420-9483
nukuhiva.nl
A small shop founded by Dutch TV host Floortje Dessing, well known in the Netherlands for her travel programs. Frequently confronted with poverty during her travels, Dessing opened this shop to sell "fair fashion"—clothing made sustainably with organic materials by fair-trade manufacturers.

Salon Heleen Hülsmann

De Lairessestraat 13B
tel 650-640994
salonheleenhulsmann.nl
A bright, minimalist salon that fea-tures secondhand designer pieces from fashion houses such as Lanvin, Chanel, Gucci, Christian Dior, and Mulberry. The salon operates on an appointment basis only, so contact Hülsmann in advance if you wish to admire her collection.

Flowers

Bloemenmarkt Singel

The Bloemenmarkt (Flower Market) consists of some 15 stands operating from floating pontoons moored in the Singel canal between Koningsplein and Vijzelstraat. The florists here sell potted plants, cut flowers, bulbs, seeds, and garden plants (from flowering shrubs to clipped topiary). They are knowledgeable about export laws, so they will be able to advise you on suit-able plants, bulbs, or flowers to take home, and will package them to withstand handling on the trip.

Food

Albert Heijn

Over 40 branches across
Amsterdam
ah.nl
If you are self-catering while in Amsterdam, or looking for picnic food or a cheap alternative to eating in a café or restaurant, this national supermarket chain is worth getting to know. The Nieuwezijds Voorburgwal branch (behind the Royal Palace, on the opposite side of the road to the Magna Plaza shopping center) is fronted by a food court selling all sorts of take-out goodies, from seafood platters to barbecue ribs and sausages. The stores have a good range of deli-style foods, bread, fruit and veggies, and beverages. None of the branches accepts credit cards, so ensure you have sufficient cash with you.

Boerenmarkt

Nordermarkt
boerenmarktamsterdam.nl
Amsterdam's farmers market takes place every Saturday in front of the Noorderkerk, and like such markets everywhere, the vendors vigorously promote their quality home-produced organic food. You can sample their cheeses, honey, fruit juices, breads, olives, and oils before you buy. Many Amsterdammers would not dream of getting their fruit and veggies anywhere else.

Chocolaterie Pompadour

Huidenstraat 12
tel 623-9554
&
Kerkstraat 148
tel 330-0981
patisseriepompadour.com
Transported from the streets of Paris to the canals of Amsterdam, these two popular patiseries and tea/lunchrooms also sell exquisite handcrafted chocolates.

De Ooievaar

Herengracht 319
tel 625-4334
de-ooievaar.nl
De Ooievaar is the last authentic distillery in Amsterdam. Founded by the Van Wees family in Den Haag in 1782, the distillery moved to its current location in the Jordaan in 1883 and specializes in Old Dutch *jenever* (gin) and liquors. The Van Wees family still run the distillery, creating 17 different jen-evers exclusively from pure, natural ingredients and aromatics. In typical Dutch style, you can sample their liquid labor of love at the distillery's original *proeflokaal* (tasting room), De Admiraal, on the Herengracht before you buy.

Holtkamp

Vijzelgracht 15
tel 624-8757
patisserieholtkamp.nl
Located in a beautifully preserved art deco building, which has housed a patisserie since 1886, this mouth-watering establishment has been run by the Holtkamp family since 1969. Expect melt-in-your-mouth pastries, handmade chocolates and cakes, and Amsterdam's "most famous" veal croquettes.

De Kaaskamer (The Cheese Room)

Runstraat 7
tel 623-3483
kaaskamer.nl
This specialist shop in the Negen Straatjes is the place to come for cheese. A good, aged Gouda travels well and is deliciously nutty—a different cheese from the flavorless slabs served up in supermarkets. The knowledgeable staff here will tell you anything you want to know about the 200 or so cheeses they have in stock, including which wines to drink with them.

Puccini Bomboni
Staalstraat 17
tel 626-5474
&
Singel 184
tel 427-8341
puccinibomboni.com
Two chic stores that are every chocolate lover's dream come true: Fresh, handmade bonbons are crafted on-site using traditional techniques. Utterly delicious and beautifully presented, the boxed packages make great gifts, although no preservatives are used in production, meaning they have to be eaten within ten days.

Jewelry
Amsterdam has been the undisputed center of the European diamond cutting and polishing industry since Jewish refugees fled to the city from Antwerp in the 16th century. Diamonds are no cheaper here than anywhere else, but there is a very wide choice, and the rival diamond companies compete to offer free factory tours that are informative and entertaining.

Coster Diamonds
Paulus Potterstraat 2–8
tel 305-5555
costerdiamonds.com
Showrooms are conveniently sited at the back of the Rijksmuseum.

Gassan Diamonds
Nieuwe Uilenbergertstraat 173–175
tel 622-5333
gassan.com
Huge factory premises in the former Jewish Quarter.

Oogst Sieraden
Tweede Tuindwarsstraat 8
tel 755-8090;
oogst-sieraden.nl
The jewelery store of designers Lotte Porrio and Ellen Philippen, Oogst Sieraden (Harvest Jewelry) showcases their one-off pieces, which are inspired by nature and handmade in the Jordaan.

Markets
See also sidebar p. 16

Albert Cuypmarkt
The biggest of them all, stretching just under a mile, the Albert Cuypmarkt is a colorful and multiethnic feast for the senses, selling everything from food to lingerie. Open daily except for Sunday.

Noordermarkt
In addition to the weekly farmers market on Saturdays, Noordermarkt hosts a Lapjesmarkt (textile market) on Mondays.

Waterlooplein
This permanent flea market has a long history, as revealed by the vintage photographs in the nearby Jewish Historical Museum. Now a popular tourist attraction, it is a good spot to pick up cheap clothes, shoes, leatherwear, fancy dress outfits, crafts, gifts, and CDs. As well as the open-air stands, there are various warehouse outlets selling new and vintage clothes and bric-a-brac. Open daily except for Sunday.

Miscellaneous
Blond Amsterdam
Gerard Doustraat 69
tel 428-4929
blond-amsterdam.nl
Fairhaired friends Femque and Janneke create their own gifts under the name Blond Amsterdam. Their appealing drawings, combined with funny text, decorated tea pots, mugs, notebooks, and clothing, draw many to their cheerful shop in De Pijp.

Condomerie het Gulden Vlies
Warmoesstraat 141
tel 627-4174
condomerie.com
Raising the display and packaging of condoms to an art form, this shop on the fringes of the Red Light District is a far-from-salacious outlet for prophylactics in every imaginable shape, size, color, and flavor, including novelty options.

De Knopenwinkel
Herengracht 383–389
tel 626-9472
knopenwinkel.net
This charming store sells jewelry, soft furnishings, scarves, textiles, and art, as well as every kind of button imaginable.

De Witte Tandenwinkel
Runstraat 5
tel 623-3443
dewittetandenwinkel.nl
An entire shop dedicated to dental hygiene, founded in 1980 and still going strong. Here you'll find everything you need for keeping your teeth white and healthy, including unusual items that might just persuade children to brush their teeth, such as glow-in-the-dark toothbrushes.

Female & Partners
Spuistraat 100
tel 620-9152
femaleandpartners.nl
Let's face it, people do come to Amsterdam for its sex shops, and this is one shop where women can indulge their curiosity without feeling threatened by a male-dominated clientele. Expect the usual range of items—magazines, videos, vibrators, and sexy clothing—but presented with more style than is usual.

Jacob Hooij

Kloveniersburgwal 10–12
tel 624-3041
jacob-hooy.nl
Culinary herbs and spices, health foods, medicinal compounds, and homeopathic remedies are the stock-in-trade of this ancient pharmacist, but Amsterdammers know it best as the home of *dropjes*, the nation's favorite licorice candy. They come in all shapes (see sidebar p. 94).

Kitsch Kitchen

Rozengracht 8–12
tel 462-0051
kitschkitchen.nl
A wonderfully quirky store that sells all manner of brightly colored and patterned objects in addition to kitchenware, from oilcloth bicycle panniers and umbrellas to children's toys. Having grown from a market stall on Noordermarkt to this large store, Kitsch Kitchen is a genuine piece of Amsterdam.

Klompenboer (Wooden Shoe Factory)

Sint Antoniesbreestraat 39–51
tel 427-3862
woodenshoefactory.nl
Well-made clogs are comfortable and durable, so if you are looking for typical Dutch footwear, it is better to buy them from specialist shoemaker Bruno than from a gift shop selling mass-produced novelties. There is also a museum on the premises.

PGC Hajenius

Rokin 92–96
tel 623-7494
hajenius.com
Smoker or not, you should visit this gloriously preserved tobacconist, with a bewildering range of cigars, clay, wood, and stone pipes, and loose tobacco. Even more impressive is the art deco interior, with its Italian marble, mahogany wall panels, and gaslit chandeliers.

Royal Delft Experience

Munttoren, Muntplien 12
tel 623-2271
royaldelftexperience.nl
The Royal Delft Experience Amsterdam includes a multimedia journey through the history of Royal Delft and the production of Delftware, a demonstration by a master painter, a tour of the historic Munttoren (Mint Tower), a visit to a museum showcasing priceless antique Delftware, and a showroom with more affordable hand-painted Delftware available for purchase.

Music

Concerto

Utrechtsestraat 54
tel 623-5228
concertomania.nl
If you are into vinyl, or want to find European tapes and CDs no longer available back home, this is the place. The stock includes classical and rock music, and both new and secondhand material.

Velvet Music

Rozengracht 40
tel 422-8777
velvetmusic.nl
An expansive shop selling vinyl, CDs, and DVDs of all genres.

Posters, Reproductions, & Prints

Foam Editions

Vijzelstraat 78
tel 551-6500
foam.org
An affiliate of the Foam Photography Museum (see sidebar p. 183), Foam Editions is a stand-alone gallery that sells a constantly changing selection of signed prints by talented young photographers and internationally acclaimed artists who have exhibited at the museum. The gallery also sells photography books, including antiquarian photo books, autographed books, and limited-edition print collections.

Van Gogh Museum

Paulus Potterstraat 7
tel 570-5200
vangoghmuseum.nl
Nearly everyone who visits the Van Gogh Museum emerges clutching one of the museum's distinctive triangular poster boxes, as it has an excellent range of reproductions of works by the artist. Housed in the museum is a well-stocked bookshop covering major artists and art movements of the last 150 years.

Entertainment & Activities

You'll never be lost for something to do in Amsterdam. From the world-renowned Concertgebouw Orchestra and the mellow harmonies of the city's jazz clubs to the carnivalesque excesses of the gay clubs, there is something here for every age and taste. Keeping track of it all is not difficult, particularly if you read the weekly A-mag, produced and sold by the VVV (tourist office) and provided free in most good hotels, and check the I amsterdam website.

You can purchase tickets for most Amsterdam events and performances from the main tourist office, located opposite Centraal Station on the Noord-Zuid Hollandse Koffiehuis (Stationsplein 10), and the OBA public library (Oosterdokskade 143). If you can be flexible, the Last Minute Ticket Shop on Leidseplein 26 *(lastminuteticketshop.nl)* sells half-price tickets to concerts, theater performances, and other events taking place that day.

ENTERTAINMENT
Ballet
Dutch National Ballet
Muziektheater, Waterlooplein 22
tel 551-8225 (information) &
900-0191 (box office)
het-ballet.nl
The Dutch National Ballet occupies a leading position in the culture of the Netherlands, and with approximately 78 international dancers, it has developed into one of the world's most respected ballet companies. The ballet gives some 70 performances in Amsterdam each year, typically accompanied by the Holland Symfonia orchestra.

Cinema
Most movies are shown in their original language (usually English) unless the words *Nederlands gesproken* appear under the title; this indicates that they are homegrown Dutch movies or dubbed.

EYE Film Institute
IJpromenade 1
tel 589-1400
eyefilm.nl
A large cinematography museum

containing the Dutch national film archive, which houses 35,000 films, fragments of which are displayed in the basement and cover the history of cinema (entrance is free). The EYE Film Institute further encompasses four film auditoriums, in which classic and art-house movies are screened, a shop, and a café.

The Movies
Haarlemmerdijk 161
tel 638-6016
themovies.nl
This art deco cinema first opened in 1928 and, complete with its original fittings, still shows art-house movies that have made the breakthrough to commercial success. The cinema has its own highly regarded restaurant, so you can eat out and see a show in one venue.

Tuschinski Theater
Reguliersbreestraat 26–28
tel 0900-1458
pathe.nl/bioscoop/tuschinski
Six separate screens are housed within this glorious art deco cinema complex, which opened in 1921 and is often used for movie premieres. You can share in the glamour by joining with friends to secure one of the eight-person boxes, then sit back and watch the movie while sipping champagne.

Classical Music
Concertgebouw
Concertgebouwplein 10
tel 573-0573 (information) &
671-8345 (box office)
concertgebouw.nl
The Concertgebouw celebrated its 125th birthday in 2013 and is renowned for the quality of its

acoustics, which are exploited to the full by the famous Royal Concertgebouw Orchestra. Hearing the orchestra perform the big works of Mahler or Strauss is an unforgettable experience, and tickets are understandably in great demand, so reserve well in advance.

Holland Symfonia
Muziektheater, Waterlooplein 22
tel 551-8225 (information)
Holland Symfonia, the Dutch Ballet and Symphonic Orchestra, was formed in January 2002, by merging the Nederlands Balletorkest (Dutch Ballet Orchestra) and the Noordhollands Philharmonisch Orkest (North Holland Philharmonic Orchestra). Holland Symfonia not only accompanies the Dutch Ballet, Opera, and Theater groups but also performs standalone symphonic concerts. While these typically take place at the Symfonia's home, the Philharmonie concert hall in Haarlem, performances also take place at the Muziektheater in Amsterdam.

Muziekgebouw aan 't IJ
Piet Heinkade 1
tel 620-2000
muziekgebouw.nl
Housed in a strikingly modern glass building perched on the shores of the IJ Bay, the Muziekgebouw aan 't IJ (Music Building on the IJ) is dedicated to music of all genres but is best known for its classical performances. Its state-of-the-art concert hall has rapidly gained an international reputation for exceptional acoustics, while its panoramic seafood restaurant, Zouthaven, is a great spot for a preconcert dinner.

Netherlands Kamerorkest (NKO)

Concertgebouwplein 10
tel 521-7500 (information)
orkest.nl
The Netherlands Chamber Orchestra was founded in 1955 and gives some 25 concerts per year in the Amsterdam Concertgebouw, the hall considered its artistic home.

Netherlands Philharmonisch Orkest (NedPho)

Concertgebouwplein 10
tel 521-7500 (information)
orkest.nl
Formed in 1985, the Netherlands Philharmonic Orchestra now gives more than 40 concerts per season in the Grote Zaal of the Concertgebouw and at other Dutch and international venues. Together with the Netherlands Chamber Orchestra, NedPho performs the majority of operas presented by De Nederlandse Opera in the Muziektheater. The NedPho merged with the Dutch Ballet Orchestra in 2002.

Festivals

See also When to Go, p. 236

Amsterdam Dance Event (ADE)

amsterdam-dance-event.nl
The world's biggest club festival and Europe's leading electronic music conference, held over five days in October.

Dutch Theater Festival & Amsterdam Fringe Festival

tel 523-7798
tf.nl
A festival in early September, which shows theater performances hailed by critics and audiences as the best of the season, attended by the biggest names in Dutch and Belgian theater. The Amsterdam Fringe Festival runs alongside the Theater Festival, celebrating the avant-garde with some 80 productions in locations across the city.

Grachtenfestival (Canal Festival)

tel 421-4542
grachtenfestival.nl
An annual ten-day classical music festival, with performances given in imaginative locations in the canal belt and Amsterdam Noord.

Holland Festival

tel 523-7787
hollandfestival.nl
One of the most important cultural festivals in the Netherlands, Holland Festival runs through the month of June. Performances of music, theater, dance, opera, film, and visual arts, as well as Western and non-Western performance pieces in many languages, take place in locations across the city.

Robeco Summer Concert Series

tel 573-0573 (information) &
671-8345 (box office)
concertgebouw.nl
This acclaimed concert series runs from July through August, with diverse performances at the Concertgebouw from the Netherlands Symphony Orchestra and Jazz Orchestra and visiting international orchestras and guests.

Roots Festival

tel 531-8181
amsterdamroots.nl
An extensive, diverse festival held in July, with indoor performances given by international bands in music venues across the city, such as Melkweg, Paradiso, Bimhuis, and the Muziekgebouw aan 't IJ, and a open-air concert performed in the Oosterpark.

Uitmarkt

tel 621-1311
amsterdamsuitburo.nl
A large, free, and family-friendly festival, held on the last weekend of August, that rings in the start of the new cultural season each year, with 450 performances by some 2,000 artists, as well as stalls selling books, art, music, and food.

Nightlife

Bimhuis

Piet Heinkade 3
tel 788-2188
bimhuis.nl
Amsterdam's iconic jazz and improv club is better than ever in its new home, a raised "black box" jutting out from the Muziekgebouw aan 't IJ with spectacular views over the old city and a spacious bar overlooking the IJ. It also has its own café and restaurant.

Escape

Rembrandtplein 11
tel 622-1111
escape.nl
Large and slightly jaded nightclub (capacity 2,000) with resident DJs and international guests.

Hotel Arena

's-Gravesandestraat 51
tel 850-2400
hotelarena.nl
The hip and trendy Hotel Arena combines smart guest rooms with a bar, restaurant, and rocking nightclub. The last is located in an old chapel and retains the original marble pillars, ceiling frescoes, and arches under which hot new DJs and bands play.

Jazz Café Alto

Korte Leidsedwarsstraat 115
tel 626-03249
jazz-cafe-alto.nl
Atmospheric, authentic jazz café just off Leidseplein, which has welcomed international stars including Chet Baker, Bill Clinton, Liza Minnelli, and Rosa King over the past 50 years. Open seven days a week.

Maloe Melo

Lijnbaansgracht 160
tel 420-4592;
maloemelo.nl
Long-established blues café with popular jamming sessions. Open seven days a week until late.

Meervaart

Meer en Vaart 300
tel 410-7700 (information) &
410-7777 (reservations)
meervaart.nl

A large theater and meeting center in Amsterdam New-West, which shows live music performances, comedy, and theater.

Melkweg

Lijnbaansgracht 234a
tel 624-1777
melkweg.nl

Housed in the city's former dairy, Melkweg (Milky Way) stages a diverse program of events, from cutting-edge contemporary dance, video, and cinema and theater programs to pop, reggae, dub, and house.

Odeon

Singel 460
tel 624-9711
odeontheater.nl

This nightclub is housed in a Philips Vingboons–designed canal house dating back to 1662. Guests dance to genres from disco and acid house to rave music and Chicago house under the building's original baroque ceiling and balcony.

Panama

Oostelijke Handelskade 4
tel 311-8686
panama.nl

Housed in a former port authority building in the Eastern Dock-lands, Panama is a concert venue, nightclub for local and international house and techno talent, and res-taurant for preclubbing fine dining.

Paradiso

Weteringschans 6–8
tel 626-4521
paradiso.nl

Paradiso is a converted church offering an intimate space for live bands, disco, and DJ events.

Opera

De Nederlandse Opera (DNO)

Muziektheater, Waterlooplein 22
tel 551-8225 (information) &
625-5455 (box office)
dno.nl

De Nederlandse Opera (DNO) is the Netherlands' largest opera company, based in the Muziek-theater. The DNO has produced many audacious performances, such as the first Dutch staging of Wagner's *Der Ring des Nibelungen*. While most DNO performances are given in the Muziektheater, operas are occasionally staged in other venues, including the Stadsschouwburg Amsterdam, Koninklijk Theater Carré, and Muziekgebouw aan 't IJ.

Theater

Boom Chicago

Rozentheater, Rozengracht 117
tel 217-0400
boomchicago.nl

Founded in 1993, this English-language comedy theater offers nightly shows. It has partnered with three top restaurants nearby to offer set menus for preshow dinners with show tickets.

Comedy Café

Max Euweplein 43–45
tel 638-3971
comedycafe.nl

Stand-up comedy in English and Dutch. Free on Wed. evenings when new acts are given the mic and new material is performed; improvisation on Sun. and estab-lished acts Thurs.–Sat.

Koninklijk Theater Carré

Amstel 115–125
tel 524-9494
carre.nl

Beautiful 19th-century theater originally built to house the Carré winter circus, which now hosts varied performances including theater, dance, cabaret, comedy, opera, operetta, classical concerts, pop concerts, and poetry.

Sugar Factory

Lijnbaansgracht 238
tel 627-0008
sugarfactory.nl

A multipurpose theater dedicated to espousing creative and experimental performing arts. Expect everything from poetry readings and cabaret to techno music concerts.

ACTIVITIES

Ice-skating

Ice-skating and ice hockey are very popular hobbies and specta-tor sports in the Netherlands. Watch the local team, the Amstel Tijgers, in action at the Jaap Eden IJsbaan center (*Radioweg 64, tel 0900/724-2287, jaapeden.nl*).

Soccer

The Dutch club that every sports fan knows is Ajax of Amsterdam. Tickets for home matches at the Amsterdam ArenA in the Bijlmer area are hard, but not impossible, to come by (*Arena Boulevard 1, tel 311-1333, amsterdamarena .nl*). Soccer fans can also visit the stadium's World of Ajax museum.

Swimming

The Marnixbad 25m indoor pool (*Marnixplein 9, tel 524-6000, hetmarnix.nl*) is the best for serious swimmers. Mirandabad (*De Mirandalaan 9, tel 252-4444, mirandabad.nl*) has the full tropi-cal works: pebble beach, wave machine, waterslides, whirlpool, and restaurant.

INDEX

Boldface indicates illustrations.
CAPS indicates thematic categories.

A
Activities & entertainment 262–264
Afsluitdijk (Enclosing Dike) 169, 219
Air travel 236–237
Albert Cuypmarkt 16, 206, 260
Alcohol 238–239
Allard Pierson Museum **37**, 63, 76, 78–79, **79**
Almshouses 135, 140, 143, 223
Alteration of 1578 59
American Hotel 172–173
AMRO Bank 170
Amstel River
    Magere Brug **157, 186,** 187
    walk **186,** 186–188, **188**
Amstelkerk 186
Amstelpark 208
The Amsterdam (ship) 120, **121**
Amsterdam Museum 60, 61–62, **64,** 64–67, **66**
Amsterdam School (architecture) 153
Amsterdamse Bos 33, 209
Anne Frank Huis 135, **136–137,** 136–138
Antiques, shopping for 174–175, 256
De Appel Arts Centre 98
Apps
    Anne's Amsterdam 138
    Museum App 65
Aquarium 113
ARCAM 120–121
Archangelsk Pakhuizen 168
Architectura et Natura (bookshop) 130
Architecture 36, 38–41
    Amsterdam School 153
    ARCAM 120–121
    Beurs van Berlage 53
    canalside houses 38–39, 40, 131, **132,** 133, 134
    nicknames 23
Arendsnest 149
Art galleries *see* **MUSEUMS**
Artis Zoo **112,** 112–113, 116
Arts
    introduction 23, 41–44
    painting 41–44
    painting workshops 105
    performing arts 44
    shopping for 256
Automobiles *see* **DRIVES**

B
De Badcuyp 207
De Bakkerswinkel 156, **156,** 254
Ballet 262
Bank van Lening 75
Bantammerbrug 97
Batavia 96
Bavo, Haarlem 222–223
Beaches 223

Beatrix, Princess (formerly Queen Beatrix) 35, **35,** 55
Begijnhof 62, 70
Begijnhofkapel 62
Berenstraat 165
Beurs van Berlage 52–53, **53**
Bickerseiland 155
Bijbels Museum 167, **167**
Biking 69, **76,** 238
    Rijkmuseum's cycle path 193
    tours 42
    in Waterland **214,** 214–217, **217**
    to Zandvoort Beach 223
Binnenhof, Den Haag **228,** 228–229
Blauwbrug 188
Blauwburgwal 146
Bloemenmarkt 16, 63, **63,** 170, **170,** 259
Bloemgracht **130**
Boat trips
    to Amsterdam 237
    canal boats 68
    dinner cruises 175
    guided canal tours 68, **68**
    museum boat 49
    Pannenkoekenboot 49
    rentals 68–69
    Rijksmuseum waterborne art history tour 195
    water taxi 238
    wetlands canoe safari 216
Books
    recommended 241
    shopping for 256–257
Borneo Island 125
Botanical gardens *see* **GARDENS**
De Brakke Grond 75
Broek **214,** 214–215
Brouwerij't IJ 121
Brouwersgracht 145, 146–147
Bruin (brown) cafés **148,** 148–149
Bulbs **224,** 224–225
Bus travel 237–238

C
Café Americain 172–173, **173**
Café culture 25
Café de Balie 173
Café de Still 149
Café de Twee Zaantjes 149
Café Hoppe 149
Café In de Waag 93
Café 't Smalle **127,** 144, **148,** 149
Cake Under My Pillow (bed & breakfast) 207, 252
Calvinism 28, 29
Canal Bus (cruise operator) 49, 238
Canal Festival (Grachtenfestival) 165
Canal house museums **182,** 182–183
Canals **2–3,** 15, 38–39, **68,** 68–69, 175
Canoe trips 216
Car travel *see* **DRIVES**
Carillon concerts 59
Catholicism 28, 29–30

Centraal Station **27, 45,** 47, **48,** 48–49
Children, activities for *see* Families, activities for
Chinatown 91
CHURCHES
    Amstelkerk 186
    Begijnhofkapel 62
    De Papegaai 61
    Engelsekerk 62
    English Episcopal Church 95
    free concerts 59
    Grote Kerk, Haarlem 222
    Het Oude Huis 88, **88–89**
    Mozes en Aäronkerk 108
    Museum Ons' Lieve Heer op Solder **86,** 86–87
    Nieuwe Kerk 46, 57–59, **58**
    Noorderkerk 134, **135,** 142
    Oude Kerk 59, **71, 84,** 84–85
    Oude Lutherse Kerk 62, 161
    Posthoornkerk 151
    Ronde Lutherse Kerk 147
    Sint Nicolaaskerk 96, **96**
    St. Francis Xavier 161
    Vondelkerk 204–205
    Westerkerk 59, **95,** 135, 139, **139,** 143
    Zuiderkerk 94–95
Cinema 126, 262
Classical music 262–263
Climate 10, 236
Clogs **8,** 261
Cobra Museum of Modern Art 209
Coffee 25, 111
Coffee shops 82, 83, **83, 150**
Collectie Six 179
Concertgebouw 44, 204, 261
Coster Diamonds 199, 204, 260
Credit cards 11, 240–241
Cruise ships 237
Currency 238
De Cuyp 206
Cycling *see* Biking

D
De Dageraad 42, 209
Dam Square 46, 54–59, 60
    Koninklijk Paleis 46, 54–57, **57**
    Nationaal Monument **54,** 57
    Nieuwe Kerk 46, 57–59, **58**
Damrak & Warmoesstraat **50,** 50–53, **53**
De Badcuyp 207
De Bakkerswinkel 156, **156,** 254
De Brakke Grond 75
De Cuyp 206
De Dageraad 42, 209
De Dierencapel 155
De Drie Fleschjes 58
De Gouden Spiegel 147
De Kaaskamer **140,** 259
De Keyser, Hendrick 133
De Krijberg *see* St. Francis Xavier
De Leeuwenburg 81

De Negen Straatjes 163–164
De Papegaai 61
De Pijp **206,** 206–207
De Porcelyne Fles, Delft 231
De Rokerij 83
De Silveren Spiegel 147
De Taart van m'n Tante 207
De Vrije Academie 105
De Wallen 80–81, 82
De Wildeman 149
Delfshaven, Rotterdam 233–234
Delft 31, **211, 230,** 230–231, 253
Den Haag **228,** 228–229, 254
Department stores & malls 257
Design & interiors (shopping) 258
Diamond industry 199, 204, 260
De Dierencapel 155
Dikker & Thijs Fenice Hotel 171
Dinner cruises 175
Discount cards 10, 239
Douwes Dekker, Eduard 145–146, 147
De Drie Fleschjes 58
DRIVES
    bulb fields of Haarlem **224,** 224–225
    driving information 237
Drugs 18, 82–83, 238–239
Dutch East India Company 30, 77, 221
Dutch gin 148, 149
Dutch West India Company 111, 150
Dylan Hotel 166, 175, 249

E
East India House **74,** 77–78
Eenhoornsluis 151
Eetcafé Singel 404 62, 251
Electricity 238
Electrische Museumtramlijn 209
Embassies & consulates 240
Emergencies 240
Engelsekerk 62
English Episcopal Church 95
Enkhuizen **218,** 218–221, **220**
Entertainment & activities 39, 103, 262–264
Erotic Museum 81
Ethnic Amsterdam 22–23
Euromast, Rotterdam 233, 254
Events see Entertainment & activities; Festivals; Holidays
Excursions 211–235
    biking in Waterland **214,** 214–217, **217**
    bulb fields of Haarlem **224,** 224–225
    Delft 31, **211, 230,** 230–231, 253
    Den Haag **228,** 228–229, 254
    Enkhuizen **218,** 218–221, **220**
    Haarlem **222,** 222–225, **224,** 253
    hotels & restaurants 253–255
    introduction 11
    Leiden **212, 226,** 226–227, 254

maps 213, 214–215, 225
Rotterdam 34, **232,** 232–234, 254–255
EXPERIENCES
    Amsterdam's largest sandwich 62
    apple cake 144
    biking to Zandvoort Beach 223
    café culture 25
    Canal Festival 165
    church concerts 59
    create your own Delft pottery 231
    De Taart van m'n Tante 207
    eat fresh herring 151
    Euromast romance 233
    free lunchtime concerts 103
    High Wine, Dylan Hotel 166
    King's Day 19
    local parks 208, **208**
    markets 16
    mass at Ons' Lieve Heer op Solder 87
    Museum Boat and Pancake Boat 49
    Openbare Library 123
    painting workshops 105
    private gardens 41
    Rijksmuseum waterborne art history tour 195
    sloep (boat) rentals 69
    Stille Omgang (Silent Procession) 85
    walking or biking tour 42
    wetlands canoe safari 216
EYE Film Institute Netherlands 126, 262

F
Families, activities for
    De Dierencapel (children's farm) 155
    Little Orphanage, Amsterdam Museum 67
    Madurodam, Den Haag 229
    NEMO museum 120, **122,** 122–123
    steam train/paddle steamer to Enkhuizen **218,** 218–219
    Stedelijk Museum **202,** 202–203, 204
    Tropenmuseum Junior 115
Fashion, shopping for 258–259
Felix Meritis Building 166
Ferries 237
Festivals 19, 165, 264
Flea markets **60,** 103
Flowers
    drive through bulb fields of Haarlem **224,** 224–225
    markets 63, **63,** 259
Foam Photography Museum 183, 261
Food & drink
    apple cake **24,** 144
    Dutch gin 148, 149
    herring 151
    High Wine, Dylan Hotel 166

introduction 24–25
shopping for 259–260
Frank, Anne 34, 136–138, **137,** 139
    see also Anne Frank Huis
Frans Hals Museum, Haarlem 223

G
Galerie Lieve Hemel 175
GARDENS
    Haarlem bulb fields **224,** 224–225
    Hortus Botanicus 110–111
    Hortus Botanicus, Leiden 227
    Keukenhof **40,** 224
    Open Tuinen Dagen (Open Gardens Days) 41
    Rijksmuseum 196–197
Gassan Diamond Works 102–103, 260
Gay Amsterdam 18, 91
Gemeentemuseum Den Haag 229
Geologisch Museum 112
Geotourism 6
Gin 148, 149
Gouden Bocht (Golden Bend) 169, **176,** 176–179, **179**
De Gouden Spiegel 147
Grachtenfestival (Canal Festival) 165, 263
Grachtengordel North **130,** 130–135, **133, 135**
Grachtengordel South **162,** 162–167, **164, 167**
Grand Hotel 74–75
Grand Hotel Amrâth Amsterdam 244
Groenland Pakhuizen 133–134
Grote Kerk, Haarlem 222
Grote Markt Square, Haarlem 222, **222**

H
Haarlem **222,** 222–225, **224,** 253
Haarlemmerbuurt **150,** 150–151
Haarlemmerdijk 151
Haarlemmerplein 151
The Hague see Den Haag
Hals, Frans 42
Hash Marihuana Hemp Museum 80
He Hua Buddhist Temple **90,** 91
Health & medicine 240
Heilige Stede 63
Heiligeweg 62
Heineken brewery 206–207, 210
Heineken Experience 210, **210**
Herengracht 176–177
Hermitage Amsterdam 184
Herring 151
Het Arsenaal 109
Het Grachtenhuis Museum 182
Het Houten Huis 62
Het Huis met de Hoofden (House with the Heads) 130, 131
Het Huys met de Gaeper 58
Het Oude Huis 88, **88–89**
History of Amsterdam 26–35
Hof Vijver, Den Haag 228, **228**

Holidays 19, 239
Hollandsche Manege 205
Hollandsche Schouwburg 109
Homomonument 139
Hoorn 220–221
Hortus Botanicus 110–111
Hortus Botanicus, Leiden 227
Hotel De Doelen **13**
HOTELS 242–255
    excursions 233, 253–255
    Jodenbuurt, Plantage, Oostelijk
        Havengebied, & Environs 246
    Museum Quarter, Vondelpark, &
        De Pijp 251–252
    Nieuwe Zijde 243
    Northern Canals 247–248
    Oude Zijde 244–245
    overview 242
    Rotterdam 233
    Southern Canals 164–165,
        249–250
Houseboat Museum **164**, 165, 185
Houseboats 185, **185**
Huis Bartolotti 130, 131
Huis op de Drie Grachten 76
Huys Zitten Weduwen Hofje 143

I
I amsterdam City Card 8, 10, 237,
    238, 239
Ice-skating 20, 264
IJsselmeer 219
In de Mooriaantjes 178
In de Olofspoort (tavern) 51
Information, tourist 9, 240
Itineraries, suggested 8–11

J
Jacob Hooij herbalist shop 94,
    260–261
Java & KNSM Island 125
Jewelry, shopping for 260
Jewish Cultural Quarter 109
Jewish District see Jodenbuurt
Jewish Historical Museum 108, **108**
Jodenbuurt (Jewish District) 102–
    105, 108–109
    Gassan Diamond Works 102–
        103, 260
    introduction 100
    Jewish Cultural Quarter 109
    Jewish Historical Museum
        108, **108**
    Museum Het Rembrandthuis **99**,
        103–105, **104**
    Stadhuis–Muziektheater 102,
        102, 105, 108
    Waterlooplein 102–103, 260
Jodenbuurt, Plantage, Oostelijk
    Havengebied, & Environs
    99–126
    hotels 246
    Jodenbuurt **99**, 100, **102**, 102–
        105, **104**, **108**, 108–109, 260
    maps 101, 117
    maritime Amsterdam **116**,
        116–117

Noord 126
    Oostelijk Havengebied 100, **118**,
        118–125, **121**, **122**, **124**
    Plantage 100, **110**, 110–114,
        112, **114**, **116**, 116–117
    restaurants 113, 120, 246–247
    Tropenmuseum **114**, 115
Jordaan **127**, **130**, **140**, 140–144,
    142

K
De Kaaskamer **140**, 259
Kandinsky (coffee shop) 83
Kasteel Teylingen, Sassenheim
    224–225
KattenKabinet 177
Keizersgracht 164, **168**, 188, **188**
Keukenhof **40**, 224
King's Day 19, **19**
Kleine Trippenhuis 94
Koningsdag (King's Day) 19, **19**
Koningsplein **170**, 170–173, **173**
Koninklijk Paleis 46, 54–57, **57**
De Krijtberg see St. Francis Xavier

L
De Leeuwenburg 81
Leiden **212**, **226**, 226–227, 254
Leiden American Pilgrim Museum
    227
Leidsebos park 172
Leidsegracht **168**, 168–169
Leidsekadebrug 173
Leidseplein **170**, 170–173, **173**
Lely, Cornelis 169
Licorice 94
Liquor 238–239
Lisse 224
Loods 6 (building) 125
Lost property 241
Lovers (cruise operator) 49, 238

M
Madame Tussauds 60, 70
Madurodam, Den Haag 229
Magere Brug (Skinny Bridge) **157**,
    186, 187
Magna Plaza 160, **160**, 257
Maps
    excursions 213, 214–215, 225
    Haarlem bulb fields 225
    Jodenbuurt, Plantage, Oostelijk
        Havengebied, & Environs
        101, 117
    Jordaan district 141
    Museum Quarter, Vondelpark, &
        De Pijp 190–191, 205
    Nieuwe Zijde 46–47, 61
    Northern Canals 128–129, 141
    Oude Zijde 72–73, 97
    Southern Canals 158–159, 187
    Waterland biking 214–215
Maritiem Museum Rotterdam 234
Maritime Amsterdam 116–117
Marken 216
Markets 16, 260
    Albert Cuypmarkt 16, 206, 260

Bloemenmarkt 16, 63, **63**, 170,
    170, 259
flea markets **60**, 103
Noordermarkt 16, **142**, 142–
    143, 144, 260
Mauritshuis, Den Haag 228
Max Euweplein 173
Máxima, Queen **35**
Media 239
Medicine & health 240
Melkweg arts center 44, 169, 264
Metro 237–238
Metz & Co. Building 171
Molenmuseum de Valk, Leiden
    226, **226**
Money matters 11, 238
Montelbaanstoren 98, **98**
Mozes en Aäronkerk 108
Multatuli (Eduard Douwes Dekker)
    145–146
Multatuli Huis Museum 147
Munttoren (church) 59, 63
Museum Boijmans van Beuningen,
    Rotterdam 232–233
Museum de Cruquius, Hoofddorp
    225
Museum de Lakenhal, Leiden 226
Museum de Noord 126
Museum de Zwarte Tulp, Lisse 224
Museum Het Prinsenhof, Delft
    230–231
Museum Het Rembrandthuis **99**,
    103–105, **104**
Museum Het Schip 42, 152–153
Museum Ons' Lieve Heer op Solder
    81, **86**, 86–89, **88–89**
Museum Quarter, Vondelpark,
    & De Pijp 189–210
    Amsterdamse Bos 33, 209
    Cobra Museum of Modern
        Art 209
    De Dageraad 42, 209
    De Pijp **206**, 206–207
    Electrische Museumtramlijn
        209
    Heineken Experience 210, **210**
    hotels 251–252
    maps 190–191, 205
    restaurants 206–207, 252–253
    Rijksmuseum **107**, **189**, **192**,
        192–197, **194**, **195**, **197**
    Stedelijk Museum **202**, 202–203,
        204
    Van Gogh Museum **198**, 198–
        200, 204, 261
    walk **204**, 204–205
    Wilhelmina Gasthuis Terrein 210
Museum Van Loon 181, **182**, 183
Museum Volkenkunde, Leiden 226
Museum Willet-Holthuysen 183,
    188
Museumpark, Rotterdam 232–233
Museumplein 204, **204**
MUSEUMS
    canal boats 49
    discount cards 8, 10, 237,
        238, 239

Allard Pierson Museum **37,** 63, 76, 78–79, **79**
Amsterdam Museum 60, 61–62, **64,** 64–67, **66**
Anne Frank Huis 135, **136–137,** 136–138
Bijbels Museum 167, **167**
canal house museums **182,** 182–183
Cobra Museum of Modern Art 209
Collectie Six 179
Electrische Museumtramlijn 209
Erotic Museum 81
EYE Film Institute Netherlands 126, 262
Foam Photography Museum 183, 261
Frans Hals Museum, Haarlem 223
Gemeentemuseum Den Haag 229
Geologisch Museum 112
Hash Marihuana Hemp Museum 80
Het Grachtenhuis Museum 182
Houseboat Museum **164,** 165, 185
Jewish Historical Museum 108, **108**
Leiden American Pilgrim Museum 227
Madame Tussauds 60, 70
Maritiem Museum Rotterdam 234
Molenmuseum de Valk, Leiden 226, **226**
Multatuli Huis Museum 147
Museum App (smart phone app) 65
Museum Boijmans van Beuningen, Rotterdam 232–233
Museum de Cruquius, Hoofddorp 225
Museum de Lakenhal, Leiden 226
Museum de Noord 126
Museum de Zwarte Tulp, Lisse 224
Museum Het Prinsenhof, Delft 230–231
Museum Het Rembrandthuis **99,** 103–105, **104**
Museum Het Schip 42, 152–153
Museum Ons' Lieve Heer op Solder 81, **86,** 86–89, **88–89**
Museum Van Loon 181, **182,** 183
Museum Volkenkunde, Leiden 226
Museum Willet-Holthuysen 183, 188
Museumpark, Rotterdam 232–233
Museumwerf 't Kromhout 116–117
Nationaal Vakbondsmuseum **110,** 111, 116

NEMO museum 120, **122,** 122–123
Prostitution Information Center 81
Rijksmuseum **107, 189, 192,** 192–197, **194, 195, 197**
Rijksmuseum van Oudheden, Leiden 227
Scheepvaartmuseum 117, **121**
Sexmuseum Amsterdam "Venustempel" 70
Stedelijk Museum **202,** 202–203, 204
Tassenmuseum (Museum of Bags and Purses) 178, **179**
Teylers Museum, Haarlem 223
Tropenmuseum **114,** 115
Van Gogh Museum **198,** 198–200, 204, 261
Vereniging Museumhaven Amsterdam 121
Vermeer Centrum Delft 231
Verzetsmuseum (Resistance Museum) 114, 116
W139 (exhibition space) 51
Westfries Museum, Hoorn 221
Zuiderzeemuseum, Enkhuizen 220, **220**
Museumwerf 't Kromhout 116–117
Music
Canal Festival 165
church concerts 59
classical music 262–263
free lunchtime concerts 103
opera 264
shopping for 261
Muziekgebouw aan 't IJ **124,** 125, 262

N
Napoléon Bonaparte 166, 177, 214–215
Narcotics 238–239
Nationaal Monument **54,** 57
Nationaal Park Zuid-Kennemerland 223
Nationaal Vakbondsmuseum **110,** 111, 116
Nazis 34, 114
De Negen Straatjes **162,** 163–164
NEMO museum 120, **122,** 122–123
NH Carlton Hotel 179
Nieuwe Kerk (New Church) 46, 57–59, **58**
Nieuwe Zijde 45–70
Amsterdam Museum 60, 61–62, **64,** 64–67, **66**
Begijnhof 62, 70
Centraal Station **27, 45,** 47, **48,** 48–49
Dam Square 46, **54,** 54–59, **57, 58,** 60
Damrak & Warmoesstraat **50,** 50–53, **53**
hotels 243
Madame Tussauds 60, 70

maps 46–47, 61
restaurants 49, 244
Sexmuseum Amsterdam "Venustempel" 70
walk through the heart of Amsterdam **60,** 60–63, **63**
Nieuwmarkt **92,** 92–95, **95**
Nightlife **12,** 58, 264–265
Noord 126
Noorderkerk 134, **135,** 142
Noordermarkt 16, **142,** 142–143, 144, 260
Northern Canals 127–156
Anne Frank Huis 135, **136–137,** 136–138
Brouwersgracht 145, 146–147
Café 't Smalle **127,** 144, **148,** 149
Grachtengordel North **130,** 130–135, **133, 135**
Haarlemmerbuurt **150,** 150–151
hotels 247–248
Jordaan **127, 130, 140,** 140–144, **142**
maps 128–129, 141
restaurants 248–249
Singel 37, **145,** 145–147
Spaarndammerbuurt **152,** 152–153
walk through Jordaan **140,** 140–144, **142**
Westelijke Eilanden **154,** 154–155
Westerkerk 59, **95,** 135, 139, **139,** 143
Westerpark 156, **156**

O
OBA (Openbare Bibliotheek Amsterdam) 123
1e Klas (café) 49, 244
Oostelijk Havengebied (Eastern Docklands) 118–125, **124**
ARCAM 120–121
introduction 100
NEMO museum 120, **122,** 122–123
Oost 124–125
Scheepvaartmuseum 117, **118,** 118–120, **121**
Oosterpark 208
Oostindisch Huis (East India House) **74,** 77–78
Openbare Bibliotheek Amsterdam (OBA) 123
Opening hours 239, 256
Opera 264
Oude Kerk 59, **71, 84,** 84–85
Oude Lutherse Kerk 62, 161
Oude Vleeshuis 75
Oude Zijde (Old Side) 71–98
hotels 244–245
maps 72–73, 97
Museum Ons' Lieve Heer op Solder 81, **86,** 86–89, **88–89**
Nieuwmarkt **92,** 92–95, **95**
Oude Kerk 59, **71, 84,** 84–85

Red Light District 20–21, 72, **80,** 80–81, **82,** 83
restaurants 93, 245–246
University Quarter **74,** 74–79, **76, 79**
waterside stroll **96,** 96–98, **98**
Zeedijk 72, **90,** 90–91, 216
Oudemannhuis 76–77
Oudezijds Voorburgwal canal **96**

P
Paleis van Justitie 171
Pannenkoekenboot (Pancake Boat) 49
Panorama Mesdag, Den Haag 229
De Papegaai 61
Paradox (coffee shop) 83
Park Frankendael 208
PARKS
Amsterdamse Bos 33, 209
Keukenhof **40,** 224
Leidsebos park 172
local parks 208, **208**
Max Euweplein 173
Nationaal Park Zuid-Kennemerland 223
Vondelpark 205, 208, **208**
Wertheimpark 116, **116**
Westerpark 156, **156**
Passports & visas 236
Pawnbrokers 75
Performing arts 44
Peter the Great, Tsar (Russia) 117, 165, 177, 184
Pieter Jansz Suyckerhoff 142
De Pijp **206,** 206–207
Plantage 100, **110,** 110–114, **112, 114, 116,** 116–117
Police 240
Pols Potten 125, 258
De Porcelyne Fles, Delft 231
Portugees-Israëlitische Synagoge 109
Post offices 239
Posthoornkerk 151
Prinseneiland **154,** 154–155
Prinsengracht 134–135
Proeflokaal Wijnand Fockink 149
Proeflokaals 149
Project 1012 20–21, 80, 81, 83
Prostitution 18, 20–21, 82
    see also Red Light District
Prostitution Information Center 81
Protestant revolution 28
Public transportation see Transportation
Pulitzer Hotel 164–165, 249
Python Bridge 125

R
Rain Restaurant **180**
Ransdorp 216–217
Rasphuis (prison) 62
Reading, recommended 241
Realeneiland 155
Red Light District 20–21, 72, **80,** 80–81, **82,** 83

Reestraat 164–165
Reguliersgracht 181
Rembrandt van Rijn 42, 93, **99,** 106–107, 195
Rembrandthuis see Museum Het Rembrandthuis
Rembrandtpark 208
Rembrandtplein **180,** 180–181
Restaurant Stalpaert 120
RESTAURANTS 242–255
Amsterdam's largest sandwich 62
café culture 25
excursions 227, 253–255
Jodenbuurt, Plantage, Oostelijk Havengebied, & Environs 113, 120, 246–247
Leiden's floating restaurants 227
Museum Quarter, Vondelpark, & De Pijp 206–207, 252–253
Nieuwe Zijde 49, 244
Northern Canals 248–249
Oude Zijde 93, 245–246
overview 242–243
Southern Canals 172–173, **173,** 250–251
tipping 240
Restrooms 239
Rijksmuseum **107, 189, 192,** 192–197, **194, 195, 197**
Asian Pavilion 195–196
cycling path 193
Dutch Masters 193–195, **197**
gardens 196–197
Great Hall **194**
history 196
Philips Wing 197
Spanish influence 193
20th-Century Galleries 195–196
Rijksmuseum van Oudheden, Leiden 227
De Rokerij 83
Ronde Lutherse Kerk 147
Rotterdam 34, **232,** 232–234, 254–255
Royal Theater Carré 188

S
Saaihal 95
Safety 241
Sailors' Quarter 90–91
St. Francis Xavier 161
Sandwiches 62
Sassenheim 224–225
Scheepvaarthuis 98
Scheepvaartmuseum 117, **121**
Scheveningen 229
Schreierstoren 96–97, 119
Sex & drugs 82–83
Sex shops see Red Light District
Sexmuseum Amsterdam "Venustempel" 70
Shopping 52, 125, 239, 256–261
De Silveren Spiegel 147
Singel 37, **145,** 145–147, **160,** 160–161
Sint Nicolaaskerk 96, **96**
Sint Olofskapel 91

Sissy-Boy Homeland 125
Sloep (aluminum boat) 69
Sloepdelen 69
Smart phone apps
Anne's Amsterdam 138
Museum App 65
Smits Noord-Zuid Hollandsch Koffiehuis 49
Smoking 239
Soccer **11, 22,** 264
Southern Canals 157–188
canal house museums **182,** 182–183
Gouden Bocht 169, **176,** 176–179, **179**
Grachtengordel South **162,** 162–167, **164, 167**
Hermitage Amsterdam 184
hotels 164–165, 249–250
houseboats 185, **185**
Koningsplein & Leidseplein **170,** 170–173, **173**
Leidsegracht **168,** 168–169
Magere Brug (Skinny Bridge) **157, 186,** 187
maps 158–159, 187
Rembrandtplein & Thorbeckeplein **180,** 180–181, 256
restaurants 172–173, **173,** 250–251
Southern Singel & Spuistraat **21, 160,** 160–161
Spiegelkwartier **174,** 174–175, 256
walk along the Amstel River **186,** 186–188, **188**
Southern Singel **160,** 160–161
Spaarndammerbuurt **152,** 152–153
Spiegelkwartier **174,** 174–175, 256
Spinhuis 77
Sporenburg 125
Sports see Activities & entertainment
Spuistraat **21,** 161
St. Francis Xavier 161
Stadhuis–Muziektheater 102, **102,** 105, 108, 188
Stadsschouwburg 44, 172
Stadts Magazijn 161
Stedelijk Museum **202,** 202–203, 204
Steen, Jan 43
Stille Omgang (Silent Procession) 85
Stopera see Stadhuis–Muziektheater
Supperclub **12**
Swimming 264
Synagogues 109

T
De Taart van m'n Tante 207
Tassenmuseum (Museum of Bags and Purses) 178, **179**
Taxis 238, 240
Telephones 239
    see also Apps
Teylers Museum, Haarlem 223
Theater 264

Thorbeckeplein **180,** 180–181, 256
Time differences 240
Tipping 11, 240
Toilets 239
Tolhuistuin 126
Torensluis 145
Tourist information 9, 240
Transportation
    in Amsterdam 8, 237–238
    to Amsterdam 236–237
    discount card 8, 10, 237, 238, 239
    trains **218,** 237
    trams **235,** 237–238
Trippenhuis 93–94
Tropenmuseum **114,** 115
Tulips **4,** 16, 52, 224–225
Tuschinski Theater 180–181, 262
Twee Zusjes 169

U
University Quarter **74,** 74–79, **76, 79**

V
Van Brienenhofje 135
Van Gogh, Vincent 200, 201, **201**
Van Gogh Museum **198,** 198–200,
    204, 261
Verenigde Oost-Indische Compagnie
    77
Vereniging Museumhaven
    Amsterdam 121
Vermeer, Johannes 42, 231
Vermeer Centrum Delft 231
Verweyhal, Haarlem 223
Verzetsmuseum (Resistance
    Museum) 114, 116

Visas & passports 236
Visitor information 9, 240
Vondelkerk 204–205
Vondelpark 205, 208, **208**
De Vrije Academie 105

W
W139 (exhibition space) 51
Waag 92–93
WALKS
    Amstel River **186,** 186–188, **188**
    heart of Amsterdam **60,** 60–63,
        63
    Jordaan **140,** 140–144, **142**
    Museum Quarter, Vondelpark, &
        De Pijp **204,** 204–205
    Oude Zijde waterside stroll **96,**
        96–98, **98**
    Plantage & Maritime Amsterdam
        116, 116–117
    tours 42
De Wallen 80–81, 82
Warmoesstraat 50–53
Water Taxi 68, 238
Waterland, biking in **214,** 214–217,
    217
Waterlooplein 102–103, 260
Weather 10, 236
Websites 240
Wertheimpark 116, **116**
West Indische Huis 150
Westelijke Eilanden **154,** 154–155
Westerkerk 59, 135, 139, **139,** 143
Westerpark 156, **156**
Westfries Museum, Hoorn 221
Wetlands canoe safari 216

WG Terrein 210
De Wildeman 149
Wilhelmina Gasthuis Terrein 210
Willem-Alexander, King 35, **35,** 55
Winkel Café 144
Wooden shoes **8,** 261

Z
Zaanhof 152–153
Zandvoort Beach 223
Zeedijk 72, **90,** 90–91, 216
Zonshofje 135
Zoo **112,** 112–113
Zuiderkerk 59, 94–95, **95**
Zuiderwoude 215–216
Zuiderzee 219
Zuiderzeemuseum, Enkhuizen 220,
    220

ACKNOWLEDGMENTS

The authors wish to express sincerest thanks to Rianne Ojeh of the NTBC and all the team at I amsterdam for their invaluable support. Thanks also to Pancras Dijk and all at *National Geographic Netherlands* and *National Geographic Traveler in the Netherlands* for their knowledge and expertise. Thanks to Charlotte Wierdsma at the Dylan Hotel and Tonko Grever at the Museum van Loon for their time and generosity and for sharing their encyclopedic knowledge of Amsterdam. And finally to Hugo Le Breton for his unfailing hospitality.

ILLUSTRATIONS CREDITS

National Geographic
TRAVELER
Amsterdam

Published by the National Geographic Society
John M. Fahey, *Chairman of the Board and Chief Executive Officer*
Declan Moore, *Executive Vice President; President, Publishing and Travel*
Melina Gerosa Bellows, *Executive Vice President; Chief Creative Officer, Books, Kids, and Family*
Lynn Cutter, *Executive Vice President, Travel*
Keith Bellows, *Senior Vice President and Editor in Chief, National Geographic Travel Media*

Prepared by the Book Division
Hector Sierra, *Senior Vice President and General Manager*
Janet Goldstein, *Senior Vice President and Editorial Director*
Jonathan Halling, *Design Director, Books and Children's Publishing*
Marianne R. Koszorus, *Design Director, Books*
Barbara A. Noe, *Senior Editor, National Geographic Travel Books*
R. Gary Colbert, *Production Director*
Jennifer A. Thornton, *Director of Managing Editorial*
Susan S. Blair, *Director of Photography*
Meredith C. Wilcox, *Director, Administration and Rights Clearance*

Staff for This Book
Larry Porges, *Project Editor*
Justin Kavanagh, *Text Editor*
Linda Makarov, *Designer*
Gabe Dinsmoor, *Photo Assistant*
Carl Mehler, *Director of Maps*
Mike McNey & Mapping Specialists, *Map Production*
Marshall Kiker, *Associate Managing Editor*
Gary Colbert, *Production Manager*
Galen Young, *Rights Clearance Specialist*
Hannah Lauterback, *Contributor*

Manufacturing and Quality Management
Phillip L. Schlosser, *Senior Vice President*
Chris Brown, *Vice President, NG Book Manufacturing*
George Bounelis, *Vice President, Production Services*
Nicole Elliott, *Manager*
Rachel Faulise, *Manager*
Robert L. Barr, *Manager*

The information in this book has been carefully checked and to the best of our knowledge is accurate. However, details are subject to change, and the National Geographic Society cannot be responsible for such changes, or for errors or omissions. Assessments of sites, hotels, and restaurants are based on the authors' subjective opinions, which do not necessarily reflect the publisher's opinion.

The National Geographic Society is one of the world's largest nonprofit scientific and educational organizations. Founded in 1888 to "increase and diffuse geographic knowledge," the Society works to inspire people to care about the planet. National Geographic reflects the world through its magazines, television programs, films, music and radio, books, DVDs, maps, exhibitions, live events, school publishing programs, interactive media, and merchandise. *National Geographic* magazine, the Society's official journal, published in English and 33 local-language editions, is read by more than 60 million people each month. The National Geographic Channel reaches 435 million households in 37 languages in 173 countries. National Geographic Digital Media receives more than 19 million visitors a month. National Geographic has funded more than 10,000 scientific research, conservation, and exploration projects and supports an education program promoting geography literacy. For more information, visit www.nationalgeographic.com.

For more information, please call 1-800-NGS LINE (647-5463) or write to the following address:

National Geographic Society
1145 17th Street N.W.
Washington, D.C. 20036-4688 U.S.A.

For information about special discounts for bulk purchases, please contact National Geographic Books Special Sales: ngspecsales@ngs.org

For rights or permissions inquiries, please contact National Geographic Books Subsidiary Rights: ngbookrights@ngs.org

National Geographic Traveler: Amsterdam (Second Edition)
ISBN: 978-1-4262-1185-0

Printed in Hong Kong

13/THK/1